Algorithms and
Parallel Computing

Algorithms and Parallel Computing

Fayez Gebali
University of Victoria, Victoria, BC

A John Wiley & Sons, Inc., Publication

Library of Congress Cataloging-in-Publication Data

Gebali, Fayez.
    Algorithms and parallel computing/Fayez Gebali.
      p. cm.—(Wiley series on parallel and distributed computing ; 82)
    Includes bibliographical references and index.
    ISBN 978-0-470-90210-3 (hardback)
  1. Parallel processing (Electronic computers) 2. Computer algorithms. I. Title.
    QA76.58.G43 2011
    004'.35—dc22

2010043659

Printed in Singapore

10 9 8 7 6 5 4 3 2 1

*To my children: Michael Monir, Tarek Joseph,
Aleya Lee, and Manel Alia*

Contents

9 z-Transform Analysis   159

10 Dependence Graph Analysis   167

11 Computational Geometry Analysis   185

Preface

ABOUT THIS BOOK

There is a *software gap* between hardware potential and the performance that can be attained using today's software parallel program development tools. The tools need manual intervention by the programmer to parallelize the code. This book is intended to give the programmer the techniques necessary to explore parallelism in algorithms, serial as well as iterative. Parallel computing is now moving from the realm of specialized expensive systems available to few select groups to cover almost every computing system in use today. We can find parallel computers in our laptops, desktops, and embedded in our smart phones. The applications and algorithms targeted to parallel computers were traditionally confined to weather prediction, wind tunnel simulations, computational biology, and signal processing. Nowadays, just about any application that runs on a computer will encounter the parallel processors now available in almost every system.

Parallel algorithms could now be designed to run on special-purpose parallel processors or could run on general-purpose parallel processors using several multi-level techniques such as parallel program development, parallelizing compilers, multithreaded operating systems, and superscalar processors. This book covers the first option: design of special-purpose parallel processor architectures to implement a given class of algorithms. We call such systems accelerator cores. This book forms the basis for a course on design and analysis of parallel algorithms. The course would cover Chapters 1–4 then would select several of the case study chapters that constitute the remainder of the book.

Although very large-scale integration (VLSI) technology allows us to integrate more processors on the same chip, parallel programming is not advancing to match these technological advances. An obvious application of parallel hardware is to design special-purpose parallel processors primarily intended for use as accelerator cores in multicore systems. This is motivated by two practicalities: the prevalence of multicore systems in current computing platforms and the abundance of simple parallel algorithms that are needed in many systems, such as in data encryption/decryption, graphics processing, digital signal processing and filtering, and many more.

It is simpler to start by stating what this book is *not* about. This book does not attempt to give a detailed coverage of computer architecture, parallel computers, or algorithms in general. Each of these three topics deserves a large textbook to attempt to provide a good cover. Further, there are the standard and excellent textbooks for each, such as *Computer Organization and Design* by D.A. Patterson and J.L.

Hennessy, *Parallel Computer Architecture* by D.E. Culler, J.P. Singh, and A. Gupta, and finally, *Introduction to Algorithms* by T.H. Cormen, C.E. Leiserson, and R.L. Rivest. I hope many were fortunate enough to study these topics in courses that adopted the above textbooks. My apologies if I did not include a comprehensive list of equally good textbooks on the above subjects.

This book, on the other hand, shows how to systematically design special-purpose parallel processing structures to implement algorithms. The techniques presented here are general and can be applied to many algorithms, parallel or otherwise.

This book is intended for researchers and graduate students in computer engineering, electrical engineering, and computer science. The prerequisites for this book are basic knowledge of linear algebra and digital signal processing. The objectives of this book are (1) to explain several techniques for expressing a parallel algorithm as a dependence graph or as a set of dependence matrices; (2) to explore scheduling schemes for the processing tasks while conforming to input and output data timing, and to be able to pipeline some data and broadcast other data to all processors; and (3) to explore allocation schemes for the processing tasks to processing elements.

CHAPTER ORGANIZATION AND OVERVIEW

Chapter 1 defines the two main classes of algorithms dealt with in this book: serial algorithms, parallel algorithms, and regular iterative algorithms. Design considerations for parallel computers are discussed as well as their close tie to parallel algorithms. The benefits of using parallel computers are quantified in terms of speedup factor and the effect of communication overhead between the processors. The chapter concludes by discussing two applications of parallel computers.

Chapter 2 discusses the techniques used to enhance the performance of a single computer such as increasing the clock frequency, parallelizing the arithmetic and logic unit (ALU) structure, pipelining, very long instruction word (VLIW), superscalar computing, and multithreading.

Chapter 3 reviews the main types of parallel computers discussed here and includes shared memory, distributed memory, single instruction multiple data stream (SIMD), systolic processors, and multicore systems.

Chapter 4 reviews shared-memory multiprocessor systems and discusses two main issues intimately related to them: cache coherence and process synchronization.

Chapter 5 reviews the types of interconnection networks used in parallel processors. We discuss simple networks such as buses and move on to star, ring, and mesh topologies. More efficient networks such as crossbar and multistage interconnection networks are discussed.

Chapter 6 reviews the concurrency platform software tools developed to help the programmer parallelize the application. Tools reviewed include Cilk++, OpenMP, and compute unified device architecture (CUDA). It is stressed, however, that these tools deal with simple data dependencies. It is the responsibility of the programmer to ensure data integrity and correct timing of task execution. The techniques developed in this book help the programmer toward this goal for serial algorithms and for regular iterative algorithms.

Chapter 7 reviews the ad hoc techniques used to implement algorithms on parallel computers. These techniques include independent loop scheduling, dependent loop spreading, dependent loop unrolling, problem partitioning, and divide-and-conquer strategies. Pipelining at the algorithm task level is discussed, and the technique is illustrated using the coordinate rotation digital computer (CORDIC) algorithm.

Chapter 8 deals with nonserial–parallel algorithms (NSPAs) that cannot be described as serial, parallel, or serial–parallel algorithms. NSPAs constitute the majority of general algorithms that are not apparently parallel or show a confusing task dependence pattern. The chapter discusses a formal, very powerful, and simple technique for extracting parallelism from an algorithm. The main advantage of the formal technique is that it gives us the best schedule for evaluating the algorithm on a parallel machine. The technique also tells us how many parallel processors are required to achieve maximum execution speedup. The technique enables us to extract important NSPA performance parameters such as work (W), parallelism (P), and depth (D).

Chapter 9 introduces the z-transform technique. This technique is used for studying the implementation of digital filters and multirate systems on different parallel processing machines. These types of applications are naturally studied in the z-domain, and it is only natural to study their software and hardware implementation using this domain.

Chapter 10 discusses to construct the dependence graph associated with an iterative algorithm. This technique applies, however, to iterative algorithms that have one, two, or three indices at the most. The dependence graph will help us schedule tasks and automatically allocate them to software threads or hardware processors.

Chapter 11 discusses an iterative algorithm analysis technique that is based on computation geometry and linear algebra concepts. The technique is general in the sense that it can handle iterative algorithms with more than three indices. An example is two-dimensional (2-D) or three-dimensional (3-D) digital filters. For such algorithms, we represent the algorithm as a convex hull in a multidimensional space and associate a dependence matrix with each variable of the algorithm. The null space of these matrices will help us derive the different parallel software threads and hardware processing elements and their proper timing.

Chapter 12 explores different parallel processing structures for one-dimensional (1-D) finite impulse response (FIR) digital filters. We start by deriving possible hardware structures using the geometric technique of Chapter 11. Then, we explore possible parallel processing structures using the z-transform technique of Chapter 9.

Chapter 13 explores different parallel processing structures for 2-D and 3-D infinite impulse response (IIR) digital filters. We use the z-transform technique for this type of filter.

Chapter 14 explores different parallel processing structures for multirate decimators and interpolators. These algorithms are very useful in many applications, especially telecommunications. We use the dependence graph technique of Chapter 10 to derive different parallel processing structures.

Chapter 15 explores different parallel processing structures for the pattern matching problem. We use the dependence graph technique of Chapter 10 to study this problem.

Chapter 16 explores different parallel processing structures for the motion estimation algorithm used in video data compression. In order to delay with this complex algorithm, we use a hierarchical technique to simplify the problem and use the dependence graph technique of Chapter 10 to study this problem.

Chapter 17 explores different parallel processing structures for finite-field multiplication over $GF(2^m)$. The multi-plication algorithm is studied using the dependence graph technique of Chapter 10.

Chapter 18 explores different parallel processing structures for finite-field polynomial division over $GF(2)$. The division algorithm is studied using the dependence graph technique of Chapter 10.

Chapter 19 explores different parallel processing structures for the fast Fourier transform algorithm. Pipeline techniques for implementing the algorithm are reviewed.

Chapter 20 discusses solving systems of linear equations. These systems could be solved using direct and indirect techniques. The chapter discusses how to parallelize the forward substitution direct technique. An algorithm to convert a dense matrix to an equivalent triangular form using Givens rotations is also studied. The chapter also discusses how to parallelize the successive over-relaxation (SOR) indirect technique.

Chapter 21 discusses solving partial differential equations using the finite difference method (FDM). Such equations are very important in many engineering and scientific applications and demand massive computation resources.

ACKNOWLEDGMENTS

I wish to express my deep gratitude and thank Dr. M.W. El-Kharashi of Ain Shams University in Egypt for his excellent suggestions and encouragement during the preparation of this book. I also wish to express my personal appreciation of each of the following colleagues whose collaboration contributed to the topics covered in this book:

Dr. Esam Abdel-Raheem
University of Windsor, Canada

Dr. Turki Al-Somani
Al-Baha University, Saudi Arabia

Dr. Atef Ibrahim
Electronics Research Institute, Egypt

Dr. Mohamed Fayed
Al-Azhar University, Egypt

Mr. Brian McKinney
ICEsoft, Canada

Dr. Newaz Rafiq
ParetoLogic, Inc., Canada

Dr. Mohamed Rehan
British University, Egypt

Dr. Ayman Tawfik
Ajman University, United Arab Emirates

COMMENTS AND SUGGESTIONS

This book covers a wide range of techniques and topics related to parallel computing. It is highly probable that it contains errors and omissions. Other researchers and/or practicing engineers might have other ideas about the content and organization of a book of this nature. We welcome receiving comments and suggestions for consideration. If you find any errors, we would appreciate hearing from you. We also welcome ideas for examples and problems (along with their solutions if possible) to include with proper citation.

Please send your comments and bug reports electronically to fayez@uvic.ca, or you can fax or mail the information to

Dr. FAYEZ GEBALI
Electrical and Computer Engineering Department
University of Victoria, Victoria, B.C., Canada V8W 3P6
Tel: 250-721-6509
Fax: 250-721-6052

List of Acronyms

1-D	one-dimensional
2-D	two-dimensional
3-D	three-dimensional
ALU	arithmetic and logic unit
AMP	asymmetric multiprocessing system
API	application program interface
ASA	acyclic sequential algorithm
ASIC	application-specific integrated circuit
ASMP	asymmetric multiprocessor
CAD	computer-aided design
CFD	computational fluid dynamics
CMP	chip multiprocessor
CORDIC	coordinate rotation digital computer
CPI	clock cycles per instruction
CPU	central processing unit
CRC	cyclic redundancy check
CT	computerized tomography
CUDA	compute unified device architecture
DAG	directed acyclic graph
DBMS	database management system
DCG	directed cyclic graph
DFT	discrete Fourier transform
DG	directed graph
DHT	discrete Hilbert transform
DRAM	dynamic random access memory
DSP	digital signal processing
FBMA	full-search block matching algorithm
FDM	finite difference method
FDM	frequency division multiplexing
FFT	fast Fourier transform
FIR	finite impulse response
FLOPS	floating point operations per second
FPGA	field-programmable gate array
$GF(2^m)$	Galois field with 2^m elements
GFLOPS	giga floating point operations per second
GPGPU	general purpose graphics processor unit
GPU	graphics processing unit

HCORDIC	high-performance coordinate rotation digital computer
HDL	hardware description language
HDTV	high-definition TV
HRCT	high-resolution computerized tomography
HTM	hardware-based transactional memory
IA	iterative algorithm
IDHT	inverse discrete Hilbert transform
IEEE	Institute of Electrical and Electronic Engineers
IIR	infinite impulse response
ILP	instruction-level parallelism
I/O	input/output
IP	intellectual property modules
IP	Internet protocol
IR	instruction register
ISA	instruction set architecture
JVM	Java virtual machine
LAN	local area network
LCA	linear cellular automaton
LFSR	linear feedback shift register
LHS	left-hand side
LSB	least-significant bit
MAC	medium access control
MAC	multiply/accumulate
MCAPI	Multicore Communications Management API
MIMD	multiple instruction multiple data
MIMO	multiple-input multiple-output
MIN	multistage interconnection networks
MISD	multiple instruction single data stream
MIMD	multiple instruction multiple data
MPI	message passing interface
MRAPI	Multicore Resource Management API
MRI	magnetic resonance imaging
MSB	most significant bit
MTAPI	Multicore Task Management API
NIST	National Institute for Standards and Technology
NoC	network-on-chip
NSPA	nonserial–parallel algorithm
NUMA	nonuniform memory access
NVCC	NVIDIA C compiler
OFDM	orthogonal frequency division multiplexing
OFDMA	orthogonal frequency division multiple access
OS	operating system
P2P	peer-to-peer
PA	processor array
PE	processing element

PRAM	parallel random access machine
QoS	quality of service
RAID	redundant array of inexpensive disks
RAM	random access memory
RAW	read after write
RHS	right-hand side
RIA	regular iterative algorithm
RTL	register transfer language
SE	switching element
SF	switch fabric
SFG	signal flow graph
SIMD	single instruction multiple data stream
SIMP	single instruction multiple program
SISD	single instruction single data stream
SLA	service-level agreement
SM	streaming multiprocessor
SMP	symmetric multiprocessor
SMT	simultaneous multithreading
SoC	system-on-chip
SOR	successive over-relaxation
SP	streaming processor
SPA	serial–parallel algorithm
SPMD	single program multiple data stream
SRAM	static random access memory
STM	software-based transactional memory
TCP	transfer control protocol
TFLOPS	tera floating point operations per second
TLP	thread-level parallelism
TM	transactional memory
UMA	uniform memory access
VHDL	very high-speed integrated circuit hardware description language
VHSIC	very high-speed integrated circuit
VIQ	virtual input queuing
VLIW	very long instruction word
VLSI	very large-scale integration
VOQ	virtual output queuing
VRQ	virtual routing/virtual queuing
WAN	wide area network
WAR	write after read
WAW	write after write
WiFi	wireless fidelity

Chapter 1

Introduction

1.1 INTRODUCTION

The idea of a single-processor computer is fast becoming archaic and quaint. We now have to adjust our strategies when it comes to computing:

- It is impossible to improve computer performance using a single processor. Such processor would consume unacceptable power. It is more practical to use many simple processors to attain the desired performance using perhaps thousands of such simple computers [1].

- As a result of the above observation, if an application is not running fast on a single-processor machine, it will run even slower on new machines unless it takes advantage of parallel processing.

- Programming tools that can detect parallelism in a given algorithm have to be developed. An algorithm can show regular dependence among its variables or that dependence could be irregular. In either case, there is room for speeding up the algorithm execution provided that some subtasks can run concurrently while maintaining the correctness of execution can be assured.

- Optimizing future computer performance will hinge on good parallel programming at all levels: algorithms, program development, operating system, compiler, and hardware.

- The benefits of parallel computing need to take into consideration the number of processors being deployed as well as the communication overhead of processor-to-processor and processor-to-memory. Compute-bound problems are ones wherein potential speedup depends on the speed of execution of the algorithm by the processors. Communication-bound problems are ones wherein potential speedup depends on the speed of supplying the data to and extracting the data from the processors.

- Memory systems are still much slower than processors and their bandwidth is limited also to one word per read/write cycle.

Algorithms and Parallel Computing, by Fayez Gebali
Copyright © 2011 John Wiley & Sons, Inc.

- Scientists and engineers will no longer adapt their computing requirements to the available machines. Instead, there will be the practical possibility that they will adapt the computing hardware to solve their computing requirements.

This book is concerned with algorithms and the special-purpose hardware structures that execute them since software and hardware issues impact each other. Any software program ultimately runs and relies upon the underlying hardware support provided by the processor and the operating system. Therefore, we start this chapter with some definitions then move on to discuss some relevant design approaches and design constraints associated with this topic.

1.2 TOWARD AUTOMATING PARALLEL PROGRAMMING

We are all familiar with the process of algorithm implementation in software. When we write a code, we do not need to know the details of the target computer system since the compiler will take care of the details. However, we are steeped in thinking in terms of a single central processing unit (CPU) and sequential processing when we start writing the code or debugging the output. On the other hand, the processes of implementing algorithms in hardware or in software for parallel machines are more related than we might think. Figure 1.1 shows the main phases or layers of implementing an application in software or hardware using parallel computers. Starting at the top, *layer 5* is the application layer where the application or problem to be implemented on a parallel computing platform is defined. The specifications of inputs and outputs of the application being studied are also defined. Some input/output (I/O) specifications might be concerned with where data is stored and the desired timing relations of data. The results of this layer are fed to the lower layer to guide the algorithm development.

Layer 4 is algorithm development to implement the application in question. The computations required to implement the application define the tasks of the algorithm and their interdependences. The algorithm we develop for the application might or might not display parallelism at this state since we are traditionally used to linear execution of tasks. At this stage, we should not be concerned with task timing or task allocation to processors. It might be tempting to decide these issues, but this is counterproductive since it might preclude some potential parallelism. The result of this layer is a dependence graph, a directed graph (DG), or an adjacency matrix that summarize the task dependences.

Layer 3 is the parallelization layer where we attempt to extract latent parallelism in the algorithm. This layer accepts the algorithm description from layer 4 and produces thread timing and assignment to processors for software implementation. Alternatively, this layer produces task scheduling and assignment to processors for custom hardware very large-scale integration (VLSI) implementation. The book concentrates on this layer, which is shown within the gray rounded rectangle in the figure.

Layer 2 is the coding layer where the parallel algorithm is coded using a high-level language. The language used depends on the target parallel computing platform. The right branch in Fig. 1.1 is the case of mapping the algorithm on a general-purpose parallel computing platform. This option is really what we mean by *parallel programming*. Programming parallel computers is facilitated by what is called *concurrency platforms*, which are tools that help the programmer manage the threads and the timing of task execution on the processors. Examples of concurrency platforms include Cilk++, openMP, or compute unified device architecture (CUDA), as will be discussed in Chapter 6.

The left branch in Fig. 1.1 is the case of mapping the algorithm on a custom parallel computer such as systolic arrays. The programmer uses hardware description language (HDL) such as Verilog or very high-speed integrated circuit hardware (VHDL).

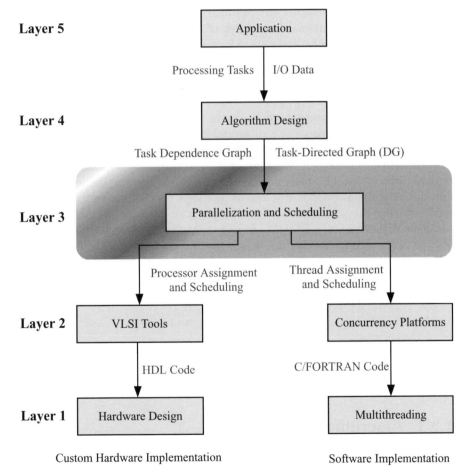

Figure 1.1   The phases or layers of implementing an application in software or hardware using parallel computers.

Layer 1 is the realization of the algorithm or the application on a parallel computer platform. The realization could be using multithreading on a parallel computer platform or it could be on an application-specific parallel processor system using application-specific integrated circuits (ASICs) or field-programmable gate array (FPGA).

So what do we mean by automatic programming of parallel computers? At the moment, we have automatic serial computer programming. The programmer writes a code in a high-level language such as C, Java, or FORTRAN, and the code is compiled without further input from the programmer. More significantly, the programmer does not need to know the hardware details of the computing platform. Fast code could result even if the programmer is unaware of the memory hierarchy, CPU details, and so on.

Does this apply to parallel computers? We have parallelizing compilers that look for simple loops and spread them among the processors. Such compilers could easily tackle what is termed *embarrassingly parallel algorithms* [2, 3]. Beyond that, the programmer must have intimate knowledge of how the processors interact among each and when the algorithm tasks are to be executed.

1.3 ALGORITHMS

The IEEE Standard Dictionary of Electrical and Electronics Terms defines an algorithm as "A prescribed set of well-defined rules or processes for the solution of a problem in a finite number of steps" [4]. The tasks or processes of an algorithm are interdependent in general. Some tasks can run concurrently in parallel and some must run serially or sequentially one after the other. According to the above definition, any algorithm is composed of a serial part and a parallel part. In fact, it is very hard to say that one algorithm is serial while the other is parallel except in extreme trivial cases. Later, we will be able to be more quantitative about this. If the number of tasks of the algorithm is W, then we say that the *work* associated with the algorithm is W.

The basic components defining an algorithm are

1. the different tasks,
2. the dependencies among the tasks where a task output is used as another task's input,
3. the set of primary inputs needed by the algorithm, and
4. the set of primary outputs produced by the algorithm.

1.3.1 Algorithm DG

Usually, an algorithm is graphically represented as a DG to illustrate the data dependencies among the algorithm tasks. We use the DG to describe our algorithm in preference to the term "dependence graph" to highlight the fact that the algorithm

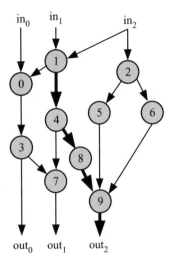

Figure 1.2 Example of a directed acyclic graph (DAG) for an algorithm.

variables flow as data between the tasks as indicated by the arrows of the DG. On the other hand, a dependence graph is a graph that has no arrows at its edges, and it becomes hard to figure out the data dependencies.

Definition 1.1 A dependence graph is a set of nodes and edges. The nodes represent the tasks to be done by the algorithm and the edges represent the data used by the tasks. This data could be input, output, or internal results.

Note that the edges in a dependence graph are undirected since an edge connecting two nodes does not indicate any input or output data dependency. An edge merely shows all the nodes that share a certain instance of the algorithm variable. This variable could be input, output, or I/O representing intermediate results.

Definition 1.2 A DG is a set of nodes and directed edges. The nodes represent the tasks to be done by the algorithm, and the directed edges represent the data dependencies among the tasks. The start of an edge is the output of a task and the end of an edge the input to the task.

Definition 1.3 A directed acyclic graph (DAG) is a DG that has no cycles or loops.

Figure 1.2 shows an example of representing an algorithm by a DAG. A DG or DAG has three types of edges depending on the sources and destinations of the edges.

Definition 1.4 An input edge in a DG is one that terminates on one or more nodes but does not start from any node. It represents one of the algorithm inputs.

Referring to Fig. 1.2, we note that the algorithm has three input edges that represent the inputs in_0, in_1, and in_2.

Definition 1.5 An output edge in a DG is one that starts from a node but does not terminate on any other node. It represents one of the algorithm outputs.

Referring to Fig. 1.2, we note that the algorithm has three output edges that represent the outputs out_0, out_1, and out_2.

Definition 1.6 An internal edge in a DG is one that starts from a node and terminate one or more nodes. It represents one of the algorithm internal variables.

Definition 1.7 An input node in a DG is one whose incoming edges are all input edges.

Referring to Fig. 1.2, we note that nodes 0, 1, and 2 represent input nodes. The tasks associated with these nodes can start immediately after the inputs are available.

Definition 1.8 An output node in a DG is whose outgoing edges are all output edges.

Referring to Fig. 1.2, we note that nodes 7 and 9 represent output nodes. Node 3 in the graph of Fig. 1.2 is not an output node since one of its outgoing edges is an internal edge terminating on node 7.

Definition 1.9 An internal node in a DG is one that has at least one incoming internal edge and at least one outgoing internal edge.

1.3.2 Algorithm Adjacency Matrix A

An algorithm could also be represented algebraically as an *adjacency matrix* **A**. Given W nodes/tasks, we define the 0–1 adjacency matrix **A**, which is a square $W \times W$ matrix defined so that element $a(i, j) = 1$ indicates that node i depends on the output from node j. The source node is j and the destination node is i. Of course, we must have $a(i, i) = 0$ for all values of $0 \leq i < W$ since node i does not depend on its own output (self-loop), and we assumed that we do not have any loops. The definition of the adjacency matrix above implies that this matrix is asymmetric. This is because if node i depends on node j, then the reverse is not true when loops are not allowed.

As an example, the adjacency matrix for the algorithm in Fig. 1.2 is given by

$$
\mathbf{A} = \begin{bmatrix}
0 & 0 & 0 & 0 & 0 & 0 & 0 & 0 & 0 & 0 \\
0 & 0 & 0 & 0 & 0 & 0 & 0 & 0 & 0 & 0 \\
0 & 0 & 0 & 0 & 0 & 0 & 0 & 0 & 0 & 0 \\
1 & 0 & 0 & 0 & 0 & 0 & 0 & 0 & 0 & 0 \\
0 & 1 & 0 & 0 & 0 & 0 & 0 & 0 & 0 & 0 \\
0 & 0 & 1 & 0 & 0 & 0 & 0 & 0 & 0 & 0 \\
0 & 0 & 1 & 0 & 0 & 0 & 0 & 0 & 0 & 0 \\
0 & 0 & 0 & 1 & 1 & 0 & 0 & 0 & 0 & 0 \\
0 & 0 & 0 & 0 & 1 & 0 & 0 & 0 & 0 & 0 \\
0 & 0 & 0 & 0 & 0 & 1 & 1 & 0 & 1 & 0
\end{bmatrix}. \tag{1.1}
$$

Matrix **A** has some interesting properties related to our topic. An input node i is associated with row i, whose elements are all zeros. An output node j is associated with column j, whose elements are all zeros. We can write

$$\text{Input node } i \Rightarrow \sum_{j=0}^{W-1} a(i, j) = 0 \tag{1.2}$$

$$\text{Output node } j \Rightarrow \sum_{i=0}^{W-1} a(i, j) = 0. \tag{1.3}$$

All other nodes are internal nodes. Note that all the elements in rows 0, 1, and 2 are all zeros since nodes 0, 1, and 2 are input nodes. This is indicated by the bold entries in these three rows. Note also that all elements in columns 7 and 9 are all zeros since nodes 7 and 9 are output nodes. This is indicated by the bold entries in these two columns. All other rows and columns have one or more nonzero elements to indicate internal nodes. If node i has element $a(i, j) = 1$, then we say that node j is a parent of node i.

1.3.3 Classifying Algorithms Based On Task Dependences

Algorithms can be broadly classified based on task dependences:

1. **Serial algorithms**
2. **Parallel algorithms**
3. **Serial–parallel algorithms (SPAs)**
4. **Nonserial–parallel algorithms (NSPAs)**
5. **Regular iterative algorithms (RIAs)**

The last category could be thought of as a generalization of SPAs. It should be mentioned that the level of data or task granularity can change the algorithm from one class to another. For example, adding two matrices could be an example of a serial algorithm if our basic operation is adding two matrix elements at a time. However, if we add corresponding rows on different computers, then we have a row-based parallel algorithm.

We should also mention that some algorithms can contain other types of algorithms within their tasks. The simple matrix addition example serves here as well. Our parallel matrix addition algorithm adds pairs of rows at the same time on different processors. However, each processor might add the rows one element at a time, and thus, the tasks of the parallel algorithm represent serial row add algorithms. We discuss these categories in the following subsections.

1.3.4 Serial Algorithms

A serial algorithm is one where the tasks must be performed in series one after the other due to their data dependencies. The DG associated with such an algorithm looks

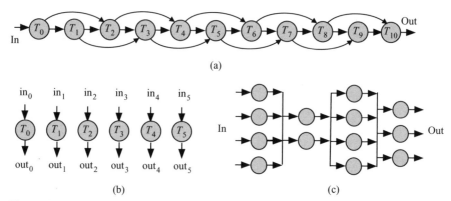

(a)

(b)   (c)

Figure 1.3 Example of serial, parallel, and serial–parallel algorithms. (a) Serial algorithm. (b) Parallel algorithm. (c) Serial–parallel algorithm.

like a long string or queue of dependent tasks. Figure 1.3a shows an example of a serial algorithm. The algorithm shown is for calculating Fibonnaci numbers. To calculate Fibonacci number n_{10}, task T_{10} performs the following simple calculation:

$$n_{10} = n_8 + n_9, \tag{1.4}$$

with $n_0 = 0$ and $n_1 = 1$ given as initial conditions. Clearly, we can find a Fibonacci number only after the preceding two Fibonacci numbers have been calculated.

1.3.5 Parallel Algorithms

A parallel algorithm is one where the tasks could all be performed in parallel at the same time due to their data independence. The DG associated with such an algorithm looks like a wide row of independent tasks. Figure 1.3b shows an example of a parallel algorithm. A simple example of such a purely parallel algorithm is a web server where each incoming request can be processed independently from other requests. Another simple example of parallel algorithms is multitasking in operating systems where the operating system deals with several applications like a web browser, a word processor, and so on.

1.3.6 SPAs

An SPA is one where tasks are grouped in stages such that the tasks in each stage can be executed concurrently in parallel and the stages are executed sequentially. An SPA becomes a parallel algorithm when the number of stages is one. A serial-parallel algorithm also becomes a serial algorithm when the number of tasks in each stage is one. Figure 1.3c shows an example of an SPA. An example of an SPA is the CORDIC algorithm [5–8]. The algorithm requires n iterations and at iteration i, three operations are performed:

$$x_{i+1} = x_i + my_i\delta_i$$
$$y_{i+1} = y_i - x_i\delta_i \qquad\qquad (1.5)$$
$$z_{i+1} = z_i + \theta_i,$$

where x, y, and z are the data to be updated at each iteration. δ_i and θ_i are iteration constants that are stored in lookup tables. The parameter m is a control parameter that determines the type of calculations required. The variable θ_i is determined before the start of each iteration. The algorithm performs other operations during each iteration, but we are not concerned about this here. More details can be found in Chapter 7 and in the cited references.

1.3.7 NSPAs

An NSPA does not conform to any of the above classifications. The DG for such an algorithm has no pattern. We can further classify NSPA into two main categories based on whether their DG contains cycles or not. Therefore, we can have two types of graphs for NSPA:

1. **DAG**
2. Directed cyclic graph (DCG)

Figure 1.4a is an example of a DAG algorithm and Fig. 1.4b is an example of a DCG algorithm. The DCG is most commonly encountered in discrete time feedback control systems. The input is supplied to task T_0 for prefiltering or input signal conditioning. Task T_1 accepts the conditioned input signal and the conditioned feedback output signal. The output of task T_1 is usually referred to as the error signal, and this signal is fed to task T_2 to produce the output signal.

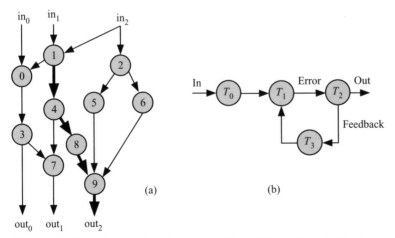

Figure 1.4 Example directed graphs for nonserial–parallel algorithms. (a) Directed acyclic graph (DAG). (b) Directed cyclic graph (DCG).

The NSPA graph is characterized by two types of constructs: the *nodes*, which describe the tasks comprising the algorithm, and the *directed edges*, which describe the direction of data flow among the tasks. The lines exiting a node represent an output, and when they enter a node, they represent an input. If task T_i produces an output that is used by task T_j, then we say that T_j depends on T_i. On the graph, we have an arrow from node i to node j.

The DG of an algorithm gives us three important properties:

1. *Work* (W), which describes the amount of processing work to be done to complete the algorithm

2. *Depth* (D), which is also known as the *critical path*. Depth is defined as the maximum path length between any input node and any output node.

3. *Parallelism* (P), which is also known as the *degree of parallelism* of the algorithm. Parallelism is defined as the maximum number of nodes that can be processed in parallel. The maximum number of parallel processors that could be active at any given time will not exceed B since anymore processors will not find any tasks to execute.

A more detailed discussion of these properties and how an algorithm can be mapped onto a parallel computer is found in Chapter 8.

1.3.8   RIAs

Karp et al. [9, 10] introduced the concept of RIA. This class of algorithms deserves special attention because they are found in algorithms from diverse fields such as signal, image and video processing, linear algebra applications, and numerical simulation applications that can be implemented in grid structures. Figure 1.5 shows the *dependence graph* of a RIA. The example is for pattern matching algorithm. Notice that for a RIA, we do not draw a DAG; instead, we use the dependence graph concept.

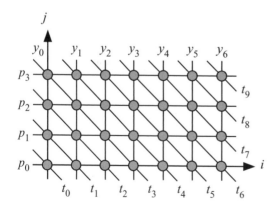

Figure 1.5   Dependence graph of a RIA for the pattern matching algorithm.

A dependence graph is like a DAG except that the links are not directed and the graph is obtained according to the methodology explained in Chapters 9, 10, and 11.

In a RIA, the dependencies among the tasks show a fixed pattern. It is a trivial problem to parallelize a serial algorithm, a parallel algorithm, or even an SPA. It is not trivial to explore the possible parallelization options of a RIA. In fact, Chapters 9–11 are dedicated to just exploring the parallelization of this class of algorithms.

A simple example of a RIA is the matrix–matrix multiplication algorithm given by Algorithm 1.1.

Algorithm 1.1   Matrix–matrix multiplication algorithm.

Require: Input: matrices A and B

 1: **for** $i = 0 : I - 1$ **do**

 2:   **for** $j = 0 : J - 1$ **do**

 3:     $temp = 0$

 4:     **for** $k = 0 : K - 1$ **do**

 5:       $temp = \text{temp} + A(i, k) \times B(k, j)$

 6:     **end for**

 7:     $C(i, j) = temp$

 8:   **end for**

 9: **end for**

10: **RETURN** C

The variables in the RIA described by Algorithm 1.1 show regular dependence on the algorithm indices i, j, and k. Traditionally, such algorithms are studied using the dependence graph technique, which shows the links between the different tasks to be performed [10–12]. The dependence graph is attractive when the number of algorithm indices is 1 or 2. We have three indices in our matrix–matrix multiplication algorithm. It would be hard to visualize such an algorithm using a three-dimensional (3-D) graph. For higher dimensionality algorithms, we use more formal techniques as will be discussed in this book. Chapters 9–11 are dedicated to studying such algorithms.

1.3.9 Implementing Algorithms on Parallel Computing

The previous subsections explained different classes of algorithms based on the dependences among the algorithm tasks. We ask in this section how to implement these different algorithms on parallel computing platforms either in hardware or in software. This is referred to as parallelizing an algorithm. The parallelization strategy depends on the type of algorithm we are dealing with.

Serial Algorithms

Serial algorithms, as exemplified by Fig. 1.3a, cannot be parallelized since the tasks must be executed sequentially. The only parallelization possible is when each task is broken down into parallelizable subtasks. An example is to perform bit-parallel add/multiply operations.

Parallel Algorithms

Parallel algorithms, as exemplified by Fig. 1.3b, are easily parallelized since all the tasks can be executed in parallel, provided there are enough computing resources.

SPAs

SPAs, as exemplified by Fig. 1.3c, are parallelized by assigning each task in a stage to a software thread or hardware processing element. The stages themselves cannot be parallelized since they are serial in nature.

NSPAs

Techniques for parallelizing NSPAs will be discussed in Chapter 8.

RIAs

Techniques for parallelizing RIAs will be discussed in Chapters 9–11.

1.4 PARALLEL COMPUTING DESIGN CONSIDERATIONS

This section discusses some of the important aspects of the design of parallel computing systems. The design of a parallel computing system requires considering many design options. The designer must choose a basic *processor architecture* that is capable of performing the contemplated tasks. The processor could be a simple element or it could involve a superscalar processor running a multithreaded operating system.

The processors must communicate among themselves using some form of an *interconnection network*. This network might prove to be a bottleneck if it cannot support simultaneous communication between arbitrary pairs of processors. Providing the links between processors is like providing physical channels in telecommunications. How data are exchanged must be specified. A bus is the simplest form of interconnection network. Data are exchanged in the form of words, and a system clock informs the processors when data are valid. Nowadays, buses are being replaced by *networks-on-chips* (NoC) [13]. In this architecture, data are exchanged on the chip in the form of *packets* and are routed among the chip modules using *routers*.

Data and programs must be stored in some form of *memory system*, and the designer will then have the option of having several memory modules shared among the processors or of dedicating a memory module to each processor. When processors need to share data, mechanisms have to be devised to allow reading and writing data in the different memory modules. The order of reading and writing will be important to ensure data integrity. When a shared data item is updated by one processor, all other processors must be somehow informed of the change so they use the appropriate data value.

Implementing the tasks or programs on a parallel computer involves several design options also. *Task partitioning* breaks up the original program or application into several segments to be allocated to the processors. The level of partitioning determines the workload allocated to each processor. *Coarse grain partitioning* allocates large segments to each processor. Fine grain partitioning allocates smaller segments to each processor. These segments could be in the form of separate *software processes* or *threads*. The programmer or the compiler might be the two entities that decide on this partitioning. The programmer or the operating system must ensure proper *synchronization* among the executing tasks so as to ensure program correctness and data integrity.

1.5 PARALLEL ALGORITHMS AND PARALLEL ARCHITECTURES

Parallel algorithms and parallel architectures are closely tied together. We cannot think of a parallel algorithm without thinking of the parallel hardware that will support it. Conversely, we cannot think of parallel hardware without thinking of the parallel software that will drive it. Parallelism can be implemented at different levels in a computing system using hardware and software techniques:

1. *Data-level parallelism*, where we simultaneously operate on multiple bits of a datum or on multiple data. Examples of this are bit-parallel addition multiplication and division of binary numbers, vector processor arrays and systolic arrays for dealing with several data samples. This is the subject of this book.

2. *Instruction-level parallelism (ILP)*, where we simultaneously execute more than one instruction by the processor. An example of this is use of instruction pipelining.

3. *Thread-level parallelism (TLP)*. A thread is a portion of a program that shares processor resources with other threads. A thread is sometimes called a lightweight process. In TLP, multiple software threads are executed simultaneously on one processor or on several processors.

4. *Process-level parallelism*. A process is a program that is running on the computer. A process reserves its own computer resources such as memory space and registers. This is, of course, the classic multitasking and time-sharing computing where several programs are running simultaneously on one machine or on several machines.

1.6   RELATING PARALLEL ALGORITHM AND PARALLEL ARCHITECTURE

The IEEE Standard Dictionary of Electrical and Electronics Terms [4] defines "parallel" for software as "simultaneous transfer, occurrence, or processing of the individual parts of a whole, such as the bits of a character and the characters of a word using separate facilities for the various parts." So in that sense, we say an algorithm is parallel when two or more parts of the algorithms can be executed independently on hardware. Thus, the definition of a parallel algorithm presupposes availability of supporting hardware. This gives a hint that parallelism in software is closely tied to the hardware that will be executing the software code. Execution of the parts can be done using different threads or processes in the software or on different processors in the hardware. We can quickly identify a potentially parallel algorithm when we see the occurrence of "FOR" or "WHILE" loops in the code.

On the other hand, the definition of parallel architecture, according to *The IEEE Standard Dictionary of Electrical and Electronics Terms* [4], is "a multi-processor architecture in which parallel processing can be performed." It is the job of the programmer, compiler, or operating system to supply the multiprocessor with tasks to keep the processors busy. We find ready examples of parallel algorithms in fields such as

- scientific computing, such as physical simulations, differential equations solvers, wind tunnel simulations, and weather simulation;
- computer graphics, such as image processing, video compression; and ray tracing; and,
- medical imaging, such as in magnetic resonance imaging (MRI) and computerized tomography (CT).

There are, however, equally large numbers of algorithms that are not recognizably parallel especially in the area of information technology such as online medical data, online banking, data mining, data warehousing, and database retrieval systems. The challenge is to develop computer architectures and software to speed up the different information technology applications.

1.7   IMPLEMENTATION OF ALGORITHMS: A TWO-SIDED PROBLEM

Figure 1.6 shows the issues we would like to deal with in this book. On the left is the space of algorithms and on the right is the space of parallel architectures that will execute the algorithms. Route A represents the case when we are given an algorithm and we are exploring possible parallel hardware or processor arrays that would correctly implement the algorithm according to some performance requirements and certain system constraints. In other words, the problem is given a parallel algorithm, what are the possible parallel processor architectures that are possible?

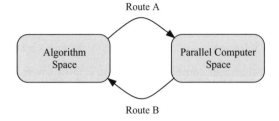

Figure 1.6   The two paths relating parallel algorithms and parallel architectures.

Route B represents the classic case when we are given a parallel architecture or a multicore system and we explore the best way to implement a given algorithm on the system subject again to some performance requirements and certain system constraints. In other words, the problem is given a parallel architecture, how can we allocate the different tasks of the parallel algorithm to the different processors? This is the realm of parallel programming using the multithreading design technique. It is done by the application programmer, the software compiler, and the operating system.

Moving along routes A or B requires dealing with

1. *mapping* the tasks to different processors,
2. *scheduling* the execution of the tasks to conform to algorithm data dependency and data I/O requirements, and
3. *identifying* the data communication between the processors and the I/O.

1.8 MEASURING BENEFITS OF PARALLEL COMPUTING

We review in this section some of the important results and benefits of using parallel computing. But first, we identify some of the key parameters that we will be studying in this section.

1.8.1 Speedup Factor

The potential benefit of parallel computing is typically measured by the time it takes to complete a task on a single processor versus the time it takes to complete the same task on N parallel processors. The speedup $S(N)$ due to the use of N parallel processors is defined by

$$S(N) = \frac{T_p(1)}{T_p(N)},\tag{1.6}$$

where $T_p(1)$ is the algorithm processing time on a single processor and $T_p(N)$ is the processing time on the parallel processors. In an ideal situation, for a fully parallelizable algorithm, and when the communication time between processors and memory is neglected, we have $T_p (N) = T_p (1)/N$, and the above equation gives

$$S(N) = N. \tag{1.7}$$

It is rare indeed to get this linear increase in computation domain due to several factors, as we shall see in the book.

1.8.2 Communication Overhead

For single and parallel computing systems, there is always the need to read data from memory and to write back the results of the computations. Communication with the memory takes time due to the speed mismatch between the processor and the memory [14]. Moreover, for parallel computing systems, there is the need for communication between the processors to exchange data. Such exchange of data involves transferring data or messages across the interconnection network.

Communication between processors is fraught with several problems:

1. *Interconnection network delay.* Transmitting data across the interconnection network suffers from bit propagation delay, message/data transmission delay, and queuing delay within the network. These factors depend on the network topology, the size of the data being sent, the speed of operation of the network, and so on.

2. *Memory bandwidth.* No matter how large the memory capacity is, access to memory contents is done using a single port that moves one word in or out of the memory at any give memory access cycle.

3. *Memory collisions*, where two or more processors attempt to access the same memory module. Arbitration must be provided to allow one processor to access the memory at any given time.

4. *Memory wall.* The speed of data transfer to and from the memory is much slower than processing speed. This problem is being solved using memory hierarchy such as

    register $\leftrightarrow$ cache $\leftrightarrow$ RAM $\leftrightarrow$ electronic disk $\leftrightarrow$ magnetic disk $\leftrightarrow$ optic disk

To process an algorithm on a parallel processor system, we have several delays as explained in Table 1.1.

1.8.3 Estimating Speedup Factor and Communication Overhead

Let us assume we have a parallel algorithm consisting of N independent tasks that can be executed either on a single processor or on N processors. Under these ideal circumstances, data travel between the processors and the memory, and there is no

Table 1.1   Delays Involved in Evaluating an Algorithm on a Parallel Processor System

Operation	Symbol	Comment
Memory read	$T_r(N)$	Read data from memory shared by N processors
Memory write	$T_w(N)$	Write data from memory shared by N processors
Communicate	$T_c(N)$	Communication delay between a pair of processors when there are N processors in the system
Process data	$T_p(N)$	Delay to process the algorithm using N parallel processors

interprocessor communication due to the task independence. We can write under ideal circumstances

$$T_p(1) = N\tau_p \tag{1.8}$$

$$T_p(N) = \tau_p. \tag{1.9}$$

The time needed to read the algorithm input data by a single processor is given by

$$T_r(1) = N\tau_m, \tag{1.10}$$

where τ_m is memory access time to read one block of data. We assumed in the above equation that each task requires one block of input data and N tasks require to read N blocks. The time needed by the parallel processors to read data from memory is estimated as

$$T_r(N) = \alpha T_r(1) = \alpha N\tau_m, \tag{1.11}$$

where α is a factor that takes into account limitations of accessing the shared memory. $\alpha = 1/N$ when each processor maintains its own copy of the required data. $\alpha = 1$ when data are distributed to each task in order from a central memory. In the worst case, we could have $\alpha > N$ when all processors request data and collide with each other. We could write the above observations as

$$T_r(N) \begin{cases} = \tau_m & \text{when} \quad \text{Distributed memory} \\ = N\tau_m & \text{when} \quad \text{Shared memory and no collisions} \\ > N\tau_m & \text{when} \quad \text{Shared memory with collisions.} \end{cases} \tag{1.12}$$

Writing back the results to the memory, also, might involve memory collisions when the processor attempts to access the same memory module.

$$T_w(1) = N\tau_m \tag{1.13}$$

$$T_w(N) = \alpha T_w(1) = \alpha N\tau_m. \tag{1.14}$$

For a single processor, the total time to complete a task, including memory access overhead, is given by

$$T_{total}(1) = T_r(1) + T_p(1) + T_w(1)$$
$$= N(2\tau_m + \tau_p) \quad . \tag{1.15}$$

Now let us consider the speedup factor when communication overhead is considered:

$$T_{total}(N) = T_r(N) + T_p(N) + T_w(N)$$
$$= 2N\alpha\tau_m + \tau_p \quad . \tag{1.16}$$

The speedup factor is given by

$$S(N) = \frac{T_{total}(1)}{T_{total}(N)}$$
$$= \frac{2\alpha N\tau_m + N\tau_p}{2N\alpha\tau_m + \tau_p}. \tag{1.17}$$

Define the *memory mismatch ratio (R)* as

$$R = \frac{\tau_m}{\tau_p}, \tag{1.18}$$

which is the ratio of the delay for accessing one data block from the memory relative to the delay for processing one block of data. In that sense, τ_p is expected to be orders of magnitude smaller than τ_m depending on the granularity of the subtask being processed and the speed of the memory.

We can write Eq. 1.17 as a function of N and R in the form

$$S(N, R) = \frac{2\alpha RN + N}{2\alpha RN + 1}. \tag{1.19}$$

Figure 1.7 shows the effect of the two parameters, N and R, on the speedup when $\alpha = 1$. Numerical simulations indicated that changes in α are not as significant as the values of R and N. From the above equation, we get full speedup when the product $RN \ll 1$. This speedup is similar to Eq. 1.7 where communication overhead was neglected.

This situation occurs in the case of trivially parallel algorithms as will be discussed in Chapter 7.

Notice from the figure that speedup quickly decreases when $RN > 0.1$. When $R = 1$, we get a communication-bound problem and the benefits of parallelism quickly vanish. This reinforces the point that memory design and communication between processors or threads are very important factors. We will also see that multicore processors, discussed in Chapter 3, contain all the processors on the same chip. This has the advantage that communication occurs at a much higher speed compared with multiprocessors, where communication takes place across chips. Therefore, T_m is reduced by orders of magnitude for multicore systems, and this should give them the added advantage of small R values.

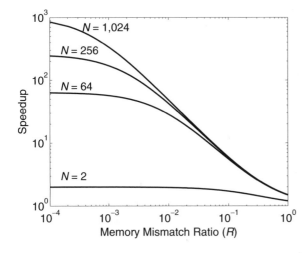

Figure 1.7 Effect of the two parameters, N and R, on the speedup when $\alpha = 1$.

The interprocessor communication overhead involves reading and writing data into memory:

$$T_c(N) = \beta N \tau_m, \tag{1.20}$$

where $\beta \geq 0$ and depends on the algorithm and how the memory is organized. $\beta = 0$ for a single processor, where there is no data exchange or when the processors in a multiprocessor system do not communicate while evaluating the algorithm. In other algorithms, β could be equal to $\log_2 N$ or even N. This could be the case when the parallel algorithm programmer or hardware designer did not consider fully the cost of interprocessor or interthread communications.

1.9 AMDAHL'S LAW FOR MULTIPROCESSOR SYSTEMS

Assume an algorithm or a task is composed of parallizable fraction f and a serial fraction $1 - f$. Assume the time needed to process this task on one single processor is given by

$$T_p(1) = N(1 - f)\tau_p + Nf\tau_p = N\tau_p, \tag{1.21}$$

where the first term on the right-hand side (RHS) is the time the processor needs to process the serial part. The second term on RHS is the time the processor needs to process the parallel part. When this task is executed on N parallel processors, the time taken will be given by

$$T_p(N) = N(1 - f)\tau_p + f\tau_p, \tag{1.22}$$

where the only speedup is because the parallel part now is distributed over N processors. Amdahl's law for speedup $S(N)$, achieved by using N processors, is given by

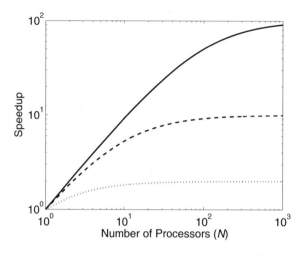

Figure 1.8 Speedup according to Amdahl's law. The solid line is for $f = 0.99$; the dashed line is for $f = 0.9$; and the dotted line is for $f = 0.5$.

$$S(N) = \frac{T_p(1)}{T_p(N)}$$

$$= \frac{N}{(1-f)N+f}$$

$$= \frac{1}{(1-f)+f/N}. \tag{1.23}$$

To get any speedup, we must have

$$1-f \ll f/N. \tag{1.24}$$

This inequality dictates that the parallel portion f must be very close to unity especially when N is large.

Figure 1.8 shows the speedup versus f for different values of N. The solid line is for $f = 0.99$; the dashed line is for $f = 0.9$; and the dotted line is for $f = 0.5$. We note from the figure that speedup is affected by the value of f. As expected, larger f results in more speedup. However, note that the speedup is most pronounced when $f > 0.5$. Another observation is that speedup saturates to a given value when N becomes large.

For large values of N, the speedup in Eq. 1.23 is approximated by

$$S(N) \approx \frac{1}{1-f} \qquad \text{when } N \gg 1. \tag{1.25}$$

This result indicates that if we are using a system with more than 10 processors, then any speedup advantage is dictated mainly by how clever we are at discovering the parallel parts of the program and how much we are able to execute those parallel parts simultaneously. The figure confirms these expectations.

For extreme values of f, Eq. 1.23 becomes

$$S(N) = 1 \quad \text{when } f = 0 \quad \text{completely serial code} \tag{1.26}$$
$$S(N) = N \quad \text{when } f = 1 \quad \text{completely parallel code.} \tag{1.27}$$

The above equation is obvious. When the program is fully parallel, speedup will be equal to the number of parallel processors we use.

What do we conclude from this? Well, we must know or estimate the value of the fraction f for a given algorithm at the start. Knowing f will give us an idea on what system speedup could be expected on a multiprocessor system. This alone should enable us to judge how much effort to spend trying to improve speedup by mapping the algorithm to a multiprocessor system.

1.10 GUSTAFSON–BARSIS'S LAW

The predictions of speedup according to Amdahl's law are pessimistic. Gustafson [15] made the observation that parallelism increases in an application when the problem size increases. Remember that Amdahl's law assumed that the fraction of parallelizable code is fixed and does not depend on problem size.

To derive Gustafson–Barsis formula for speedup, we start with the N parallel processors first. The time taken to process the task on N processors is given by

$$T_p(N) = (1 - f)\tau_p + f\tau_p = \tau_p. \tag{1.28}$$

When this task is executed on a single processor, the serial part is unchanged, but the parallel part will increase as given by

$$T_p(1) = (1 - f)\tau_p + Nf\tau_p. \tag{1.29}$$

The speedup is given now by

$$S(N) = \frac{T_p(1)}{T_p(N)}$$
$$= (1 - f) + Nf$$
$$= 1 + (N - 1)f. \tag{1.30}$$

Figure 1.9 shows the speedup versus f for different values of N. The solid line is for $f = 0.99$; the dashed line is for $f = 0.9$; and the dotted line is for $f = 0.5$. Notice that there is speedup even for very small values of f and the situation improves as N gets larger.

To get any speedup, we must have

$$f(N - 1) \gg 1. \tag{1.31}$$

Notice that we can get very decent speedup even for small values of f especially when N gets large. Compared with inequality 1.24, we note that the speedup constraints are very much relaxed according to Gustafson–Barsis's law.

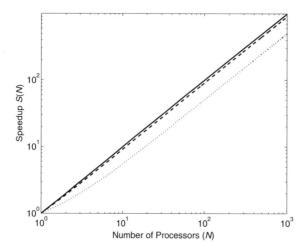

Figure 1.9   Speedup according to Gustafson–Barsis's law. The solid line is for $f = 0.99$; the dashed line is for $f = 0.9$; and the dotted line is for $f = 0.5$.

1.11   APPLICATIONS OF PARALLEL COMPUTING

The availability of inexpensive yet really powerful parallel computers is expected to make a hitherto unforeseeable impact on our lives. We are used now to parallel computers helping us access any information through web search engines. In fact, the search progresses as we are typing our search key words. However, there is room for improvement and, more importantly, for innovation, as the following sections illustrate.

1.11.1   Climate Modeling

Climate simulations are used for weather forecasting as well as for predicting global climate changes based on different phenomena or human activities. As Reference 1 points out, the resolution of today's climate models is 200 km. This is considered low resolution given the fact that some climate systems exist completely within such resolution scale.

Assume a high-resolution model for climate simulation partitions the globe using 3-D cells 1 km in size in each direction. Assume also that the total surface of the earth to be 510×10^6 km^2 and the thickness of the atmospheric layer to be approximately 1,000 km. Then, we need to simulate approximately 5×10^{11} weather cells. Assume further that each cell needs to do 200 floating point operations for each iteration of the simulation. Thus, we have to perform a total of 10^{14} floating point operations per iteration.

Let us now assume that we need to run the simulation 10^6 times to simulate the climate over some long duration of the weather cycle. Thus, we have the following performance requirements for our computing system:

Table 1.2 Parallel Multicore Computer Implementation Using Two Types of Microprocessors Needed to Perform 2.8×10^{15} FLOPS

Processor	Clock speed	GFLOPS/core	Cores needed	Power (MW)
AMD Opteron	2.8 GHz	5.6	4.9×10^5	52.0
Tensilica XTensa LX2	500.0 MHz	1.0	2.8×10^6	0.8

$$\text{Total number of operations} = 10^{14} \text{ operations/iteration} \times 10^6 \text{ iterations}$$
$$= 10^{20} \text{ floating point operations} \qquad (1.32)$$

A computer operating at a rate of 10^9 floating point operations per second (FLOPS) would complete the operations in 10^{11} seconds, which comes to about 31 centuries. Assuming that all these simulations should be completed in one workday, then our system should operate at a rate of approximately 2.8×10^{15} FLOPS. It is obvious that such performance cannot be attained by any single-processor computer. We must divide this computational task among many processors. Modeling the atmosphere using a mesh or a grid of nodes lends itself to computational parallelization since calculations performed by each node depend only on its immediate six neighboring nodes. Distributing the calculations among several processors is relatively simple, but care must be given to the exchange of data among the processors. Table 1.2 compares building a parallel processor system needed to give us a performance of 2.8×10^{15} FLOPS. We assume using desktop microprocessors versus using a simple embedded microprocessor [1].

The power advantage of using low-power, low-performance processors is obvious from the table. Of course, we need to figure out how to interconnect such a huge system irrespective of the type of processor used. The interconnection network becomes a major design issue here since it would be impossible to think of a system that uses buses and single global system clock.

1.11.2 CT

CT and magnetic resonance imaging (MRI) are techniques to obtain a high-resolution map of the internals of the body for medical diagnosis. Figure 1.10 shows a simplified view of a CT system. Figure 1.10a shows the placement of the patient on a gurney at the center of a very strong magnet and a strong X-ray source. The gurney is on a movable table in a direction perpendicular to the page. The X-ray source or emitter is placed at the top and emits a collimated beam that travels to the other side of the circle through the patient. An X-ray detector is placed diametrically opposite to where the X-ray source is. When the machine is in operation, the source/detector pair is rotated as shown in Fig. 1.10b. After completing a complete rotation and storing the detector samples, the table is moved and the process is repeated for a different section or slice of the body. The output of a certain detector at a given time

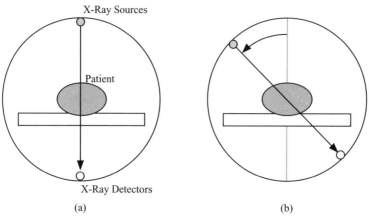

Figure 1.10 Computerized tomography (CT) system. (a) Setup of X-ray sources and detectors. (b) Schematic of the output of each sensor when a single X-ray source is active.

is affected by all the patient tissue that a certain X-ray beam encounters in its passage from the source to the detector. As things stand at the time of writing, the patient needs to be in this position for several minutes if not hours (personal experience).

Assume the image we are trying to generate is composed of $N \times N$ pixels, where N could be approximately equal to 4,000. Thus, we have approximately 10^7 pixels to generate per image, or slice, of the body scan. As the table moves, more slices should be generated. This allows for 3-D viewing of the body area of concern. For a system that generates $S = 1,000$ successive slices, $SN^2 = 10^{10}$ pixels will have to be processed. A slice will require approximately $N^2 (\log_2 N)^3$ calculations [16]. For our case, we need approximately

$$\text{Total number of operations} = 10^{10} \text{ operations/slice} \times 10^3 \text{ slices}$$
$$= 10^{13} \text{ floating point operations} \qquad (1.33)$$

Assume we need to generate these images in 1 second to allow for a real-time examination of the patient. In that case, the system should operate at a rate of approximately 10^{13} FLOPS. For an even more accurate medical diagnosis, high-resolution computerized tomography (HRCT) scans are required even at the nanoscale level where blood vessels need to be examined. Needless to say, parallel processing of massive data will be required for a timely patient treatment.

1.11.3 Computational Fluid Dynamics (CFD)

CFD is a field that is closely tied to parallel computers and parallel algorithms. It is viewed as a cost-effective way to investigate and design systems that involve flow of gas or fluids. Some examples of CFD are:

- ocean currents,
- our atmosphere and global weather,

- blood flow in the arteries,
- heart deformation during high-G maneuvers of a fighter jet,
- air flow in the lungs,
- design of airplane wings and winglets,
- seat ejection in a fighter jet,
- combustion of gases inside a car cylinder,
- jet engine air intake and combustion chamber,
- shape of a car body to reduce air drag, and
- spray from nozzles such as paint guns and rocket exhaust.

Typically, the region where the flow of interest is being studied is divided into a grid or mesh of points using the *finite element* method. The number of grid points depends on the size of the region or the desired resolution. A system of linear equations or a set differential equations is solved at each grid point for the problem unknowns. The number of unknown might be around 10^3, and each variable might require around 10^3 floating point operations at each grid point.

The targeted region of the CFD applications ranges from 10^{12} to 10^{18} FLOPS [17]. If the computer system operates at a speed of 10^9 (giga) FLOPS, then CFD applications would complete a simulation in the time period that ranges between 15 minutes and 30 years. On the other hand, a parallel computer system operating at 10^{12} (tera) FLOPS would complete the application in a time period between 1 second and 12 days. Currently, there are few supercomputer systems that operate at the rate of 10^{15} (peta) FLOPS. On such a system, the larger problem would take about 3 minutes to complete.

1.12 PROBLEMS

1.1. Assume you are given the task of adding eight numbers together. Draw the DG and the adjacency matrix for each of the following number adding algorithms:

  (1) Add the numbers serially, which would take seven steps.

  (2) Add the numbers in a binary fashion by adding each adjacent pair of numbers in parallel and then by adding pairs of the results in parallel, and continue this process.

1.2. Derive general expressions for the number of tasks required to do the number adding algorithms in Problem 1.1 when we have $N = 2^n$ numbers to be added. What conclusion do you make?

1.3. Now assume that you have a parallel computer that can add the numbers in Problem 1.1. The time required to add a pair of numbers is assumed 1. What would be the time required to perform the two algoritnms for the case $N = 2^n$? How much is the speedup?

1.4. Consider Problem 1.3. Now the parallel computers require a time C to obtain data from memory and to communicate the add results between the add stages. How much speedup is accomplished?

1.5. Which class of algorithms would the fast Fourier transform (FFT) algorithm belong to?

1.6. Which class of algorithms would the quicksort algorithm belong to?

1.7. The binary number multiplication problem in Chapter 2 could be considered as a RIA algorithm. Draw the dependence graph of such an algorithm.

1.8. The binary restoring division algorithm is based on the recurrence equation

$$r_{j+1} = 2r_j - q_{n-j-1} D \geq j < n,$$

where r_j is the partial remainder at the jth iteration; q_k is the kth quotient bit; and D is the denominator. It is assumed that the number of bits in the quotient is n and q_{n-1} is the quotient most significant bit (MSB). What type of algorithm is this division algorithm?

1.9. A processor has clock frequency f, and it requires c clock cycles to execute a single instruction. Assume a program contains I instructions. How long will the program take before it completes?

1.10. Repeat Problem 1.9 when a new processor is introduced whose clock frequency is $f' = 2f$ and $c' = 1.5c$.

1.11. Give some examples of serial algorithms.

1.12. Give some examples of parallel algorithms.

1.13. Consider the speedup factor for a fully parallel algorithm when communication overhead is assumed. Comment on speedup for possible values of α.

1.14. Consider the speedup factor for a fully parallel algorithm when communication overhead is assumed. Comment on speedup for possible values of R.

1.15. Write down the speedup formula when communication overhead is included and the algorithm requires interprocessor communications Assume that each task in the parallel algorithm requires communication between a pair of processors. Assume that the processors need to communicate with each other m times to complete the algorithm.

1.16. Consider an SPA with the following specifications:

Number of serial tasks per stage	N_s
Number of serial tasks per stage	N_p
Number of stages	n

Now assume that we have a single processor that requires τ to complete a task and it consumes W watts while in operation. We are also given $N = N_p$ parallel but very slow processors. Each processor requires $r\tau$ to complete a task and consumes W/r watts while in operation, where $r > 1$ is a performance derating factor.

(1) How long will the single processor need to finish the algorithm?

(2) How much energy will the single processor consume to finish the algorithm?

(3) How long will the multiprocessor need to finish the algorithm?

(4) How much energy will the multiprocessor system consume to finish the algorithm?

(5) Write down a formula for the speedup.

(6) Write down a formula for the energy ratio of the multiprocessor relative to the single processor.

1.17. The algorithm for floating point addition can be summarized as follows:

   (1) Compare the exponents and choose the larger exponent.

   (2) Right shift the mantissa of the number with the smaller exponent by the amount of exponent difference.

   (3) Add the mantissas.

   (4) Normalize the results.

   Draw a dependence graph of the algorithm and state what type of algorithm this is.

1.18. The algorithm for floating point multiplication can be summarized as follows:

   (1) Multiply the mantissas.

   (2) Add the two exponents.

   (3) Round the multiplication result.

   (4) Normalize the result.

   Draw a dependence graph of the algorithm and state what type of algorithm this is.

1.19. Discuss the algorithm for synthetic apperture radar (SAR).

1.20. Discuss the Radon transform algorithm in two dimensions.

Chapter 2

Enhancing Uniprocessor Performance

2.1 INTRODUCTION

In this chapter, we review techniques used to enhance the performance of a uniprocessor. A multiprocessor system or a parallel computer is composed of several uniprocessors and the performance of the entire system naturally depends, among other things, on the performance of the constituent uniprocessors. We also aim, in this chapter, to differentiate the techniques used to enhance uniprocessor performance from the techniques used to enhance multiprocessor performance, which are discussed in subsequent chapters.

Traditionally, building a computer was an expensive proposal. For almost 50 years, all effort went into designing faster single computer systems. It typically takes a microprocessor manufacturer 2 years to come up with the next central processing unit (CPU) version [1]. For the sake of the following discussion, we define a simple computer or processor as consisting of the following major components:

1. controller to coordinate the activities of the various processor components;
2. datapath or arithmetic and logic unit (ALU) that does all the required arithmetic and logic operations;
3. storage registers, on-chip cache, and memory; and
4. input/output (I/O) and networking to interface and communicate with the outside world.

The above components are sometimes referred to as the computer resources. Theses resources are shared between the different programs or processes running on the computer, and the job of the computer operating system (OS) is to organize the proper sharing and access to these resources. Making a processor run faster was accomplished through many techniques to enhance the datapath since it is the heart of any processor. We discuss datapath enhancements in the following subsections.

Algorithms and Parallel Computing, by Fayez Gebali
Copyright © 2011 John Wiley & Sons, Inc.

2.2 INCREASING PROCESSOR CLOCK FREQUENCY

Increasing the system clock frequency allows the computer to execute more instructions per unit time. However, logic gates need time to switch states and system buses need time to be charged or discharged through bus drivers. These delays are closely tied to the underlying silicon technology such as NMOS, CMOS, and bipolar. The type of gate circuits also dictate the clock speed, such as using CMOS or domino logic or current-mode logic. There is also a fundamental limit on how fast a chip could run based on dynamic power dissipation. Dynamic power dissipation is given approximately by

$$p_d = CfV^2, \tag{2.1}$$

where C is the total parasitic capacitance, f is the clock frequency, and V is the power supply voltage. Engineers developed many techniques to reduce power consumption of the chip while raising the clock frequency. One obvious solution was to reduce the value of C through finer lithographic process resolution. A bigger impact resulted when the chip power supply voltage was reduced from 5.0 to 2.2 V and then 1.2 V, and the question is how much the supply voltage can keep scaling down without affecting the gate switching noise margin.

2.3 PARALLELIZING ALU STRUCTURE

Parallel structure implies using several copies of the same hardware in the ALU. An example of use of parallelism to enhance performance is the multiplication operation. Before the days of very large-scale integration (VLSI), early computers could not afford to multiply numbers using a dedicated multiplier. They used the adder in the ALU to do multiplication through the add–shift technique. Assume the two numbers to be multiplied, a and b, have the following binary representations:

$$c = a \times b$$

$$= \sum_{i=0}^{n-1} 2^i a_i \times \sum_{j=0}^{n-1} 2^j b_j$$

$$= \sum_{i=0}^{n-1} \sum_{j=0}^{n-1} 2^{i+j} a_i b_j \tag{2.2}$$

$$= \sum_{i=0}^{n-1} \left(\sum_{j=0}^{n-1} 2^{i+j} a_i b_j \right), \tag{2.3}$$

where $a_i, b_i = \{0, 1\}$. Equation 2.2 could be thought of as the parallel implementation of the multiplication operation. Essentially, we are forming all the partial products $a_i b_j$ and then add them together with the proper binary weights. Equation 2.3 is the bit-serial implementation. Here we add the partial products over two stages first along the j index then add the results over the i index. This will be explained shortly.

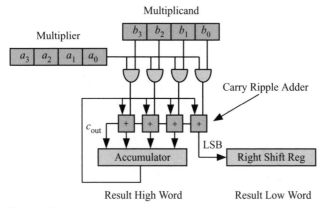

Figure 2.1   Bit-serial binary multiplication for the case $n = 4$.

Some authors refer to this operation as serial/parallel multiplication since 1 bit is used to multiply the other word.

Figure 2.1 shows the bit-serial multiplication technique for the case $n = 4$. The multiplicand b is stored in a register and the multiplier a is stored in a shift register so that at each clock cycle, 1 bit is read out starting with the least significant bit (LSB). At the first clock cycle, a partial product pp_0 is formed

$$pp_0 = \sum_{j=0}^{n-1} 2^{i+j} a_0 b_j. \tag{2.4}$$

The LSB of this partial product is extracted and stored in a right shift register, as shown at the bottom right of the figure. The remaining bits of pp_0 are stored in an accumulator to be added to the next partial product, pp_1. In general, at clock cycle i, we generate partial product pp_i:

$$pp_i = \sum_{j=0}^{n-1} 2^{i+j} a_i b_j, \tag{2.5}$$

and the accumulator performs the operation

$$Acc_i = Acc_{i-1} + pp_i' \qquad i \geq 0, \tag{2.6}$$

where Acc_i is the content of the accumulator at the end of the ith clock cycle and pp_i' is the ith partial product with the LSB removed. After $n = 4$ clock cycles, the $2n$-bit product $a \times b$ is available with the n-bit high word stored in the accumulator and the n-bit low word stored in the right shift register. The time required to perform the bit-serial multiplication is estimated roughly as

$$T_{serial} = nT_{add} = n^2 T_{fa}, \tag{2.7}$$

where T_{add} is the n-bit carry ripple adder delay and T_{fa} is the 1-bit full adder delay.

For such a processor, the clock duration is dictated by the carry ripple adder delay, and we have $T_{clk} = T_{add}$. Simple ALUs used this iterative multiplication

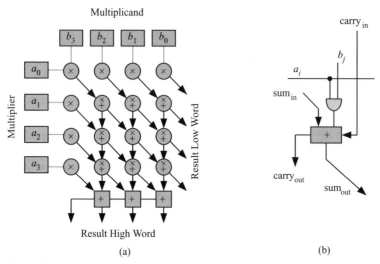

Figure 2.2   Parallel binary multiplication for the case $n = 4$. (a) The multiplier structure. (b) The details of the gray circles with + and × symbols.

technique to do many more operations that need several multiplication operations such as division and elementary function evaluation (e.g., trigonometric and hyperbolic functions and square root). In fact, the coordinate rotation digital computer (CORDIC) algorithm was invented in the late 1950s for elementary function evaluation without the need for multipliers [7, 8]. However, this CORDIC algorithm is inherently bit-serial and required many clock cycles to complete.

Thanks to VLSI technology, it is now feasible to incorporate a parallel multiplier in the ALU and thereby to speed up the processor. Figure 2.2 shows the parallel multiplication technique for the case $n = 4$. Figure 2.2a shows the parallel multiplier structure. The multiplicand b is stored in a register at the top, and the multiplier a is stored in a register at the left of the figure. Most of the parallel multiplier structure is composed of a two-dimensional (2-D) array of cells that generate the partial product bits simultaneously. At the bottom of Fig. 2.2a is a carry ripple adder. The gray squares with the $a +$ symbol indicate a 1-bit full adder. The gray circles with $a +$ and × symbols indicate an AND gate connected to a 1-bit full adder as shown in more detail in Fig. 2.2b.

The array of AND gates is responsible for generating all the bits of the partial products $a_i b_j$. The array of adders is responsible for adding up all these partial products. The diagonal lines indicated lines of equal binary weight, and the vertical lines indicate the path for the carry out signals. The time required to perform the parallel multiplication operation is

$$T_{\text{parallel}} \approx 2(n-1)T_{fa}. \tag{2.8}$$

We see that the time required for parallel multiplication is n times smaller than the bit-serial multiplication delay. However, this comes at a cost of more hardware.

The author developed a parallel CORDIC algorithm (high-performance coordinate rotation digital computer [HCORDIC]) that is faster than the bit-serial CORDIC but relies on the fact that modern ALUs contain a multiplier [5, 6]. Thus the presence of a parallel multiplier speeds up not only the multiplication operation but the evaluation of many elementary functions.

2.4 USING MEMORY HIERARCHY

An ideal memory, which is not available yet, should possess several attributes:

1. Nonvolatile so that memory contents are not lost when power is turned off
2. Short access time to match processor speed so that memory load and store operations do not require several clock cycles to complete
3. Large capacity to be able to store massive amounts of data
4. Inexpensive both in terms of the silicon real estate area they require and in price since many data have to be stored

Such an ideal memory does not exist yet. Several memory technologies exist that satisfy some of the above attributes but not all of them simultaneously. The system designer must build the computer storage requirements using a memory hierarchy to take advantage of each memory technology as shown in Fig. 2.3. The types of storage technologies used by current processors are

- registers;
- cache;
- RAM; and
- mass storage, such as magnetic, optical, and flash drives.

The processor talks directly to the fastest memory module available, which is the registers and the cache memory. The only problem is that these two memory modules do not have a large capacity and are expensive to build.

The interconnection pattern of the memory hierarchy is such that each memory module shown in the figure communicates with the neighboring modules connected

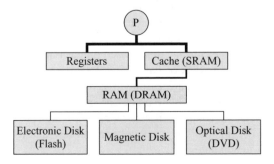

Figure 2.3   Memory hierarchy.

to it by the shown lines. Data migrate to the processor from the bottom of the hierarchy. Likewise, data from the processor migrates downwards down the hierarchy. The thickness of each line symbolizes the speed of communication of the line. For example, the processor can directly communicate with its registers and the cache at high speed, matching the clock speed of the processor. Both of these memory components are very fast since they are always implemented on the same chip as the CPU. This ensures speeds that match the processor instruction execution speeds. The goal is to make sure that the processor operates most of the time using only the data and instructions residing in its registers and cache. Whenever the processor needs data or instructions from the memory, things slow down considerably until such data migrate to the cache.

The closest memory to the CPU is the register bank memory, which is built using the same gate technology as the rest of the processor. Hence, registers are very fast and match the processor speed. It is not possible to satisfy all the system storage requirements using registers since a chip has a limited silicon area. Register memory is therefore of small capacity and most computers have a limited amount of registers. For example, Intel's Itanium processor has 96 registers.

The cache is also very close to the CPU and can communicate with the processor. Similar to registers, the cache communicates at speed matching CPU speed. The cache also communicates with the off-chip dynamic random access memory (DRAM) using slower communication links. A cache is useful because most tasks or applications display *temporal locality* and *spatial locality*. Temporal locality refers to the near future. Spatial locality refers to using data stored near the current data. For this reason, data load/store operations between the shared memory and the caches take place using *blocks* of data. Cache memory is built using static random access memory (SRAM) technology. SRAM is both fast and nonvolatile but also has limited capacity since the number of transistors to store a bit varies between four and six.

DRAM, or memory, is a slower memory but with a large capacity compared with the cache. However, DRAM is considered extremely fast compared with the mass storage disk drives. The problem with DRAM is its volatility. It loses all its content due to current leakage even when power is applied. The entire memory content must be refreshed every 1 millisecond or so. DRAM is slow because it is built on a different chip and its large capacity dictates slow data access operations. In summary DRAM constitutes the main memory of any processor. This memory is inexpensive, slower than cache, but much faster than mass disk storage.

The most inexpensive memory is mass disk storage, whether it uses magnetic storage or optical storage as in CD, DVD, Blu-ray, and so on. Disk storage is inexpensive and has a large capacity. However, it is slow since it is based on mechanical devices. A recent addition to disk storage is electronic disks based on flash memory cards. This is usually referred to as solid state disk or flash drive. Relative to magnetic disks, flash drives are high-speed devices and are starting to have a consistently large capacity. However, their speed does not match the processor speed since they are off-chip memory. We are already seeing advances in flash memory, which possesses most of the desirable features of a memory. It is nonvolatile and fast, and its capacity is increasing with advances in technology.

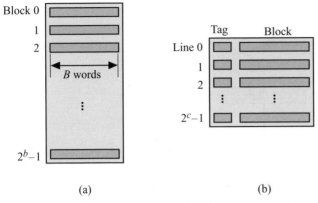

Figure 2.4   Cache and memory organization. (a) Memory organization into blocks for communicating with cache. (b) Cache organization into lines.

2.4.1 Cache Memory Operation

Communication between the main memory and the cache occurs in chunks of words called blocks. Figure 2.4 shows the organization in the main memory and the cache from the point of view of communicating between the two modules. Figure 2.4a shows that the main memory is organized in blocks having B words each. Each block is addressed by a b-bit address so that memory is divided into 2^b blocks as far as memory/cache interaction is concerned. Figure 2.4b shows that the cache is organized in *lines* where each line contains a block from the main memory and an associated *tag*. The cache capacity is much smaller than the memory and it can store only 2^c lines. The tag stores the address of the block in memory corresponding to the line in the cache. This way, a cache line is identified with the corresponding memory block.

When the processor requires to read the data, it issues a read instruction and generates the memory address of the word. If the word is in the cache, then we have a *cache hit* and the word is delivered to the processor at a very high rate. If, however, the processor does not find the word it needs in the cache, then we have a *cache miss*, and data access halts until the contents of the cache are updated from the main memory. The block containing the word is fetched from the memory and loaded into the cache. The desired word is forwarded to the processor. Communication between cache and memory is performed over blocks of data and progresses at the speed of the DRAM memory access.

2.4.2 Cache Design

We saw that processing speed is high as long as memory read/write operation concerns data and instructions that are located in the cache. Things slow down considerably if the data are not located in the cache. The design of cache memories is beyond

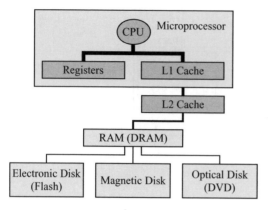

Figure 2.5 Cache hierarchy.

the scope of this book, and there are several excellent textbooks dealing with such issues as References 18 and 19. There are several factors that increase the chances of cache hits, which include

- cache size (2^c);
- mapping technique to associate the address of a block in memory with the address of a line in the cache;
- cache replacement or update policy; this policy is concerned with choosing blocks of memory to load into the cache and with removing lines from the cache; and
- using cache hierarchy, as will be discussed in the next section.

2.4.3 Cache Hierarchy

Cache memory communicates directly with the processor, and there is always the need to increase the cache capacity to prevent the penalty of cache misses. Since the memory hierarchy model proved very useful in providing the processor with the best of the different storage technologies, it is now common to use the memory hierarchy to construct a parallel model for cache hierarchy. Cache could be organized in different levels. Figure 2.5 shows the different cache levels used to construct a cache hierarchy. Level 1 cache (L1) is an on-chip cache, which is very fast but has a small capacity. This is indicated by the thick line connecting the CPU and the L1 cache. Level 2 (L2) cache is slower than L1 cache since it is off-chip but has a larger capacity. Such memory is built using fast SRAM technology but has a larger capacity compared with the smaller L1 cache.

2.4.4 Mapping Memory Blocks into Cache Lines

A mapping function establishes a correspondence between the main memory blocks and the lines in the cache [19]. Assume we have a memory of size 64 K—that is,

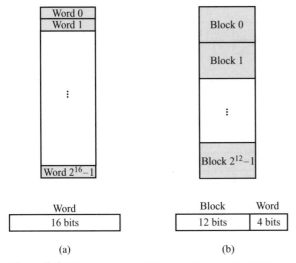

Figure 2.6   Main memory. (a) Organized into words. (b) Organized into blocks.

the memory address line has 16 bits. Figure 2.6 shows how data are addressed in memory. Figure 2.6a is the case when the memory is organized into words and a memory address specifies a specific word in memory. Sixteen bits are required to specify and access a specific word in the memory.

Figure 2.6b is the case when the memory is organized into blocks and a memory address specifies a specific block in memory. Assume that each block contains 16 words. The 16 address bits are now broken down into two fields: the most significant 12 bits are required to specify and access a specific block in the memory. The remaining least significant 4 bits specify a word in a given block.

Now assume we have a cache memory that can accommodate 128 blocks. In that case, 7 bits are needed to specify the location of a line in the cache. Now we need a mapping function that picks a block from the memory and places it at some location in the cache. There are three mapping function choices:

1. Direct mapping
2. Associative mapping (also known as fully associative mapping)
3. Set-associative mapping

Direct Mapping

In direct mapping, we take the 12-bit address of a block in memory and store it in the cache based on the least significant 7 bits as shown in Fig. 2.7. To associate a line in the cache with a block in the memory, we need 12 bits composed of 7 bits for address of the line in the cache and 5 tag bits.

Now we see that a line in the cache corresponds to 32 blocks from the main memory, which correspond to the 5-bit tag address. This is because there are exactly

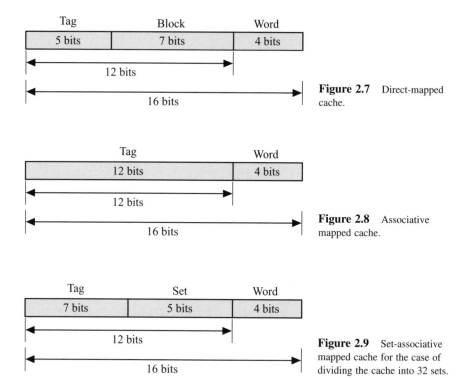

Figure 2.7 Direct-mapped cache.

Figure 2.8 Associative mapped cache.

Figure 2.9 Set-associative mapped cache for the case of dividing the cache into 32 sets.

32 blocks in the main memory whose least significant 7 bits are all identical out of the 12-bit line address.

2.4.5 Associative Mapping

In associative or fully associative mapping, we place the block of memory in any available location in the cache, in this case, the tag is used to associate a block with a line as shown in Fig. 2.8. To associate a line in the cache with a block in the memory, we need 12 bits composed of the 12 tag bits (Fig. 2.8).

2.4.6 Set-Associative Mapping

Set-associative mapping could be thought of as a combination of direct and associative mapping. We divide the cache into 2^m sets and associate a block to a set based on the m least significant bits of the block address bits. The block is mapped to any empty location in the set. For a cache with capacity of 128 blocks, if we divide the cache into 32 sets, we would be able to store four blocks per set. The breakdown of the 12-bit block address is shown in Fig. 2.9. To associate a line in the cache with a block in the memory, we need 12 bits composed of 5 bits for the address of the set in the cache and 7 tag bits.

2.4.7 Effects of Cache Size on Cache Misses

Cache misses can be classified into three categories (the three Cs) [20]:

Compulsory misses: caused when a block is initially required but has never been loaded into the cache. This type of cache miss is also called *cold-start miss*. Cache size has no effect on compulsory misses.

Capacity misses. Caused when the cache cannot hold the blocks needed during the execution of a program. In that case, blocks are replaced then later loaded back into the cache. Capacity misses are reduced by enlarging the cache size.

Conflict misses: Occur in set-associative or direct-mapped caches when the cache cannot accommodate the blocks in a set. Such misses would not have occurred in a fully associative cache. Conflict misses are also called *collision misses*. Conflict misses are reduced by increasing the associativity or by increasing the number of lines to map to in the cache. This can be accomplished either by increasing the cache size or by reducing the block size.

2.5 PIPELINING

Pipelining is a very effective technique for improving system throughput, which is defined as the rate of task completion per unit time. This technique requires two conditions to be effective:

1. It is desired to implement several instances of a task
2. Each task is divisible into several subtasks.

An often quoted example of successful pipelining is car manufacture. We note that this satisfies the two requirements of pipelining: we have many cars to manufacture and the manufacture of each car requires manufacture of several components.

A pipeline executes a task in successive stages by breaking it up into smaller tasks. It is safe to assume that a smaller task will be completed in a shorter time compared to the original task. As explained above, the idea of a pipeline is to execute a serial task using successive pipeline stages and placing registers between the stages to store the intermediate results.

2.5.1 Estimating Pipeline Speed

Figure 2.10 shows a general organization of a pipeline where the *C/L* blocks indicate combinational logic blocks composed of logic gates. The *Reg* blocks indicate edge-triggered registers to store intermediate results. The speed of that pipeline depends on the largest combinational logic delay of the *C/L* blocks. Figure 2.11 shows how the clock speed of the pipeline is calculated. The figure illustrates several delays:

T_{CL}: delay through the *C/L* blocks

τ_{setup}: setup delay for data at the input of a register

τ_d: delay of data through a register.

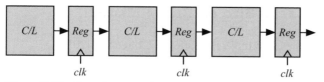

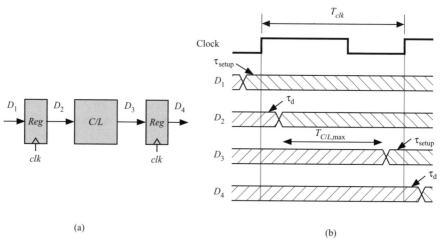

Figure 2.10   General structure for pipeline processing.

(a)   (b)

Figure 2.11   Estimating clock speed for a pipeline based on pipeline delays. (a) One stage of a pipeline. (b) Signal delays due to the registers and combinational logic blocks.

The formula for estimating the clock frequency is given by

$$\text{Clock frequency} = \frac{1}{T_{clk}} \tag{2.9}$$

$$T_{clk} = T_{C/L,\text{max}} + 2\tau_{\text{skew}} + \tau_{\text{d}} + \tau_{\text{setup}}, \tag{2.10}$$

where $T_{C/L,\text{max}}$ is the maximum delay of the combinational logic blocks, τ_{skew} is the maximum expected clock skew between adjacent registers, and τ_{setup} is the setup time for a register.

A classic example of pipelining is in the way a computer executes instructions. A computer instruction goes through four steps:

1. *Fetch* the instruction from the cache and load it in the CPU instruction register (IR).

2. *Decode* the contents of the IR using decoding logic in order to control the operations performed by the ALU or the datapath.

3. *Execute* the instruction using the data supplied to the ALU/datapath inputs.

4. *Write* the result produced by the ALU into the accumulator, registers, or memory.

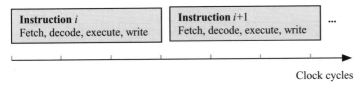

Clock cycles

Figure 2.12   Time needed for the serial processing of a computer instruction.

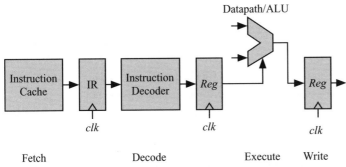

Fetch   Decode   Execute   Write

Figure 2.13   Instruction pipeline processing.

The above steps are dependent and must be executed serially in the order indicated above. We cannot reverse the order or even do these steps in parallel (i.e., simultaneously). So, without pipelining, the processor would need three clock cycles per instruction. We can see that processing computer instructions satisfies the pipeline requirements: we have several instructions and each instruction is divisible into several serial subtasks or stages.

A serial implementation of the above tasks is shown in Fig. 2.12. We see that the fetch operation of the next instruction can only start after all the operations associated with the current instruction are completed. Now we can show a sketch of a pipeline to process computer instructions as shown in Fig. 2.13. Instruction processing could be looked at in more detail than implied by the above processing stages. A nice discussion of the instruction cycle can be found in Reference 18.

Now let us see how this pipeline can speed up the instruction processing. Figure 2.14 shows the instruction pipeline during program execution. Each row in the figure shows the activities of each processing stage during the successive clock cycles. So, the first row shows the contents of the *IR* after each fetch operation. The second row shows the instructions being decoded at the different clock cycles. The third row shows the instructions being executed by the ALU during each clock cycle as well as storing the result in a register. If we trace each instruction through the pipeline stages, we conclude that each instruction requires three clock cycles to be processed. However, we also note that each hardware unit is active during each clock cycle as compared to Fig. 2.12. Therefore, the pipeline executes an instruction at each clock cycle, which is a factor of three better than serial processing. In general,

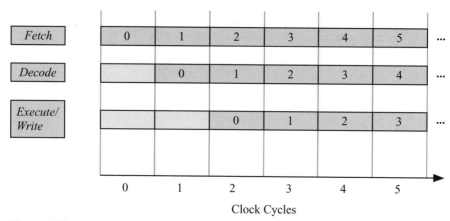

Figure 2.14   Pipeline processing of computer instructions during program execution.

when the pipeline is running with data in every pipeline stage, we expect to process one instruction every clock cycle. Therefore, the maximum speedup of a pipeline is n, where n is the number of pipeline stages.

There is one problem associated with using pipelining for processing computer instructions. Conditional branching alters the sequence of instructions that need to be executed. However, it is hard to predict the branching when the instructions are being executed in sequence by the pipeline. If the sequence of the instructions needs to be changed, the pipeline contents must be flushed out and a new sequence must be fed into the pipeline. The pipeline latency will result in the slowing down of the instruction execution.

Now we turn our attention to showing how pipelining can increase the throughput of the ALU/datapath. We use this topic to distinguish between pipelining and parallel processing. We can use the example of the inner product operation often used in many digital signal processing applications. Inner product operation involves multiplying several pairs of input vectors and adding the results using an accumulator:

$$d = \sum_{i=0}^{N-1} a_i \times b_i. \tag{2.11}$$

As mentioned before, the above operation is encountered in almost all digital signal processing algorithms. For example, the finite impulse response (FIR) digital filter algorithm given by the following equation is an example of an inner product operation (sure, it is convolution, but we are assuming here the shifted samples are stored as a vector!):

$$y(i) = \sum_{j=0}^{N-1} a(j)x(i-j) \qquad i \geq 0. \tag{2.12}$$

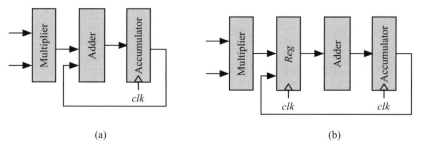

Figure 2.15   Multiply/accumulate (MAC) implementation options. (a) Parallel implementation. (b) Pipelined implementation.

We can iteratively express evaluation of $y(i)$ in the form

$$y(i, -1) = 0$$
$$y(i, k) = y(i, k-1) + a(k)x(i-k) \qquad 0 \le k < N \qquad (2.13)$$
$$y(i) = y(i, N-1).$$

The operation in Eq. 2.13 is often referred to as the multiply/accumulate (MAC) operation. Again, this operation is so important in digital signal processing that there are special MAC instructions and hardware to implement it. The FIR algorithm satisfies pipelining requirements: we have several tasks to be completed, which are the repeated MAC operations. Also, each MAC operation can be broken down into two serial subtasks: the multiply followed by the add operations.

Figure 2.15 shows how we can implement each MAC iterative step using parallel or pipelined hardware. In this diagram, we assumed that we are using a parallel multiplier to effect the multiplication operation. The parallel implementation of Fig. 2.15a shows that the multiply and add operations are done in the same clock cycle and the adder output is used to update the contents of the accumulator. The clock period or time delay for these two operations is given by

$$T_{mac}(\text{parallel}) = T_{mult} + T_{add}. \qquad (2.14)$$

Assuming that the parallel multiplier delay is double the adder delay, the above equation becomes

$$T_{mac}(\text{parallel}) = 3T_{add}. \qquad (2.15)$$

Now consider the pipelined MAC implementation Fig. 2.15b. The output of the multiplier is stored in a register before it is fed to the adder. In that case, the clock period is determined by the slowest pipeline stage. That stage is the multiplier and our clock period would be given by

$$T_{mac}(\text{pipeline}) = 2T_{add}. \qquad (2.16)$$

In effect, the pipelined design is approximately 30% faster than the parallel design. We should point out before we leave this section that many hardware design innovations are possible to obtain much better designs than those reported here. The interested reader could refer to the literature such as References 21–23.

2.6 VERY LONG INSTRUCTION WORD (VLIW) PROCESSORS

This technique is considered fine-grain parallelism since the algorithm is now parallelized at the instruction level, which is the finest level of detail one could hope to divide an algorithm into. A VLIW implies that several instructions or opcodes are sent to the CPU to be executed simultaneously. Picking the instructions to be issued in one VLIW word is done by the compiler. The compiler must ensure that there is no dependency between the instructions in a VLIW word and that the hardware can support executing all the issued instructions [20]. This presents a potential advantage over instruction pipelining since instruction scheduling is done before the code is actually run.

Figure 2.16 illustrates a processor that uses VLIW to control the operation of two datapath units. Figure 2.16a shows the schematic of the processor where the VLIW contains two instructions. Each instruction is used to control a datapath unit. Figure 2.16b shows the content of the VLIW word at different processing cycles. The figure is based on the ones presented in References 18 and 24. Each row represents a VLIW word issue. The vertical axis represents the machine cycles. A gray box indicates an instruction within the VLIW word and an empty box indicates a no-op. A no-op instruction is used when the compiler is unable to resolve the dependency among the instructions or datapath availability.

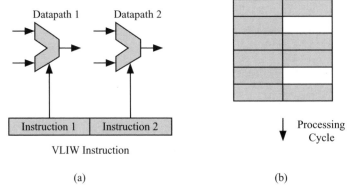

Figure 2.16 A VLIW word containing two instructions to independently control two datapath units in the same processor. (a) Schematic. (b) VLIW content at different processor cycles.

2.7 INSTRUCTION-LEVEL PARALLELISM (ILP) AND SUPERSCALAR PROCESSORS

A superscalar processor is able to simultaneously execute several instructions from independent instruction pipelines [18]. Superscalar processors have a *dynamic scheduler* that examines the instructions in the instruction cache/memory and decides which ones to be issued to each instruction pipeline. Dynamic scheduling allows out-of-order instruction issue and execution. Figure 2.17 shows a general organization of a three-way superscalar processor where the processor contains three instruction pipelines operating on three independent datapath units. A superscalar computer has several instruction pipelines and datapath units that can work in parallel to execute instructions issued to them from the CPU. Using this technique, the instruction execution rate will be greater than the clock rate. For a three-way superscalar architecture with an instruction pipeline, up to three instructions could be executed per clock cycle.

The instruction pipeline for a two-way superscalar processor shown in Fig. 2.18, which is a modification of Fig. 2.14, indicates the fact that we now have two instruction pipelines.

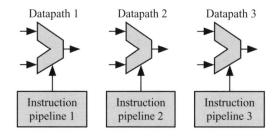

Figure 2.17   General organization of a three-way superscalar processor.

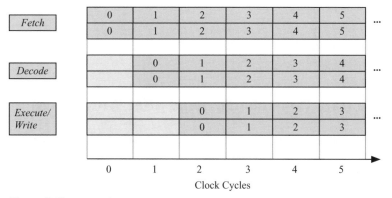

Figure 2.18   Instruction pipelines for a two-way superscalar processor.

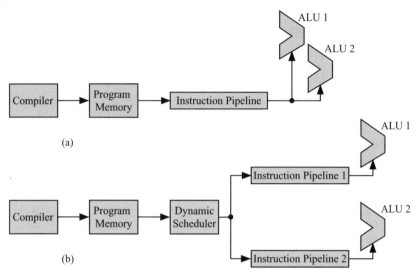

Figure 2.19   Comparing program execution on VLIW and superscalar processors. (a) VLIW processor. (b) Superscalar processor.

At this point, it is worthwhile to explain the difference between VLIW and superscalar processors. Both techniques rely on the presence of several ALUs to perform several operations in parallel. The main difference lies in how the instructions are issued. Figure 2.19 shows the flow of program instructions starting from the compilation stage all the way to the instruction execution by the parallel ALUs for VLIW and superscalar processors.

The key idea in superscalar processors is the ability to execute multiple instructions in parallel. Compilation and hardware techniques are used to maximize the number of instructions that can be used issued in parallel. However, there are limitations to achieving this level of speedup [3, 18, 20, 25]:

- True data dependencies
- Procedural dependencies
- Resource conflicts
- Output dependencies
- Antidependencies

2.7.1   True Data Dependency: Read after Write (RAW)

RAW implies that instruction i should *read* a new value from a register *after* another instruction j has performed a *write* operation.

Assume instruction I_0 produces some result and instruction I_1 uses that result. We say that I_1 has true data dependency on I_0 and the execution of I_1 must be delayed until I_0 is finished. We can represent this true data dependency or dependence as shown in Fig. 2.20a. The figure shows that I_0 reads its input arguments from registers

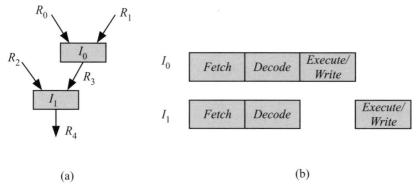

Figure 2.20   True data dependency between two instructions. (a) Dependence graph. (b) Pipeline processing of the two instructions.

I_0	Fetch	Decode	Execute/ Write			
I_1 Branch	Fetch	Decode	Execute/ Write			
I_2				Fetch	Decode	Execute/ Write
I_3					Fetch	Decode	Execute/ Write

Figure 2.21   Procedural dependency.

R_0 and R_1 and the output result is stored in R_2. If I_0 is a *load* from memory instruction, then it might have a large delay or *latency*. In that case, the *execute* phase of I_1 would have to be delayed by more than one clock cycle.

2.7.2 Procedural Dependencies

A major problem with computer instructions is the presence of branch instructions. Figure 2.21 shows the instruction pipeline has two instructions I_0 and I_1. However, I_1 is a branch instruction and it is not possible to determine which instruction to execute until I_1 produces its output. Therefore, the *fetch* phase of the next instruction has to be delayed as shown in Fig. 2.21.

2.7.3 Resource Conflicts

A resource conflict arises when two or more instructions require the same processor resource. Examples of shared processor resources are memory, cache, buses, register file, and so on. A resource conflict is resolved when the execution of the competing instructions is delayed. Figure 2.20 can be used to visualize the effect of resource conflict on the instruction pipeline. One should note that, unlike true data dependencies, a resource conflict can be eliminated by duplicating the shared resource. This might be an expensive or impractical solution. For example, eliminating

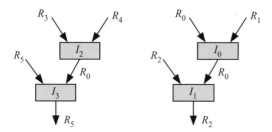

Figure 2.22 Output dependency.

floating-point unit conflicts might involve designing two floating-point units associated with each ALU. This might require a small amount of silicon real estate. Cache conflicts might be eliminated by designing a dual-ported cache or duplicating the cache. Both these options might not be practical though.

2.7.4 Output Dependencies: Write after Write (WAW)

WAW implies that instruction i *writes* an operand after instruction j has written another operand in the register. The sequence is important since the register should contain the value written by instruction j after both instructions i and j have finished an execution.

An output dependency occurs when two instructions, I_0 and I_1, store their output result in the same register. In that case, the register content at a given time depends on which instruction finished last, I_0 or I_1. We illustrate this using the following register transfer language (RTL) code fragment where op indicates any binary operation [18] requiring two input registers:

I_0: $R_0 \leftarrow R_0$ op R_1

I_1: $R_2 \leftarrow R_0$ op R_2

I_2: $R_0 \leftarrow R_3$ op R_4

I_3: $R_5 \leftarrow R_0$ op R_5

Figure 2.22 shows the dependence graph of the instructions. The figure shows two instances of true data dependencies: I_1 depends on I_0 and I_3 depends on I_2. Instructions I_0 and I_2 show output dependency since both instructions store their results in register R_0. The sequence of instructions as they are written in the RTL code fragment above indicates that our intention is that I_1 uses the content of R_0 after instruction I_0 is completed. Similarly, instruction I_3 uses the content of R_0 after I_2 is completed. We must ensure that I_2 starts its execution phase after I_0 has finished its execution phase.

2.7.5 Antidependencies: Write after Read (WAR)

WAR implies that instruction i *writes* an operand after instruction j has read the contents of the register. Antidependency is illustrated with the help of the RTL code fragment used to explain output dependencies as shown in Fig. 2.22. We note here that instruction I_1 uses content of register R_0 as an input operand. We must ensure that I_1 completes its execution before I_2 begins its execution so that the content of R_0 is not disturbed while I_1 is using it.

2.8 MULTITHREADED PROCESSOR

As defined at the start of this chapter, a thread is a portion of a program that shares processor resources with other threads. A multithreaded processor is a processor capable of running several software threads simultaneously. Of course, a simple processor has only one ALU and can manage to run one thread at a time. Ungerer et al. [24] provide a comprehensive discussion on threads. Figure 2.23a shows the case of a simple processor running an OS that allows running only one thread. We see in the figure the situation when the thread T_0 stalls, such as due to waiting for a memory access or a cache miss. Of course, the program execution halts until the memory access has been completed. Figure 2.23b shows the case of a single processor running an OS that supports multithreading. Two threads, T_0 and T_1, are available. The OS schedules T_0 for execution and when T_1 stalls, thread T_1 is immediately loaded and runs until T_0 is ready to resume. In such a case, a preemptive OS scheduler is assumed where the execution of T_1 is stopped when T_0 is ready to resume operation.

Figure 2.23c shows the case of a two-way superscalar processor running an OS that allows running only one thread. We see in the figure that thread T_0 is now running on the two ALUs assuming data dependencies have been resolved.

Figure 2.23d shows the case of a two-way superscalar processor running a multithreaded operation. We see in the figure that thread T_0 is now running on the two ALUs assuming data dependencies have been resolved. When T_0 stalls, thread T_1 is switched and starts running until T_0 is ready to resume again.

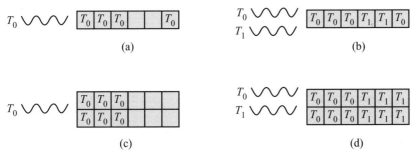

Figure 2.23   Multithreading in a single processor. (a) Single processor running a single thread. (b) Single processor running several threads. (c) Superscalar processor running a single thread. (d) Superscalar processor running multiple threads.

2.9 PROBLEMS

2.1. Estimate how long a given program will take to be executed given the following processor parameters:

- Number of instructions in the program (I)
- Number of clock cycles needed to execute an instruction (C)
- The clock period T

2.2. How many instructions per second are produced by the processor in Problem 2.1? This is referred to as the instruction throughput.

2.3. Moore's law traces the number of transistors on a chip versus the year of introduction. Obtain a plot of the number of transistors in a CPU starting around 1970–2010.

2.4. Repeat Problem 2.3 for CPU clock speed.

2.5. Repeat Problem 2.3 for CPU power consumption.

2.6. This problem is based on concepts from Patterson and Hennessy 20. For a given processor, there are four instruction classes where each instruction requires a different number of clock cycles according to the following table:

Instruction class	Clock cycles per instruction (CPI)
I_1	1
I_2	2
I_3	3
I_4	4

A program was found to contain the following proportion of instruction classes:

Instruction class	Percentage (%)
I_1	40
I_2	25
I_3	20
I_4	15

What is the average CPI for this processor?

2.7. The parallel implementation of the binary multiplication operation was shown as a directed acyclic graph (DAG). Can you obtain different pipeline structures based on that graph?

2.8. Write down the modified booth algorithm.

2.9. Draw a block diagram for the serial modified booth algorithm.

2.10. Draw a block diagram for the parallel modified booth algorithm.

2.11. Obtain a pipelined structure for the modified booth algorithm.

2.12. It is required to design a pipeline to perform the inner product operation between two vectors of length n. Discuss the pipeline design options and the operating speed of the pipeline.

2.13. Explain why multithreading improves the performance of a uniprocessor.

2.14. What are the factors that limit the performance of a superscalar processor?

2.15. Explain the meaning of the following acronyms:

- RAW
- WAW
- WAR

2.16. Explain the different types of cache misses and how each one can be reduced.

2.17. Assume a direct-mapped cache memory where n is the number of address bits for the memory, n_1 is the number of address bits for each block in the memory, and n_2 is the number of address bits for each block in the cache.

(1) What is the number of words in the memory?

(2) What is the number of blocks in the memory?

(3) What is the number of blocks in the cache?

(4) What is the number of words in a block?

(5) What is the number of words in the cache?

2.18. A cache memory has a capacity B block but actually contains b. What is the conflict miss probability for the three types of block mapping strategies?

Chapter 3

Parallel Computers

3.1 INTRODUCTION

Algorithms and multiprocessing architectures are closely tied together. We cannot think of a parallel algorithm without thinking of the parallel hardware that will support it. Conversely, we cannot think of parallel hardware without thinking of the parallel software that will drive it. Parallelism can be implemented at different levels in a computing system using hardware and software techniques:

1. *Data-level parallelism*, where we simultaneously operate on multiple bits of a datum or on multiple data. Examples of this are bit-parallel addition, multiplication, and division of binary numbers, vector processors, and systolic arrays for dealing with several data samples.

2. *Instruction-level parallelism (ILP)*, where we simultaneously execute more than one instruction by the processor. An example of this is use of instruction pipelining.

3. *Thread-level parallelism (TLP)*. A thread is a portion of a program that shares processor resources with other threads. A thread is sometimes called a lightweight process. In TLP, multiple software threads are executed simultaneously on one processor or on several processors.

4. *Process-level parallelism*. A process is a program that is running on the computer. A process reserves its own computer resources, such as memory space and registers. This is, of course, the classic multitasking and time-sharing computing where several programs are running simultaneously on one machine or on several machines.

3.2 PARALLEL COMPUTING

We attempt in this section to show the different design options available to construct a parallel computer system. The most famous processor taxonomy was proposed by Flynn [26] based on the data and the operations performed on this data:

Algorithms and Parallel Computing, by Fayez Gebali
Copyright © 2011 John Wiley & Sons, Inc.

1. *Single instruction single data stream (SISD).* This is the case of the single processor.

2. *Single instruction multiple data stream (SIMD).* All the processors execute the same instruction on different data. Each processor has its own data in a local memory, and the processors exchange data among themselves through typically simple communication schemes. Many scientific and engineering applications lend themselves to parallel processing using this scheme. Examples of such applications include graphics processing, video compression, medical image analysis, and so on.

3. *Multiple instruction single data stream (MISD).* One could argue that neural networks and data flow machines are examples of this type of parallel processors.

4. *Multiple instruction multiple data stream (MIMD).* Each processor is running its own instructions on its local data. Examples of such parallel processors are multicore processors and multithreaded multiprocessors in general.

Flynn's classification is a bit coarse, and we would like to explore more the space of parallel computers, which comprises the SIMD and MIMD categories, in more detail. The issue of synchronization among processors was not part of the classification criteria used by Flynn. Instead of exploring alternative classification schemes, we discuss in this chapter the different parallel computer architectures most commonly used. We should point out that the last type of processor is the one that is fast becoming a popular processing system:

- Shared-memory multiprocessors
- Distributed-memory multiprocessors
- SIMD processors
- Systolic processors
- Cluster computing
- Grid computing
- Multicore processors
- Streaming multiprocessor (SM)

3.3 SHARED-MEMORY MULTIPROCESSORS (UNIFORM MEMORY ACCESS [UMA])

Shared-memory processors are popular due to their simple and general programming model, which allows simple development of parallel software that supports sharing of code and data [27]. Another name for shared memory processors is parallel random access machine (PRAM). The shared-memory or shared-address space is used as a means for communication between the processors. All the processors in the shared memory architecture can access the same address space of a common memory through an interconnection network as shown in Fig. 3.1a. Typically, that interconnection network is a bus, but for larger systems, a network replaces the bus

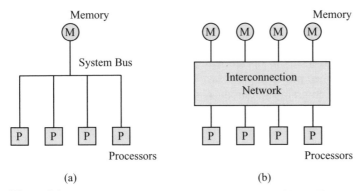

Figure 3.1   Shared-memory multiprocessor architecture (PRAM). (a) The processors are connected to the shared memory using a single bus. (b) The processors and memory modules are connected using an interconnection network.

to improve performance. The performance we are referring to is the amount of processor/memory accesses that can be performed per unit time (throughput) and the time delay between a processor requesting memory access and the time when that request is granted (delay). Examples of the types of interconnection networks and their performance analysis can be found in Reference 28.

We can immediately see that the memory bandwidth becomes the system bottleneck since only one processor can access the memory at a given time. To get around this problem, the configuration in Fig. 3.1b replaces the bus with an interconnection network that allows more than one processor to simultaneously access the network. The configuration also replaces the single memory module with a bank of memories. This allows more than one memory read/write operation to take place simultaneously.

Another problem common to shared memory systems, and parallel computers in general, is cache coherence, where any information present in the shared memory must agree with all the copies that might be present in the local caches of the different CPUs. Cache coherency protocols are used to ensure the cache coherence among the processors [20].

In a shared-memory multiprocessor, any processor can access any memory module. Figure 3.1b shows the shared memory multiprocessor architecture. Having several memory modules allows several processors to access several memory modules simultaneously. This increases the memory bandwidth subject of course to the interconnection network limitations and memory collisions. A memory collision occurs when more than one processor attempts to access the same memory module. The main problem with any memory module design is that it typically has one access port. So, no matter how large the memory module is, only one data word can be accessed at any given time.

In shared memory multiprocessors, each processor sees only one memory address space and it takes the same amount of time to access any memory module. This is referred to as UMA multiprocessor system. In many shared memory multiprocessors, the interconnection network is a simple bus. This is the case of dual and quad Pentium processors.

Developing parallel programs for shared memory multiprocessors is not too difficult since all memory read operations are invisible to the programmer and could be coded the same as in a serial program [3]. Programming write instructions are relatively more difficult since this operation requires locking the data access until a certain thread has finished processing the data. The programmer has to identify the *critical sections* in the program and introduce interprocess and interthread synchronization to ensure data integrity. Programming libraries like POSIX and directives like OpenMP support synchronization through barriers, locks, monitors, mutex, and semaphores.

A problem encountered in shared memory multiprocessor systems is cache coherence. Typically, a processor keeps a copy of the data in a memory module in its own cache. Now, if another processor changes the contents of the block in the memory module, then the cache content is out of date. A cache update policy must be implemented to ensure that all cache copies at the processors are updated.

Synchronization issues must also be implemented to ensure that writing and reading data by more than one processor do not conflict. Semaphores, mutex, and monitors are typically used to ensure data integrity. Chapter 4 discusses shared memory processors in more detail.

3.4 DISTRIBUTED-MEMORY MULTIPROCESSOR (NONUNIFORM MEMORY ACCESS [NUMA])

In a distributed-memory multiprocessor, each memory module is associated with a processor as shown in Fig. 3.2. Any processor can directly access its own memory. A *message passing (MP) mechanism* is used in order to allow a processor to access other memory modules associated with other processors. Message passing interface (MPI) is a language-independent communication protocol.

In that sense, memory access by a processor is not uniform since it depends on which memory module the processor is trying to access. This is referred to as a NUMA multiprocessor system.

If the distributed-memory multiprocessor is composed of identical processors, we say that this is a symmetric multiprocessor (SMP). If the distributed-memory multiprocessor is composed of heterogeneous processors, we say that this is an asymmetric multiprocessor (ASMP).

When the interconnection network of the distributed-memory multiprocessor is global, such as the Internet, then the distributed memory system is usually composed

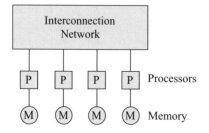

Figure 3.2 Distributed-memory multiprocessor architecture.

of thousands of computers all collaborating to solve huge scientific problems, and the system is called by different names such as massively parallel computing, distributed computing, or grid computing.

3.5 SIMD PROCESSORS

SIMD could be classified as a special case of single program multiple data stream (SPMD) [29]. SIMD processors could belong to the class of shared memory multiprocessing system or distributed-memory multiprocessing system. SIMD machines built using shared memory are suited to applications that require frequent exchange of data where one processor acts as the producer of new data and many other processors act as the consumer of this data.

Each processor executes the same task in synchrony with the other processors. The task being executed could be a simple instruction, a thread, or a process. Distributing the memory among the processors reduces the memory bandwidth problem.

Many applications lend themselves to the SIMD processing model as long as the application is parallelizable. Applications include bioinformatics, biomedical diagnosis, fluid dynamics, image processing, and video processing. SIMD provides the ability to dramatically boost the performance of an application. Some computer manufacturers are adding SIMD extensions to their processors and can run existing applications without the need for recompilation. It is also easy-to-learn programming modifications that utilize SIMD architectures such as the Intel C++ parallel exploration compiler.

An example of a parallel algorithm that is suited to the shared memory model of SIMD is recursive filters described by the equation

$$y(i) = \sum_{j=0}^{N-1} [a(j)x(i-j) - b(j)y(i-j)], \tag{3.1}$$

where $a(j)$ and $b(j)$ are the filter coefficients and N is the filter order or length. Note that $b(0) = 0$ in the above equation. All the processors implement the above equation (single instruction/program) but on different input data. Processor i would be in charge of producing filter output sample $y(i)$ and N other processors would need to read this value for their own calculations.

When the algorithm granularity is coarse, SIMD machines would be called SPMD machines.

3.6 SYSTOLIC PROCESSORS

Many authors state that systolic processors are pipeline systems. Truth of the matter is that pipeline processing is a special case of systolic processing. As we have seen in Chapter 2, a pipeline is one-dimensional and data flow is one-directional. A typical pipeline transmits data between adjacent stages. Systolic arrays could be one-, two-, or three-dimensional, or even higher if deemed necessary. Data flow among the adjacent processors along one or more directions. In a pipeline system, each pipeline stage performs a different task. In a systolic processor, all processing elements (PEs) usually perform the same task.

Typically, the interconnection pattern among the PEs is neighbor to neighbor and possibly some global interconnections. Each PE has a small memory to store data and intermediate results. systolic architectures are suited to implement algorithms that are highly regular with simple data dependencies. Examples of these algorithms include

1. linear algebra, for example, matrix–matrix and matrix–vector multiplication, and solving systems of linear equations;
2. string search and pattern matching;
3. digital filters, for example, one-, two-, and three-dimensional digital filters;
4. motion estimation in video data compression; and
5. finite field operations, such as elliptic curve operations.

Figure 3.3 shows an example of a simple SIMD processor used to implement a matrix–matrix multiplication algorithm. From the figure, we see that the matrix coefficients are stored in the PEs in a distributed memory fashion. We also see that communication between processors is neighbor to neighbor as indicated by the verti-

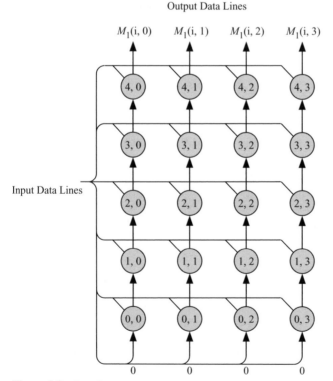

Figure 3.3   Systolic processor for the matrix multiplication algorithm.

cal arrows and by using global wires as indicated by the horizontal lines. Input data must mainly be supplied to the processors on the left edge. Output data are obtained from the processors at the top edge.

Some design issues associated with systolic architectures are the following:

1. A systolic processor is designed to implement a specific algorithm. It must be redesigned to implement a different algorithm. Even while implementing the same algorithm, a change in the problem size might require a major redesign of the system.

2. Supplying a large amount of input data to several processors is a serious constraint on the system input/output (I/O) bandwidth. In a one-dimensional systolic processor, inputs are usually fed to one processor then pipelined to the other processors. At other times, inputs are fed to the PEs through a broadcast bus or to all the PEs at one edge of the PE array. This could transform the performance of the systolic processor to an I/O-bound performance. Redundant arrays of inexpensive disks (RAIDs) can be used to provide mass storage with a large memory bandwidth. This concept can be applied to a bank of flash memory as opposed to magnetic disks.

3. Obtaining a large amount of output data from several processors is a serious constraint on the system I/O bandwidth The outputs could be obtained from one processor, from a bus connected to all the processors or from one edge of the PE array. Again, RAIDs can be used to provide mass storage with a large memory bandwidth.

Before we leave this section, it is worthwhile to compare systolic processors with SIMD processors since both types run a single instruction on multiple data on the surface. Table 3.1 compares SIMD and systolic array processors from different perspectives related to architecture, memory, and task granularity.

Table 3.1   Comparing SIMD and Systolic Processors

Feature	SIMD	Systolic
Interconnection network	Any type	Neighbor to neighbor plus some buses
Communication pattern	Depends on algorithm	Typically neighbor to neighbor
Interprocessor communication	Message passing	Simple clocked transmission
Processor	Could be simple or complex	Typically very simple
Algorithm implemented	Any parallelizable algorithm	Regular iterative algorithm (RIA)
Integration	Stand-alone	Typically part of another system
Task granularity	Typically coarse: a process or a thread	Typically fine: a simple mathematical operation or function
Memory	Distributed	Distributed and small
Layout	Not applicable	One-, two-, or three-dimensional grid

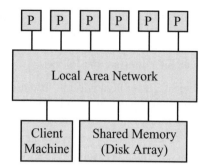

Figure 3.4 Architecture of a cluster computer system.

3.7 CLUSTER COMPUTING

A computer cluster is a collection of two or more computers used to execute a given problem or section. Typically, in a computing cluster, the interconnection network tying the computers together is a local area network (LAN). Figure 3.4 shows an architecture of a cluster computer system [30]. The computers in the cluster communicate among themselves and among the shared memory. Therefore, the processors in a cluster communicate mainly using packets over the LAN. The LAN is usually implemented using a high-speed server computer capable of supporting high-rate traffic between the processors. The shared memory must be able to communicate with many processors at the same time. Depending on the size of the shared memory, it could be implemented using RAID. The client machine distributes the tasks among the processors of the cluster and gathers the finished results.

3.8 GRID (CLOUD) COMPUTING

Grid computing refers to providing access to computing resources distributed over a wide area network (WAN). In that sense, a grid computer is a collection of a large number of processors distributed over a wide geographic area. A grid computer can handle large-scale computational problems such as N-body simulations, seismic simulations, and atmospheric and oceanic simulations. Compared with cluster computing, a grid computer is a large cluster where the LAN is now replaced with a WAN, such as the Internet. The problems at the back of the chapter summarize the main differences between cluster and cloud computing.

Some of the applications implemented using cloud computing include

- peer-to-peer (P2P) computing;
- software as a service, like Google Apps, Google Calendar, and Google mail;
- mass storage; and
- web applications and social networks.

3.9 MULTICORE SYSTEMS

A multicore system usually refers to a multiprocessor system that has all its processors on the same chip. It could also refer to a system where the processors are on different chips but use the same package (i.e., a multichip module). This close packing allows for very fast interprocessor communication without too much power consumption. For a dual or quad core system, the processors are connected using a simple bus. For a larger number of cores, the processors are interconnected using a network-on-chip (NoC) [13]. On the other hand, a multiprocessor system has its processors residing in separate chips and processors are interconnected by a backplane bus. It is possible to carry this further and to have a multiprocessor system where each chip is a multicore chip.

Multicore systems were developed primarily to enhance the system performance while limiting its power consumption. In other words, a multicore system has good performance even though its constituent cores are low-performing processors. By contrast, multiprocessor systems were developed to enhance the system performance with little regard to power consumption. A multiprocessor system has good performance and its constituent processors are high-performing processors. Table 3.2 summarizes the main differences between multicore systems and multiprocessor systems.

Figure 3.5 shows a sketch of a multicore processor. A multicore system consists of

1. general-purpose programmable cores,
2. special-purpose accelerator cores,
3. shared memory modules,
4. NoC (interconnection network), and
5. I/O interface.

Why move toward multicore systems? The main reason is scalability. As we increase the number of processors to enhance performance, multicore systems allow limiting power consumption and interprocessor communication overhead. A multicore system can be scaled by adding more CPU cores and adjusting the interconnection network. More system programming work has to be done to be able to utilize the

Table 3.2 Main Differences between Multicore Systems and Multiprocessor Systems

	Multiprocessor system	Multicore system
Integration level	Each processor in a chip	All processors on the same chip
Processor performance	High	Low
System performance	Very high	High
Processor power consumption	High	Low
Total power consumption	Relatively high	Relatively low

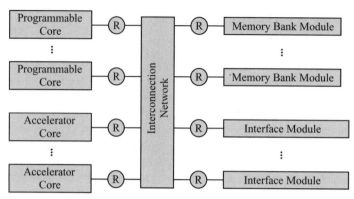

Figure 3.5   A multicore microprocessor system.

increased resources. It is one thing to increase the number of CPU resources. It is another to be able to schedule all of them to do useful tasks.

Some of the possible applications that can be efficiently implemented on multicore systems include [31]

1. general-purpose multitasking computations,
2. network protocol processing,
3. encryption/decryption processing, and
4. image processing.

3.10   SM

A stream multiprocessor is a type of SIMD or a MIMD machine where the constituent processors are streaming processors (SPs) or thread processors. A stream processor is defined as a processor that deals with data *streams*, and its instruction set architecture (ISA) contains *kernels* to process these streams [32]. The concept of stream processing is closely associated with the graphics processing unit (GPU) where the GPU is thereby able to perform general compute-intensive general-purpose computations. The GPU thus becomes a general-purpose GPU. Examples of data streams are vectors of floating point numbers or a group of frame pixels for video data processing. This type of data shows temporal and spatial localities. Temporal locality is when the input data stream is used only a few times to produce the output steam. Spatial locality is when the input data stream is located in the same memory block. A successful example of a stream multiprocessor is the new generations of GPUs like Fermi from NVIDIA [33].

Applications suited for SM must satisfy three characteristics [34]:

1. Compute intensity
2. Data parallelism
3. Consumer–producer locality, that is, temporal and spatial locality

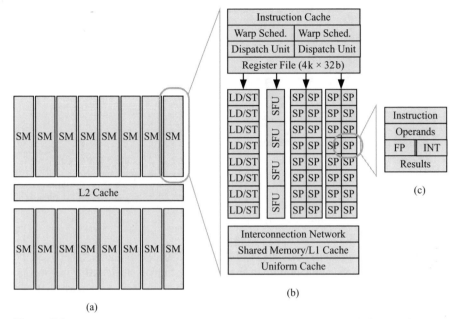

Figure 3.6   Simplified view of the Fermi GPU stream multiprocessor. (a) Block diagram of the stream multiprocessor. (b) Block diagram of the stream processor or thread processor. (c) Block diagram of the CUDA core processor. INT: integer unit; FP: floating point unit; LD: load unit; ST: store unit; SFU: special function unit. © NVIDIA Corporation 2009.

Compute intensity is defined as the number of arithmetic operations per I/O or global memory reference. In applications suitable for stream processing, this ratio could reach 50:1 and above. Data parallelism is when the same operation is performed on all data in an input stream in parallel. Producer–consumer locality is when data are read once and are used once or for a few times to produce the output stream. GPUs such as NVIDIA's Fermi can sustain tens of thousands of parallel threads.

Data suited for stream multiprocessing use the local caches without cache misses since the data exhibit locality. This eliminates the problem of long memory latency [32]. In short, an SM or a GPU is suited for applications with long sequences of data that can be executed using thousands of threads.

Figure 3.6 shows a block diagram of the Fermi GPU from NVIDIA. Fermi has 3 billion transistors and 512 cores or SPs. Fermi is capable of delivering up to 1.5 tera floating point operations per second (TFLOPS). Figure 3.6a is a simplified view of the Fermi GPU stream multiprocessor. It consists of 16 stream multiprocessor (SM) blocks sharing an L2 cache. Surrounding the SMs are six 64-bit interfaces to dynamic random access memory (DRAM) to give a 384 bits wide path to memory.

Figure 3.6b is a simplified expanded view of one of the 16 SM blocks of Fig. 3.6a. Each SM block consists of 64 stream processors or thread processors labeled SP and arranged in groups of four representing the four columns in the figure. Instructions arrive and are scheduled by the block labeled *instruction* at the top of

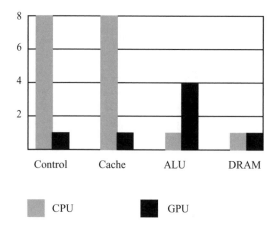

Control   Cache   ALU   DRAM

CPU   GPU

Figure 3.7 Ratio of the different resources allocated to a CPU versus a GPU.

the figure. The *interconnection network* block provides communication between the SMs and the L1 cache at the bottom of the figure. The block labeled SFU is a special function unit capable of evaluating elementary functions such as square root and trigonometric functions so common in scientific applications.

Figure 3.6c is an expanded view of one of the SP blocks in Fig. 3.6b. These blocks are called compute unified device architecture (CUDA) cores and are capable of doing a full integer arithmetic and logic unit (ALU) and floating point arithmetic operations.

Figure 3.7 compares the ratio of the different resources allocated to a CPU versus a GPU. General-purpose computers have a CPU that does sophisticated control like branch prediction. That is why the area allocated to control in a CPU is eight times larger than in a GPU. A GPU eliminates cache misses and long memory latency by using large cache to store data. The ALU resources in a GPU are more since the GPU is a stream multiprocessor that dedicates more area to ALU resources. Finally, the DRAM is almost the same size in both systems.

3.11 COMMUNICATION BETWEEN PARALLEL PROCESSORS

We review in this section how parallel processors communicate and what type of communication strategies are available. Parallel processors need to exchange data among themselves in order to complete the tasks assigned to them.

3.11.1 Types of Communication

We can identify the following types of communication modes:

1. One to one (unicast)
2. One to many (multicast)

(a)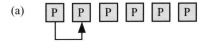

(b)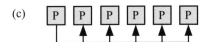

(c)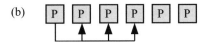

(d)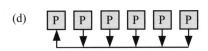

Figure 3.8 The different types or modes of communication among processors: (a) one to one, (b) one to many, (c) broadcast (one to all), and (d) gather and reduce.

3. One to all (broadcast)

4. Gather

5. Reduce

Figure 3.8 shows the different types of modes of communications.

One to One (Unicast)

One-to-one operation involves a pair of processors: the sender and the receiver. This mode is sometimes referred to as point-to-point communication. We encounter this type of communication often in SIMD machines where each processor exchanges data with its neighbor. Figure 3.8a shows the one-to-one mode of communication between processors. The figure only shows communication among a pair of processors, but typically, all processors could be performing the one-to-one communication at the same time. This operation is typically performed in each iteration and therefore must be done efficiently. Most of the time, a simple exchange of data between the source and the destination register is used, assuming clock synchronization between the adjacent processors is accomplished. In other cases, two-way (i.e., data–acknowledge) or even four-way handshaking (i.e., request–grant–data–acknowledge) might be required.

One to Many (Multicast)

One-to-many operation involves one sender processor and several receiver processors. Figure 3.8b shows the one-to-many mode of communication between processors. The figure only shows communication of one source processor to multiple receiving processors, but typically, all processors could be performing the one-to-many communication at the same time. The number of receiving processors depends on the details of the algorithm and how the mapping of tasks to processors was accomplished. This operation is typically performed in each iteration and therefore must be done efficiently. Most of the time, a simple exchange of data between the source and the destination register is used assuming clock synchronization between the adjacent processors is accomplished. In other cases, two-way (i.e., data–acknowledge) or even four-way handshaking (i.e., request–grant–data–acknowledge) might be required.

One to All (Broadcast)

Broadcast operation involves sending the same data to all the processors in the system. Figure 3.8c shows the broadcast mode of communication between processors. This mode is useful in supplying data to all processors. It might also imply one processor acting as the sender and the other processors receiving the data. We will see this type of communication in systolic arrays and also in SIMD machines.

Gather

Gather operation involves collecting data from several or all processors of the system. Figure 3.8d shows the gather mode of communication between processors. Assuming we have P processors, the time needed to gather the data could be estimated as

$$T(\text{gather}) = P\tau_c, \tag{3.2}$$

where τ_c is the time needed to transmit–receive–process one data item.

Reduce

Reduce operation is similar to gather operation except that some operation is performed on the gathered data. Figure 3.8d shows the reduce mode of communication between processors. An example of the reduce operation is when all data produced by all the processors must be added to produce one final value. This task might take a long time when there are many data to be reduced. Assuming we have P processors producing data to be added, the total time is estimated as

$$T(\text{reduce}) = T(\text{gather}) + (P-1)\tau_c, \tag{3.3}$$

where τ_c is the time needed by the processor to process a pair of received data items. It might be worthwhile to perform the reduce operation hierarchically. In that case, the reduce delay time might be

$$T(\text{reduce}) = \log_2\left[P\left(\tau_c + \tau_p\right)\right]. \tag{3.4}$$

3.11.2 Message Passing (MP) Communication Mechanism

MP is used mainly in distributed-memory machines. Passing a message between two processes involves using `send()` and `recv()` library calls. The programmer uses the send(*destination, message*) library call to specify the ID of the destination processor or process and the data to be sent. The programmer must also use the recv(*source, message type*) library call to specify the ID of the source processor or process and the type of data to be received.

In order for two processors to communicate using MP, two operations need to be performed:

1. Establish a communication link between them. Link establishment depends on the nature of the interconnection network. We can think of the link in terms of its physical properties (hardware) or its logical properties (addressing, unidirectional or bidirectional, capacity, message size, etc.)

2. Exchange messages via the send() and recv() library calls.

The MPI is a standard developed to improve the use and portability of MP mechanism.

MP synchronization ensures proper communication between the processors. Synchronization must be treated with care by the programmer since the execution of send() and recv() library calls is under the control of the operating system or systems running the processors. There are two types of synchronization strategies:

- *Synchronous or blocking*, where the sender halts execution after it executes the send() library call until the message is received. Also, the receiver halts after it executes the recv() library call until the message is available.

- *Asynchronous or nonblocking*, where the sender continues execution after it executes the send() library call. Also, the receiver continues execution after it executes the recv() library call.

MPI standard supports one-to-one and broadcast modes of communication.

3.12 SUMMARY OF PARALLEL ARCHITECTURES

The previous sections briefly explained five parallel processor systems that are widely used:

- Shared memory
- Distributed memory
- SIMD
- Systolic
- Multicore

It is hard to uniquely classify each type; for example, SIMD could be built on top of a shared memory system. We can summarize the salient features of these multi-processors in the following points:

1. All multiprocessors, except systolic processors, communicate using an interconnection network that can be easily identified.

2. Systolic processors have neighbor-to-neighbor connections and few global buses.

3. All multiprocessors, except systolic processors, are more general purpose in nature compared with SIMD. They implement all sorts of tasks and algorithms.

4. Systolic processors are designed to execute a specific algorithm. The algorithm dictates several details, such as the type of interprocessor communication, the I/O data timing, and the feeding or extraction points of the I/O data.

5. A multicore system uses accelerator cores to implement special tasks that need to be implemented at a high rate. For example, we could have a GPU in a multicore system to implement intensive graphic processing tasks. Such accelerator cores are built using systolic processors.

3.13 PROBLEMS

3.1. What is the main communication mechanism between processors in a shared memory multiprocessor system?

3.2. What are the main issues in shared memory processor systems?

3.3. What is the main disadvantage of shared memory multiprocessors?

3.4. What is the main communication mechanism between processors in a distributed-memory multiprocessor system?

3.5. Identify the main type of interprocess communication in a distributed-memory multiprocessor system.

3.6. Define what is meant by the critical section in a distributed-memory multiprocessor system.

3.7. How are threads synchronized in OpenMP?

3.8. Explain the function of #pragma reduction (operation: variable list) directive in OpenMP.

3.9. Give examples of SIMD machines.

3.10. Summarize the main difference between cluster computing and grid computing.

Chapter 4

Shared-Memory Multiprocessors

4.1 INTRODUCTION

Shared-memory processors are popular due to their simple and general programming model, which allows simple development of parallel software that supports sharing of code and data [27].

Shared-memory processors provide a single physical address space for all processors, and each processor can run its own program using its local memory and cache. The processors also have access to shared memory arranged in separate modules. The processors communicate using *shared variables*, which are stored in the shared memory to be accessible to any processor. Memory in a shared-memory multiprocessor system is organized in a hierarchical fashion as shown in Fig. 4.1. The figure shows a system with n processors and b shared memory modules. Each processor has its own internal registers, cache, and local memory. The cache stores all data currently used by the processor. The local memory stores local variables not meant to be shared with the other processors. The shared memory stores the shared variables that need to be exchanged between the processors. The interconnection network allows more than one processor to simultaneously access different shared memory modules through the network. This allows more than one memory read/write operations to take place simultaneously.

We explained in Chapter 2 that a processor communicates mainly with its cache since this is the fastest memory that matches the speed of the processor. However, these caches read or load data from the shared memory and write or store data in this memory also. This brings up two important considerations in shared-memory processors [27]:

1. Cache coherence
2. Synchronization and mutual exclusion

We discuss these two issues in the following sections.

Algorithms and Parallel Computing, by Fayez Gebali
Copyright © 2011 John Wiley & Sons, Inc.

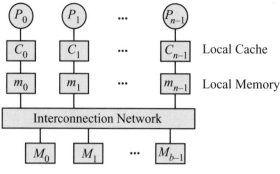

Local Cache

Local Memory

Figure 4.1 Shared-memory processors. Each processor has its local cache and local memory. All processors can access the shared memory modules through the interconnection network.

Shared Memory Modules

4.2 CACHE COHERENCE AND MEMORY CONSISTENCY

Attaching private caches to processors speeds up program execution by making memory latency match the processor speed. Thus, read/write operations take about the same time as the arithmetic and logic unit (ALU) operations. Table 4.1 summarizes the terminology used to describe cache coherence. A cache is useful because most tasks or applications display *temporal locality* and *spatial locality*. Temporal locality refers to the near future. Spatial locality refers to using data located near the current data in the near future. For this reason, data load/store operations between the shared memory and the caches take place using *blocks*. Figure 4.2 shows the relation between the blocks stored in the shared memory and their copies in the cache of a certain processor. The cache stores some blocks using a *tag*, which stores the address of the block in the shared memory. Each block stored in the cache is stored as a row called a *line*. A line contains the following components:

1. Valid bit (V) to indicate whether the data in the line are coherent with the block in the shared memory or not
2. Index, which is the address of the line in the cache
3. Tag, which refers to the address of the block in the shared memory
4. Data, which comprise the data stored in the block

For shared memory systems, caches also help eliminate memory contention when two or more processors attempt to access the same memory module [27].

Copies of the data stored in the shared memory must match those copies stored in the local caches. This is referred to as *cache coherence*. The copies of a shared variable are *coherent* if they are all equal [35]. Effectively, the caches are coherent if every read operation by a processor finds a value produced by a previous write [27]. Cache coherence is important to guarantee correct program execution and to ensure high system performance. Assume two processors, P_1 and P_2, use the same

Table 4.1   Terminology Used to Describe Cache Coherence

Term	Meaning
Block	Group of contiguous words or data stored in shared memory
Broadcast	When information is sent to all caches
Cache	A small high-speed memory implemented on the same chip as the processor to reduce memory access time and to reduce shared-memory collisions between processors
Cache coherence	The contents of a block in the shared memory and the different caches are not the same.
Cache coherence protocol	Policy implemented to maintain cache coherence
Coherent system	When every read of a block from the shared memory finds the same data produced by the last previous write by any other processor
Global data	Data stored in the shared memory
Line	A block stored in a cache along with its tag and valid bit
Local data	Data stored in the cache
Modified block	Data of block in cache have not been updated in the shared memory
Multicast	Information is sent to some, not all, caches.
Replacement	Removing a block from the cache to make room for a new block
Spatial locality	Data in the same block will be used over a short period of time.
Temporal locality	A data word in a block will be used over a short period of time.
Unicast	Information is sent to only one cache.
Valid	Block contents are up to date.
Write-back	A block in the shared memory is updated when the corresponding block in a cache is replaced.
Write-through	A block in the shared memory is updated when the corresponding block in a cache is modified.

shared variable stored in their two separate caches. If P_1 modifies its local value, we must make sure that P_2 is aware of the change.

Consider the case of a shared memory system with four processors and one shared memory module. Table 4.2 illustrates the problems that arise when a block in the shared memory is loaded by the processors and then gets modified by one or more processors. A write-through policy is assumed.

Table 4.3 illustrates the problems that arise when a block in the shared memory is loaded by the processors and then gets modified by one or more processors. A write-back policy is assumed. The cache contents at the different time instances according to the events of Table 4.2 are explained below.

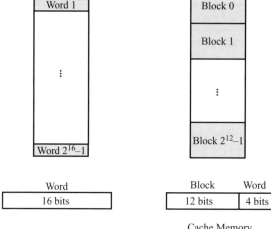

Figure 4.2 Relation between the blocks stored in the shared memory and their copies in the cache of a certain processor.

Main Memory with 16-bit word address space

Cache Memory with 12-bit block address and 4-bit word address

Table 4.2 Example of Cache Coherence Problem with Write-Through Policy

Time	Shared memory	Caches				Comment
		C_0	C_1	C_2	C_3	
0	b	b	—	—	—	Block b is loaded in C_0.
1	b	b	b	—	b	Block b is loaded in C_1 and C_3.
2	b	b	b	—	b_3	Processor P_3 modifies its copy of b. Now the system is noncoherent.
3	b_3	b	b	—	b_3	Processor P_3 performs a write-through. The system is noncoherent since C_0 and C_1 have different copies.
4	b_3	b_3	b_3	—	b_3	Shared memory controller updates C_0 and C_1. Now the system is coherent.

Time 0. The cache C_0 in processor P_0 loads block b for use during its processing.

Time 1. Both caches C_1 and C_3 also load the same block from the shared memory. Now we have three copies of b.

Time 2. Processor P_3 updates its copy of b in C_3. At this time, the data in the shared memory and the caches are not consistent.

Time 3. P_3 performs a write-through operation to make the data in C_3 and in the shared memory consistent.

Table 4.3 Example of Cache Coherence Problem with Write-Back Policy

Time	Shared memory	Caches				Comment
		C_0	C_1	C_2	C_3	
0	b	b	–	–	–	Block b is loaded in C_0.
1	b	b	b	–	b	Block b is loaded in C_1 and C_3.
2	b	b	b	–	b_3	Processor P_3 modifies its copy of b_3. Now the system is noncoherent.
3	b	b_0	b_1	–	b_3	Processors P_0 and P_1 modify their own copies of b.
4	b_1	b_0	b_1	–	b_3	P_1 performs write-back to shared memory
5	b_1	?	b_1	b_1	?	Which value of b should be used to update the memory and caches?

Time 4. Which processor should update the shared memory? With the write-back policy, this is determined by whichever processor performs a cache replacement. In this case, it happens to be P_1.

Time 5. P_2 loads block b and the central controller informs all processors of the new value b_1. What should P_0 and P_3 do? Replace their data or inform the shared memory to use their own versions of b.

It is clear from the previous two situations in Tables 4.2 and 4.3 that the cache coherence problem is very serious especially for the case of multiprocessor systems. The correct value of memory content should not be implied by which processor performed the cache store (write) into memory first. For example, in Table 4.2, we see that P_3 performed the first change in block b followed by P_0 then P_1. This might not have been the correct sequence to update block b in the shared memory. The reason for that is the processors are not synchronized with each other and the scheduling of tasks and threads in each processor is not aligned with that in the other processors. So what is the correct sequence of updating b? There are two ways to arrive at this answer:

1. Correct update of b based on sequential execution of the application

2. Correct update of b based on data dependencies

Sequential execution of the program means running the program on a single-processor sequential machine, which has no multiprocessing or multithreading capabilities. The order of accessing and updating the variable is the correct order as designed by the application developer. This sequence of variable access/update should be the one followed when implementing the application on a multiprocessor system. That sequence of access should be followed when determining how to update the shared variable in memory and in all the caches. Correct cache/memory access is correct if the results obtained by the parallel machine are always identical to the results obtained by the sequential machine.

Correct update of b based on data dependencies is a byproduct of implementing a timing sequence for the application tasks. The data scheduling strategies developed in Chapters 8–11 all identify the correct sequence for updating the algorithm variables. This serves as a guideline for determining the cache update sequencing.

Updating the values of shared variables by the processors is expected in a shared memory system. A cache coherence protocol must be used to ensure that the contents of the cache memories are consistent with the contents of the shared memory. There are two main cache coherence protocols:

1. Directory protocols

2. Snoopy protocols

4.2.1 Cache Coherence Using Directory Protocols

The main components for maintaining cache coherence using directory protocols are shown in Fig. 4.3. The local caches associated with the processors have local cache controllers to coordinate updating the copies of the shared variables stored in the local caches. The central controller is responsible for mainlining cache coherence for the system. Part of the shared memory is a directory that stores entries denoting the state of each shared block. The structure of each entry in the directory depends on the implementation details of the directory protocol used. The central controller handles local cache requests and is responsible for informing the local cache controllers of any changes in the states of the shared variables. The interconnection network enables communication between the controllers and between the caches and the shared memory.

Figure 4.4 shows the details of the full-map directory protocol. Each entry contains $n + 2$ bits, where n is the number of processors. We assumed in the figure that $n = 8$. The bit labeled D indicates whether the data are valid (0) or modified (1).

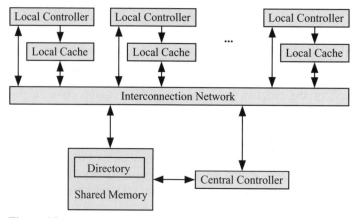

Figure 4.3 System components for cache coherence using directory protocols.

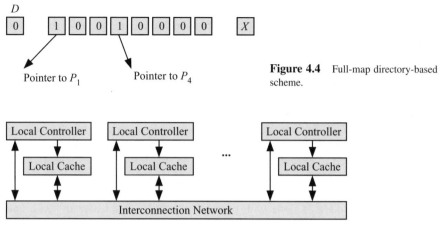

Figure 4.4 Full-map directory-based scheme.

Figure 4.5 System components for cache coherence using snoopy protocols.

The bit labeled X indicates whether to broadcast the update information (B) to each processor or that data is no-broadcast (NB). We see from the figure that if the block corresponding to the shown entry is modified, then only the caches in processors 1 and 4 will have to be informed of that change.

Full-map directory scheme knows exactly the locations of the shared blocks. The caches associated with these copies are involved in coherence actions associated with a given shared block. However, the scheme is inflexible since all coherence transactions must be routed to the central controller. This could prove to be a bottleneck. Also, the size of each entry is directly proportional to the number of processors and must be changed when the number of processors changes.

4.2.2 Cache Coherence Using Snoopy Protocols

Figure 4.5 shows the main components for cache coherence using snoopy protocols. Unlike directory protocols, snoopy protocols do not use a directory in the shared memory nor a central controller. The coherence actions associated with a block are communicated between a local cache and the shared memory. These transactions are monitored by all other local caches. The interconnection network must be able to support broadcast of the data transmissions such that every processor is able to monitor all the network activities. A shared bus is suited for this broadcast mode since each bus transaction can be easily sensed by all processors connected to the bus. The shared bus, however, has a limited bandwidth that allows only one transaction to take place at any given time.

When a memory write operation takes place by any processor, all other processors decide if this operation is relevant to them or not. The write operation by processor P_i is relevant to processor P_j if it has a copy of the block being accessed by P_i. There are two options for P_j based on its cache update policy. In the case of *invalidation-based* policy, P_j invalidates its own copy of b. It then copies b from the shared memory when it needs data from the cache. In the case of *updated-based* policy, P_j replaces its copy of *b* using the data available on the bus while the shared memory is being updated or some other time thereafter.

4.3 SYNCHRONIZATION AND MUTUAL EXCLUSION

Each process or thread operating on a shared variable has a segment of code called *critical section*, where the process operates on the shared variable by changing its value. When a process is executing its critical section, no other process on any processor is allowed to execute its critical section. Figure 4.6 shows a segment of code containing a critical section. When a process reaches the critical section code, it is allowed to enter it and to execute that code section only if it can acquire a *lock*. As soon as the process is done with the critical section, it releases the lock and proceeds to execute the code after the critical section. If two or more processes reach the critical section, only one process is allowed to acquire the lock. All other processes wait at the start of the critical section.

Dijkstra [36] and Knuth [132] showed that it is possible to provide synchronization and mutual exclusion using atomic read and write operations [37]. Atomic operations ensure that the memory read, modify, then write operation to a certain location is done without interference from other processors. This basic capability is provided by hardware and enables the construction of more elaborate software algorithms. Examples of low-level hardware atomic operations include memory load/store and test&set [38–40].

These low-level synchronization primitives can be used by software to build high-level atomic operations such as locks, semaphore, monitors, and barriers. One must be careful when a process or thread acquires a lock or barrier in a multiprocessor system. The process holding the lock must not be preempted so that other

While (Condition == 0)
{

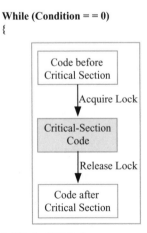

} // **End of While Loop**

Figure 4.6 Segment of code showing a critical section within a normal code.

processes waiting to acquire the lock are not delayed. One solution is to provide a preemption-safe locking [41].

Synchronization processes or threads involve three events [37–39]:

Acquire: where a process or thread tries to acquire the synchronization primitive (e.g., a mutex or barrier)

Wait: where the thread *efficiently* waits for the synchronization primitive to become available.

Release: when a thread has finished its operation, it must inform other processes or threads that the synchronization primitive is available. This allows other threads to acquire the primitive or to proceed beyond past the synchronization event.

A process or thread waiting for a synchronization primitive to become available employs a waiting algorithm. Waiting algorithm could be implemented by busy-waiting or blocking. The latter choice does not waste central processing unit (CPU) resources but carries more overhead for suspending and resuming the thread. This is the reason why busy-waiting is more appropriate when the waiting period is short and the blocking is appropriate when the wait period is long [37]. Busy-waiting in multiprocessor systems does not scale well. The waiting processes actually will test the shared lock using the copies in their own caches. However, as soon as the lock is released, all processes become aware of this new condition and will use the interconnection network while attempting to access the released shared lock in the shared memory. This will lead to increased traffic on the interconnection network and to memory contention.

4.3.1 Synchronization: Locks

Any solution to the critical section problem requires a lock [40]. A lock essentially serializes access to a shared resource so that only one process or thread reads and modifies the variable at any given time. As we mentioned at the start of this section, a process must acquire the lock before it is allowed to enter the critical section as shown in Fig. 4.6. A lock is provided in hardware to simplify program development and to move some of the processing load off the operating system.

The critical section could be handled in a single processor using interrupt prevention when a process is operating on the shared variable. This solution is not practical in a multiprocessor system since all processors must be informed of the interrupt disable. Time will be wasted while this message is being broadcast among the processors.

A lock is provided in hardware by a special atomic `TestAndSet ()` instruction. That instruction returns the value of the lock (the `test` part) and then sets the value of the lock to 1 upon completion.

The lock is a value in memory where the operation read–modified–write is performed atomically using that instruction. The atomic `TestAndSet ()` function is implemented in hardware but a pseudocode is illustrated as follows [37, 40]:

```
1: boolean TestAndSet (boolean *lock)
2: {
3:   boolean v = *lock; // Test (read) operation
4:   *lock = TRUE; // Modify (set) and Write operations
5:   return v;
6: }
```

Line 1 declares the function and defines its body.

Line 3 performs the test portion of the atomic instruction by reading the value of the lock.

Line 4 modifies the lock and updates the value of the lock. If the lock was originally TRUE, no harm is done by writing TRUE again. However, if the lock was FALSE, then the lock becomes available and the process is informed of this fact through the variable *v*. The process also atomically sets the lock to TRUE to make it unavailable to other processes.

Line 5 returns the original value of the lock to be used by the process to decide whether to enter the critical section or not.

The TestAndSet () function can now be used to by a process to control entering the critical section when the lock is available or when waiting for the lock to become available as follows:

```
 1: Code before critical section
 2:
 3: // Attempt to acquire lock
 4: while (TestAndSet (&lock))
 5: ; // no action and continue testing lock
 6:
 7: // Start of critical section
 8: critical section code
 9: // End of critical section
10: lock = FALSE; // release lock
11:
12: Code after critical section
```

Line 1 represents the normal code just before the critical section.

Line 4 is where the process tests the value of the lock in an infinite WHILE loop. The loop ends if the lock value is FALSE and the process acquires the lock and proceeds to execute its critical section. Line 8 represents the critical section.

Line 10 releases the lock at the end of the critical section. Line 12 is the code after the critical section.

The similarity of processes attempting to acquire the lock and the medium access control (MAC) problem in computer communications or networks should be noted here. Table 4.4 summarizes the similarities between mutual exclusion and MAC in telecommunications.

4.3.2 Synchronization: Mutex

A mutex *M* is a binary number that can have the values 0 and 1, which proves useful in mutual exclusion. The mutex is initially given the value 1 to allow any thread

Table 4.4   Similarities between Mutual Exclusion and MAC

Mutual exclusion	MAC
Critical section	Transmitted packet
Process/thread	User/node
Lock	Channel
Lock acquired	Channel acquired by node
Lock available	Channel free
Lock unavailable	Channel busy
Release lock	End of transmission
Test lock	Check channel state
Busy-waiting	User in backoff mode

that needs it to enter its critical section. When a thread acquires the mutex and enters its critical section, it locks it by decrementing its value. When the thread is finished with its critical section, it releases the mutex by incrementing its value. Any thread arriving at the critical region while the lock is in use will wait because the mutex is already at 0. The result is that at most, one thread can enter into the critical section and only after it leaves can another enter. This sort of locking strategy is often used to serialize code that accesses a shared global variable and to ensure mutual exclusion.

There are two basic atomic operations to apply to the mutex: wait() and signal(). The pseudocodes for these two operations are as follows:

```
1:  wait (M)                       1:  signal (M)
2:  while M <= 0                    2:  {
3:  {                              3:     M++; // increment M
4:    ; // do nothing              4:  }
5:    M--; // decrement M if it is 1
6:  }
```

wait() effectively prevents the thread from entering its critical section while the mutex $M = 0$. As soon as $M = 1$, the thread can proceed to execute its critical section.

In the thread library POSIX, the wait() function is implemented using the library call pthread mutex lock(mutex *M). The signal() function is implemented using the library call pthread mutex unlock(mutex *M).

The wait() and signal() functions can now be used by a process to control entering the critical section when the lock is available or when waiting for the lock to become available as follows:

```
1:  Code before critical section
2:
3:  // Attempt to acquire mutex
4:  wait(M);
5:  ; // no action and continue testing mutex
6:
```

```
 7: // Start of critical section
 8: critical section code
 9: // End of critical section
10: signal(M); // release mutex
11:
12: Code after critical section
```

Needless to say, the programmer must ensure that the critical section is surrounded by the correct `wait()` and `signal()` function calls and in the correct order. Failure to do so will result in wrong results that are difficult to track down.

4.3.3 Synchronization: Barriers

The examples of locks and mutexes we discussed in the previous two sections were used when several tasks or threads operated on shared variables in their critical sections. A synchronization barrier, on the other hand, is used when several *independent* tasks or threads are employed to perform several chores in parallel. There are no shared variables between those threads. The synchronization barrier is used for event synchronization where a specified number of tasks must be completed before the rest of the tasks are allowed to proceed. A barrier would be very useful to implement serial–parallel algorithms (SPAs) where several parallel tasks must be completed before moving on to the next state of algorithm execution. Figure 4.7 shows an example of a SPA where barriers are used between the parallel tasks. In the figure, we have the SPA consisting of five stages and we assumed that each task is to be executed by a thread. The number of parallel tasks executed at each stage varies from two to four. To ensure the tasks at each stage are completed before we move to the next task, we place barriers as shown. The command `barrier(j)` indicates that j tasks/threads must reach the barrier before the next set of tasks can proceed.

The POSIX thread library specifies the barrier object along with functions to create it and creates the threads that will use it for synchronization.

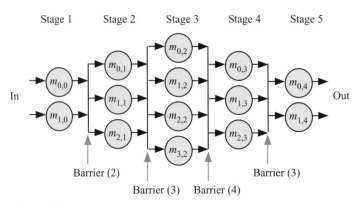

Figure 4.7 Example of using synchronization barriers in serial–parallel algorithms. Each task is to be executed by its own thread.

To initialize the barrier, the following routine is used [42]:

```
1: #include <pthread.h>
2: pthread barrier t barrier;
3: pthread barrierattr t attribute;
4: unsigned count;
5: int return value;
6: return value = pthread barrier init(&barrier, &attri-
bute, count);
```

Line 1 adds the functions and data types associated with the pthread library.
Line 2 defines `barrier` to be of the type barrier.

Line 3 defines `attributes` to be of type barrier attributes.

Lines 4 and 5 define other data types where `count` is the number of threads
that must arrive at the barrier before they can proceed any further.

Line 6 initializes the barrier and returns the variable `return value` to monitor
the success of the function call. The return value is zero for successful
completion.

The threads being synchronized by the barrier include the following code:

```
1: Code before the barrier
2:
3: // Wait at the barrier
4: ret = pthread barrier wait(&barrier);
5:
6: Code after the barrier
```

where the type `barrier` was initialized using the `pthread barrier init()`
routine.

4.3.4 Comparing the Synchronization Primitives

The most basic synchronization primitive is the *lock* and is the most efficient in its
memory use and execution time [42]. The lock is essentially used to serialize access
to a shared resource or shared variable.

The *mutex* uses more memory than a lock. The mutex must be acquired before
the shared variable is modified. After a thread is finished with its critical section, it
must release the mutex so that other threads can proceed with their critical
sections.

The *barrier* is used as an event synchronization mechanism so that all threads
arrive at a certain point before the rest of the code is executed.

4.4 PROBLEMS

4.1. A shared-memory parallel processor system has n processors and b shared memory
modules with $n \leq b$. Assume all processors need to update their caches by accessing the
memory modules. Assume a uniform probability that a processor requests to access data
from a particular memory module.

   (1) What is the value of the probability that a processor requests to access data from a particular memory module?

   (2) What is the probability that a memory access collision takes place for a particular memory module?

   (3) What is the probability that a memory access collision takes place for the shared memory as a whole?

   (4) What is the probability that a memory access collision takes place for the shared memory as a whole for the case when $n > b$?

4.2. What are the two main advantages for using the local cache in shared-memory multiprocessor systems?

4.3. Explain the two reasons for maintaining cache coherence in shared-memory multiprocessor systems?

4.4. A shared-memory system consists of n processors, one shared memory module, and a system-wide bus connecting all the components. Assume a as the probability that a processor requests access to the shared memory to update its cache at a given time step. What is the probability that a bus collision takes place?

4.5. Assume in a shared memory system that the probability that a data is not in the cache is α. And $1 - \alpha$ is the probability the data are in the cache. What is the average memory access time?

4.6. The three Cs for single-processor cache misses were discussed in a previous chapter. Investigate if there are other causes for cache misses in a shared memory system.

4.7. Cache misses in a shared memory system show a "U" pattern versus block size for a fixed cache capacity. Explain why this behavior is expected.

Chapter 5

Interconnection Networks

5.1 INTRODUCTION

We saw in Chapter 3 that parallel computers require an interconnection network to allow exchange of data between the processors and between the processors and common shared or distributed memories. Interconnection networks connect processors in a parallel computer system. The main factors that affect the interconnection network performance are

1. network links, which could be wires, wireless, or even optic channels or media;

2. switches that connect the links together;

3. the protocol software/firmware that is used to route the packets or messages between the processors through the switches and links; and

4. the network topology, which is the way the switches are connected together.

The capabilities and characteristics of the interconnection network have a direct influence on the resulting performance of the multiprocessor system. The following sections discuss the different types of networks used in multiprocessor systems. We should mention here that multicore processors have all the cores and their interconnection network on the same chip. Thus, the network is called network-on-chip (NoC). We discuss in this chapter interconnection networks based on their topology. Topology defines how the processor or nodes are connected. The topology impacts system performance parameters such as data throughput, delay, and network power consumption.

We define the interconnection network *diameter* as the longest distance between two nodes in the graph. The diameter represents the number of switches or nodes a message takes to travel from a source to a destination node.

Algorithms and Parallel Computing, by Fayez Gebali
Copyright © 2011 John Wiley & Sons, Inc.

5.2 CLASSIFICATION OF INTERCONNECTION NETWORKS BY LOGICAL TOPOLOGIES

The interconnection network topology is usually drawn as a graph with nodes representing the switches or processors and the edges representing the communication links between the switches or processors. There are major well-known network topologies that are summarized in the following sections.

5.2.1 Bus

A bus is the simplest type of interconnection network as shown in Fig. 5.1. The shaded squares represent medium access control (MAC) controllers. These controllers could be simple arbiters or they could be ethernet controllers if the bus is an ethernet local area network (LAN). They could also represent wireless devices if the bus physical medium is a wireless channel.

All processors and memory modules are connected to the bus, and communication between any pair of processors takes the same amount of time no matter how far apart they are. The bus, however, allows only one processor to access the shared medium at any given time so as to prevent bus access *collisions*. Each module connected to the bus is characterized by its own unique MAC address for identification. The source processor communicates with another processor or memory module by specifying the destination MAC address. Some form of MAC arbitration scheme must be enforced to prevent bus access collisions. There are many arbitration schemes that affect the overall performance of the system [43].

The performance of the bus interconnection network depends very heavily on the following factors:

1. the number of processors connected to the bus; as the network size scales up, performance degrades;

2. the statistics of the network access requests issued by the processors; and

3. the type of MAC arbitration protocol being used.

The traffic statistics depend on the algorithm being implemented and could follow any type of traffic distribution, such as constant bit rate, Poisson process, bursty distribution, and so on.

The arbitration protocol can be chosen to be [43] round robin, fixed priority, rotating priority, random access, and so on.

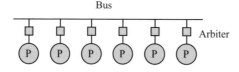

Figure 5.1 A bus interconnection network. The shaded squares represent MAC controllers.

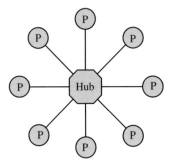

Figure 5.2   A star interconnection network.

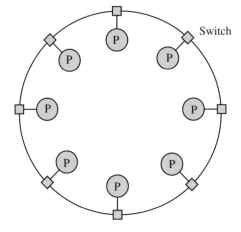

Figure 5.3   A ring interconnection network.
The shaded squares represent MAC controllers.

5.2.2 Star

Figure 5.2 shows an example of a star interconnection network, all processors are connected to a central *hub*. All network traffic between the processors must pass through the hub. The hub limits the communication performance of the system since it must communicate with all the processors and must handle their requests. It is a simple matter to add more processors, but the hub must be able to accommodate the extra links.

5.2.3 Ring

Figure 5.3 shows an example of a ring interconnection network, where each processor is connected to the ring through a switch. The shaded squares represent MAC controllers. Each switch is aware of the MAC address of the processor that is connected to it. The switches allow more than one processor to transmit and receive messages or data at the same time. The sending processor sends its data to the switch it is connected to. The switch forwards the message to a neighboring switch and the message travels between the switches until it reaches its destination.

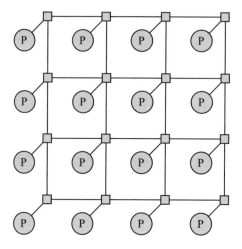

Figure 5.4 A two-dimensional mesh interconnection network. The shaded squares represent MAC controllers.

5.2.4 Mesh

A two-dimensional mesh network is shown in Fig. 5.4. The shaded squares represent MAC controllers. Messages travel from source processor to destination processor through a *routing algorithm* that is implemented in each switch or router. There are several message routing algorithms such as deterministic routing, where the route between source and destination is predetermined and fixed. Another routing algorithm is adaptive routing, where the route taken by the message is controlled by the state of the switches in the network.

The mesh network performance depends on the traffic pattern in the mesh, the buffer size in each switch, and the arbitration scheme used in the switches.

5.2.5 Crossbar Network

Crossbar networks have not been well represented in the literature, with the exception of Furhmann [44], perhaps due to the original article by Clos [45] in which he claimed that a crossbar network is very expensive to implement. With the current state of very large-scale integration (VLSI) technology, it is possible to place several switching elements (SEs) and their state registers on a single chip with the only limitation being the number of input/output (I/O) pins and pad size [46].

An $N \times N$ crossbar network consists of N inputs and N outputs. It can connect any input to any free output without blocking. Figure 5.5 shows a 6×6 crossbar network. The network consists of an array of crosspoints (*CP*) connected in a grid fashion. $CP(i, j)$ lies at the intersection of row i with column j. Each *CP* operates in one of two configurations as shown in Fig. 5.6. The *X* configuration is the default configuration where the SE allows simultaneous data flow in the vertical and horizontal directions without interference. If $CP(3, 5)$ was in the *X* configuration, then

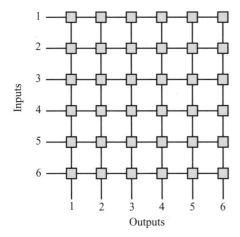

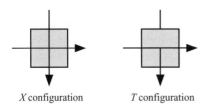

Figure 5.5 A 6 × 6 crossbar interconnection network.

Figure 5.6 States of the crosspoint (CP) in a crossbar network.

data flowing horizontally originate at input 3 and are sent to all the intersection points at this row. Data flowing vertically in column 5 could have originated from any input above or below row 3.

In the *T* configuration, the *CP* allows data flow in the horizontal direction and interrupts data flow in the vertical direction. Data flowing vertically at the output are a copy of the horizontal data. For example, if *CP*(3, 5) was in the *T* configuration, then data flowing horizontally originate at input 3. Data flowing downward at the output are a copy of the horizontal data coming from row 3. This way, output at column 5 sees a copy of the data that were moving on row 3.

A crossbar network supports high capacity due to the *N* simultaneous connections it can provide. This comes at the expense of the number of *CP* that grows as N^2. This is one reason why a crossbar network is used mainly for demanding applications that require a relatively small value of *N* (about 10). However, advances in VLSI technology and electro-optics make crossbar switches a viable switching alternative.

Data multicast in a crossbar network can be easily accomplished. Suppose that input 3 requests to multicast its data to outputs 1, 2, and 5. Input 3 would then request to configure *CP*(3, 1), (3, 2), and (3, 5) into the *T* configuration and all other *CP* in row 3 would remain in the default *X* configuration.

5.2.6 Crossbar Network Contention and Arbitration

Suppose that two or more inputs request access to the same output. In that case, contention arises and some arbitration mechanism has to be provided to settle this dispute. In fact, we have to provide N arbiters such that each one is associated with a column in the crossbar network. For example, when input 1 requests to communicate with output 3, it requests to configure $CP(1, 3)$ into the T configuration and must wait until the arbiter in column 3 issues a grant to that input. At the same time, the arbiter in column 3 must inform all other inputs that they cannot access column 3 in that time step. This happens only after the arbiter checks to see if there are any requests coming from other inputs demanding access to output 3. These arbiters slow down the system especially for large networks where signal propagation up and down the columns takes a substantial amount of time.

5.2.7 Multistage Interconnection Networks (MINs)

Figure 5.7 shows that an $N \times N$ MIN consists of n stages with stage i connected to stages $i - 1$ and $i + 1$ through some pattern of connection lines. Each stage has w crossbar SEs that vary in size from 2×2 and up. The SEs in each stage are numbered starting at the top as shown. For the MIN in the figure, we have $N = 4$, $n = 3$, and $w = 4$. The labeling of the stages and switches is also shown in the figure.

Typically, the number of stages is $n = \lg N$. The design parameters for a MIN are the size of the network N, the number of stages n, the number of switches per stage w, and the size of each switch. These four factors determine the MIN *complexity*. Another important measure of the cost of a MIN is the number and length of the wires in the connection links between the stages. This last factor determines the required number of pins or connections at every level of integration or packaging.

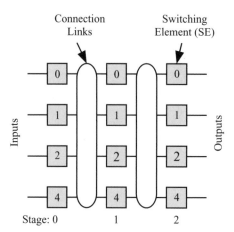

Figure 5.7   A 4 × 4 MIN with three stages and four switches per stage.

5.2.8 The Banyan Network

Figure 5.8 shows an 8×8 banyan network. For an $N \times N$ network, the number of stages is $n + 1$, where $n = \lg N$, and the number of SEs in each stage is N. Each SE is a 2×2 crossbar switch and the number of links between the stages is $2N$.

An $N \times N$ banyan network is built using one to two selectors in the input stage $(i = 0)$, 2×2 crossbar SEs in the $n - 1$ internal stages $(0 < i < n)$, and two to one concentrators in the output stage $(i = n)$. However, the banyan network is a blocking network and provides only one path from any input to any output. As such, it possesses no tolerance for faults.

$SE(i, j)$ at stage i and row position j is connected to $SE(i + 1, k)$ such that k is is given by

$$k = \begin{cases} j & \text{Straight connection} \\ C^i(j) & \text{Cube connection} \end{cases} \tag{5.1}$$

where $0 \leq i < n$. Thus, at stage 1, we see that $SE(1, 2)$ is connected to switches $SE(2, 2)$, the straight connection, and switch $SE(2, 0)$, the $C^1(2)$ connection.

The cube function C^i complements the ith bit (a_i) of the binary number, leaving all other bits intact.

$$A = a_{n-1} \quad \cdots \quad a_{i+1} \quad a_i \quad a_{i-1} \quad \cdots \quad a_0$$
$$C^i(A) = a_{n-1} \quad \cdots \quad a_{i+1} \quad \overline{a_i} \quad a_{i-1} \quad \cdots \quad a_0$$

The banyan network provides one unique path from any input to any output based on the input row address and the destination address. Figure 5.9 shows the two types of connections that could be established for the two inputs of an SE at stage i:

Straight connection. The packet enters and exits at the same row location.

Cube connection. The packet enters at row location R and exits at row location $C^i(R)$.

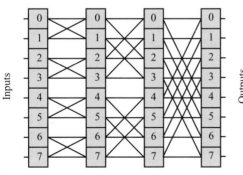

Stage: 0   1   2   3

Figure 5.8 An 8×8 banyan network.

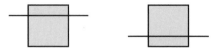

The straight connection for
each input

The cube connection for each
input

Figure 5.9   The straight and cube connections
for each input of an *SE* in a banyan network.

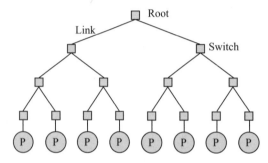

Figure 5.10   A binary tree
interconnection network.

Straight connection. The packet enters and exits at the same row location.

Cube connection. The packet enters at row location R and exits at row location
$C^i(R)$.

5.2.9 Tree Network

Figure 5.10 shows a binary tree network. The tree supports communication among
P processors using $2P - 1$ switches or routers. The processors are located at the
leaves of the tree and the switches have three links except for the switch at the root
of the tree and the switches at the bottom of the tree connected to the processors.
For the binary tree, the diameter is $2\log_2 P$.

5.2.10 Random Topology

Random topology implies that the interconnection network links do not follow a
well-defined pattern. The Internet is an example of such a random type of network.
Figure 5.11 shows the main component of the Internet. The white circles represent
core switches, which are specialized high-speed computers capable of maintaining
traffic in the gigabit range and higher. The gray circles represent switches at the edge

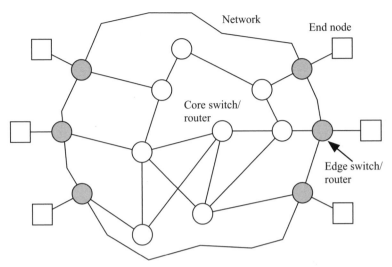

Figure 5.11   The main components of the Internet.

of the Internet. These switches connect the Internet service providers (ISPs) to the Internet cloud. In turn, the ISPs have their own network of subscribers that access the Internet through subscription to the services provided by the ISP. The end nodes could be thought of as LANs with many Internet users.

The main protocol used to transmit packets across the Internet is the transfer control protocol/Internet protocol (TCP/IP) protocol. This is a session-oriented protocol and guarantees the delivery of the transmitted packets. The average time for delivering packets across the Internet is on the order of 10 ms [47].

5.3 INTERCONNECTION NETWORK SWITCH ARCHITECTURE

As was explained above, networks rely on switches to perform their functions. Thus, it is worthwhile to study the construction of switches in more detail. A switch is a hardware device that accepts messages or packets at its inputs and routes them to its outputs according to the routing information provided in the message header and the switch routing table. Figure 5.12 is a block diagram showing the main components of a switch. The switch has the following main architectural components:

1. Controller
2. Input ports
3. Switch fabric (SF)
4. Buffers
5. Output ports

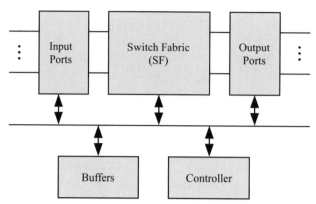

Figure 5.12 Basic components of a switch.

Notice that although the switch is a part of the interconnection network, it also has its own switching network! Typically, it is called the SF. In the following discussion, we shall refer to the units of data communicated between processors as *packets*.

Controller. The controller controls the operation of the switch and routing packet streams through a *lookup table* that knows how to route a packet based on its source and destination processor addresses.

Buffers. The incoming packets must be stored within the processor since a certain delay is encountered while determining the packet route. Also, due to collisions, an incoming packet might not be able to access the desired output port and must wait for later routing. The design of the buffer has great influence on the performance of the switch and consequently on the performance of the interconnection network.

SF. The SF routes packets from the input ports to the output ports. The setup of the proper packet rout is determined by the controller.

Input ports. The input ports accept packets arriving from input links.

Output ports. The output ports deliver packets to output links.

There are different types of switches depending on where the buffers are located as we discuss in the following sections.

5.3.1 Input Queuing Switch

Figure 5.13 shows an input queuing switch. Each input port has a dedicated first-in, first-out (FIFO) buffer to store incoming packets. The arriving packets are stored at the tail of the queue and only move up when the packet at the head of the queue is routed through the SF to the correct output port.

A controller at each input port classifies each packet by examining its header to determine the appropriate path through the SF. The controller must also perform traffic management functions.

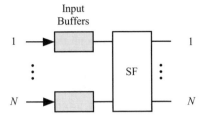

Figure 5.13 Input queuing switch. Each input has a queue for storing incoming packets.

In one time step, an input queue must be able to support one write and one read operation, which is a nice feature since the memory access time is not likely to impose any speed bottlenecks.

Assuming an $N \times N$ switch, the SF must connect N input ports to N output ports. Only a space division $N \times N$ switch can provide simultaneous connectivity.

The main advantages of input queuing are

1. low memory speed requirement;
2. distributed traffic management at each input port;
3. distributed lookup table at each input port; and
4. support of broadcast and multicast does not require duplicating the data.

The main disadvantages of input queuing are

1. head of line (HOL) problem, as discussed below;
2. difficulty of implementing data broadcast or multicast since this will further slow down the switch due to the multiplication of an HOL problem;
3. difficulty of implementing quality of service (QoS) or differentiated services support, as discussed below; and
4. difficulty of implementing scheduling strategies since this involves extensive communications between the input ports.

An HOL problem arises when the packet at the head of the queue is blocked from accessing the desired output port [28]. This blockage could arise because the SF cannot provide a path (*internal blocking*) or if another packet is accessing the output port (*output blocking*). When HOL occurs, other packets that may be queued behind the blocked packet are consequently blocked from reaching possibly idle output ports. Thus, HOL limits the maximum throughput of the switch [28].

The switch throughput can be increased if the queue service discipline examines a window of w packets at the head of the queue instead of only the HOL packet. The first packet out of the top w packets that can be routed is selected and the queue size decreases by one such that each queue sends only one packet to the switching fabric. To achieve multicast in an input queuing switch, the HOL packet must remain at the head of the queue until all the multicast ports have received their own copies at different time steps. Needless to say, this aggravates the HOL problem since now we must deal with multiple blocking possibilities for the HOL packet before it finally leaves the queue. Alternatively, the HOL packet might make use of the multicast capability of the switching fabric if one exists.

Packet scheduling is difficult because the scheduler has to scan all the packets in all the input ports. This requires communication between all the inputs, which limits the speed of the switch. The scheduler will find it difficult to maintain bandwidth and buffer space fairness when all the packets from different classes are stored at different buffers at the inputs. For example, packets belonging to a certain class of service could be found in different input buffers. We have kept a tally of the buffer space used up by this service class.

In input queuing, there are three *potential* causes for packet loss:

1. *Input queue is full.* An arriving packet has no place in the queue and is discarded.

2. *Internal blocking.* A packet being routed within the SF is blocked inside the SF and is discarded. Of course, this type of loss occurs only if the input queue sends the packet to the SF without waiting to verify that a path can be provided.

3. *Output blocking.* A packet that made it through the SF reaches the desired output port, but the port ignores it since it is busy serving another packet. Again, this type of loss occurs only if the input queue sends the packet to the output without waiting to verify that the output link is available.

5.3.2 Output Queuing Switch

To overcome the HOL limitations of input queuing, the standard approach is to abandon input queuing and to place the buffers at the output ports as shown in Fig. 5.14. Notice however, that an output queuing switch must have small buffers at its inputs to be able to temporarily hold the arriving packets while they are being classified and processed for routing.

An incoming packet is stored at the input buffer, and the input controller must read the header information to determine which output queue is to be updated. The packet must be routed through the SF to the correct output port. The controller must also handle any contention issues that might arise if the packet is blocked from leaving the buffer for any reason.

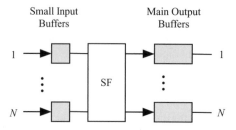

Figure 5.14   Output queuing switch. Each output has a queue for storing the packets destined to that output. Each input must also have a small FIFO buffer for storing incoming packets for classification.

A controller at each input port classifies each packet by examining the header to determine the appropriate path through the SF. The controller must also perform traffic management functions.

In one time step, the small input queue must be able to support one write and one read operation, which is a nice feature since the memory access time is not likely to impose any speed bottlenecks. However, in one time step, the main buffer at each output port must support N write and one read operations.

Assuming an $N \times N$ switch, the SF must connect N input ports to N output ports. Only a space division $N \times N$ switch can provide simultaneous connectivity.

The main advantages of output queuing are

1. distributed traffic management,

2. distributed lookup table at each input port,

3. ease of implementing QoS or differentiated services support, and

4. ease of implementing distributed packet scheduling at each output port.

The main disadvantages of output queuing are

1. high memory speed requirements for the output queues;

2. difficulty of implementing data broadcast or multicast since this will further slow down the switch due to the multiplication of a HOL problem;

3. support of broadcast and multicast requires duplicating the same data at different buffers associated with each output port; and

4. HOL problem is still present since the switch has input queues.

The switch throughput can be increased if the switching fabric can deliver more than one packet to any output queue instead of only one. This can be done by increasing the operating speed of the SF, which is known as *speedup*. Alternatively, the SF could be augmented using duplicate paths, or by choosing an SF that inherently has more than one link to any output port. When this happens, the output queue has to be able to handle the extra traffic by increasing its operating speed or by providing separate queues for each incoming link.

As we mentioned before, output queuing requires that each output queue must be able to support one read and N write operations in one time step. This of course could become a speed bottleneck due to cycle time limitations of current memory technologies.

To achieve multicast in an output queuing switch, the packet at an input buffer must remain in the buffer until all the multicast ports have received their own copies at different time steps. Needless to say, this leads to increased buffer occupancy since now we must deal with multiple blocking possibilities for the packet before it finally leaves the buffer. Alternatively, the packet might make use of the multicast capability of the switching fabric if one exists.

In output queuing, there are four potential causes for packet loss:

1. *Input buffer is full.* An arriving packet has no place in the buffer and is discarded.

2. *Internal blocking.* A packet being routed within the SF is blocked inside the SF and is discarded.

3. *Output blocking.* A packet that made it through the SF reaches the desired output port, but the port ignores it since it is busy serving another packet.

4. *Output queue is full.* An arriving packet has no place in the queue and is discarded.

5.3.3 Shared Buffer Switch

Figure 5.15 shows a shared buffer switch design that employs a single common buffer in which all arriving packets are stored. This buffer *queues* the data in separate queues that are located within one common memory. Each queue is associated with an output port. Similar to input and output queuing, each input port needs a local buffer of its own in which to store incoming packets until the controller is able to classify them.

A flexible mechanism employed to construct queues using a regular random access memory is to use the *linked list* data structure. Each linked list is dedicated to an output port. In a linked list, each storage location stores a packet and a pointer to the next packet in the queue as shown. Successive packets need not be stored in successive memory locations. All that is required is to be able to know the address of the next packet though the pointer associated with the packet. This pointer is indicated by the solid circles in the figure. The lengths of the linked lists need not be equal and depend only on how many packets are stored in each linked list. The memory controller keeps track of the location of the last packet in each queue, as shown by the empty circles. There is no need for an SF since the packets are effectively "routed" by being stored in the proper linked list.

When a new packet arrives at an input port, the buffer controller decides which queue it should go to and stores the packet at any available location in the memory then appends that packet to the linked list by updating the necessary pointers. When

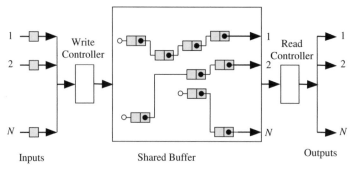

Figure 5.15 Shared buffer switch. Solid circles indicate next packet pointers. Empty circles indicate pointers to the tail end of each linked list.

a packet leaves a queue, the pointer of the next packet now points to the output port and the length of the linked list is reduced by one.

The main advantages of shared buffering are

1. the ability to assign a different buffer space for each output port since the linked list size is flexible and limited only by the amount of free space in the shared buffer;
2. a switching fabric is not required;
3. distributed lookup table at each input port;
4. there is no HOL problem in the shared buffer switch since each linked list is dedicated to one output port;
5. ease of implementing data broadcast or multicast;
6. ease of implementing QoS and differentiated services support; and
7. ease of implementing scheduling algorithms at each linked list.

The main disadvantages of shared buffering are

1. high memory speed requirements for the shared buffer;
2. centralized scheduler function implementation, which might slow down the switch;
3. support of broadcast and multicast requires duplicating the same data at different linked lists associated with each output port; and
4. the use of a single shared buffer makes the task of accessing the memory very difficult for implementing scheduling algorithms, traffic management algorithms, and QoS support.

The shared buffer must operate at a speed of at least $2N$ since it must perform a maximum of N write and N read operations at each time step.

To achieve multicast in a shared buffer switch, the packet must be duplicated in all the linked lists on the multicast list. This needlessly consumes storage area that could otherwise be used. To support differentiated services, the switch must maintain several queues at each input port for each service class being supported.

In shared buffering, there are two potential causes for packet loss:

1. *Input buffer is full.* An arriving packet has no place in the buffer and is discarded.
2. *Shared buffer is full.* An arriving packet has no place in the buffer and is discarded.

5.3.4 Multiple Input Queuing Switch

To overcome the HOL problem in input queuing switch and still retain the advantages of that switch, m input queues are assigned to each input port as shown in Fig. 5.16. If each input port has a queue that is dedicated to an output port (i.e.,

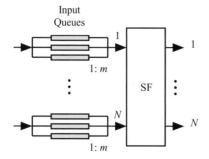

Figure 5.16 Multiple input queue switch. Each input port has a bank of FIFO buffers. The number of queues per input port could represent the number of service classes supported or it could represent the number of output ports.

$m = N$), the switch is called a *virtual output queuing* (VOQ) switch. In that case, the input controller at each input port will classify an arriving packet and place it in the FIFO buffer belonging to the destination output port. In effect, we are creating output queues at each input and hence the name "VOQ."

This approach removes the HOL problem and the switch efficiency starts to approach 100% depending only on the efficiency of the SF and the scheduling algorithm at each output port. Multicast is also very easily supported since copies of an arriving packet could be placed at the respective output queues. Distributed packet classification and traffic management are easily implemented in that switch also.

There are, however, several residual problems with this architecture. Scheduling packets for a certain output port becomes a major problem. Each output port must choose a packet from N virtual queues located at N input ports. This problem is solved in the VRQ switch, which is discussed later. Another disadvantage associated with multiple input queues is the contention between all the queues to access the switching fabric. Dedicating a direct connection between each queue and the SF results in a huge SF that is of dimension $N^2 \times N$, which is definitely not practical.

In multiple input queuing, there are three potential causes for packet loss:

1. *Input buffer is full.* An arriving packet has no place in the buffer and is discarded.

2. *Internal blocking.* A packet being routed within the SF is blocked inside the SF and is discarded.

3. *Output blocking.* A packet that made it through the SF reaches the desired output port, but the port ignores it since it is busy serving another packet.

5.3.5 Multiple Output Queuing Switch

To support sophisticated scheduling algorithms, n output queues are assigned to each output port as shown in Fig. 5.17. If each output port has a queue that is dedicated to an input port (i.e., $n = N$), the switch is called a *virtual input queuing* (VIQ) switch. In that case, the output controller at each output port will classify an arriving

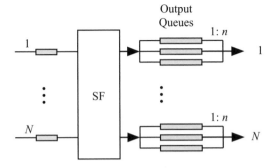

Figure 5.17 Multiple output queuing switch. Each output port has a bank of FIFO buffers. The number of queues per output port could represent the number of service classes supported or it could represent the number of connections supported.

packet and place it in the FIFO buffer belonging to the input port it came on. In effect, we are creating input queues at each output and hence the name "VIQ." Another advantage of using several output queues is that the FIFO speed need not be N times the line rate as was the case in output queuing switch with a single buffer per port.

Several disadvantages are not removed from output queue switch using this approach. The HOL problem is still present and packet broadcast still aggravates the HOL problem. Another disadvantage associated with multiple output queues is the contention between all the queues to access the switching fabric. Dedicating a direct connection between each queue and the SF results in a huge SF that is of dimension $N \times N^2$, which is definitely not practical.

This problem is solved in the virtual routing/virtual queuing (VRQ) switch, which is discussed later. In multiple output queuing, there are four potential causes for packet loss:

1. *Input buffer is full.* An arriving packet has no place in the buffer and is discarded.

2. *Internal blocking.* A packet being routed within the SF is blocked inside the SF and is discarded.

3. *Output blocking.* A packet that made it through the SF reaches the desired output port, but the port ignores it since it is busy serving another packet.

4. *Output queue is full.* An arriving packet has no place in the queue and is discarded.

5.3.6 Multiple I/O Queuing Switch

To retain the advantages of multiple input and multiple output queuing and to avoid their limitations, multiple queues could be placed at each input and output port as shown in Fig. 5.18. An arriving packet must be classified by the input controller at each input port to be placed in its proper input queue. Packets destined to a certain output port travel through the SF and the controller at each output port classifies

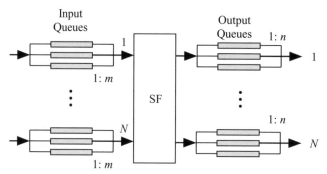

Figure 5.18   Multiple input and output queuing switch. Each input port has a bank of FIFO buffers and each output port has a bank of FIFO buffers.

them, according to their class of service, and places them in their proper output queue.

The advantages of multiple queues at the input and the output are removal of HOL problem, distributed lookup table, distributed traffic management, and ease of implementation of differentiated services. Furthermore, the memory speed of each queue could match the line rate.

The disadvantage of the multiple input and output queue switch is the need to design an SF that is able to support a maximum of $N^2 \times N^2$ connections simultaneously. This problem is solved in the VRQ switch, which is discussed later.

In multiple input and output queuing, there are four potential causes for packet loss:

1. *Input buffer is full.* An arriving packet has no place in the buffer and is discarded.

2. *Internal blocking.* A packet being routed within the SF is blocked inside the SF and is discarded.

3. *Output blocking.* A packet that made it through the SF reaches the desired output port, but the port ignores it since it is busy serving another packet.

4. *Output queue is full.* An arriving packet has no place in the queue and is discarded.

5.3.7 VRQ Switch

We saw in the previous sections the many alternatives for locating and segmenting the buffers. Each design had its advantages and disadvantages. The VRQ switch has been proposed by the author such that it has all the advantages of earlier switches but none of their disadvantages. In addition, the design has extra features such as low power, scalability, and so on [28].

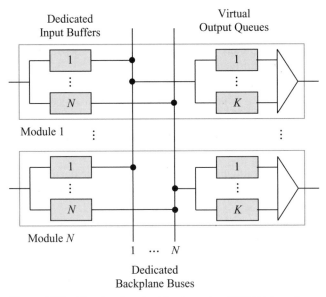

Figure 5.19 The virtual routing/virtual queuing (VRQ) high-performance switch.

Figure 5.19 shows the main components of that switch. Each input port has N buffers (not queues) where incoming packets are stored after being classified. Similarly, each output port has K FIFO queues, where K is determined by the number of service classes or sessions that must be supported. The SF is an array of backplane buses. This gives the best throughput compared with any other previously proposed SF architecture including crossbar switches.

The input buffers store incoming packets, which could be variable in size. The input controller determines which output port is desired by the packet and sends a *pointer* to the destination output port. The pointer indicates to the output port the location of the packet in the input buffer, which input port it came from, and any other QoS requirements. The output controller queues that pointer—the packet itself remains in the input buffer. The buffer storage requirements for the output queues are modest since they store pointer information, which is small in size compared to the size of the packets stored in the input buffers.

When a pointer is selected from an output queue, the location of the corresponding packet is determined and the packet is selected to access the SF. We call this mode of operation *output-driven routing*, which never leads to SF contention. The classic or usual way of accessing the SF is called *input-driven routing*, which is guaranteed to lead to contention as we have seen in each switch design we have studied so far.

Let us see how the VRQ switch is able to overcome all the limitations of earlier designs:

1. Traffic management, scheduling, and congestion control are all distributed among the input and output ports. This allows more time for the algorithms

to complete their operations and for the designer to implement more sophisticated algorithms.

2. The HOL problem is completely eliminated because the VRQ switch is output driven and not input driven.

3. The input buffers operate at the line rate, and each output queue needs to process at most N pointers, which is much simpler than processing N packets.

4. Packets are stored at the inputs in regular memory, not FIFO memory, which is much simpler to implement.

5. There is great freedom in configuring the output queues. The queues could be constructed based on a per-connection basis, per-input basis, or per-service class basis.

6. Data broadcast is very simple to implement and no extra copies of a packet need to be stored.

7. An incoming packet does not leave its location in the input buffer until it is ready to be moved through the switch. This reduces power and storage requirements.

8. Internal blocking is completely removed since each input port has its own dedicated bus.

9. Output blocking is completely removed since each output port is able to process all the pointers that arrive to it.

10. The backplane buses operate at the line rate in a bit-serial fashion with no need whatsoever for internal speedup or use of parallel data lines.

11. The SF is contentionless since it is based on a matrix of *dedicated buses* that are *output driven*.

Table 5.1 summarizes the desirable features to be supported by a switch and switch type that can support these features. From the table, we see that both the shared buffer switch and the VRQ switch can easily implement most of the functionalities of a high-speed switch.

Table 5.1   Switch Types Capable of Supporting the Different Switch Features

Feature	Input	Output	Shared	VRQ
QoS support		X	X	X
HOL elimination			X	X
Scheduling support		X	X	X
Broadcast support			X	X
Memory speed	X			X
Scalability	X			X
Contentionless SF			X	X

5.4 PROBLEMS

5.1. This problem is adapted from Quinn [48]. Draw hypercube networks with two, four, and eight nodes.

5.2. Explain how a path is established in the crossbar switch and explain why the switch is nonblocking.

5.3. A blocking interconnection network is one where a connection between an input and an output is not available if another input is accessing another output. Show which of the networks discussed in this chapter are blocking networks and which are not.

5.4. Discuss the need for arbitration in a crossbar network and propose some techniques for resolving output contention. Discuss the advantages and disadvantages of the arbitration techniques you propose from the point of view of hardware complexity and speed.

5.5. Derive the performance parameters of the bus interconnection network. Assume that network access requests are issued randomly with probability a per time slot and that there are P processors in the system.

5.6. Derive the performance parameters of the star interconnection network. Assume that network access requests are issued randomly with probability a per time slot and that there are P processors in the system.

Chapter 6

Concurrency Platforms

6.1 INTRODUCTION

There is a *software gap* [49] between hardware potential and the performance that can be attained using today's software tools. There are now concurrency platforms that support multithreading, such as Cilk++ [50] and Open Multi-Processing (OpenMP) [51] and standard libraries like POSIX threads (Pthreads) [38–40, 52, 53] and WinAPI threads [40]. Using these tools, the program developer is able to control the number of threads and the workload assigned to each thread. The program developer can also control synchronization of the different threads to ensure proper program execution. Using such techniques, the programmer is able to generate a *parallel code*—that is, a code that contains several threads. However, this code might not automatically result in a *concurrent code*—that is, a code that runs simultaneously on several cores or processors. Concurrency is controlled ultimately by the operating system [54]. The application developers cannot rely on the software to explore algorithm speedup. Rather, the developer must use special directives to control the progress of tasks even in the presence of operating system uncertainties.

The above tools rely on the application developer or the programmer being able to identify parallelism and to ensure proper program sequencing. This might be easy to do for the simplest cases. For other cases, the programmer needs other tools to investigate the alternative ways to explore possible parallelism. The purpose of this book is to provide such tools to programmers so they can intelligently control the concurrency platforms.

6.2 CONCURRENCY PLATFORMS

An alternative to these low-level do-it-yourself tools is the *concurrency platform*—this is a software that allows coordination, scheduling, and management of multicore resources. Examples of concurrency platforms include [55]

Algorithms and Parallel Computing, by Fayez Gebali
Copyright © 2011 John Wiley & Sons, Inc.

- .NET ThreadingPool class [56]
- message-passing libraries such as message passing interface (MPI) [57]
- data-parallel programming languages such as NESL [58], Ct from RapidMind/ Intel [59];
- task parallel libraries such as Intel's Threading Building Blocks (TBB) [60], Microsoft's Task Parallel Library (TPL) [61], and Microsoft's Concurrency Runtime; and
- extensions to programming languages such as OpenMP [51], Cilk++ [50], C++ [62], and Microsoft's Parallel Patterns Library (PPL) [63].

In the following sections, we illustrate using concurrency platforms.

6.3   CILK++

Cilk++ is a language extension programming tool. Cilk++ is suited for divide-and-conquer problems where the problem can be divided into parallel independent tasks and the results can be combined afterward. As such, the programmer bears the responsibility of structuring the program to expose its inherent parallelism. Cilk's runtime system bears the responsibility of scheduling the computational tasks on the parallel processor system. The techniques we discuss in this book give the programmer insight on the alternative parallelism options available for a given algorithm. The application developer can use a few key words provided by Cilk++ to convert a standard serial program into a parallel program. A standard C++ program can be converted to a Cilk++ program running Intel's Cilk++ system developers kit (SDK) by doing these initial steps [64]:

1. Ensure that the serial C++ program is bug free.
2. Rename source file extension from `.cpp` to `.cilk`.
3. Add `#include <cilk.h>`.
4. Rename the `main()` function to `cilk_main()`.

At this stage, the program is a program that has no parallelism yet. The programmer must add a few key words to the program, such as

- **cilk**, which alerts the compiler that this is a parallel program;
- **cilk_spawn**, which creates a locally spawned function that can be executed in parallel with other tasks;
- **cilk_sync**, which forces the current threads to wait for all locally spawned functions to be completed; thus, all `cilk_spawn` function must be completed first before the `cilk_sync` function can continue. This is equivalent to the join statement in the pthread library; and
- **cilk for**, which is a parallel version of the serial `for` loop statement.

The Cilk++ constructs discussed above specify logical parallelism in the program. The operating system will map the tasks into processes or threads and schedules them for execution. Listing 6.1 is the pseudocode for the Fibonacci algorithm implemented using Cilk:

Listing 6.1   Pseudocode for the evaluation of Fibonacci numbers

```
 1: int fib (int n)
 2: {
 3: if n < 2 then
 4:    return n;
 5: else
 6:    {
 7:      int x, y;
 8:      x = cilk_spawn fib(n - 1);
 9:      y = cilk_spawn fib(n - 2);
10:      cilk_sync
11:      return (x + y);
12:    }
13: end if
14: }
```

The key words in italics in lines 8 and 9 indicate that the fib() function call can be done in parallel. The key word in line 10 ensures that the add operation in line 11 can be performed only after two function calls in lines 8 and 9 have been completed.

6.3.1 Cilk++ Parallel Loop: cilk_for

The syntax of the Cilk++ for loop is very much similar to that of the C++ for loop.

```
cilk for (i = start_value; i < end_value; i++){
  statement_1;
  statement_2;
    .
    .
    .
}
```

The end-of-iteration comparison could be one of the usual relational operators:

$$<, \quad <=, \quad !=, \quad >=, \quad or \; >.$$

Cilk++ for does not have a break statement for early exit from the loop. Cilk++ divides the iterations of the loop into *chunks* where each chunk consists of few iterations of the loop. An implied cilk_spawn statement creates a thread or a strand for each chunk. Thus, the loop is parallelized since chunk strands will be executed in parallel using a work-stealing scheduler [65]. The chunk size is called the *grain size*. if the grain size is large, parallelism is reduced since the number of chunks will be small. If the grain size is small, then the overhead to deal with too many strands reduces the performance. The programmer can override the default grain size through the compiler directive statement

$$\text{\#pragma cilk\_grain size = expression,}$$

where expression is any valid C++ expression that yields an integer value. The pragma should immediately precede the cilk_for loop [66].

6.3.2 Data Races and Program Indeterminacy

A data race occurs when two threads attempt to access the same variable in memory and one of them performs a write operation. This is the problem of shared or nonlocal variables. Nonlocal variables are variables that are declared outside the scope where it is used. A global variable is a nonlocal variable declared in the outermost scope of the program [49]. It is hard to rewrite a code that avoids the use of nonlocal variables. This occurs when a function call has side effects and changes a variable declared outside the function. The obvious solution is to use local variables by passing the variable as a parameter of the function. Most of us know that this will lead to functions with a long argument list. The problem is that with multicores, nonlocal variables will lead to race bugs. Parallel processors that share variables must guard against race bugs that compromise data integrity.

A simple race bug is a *determinacy race*. A program is *deterministic* if the output is the same for any multicore *strand* scheduling strategy. A strand is defined as a sequence of executed instructions containing no parallel control [67]. On the other hand, a program is *nondeterministic* if it produces different results for every run.

Consider the following serial code as an example of determinacy race:

```
1:  #include <iostream>
2:  using namespace std;
3:  void swap (int &x, int &y);
4:  int main()
5:  {
6:      int x = 1, y = 10;
7:      swap (x, y);
8:      x = 2 * x;
9:      cout << "x = " << x << endl;
10:     cout << "y = " << y << endl;
11: }
12: void swap (int &x, int &y)
13: {
14:     int temp;
15:     temp = x;
16:     x = y;
17:     y = temp;
18: }
```

The output of the serial program is $x = 20$ and $y = 1$ because x and y will get swapped first then x is doubled according to lines 7 and 8, respectively.

Now consider a similar code executed on a parallel computing platform with the directive `cilk_spawn`:

```
 1:  #include <iostream>
 2:  using namespace std;
 3:  void swap (int &x, int &y);
 4:  int main()
 5:  {
 6:    int x = 1, y = 10;
 7:    cilk_spawn swap (x, y);
 8:    x = 2 * x;
 9:    cilk_sync;
10:    cout << "x = " << x << endl;
11:    cout << "y = " << y << endl;
12:  }
13:  void swap (int &x, int &y)
14:  {
15:    int temp;
16:    temp = x;
17:    x = y;
18:    y = temp;
19:  }
```

The output of the parallel program has a race bug and the output might be $x = 20$ and $y = 1$ sometime and $x = 10$ and $y = 2$ at another time. Figure 6.1 shows the breakdown of the parallel program into strands A, B, C, and D. Strand A begins at the start of the program and ends at the `cilk_spawn` statement. The `cilk_spawn` statement creates the strands B and C. Strand B executes the statement $x = 2 * x$ and strand C executes the swap(x, y); statement. Strand D begins after the `cilk_sync` statement to the end of the program.

The race condition occurs because strands B and C both involve reading and writing the same variable x. This will most certainly lead to data inconsistency of the types discussed in Chapter 2, such as

1. *output dependencies:* write after write (WAW),

2. *antidependencies:* write after read (WAR),

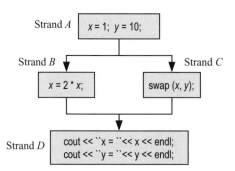

Figure 6.1   Splitting of a program into strands using the directive `cilk_spawn` and merging the strands using `cilk_sync` statements.

3. *true data dependency:* read after write (RAW), and

4. *procedural dependencies.*

Any of the following race conditions could take place depending on the operating system:

- Strand *B* executes completely before strand *C*.
- Strand *C* executes completely before strand *B*.
- Strand *B* partially executes, then strand *C* starts.
- Strand *C* partially executes, then strand *B* starts.

Cilk Arts provides a tool called Cilkscreen to detect and report data races.

To get rid of data races, traditional programming uses mutexes. These, however, might cause locks and lose potential parallelism. Cilk++ provides hyperobjects to eliminate data races without the use of mutex or rewriting the program. A nonlocal variable is declared to be a hyperobject of the appropriate type to eliminate data races on the nolocal variable [67]. Hyperobjects are not defined within Cilk++. Rather, they are specified as common C++ classes.

6.3.3   Cilk++ Components for Parallelizing a Serial Code

Cilk++ has several components to help the programmer parallelize a serial code and debug the resulting program:

1. Cilk++ compiler

2. Cilk++ libraries to be used by the Cilk++ compiler

3. Cilkscreen the Cilk++ race detector

4. Performance analysis tools

5. Debugging tools

6. Cilk++ documentation

As mentioned before, `Cilkscreen` finds all the data races. In addition, Cilkscreen performance profiler measures the *work*, *depth*, and parallelism, which is defined here as work divided by depth.

We should stress that it is the programmer's responsibility to strategically place the `cilk_spawn` and `cilk_sync` statements in the program to optimize its performance on a given multicore system. The algorithm analysis tools provided in this book can help the programmer find out the alternative ways to place those statements while preserving the algorithm correctness.

Some guidelines proposed in using Cilk++ are the following [68]

1. Write the fastest correct serial program.

2. Introduce Cilk++ key words to make the program parallel.

3. Use the Cilkscreen race detector to find and correct any data races.

4. Use the Cilkscreen performance profiler to predict performance, looking for ways to reduce the span to increase the parallelism.

6.3.4 Applying Cilk++ to Matrix–Matrix Multiplication

Listing 6.2 shows the pseudocode for the matrix–matrix multiplication algorithm.

Listing 6.2   The pseudocode for the standard algorithm for multiplying two $n \times n$ matrices, **A** and **B**, to produce matrix **C** is given by

```
multiply (A, B, C, n) {
if n = 1 then
  C = A * B
else
  for i = 0; i < n; i++ do
    for j = 0; j < n; i++ do
      for k = 0; j < n; k++ do
        C(i, j) = C(i, j) + A(i, k) * B(k, j)
      end for
    end for
  end for
end if
return C
}.
```

This algorithm requires n^3 multiplications and $(n - 1)n^2$ additions. We can partition our input matrices and the product would be given by

$$\begin{bmatrix} C_{11} & C_{12} \\ C_{21} & C_{22} \end{bmatrix} = \begin{bmatrix} A_{11} & A_{12} \\ A_{21} & A_{22} \end{bmatrix} \times \begin{bmatrix} B_{11} & B_{12} \\ B_{21} & B_{22} \end{bmatrix}. \tag{6.1}$$

The parallelized pseudocode for partitioned matrix–matrix multiplication using Cilk++ would be given by Listing 6.3. The code requires the definition of two functions, `multiply()` and `add()`. Notice that each of these functions calls itself recursively.

Listing 6.3   Pseudocode for Cilk++ parallelization of the partitioned matrix–matrix multiplication algorithm

```
1: multiply (A, B, C, n) {
2: if n = 1 then
3:   C = A * B
4: else
5:   define a temporary matrix T
6:   partition A, B, C and T into n/2 × n/2 submatrices
7:   cilk_spawn multiply (A₁₁, B₁₁, C₁₁, n/2)
8:   cilk_spawn multiply (A₁₁, B₁₂, C₁₂, n/2)
```

```
 9:     cilk_spawn multiply (A₂₁, B₁₁, C₂₁, n/2)
10:     cilk_spawn multiply (A₂₁, B₁₂, C₂₂, n/2)
11:     cilk_spawn multiply (A₁₁, B₁₁, C₁₁, n/2)
12:     cilk_spawn multiply (A₁₁, B₁₂, T₁₂, n/2)
13:     cilk_spawn multiply (A₂₁, B₁₁, T₂₁, n/2)
14:     cilk_spawn multiply (A₂₁, B₁₂, T₂₂, n/2)
15:     cilk_sync
16:     cilk_spawn add(C, T, n)
17:     cilk_sync
18: end if
19: return C
20: }
21:
22: add(C, T, n){
23: if n =1 then
24:     C = C + T
25: else
26:     partition B, and T into n/2 × n/2 submatrices
27:     cilk_spawn add (C₁₁, T₁₁, n/2)
28:     cilk_spawn add (C₁₂, T₁₂, n/2)
29:     cilk_spawn add (C₂₁, T₂₁, n/2)
30:     cilk_spawn add (C₂₂, T₂₂, n/2)
31:     cilk_sync
32: end if
33: }
```

Line 6 will define the partitioning of the matrices into submatrices. Lines 7–17 produce eight strands, and each strand is in charge of doing a $n/2 \times n/2$ matrix multiplication. Each submatrix multiplication operation produces its own strands to multiply smaller partitioned matrices of size $n/4 \times n/4$. And this is done recursively.

We do not do the final add on line 16 until all the strands on lines 7–14 have finished their operations. Similarly, the addition of the resulting partial matrices is done in a hierarchical fashion as shown by lines 22–33 of the algorithm.

6.4 OpenMP

OpenMP is a concurrency platform for multithreaded, shared-memory parallel processing architecture for C, C++, and Fortran. By using OpenMP, the programmer is able to incrementally parallelize the program with little programming effort. The programmer manually inserts compiler directives to assist the compiler into generating threads for the parallel processor platform. The user does not need to create the threads nor worry about the tasks assigned to each thread. In that sense, OpenMP is a higher-level programming model compared with pthreads in the POSIX library.

At the current state of the art, there is something to be gained using manual parallelization. Automatic parallelizing compilers cannot compete with a hand-coded parallel program. OpenMP uses three types of constructs to control the parallelization of a program [69]:

1. Compiler directives
2. Runtime library routines
3. Environment variables

To compile an OpenMP program, one would issue the command

`gcc -openmp file.c -o file.`

Listing 6.4 The following pseudocode is a sketch of how OpenMP parallelizes a serial code [69]:

```
1:  #include <omp.h>
2:  main () {
3:    int var1, var2, var3;
4:    Serial code executed by master thread
5:    :
6:    #pragma    omp    parallel    private(var1,    var2)
    shared(var3)
7:    {
8:      Parallel section executed by all threads
9:      :
10:   }
11:   Resume serial code
12: }
```

Line 1 is an include file that defines the functions used by OpenMP. Lines 2–5 is a serial code just like in any C or C++ program. Line 6 is an OpenMP compiler directive instructing the compiler to parallelize the lines of code enclosed by the curly brackets spanning lines 7–10. The directive forks a team of threads and specifies variable scoping; some variables are private to each thread, and some are shared between the threads. Another name for a compiler directive is *pragma*.

Line 7 is the start of the parallel code block indicated by the left curly bracket. The code block is duplicated and all newly forked threads execute that code in parallel. Line 8 is the start of parallel section instructions. Line 10 is the end of the parallel code block indicated by the right curly bracket. All threads join the master thread and disband. Lines 11–12 are the start of another serial code block.

Figure 6.2 shows breaking up a serial single-thread code into multithreads. Figure 6.2a shows the original serial code composed of several code sections as indicated by the numbered blocks. Indicated on the figure also are the compiler directives manually inserted by the programmer at the start of a group of code sections instructing the compiler to fork threads at this point. Figure 6.2b shows how the compiler forks as many threads as required to parallelize each code section that follows each compiler fork directive. A join synchronization compiler directive ensures that the program resumes after the parallel threads have finished executing their tasks. There is a master thread, indicated by the solid thick line, which forks the other threads. Each thread is identified by an "ID" integer and the master thread has an ID value of "0".

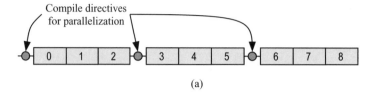

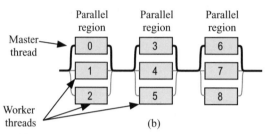

Figure 6.2 Breaking up a serial code into parallel threads. (a) Original serial code that has one master thread. (b) Forking parallel threads to be executed concurrently.

OpenMP consists of the following major components:

- Compiler directives instructing the compiler on how to parallelize the code
- Runtime library functions to modify and check the number of threads and to check how may processors there are in the multiprocessor system
- Environment variables to alter the execution of OpenMP applications

Like Cilk++, OpenMP does not require restructuring the serial program. The use only needs to add compiler directives to reconstruct the serial program into a parallel one.

6.4.1 OpenMP Compiler Directives

The user tells the compiler to recognize OpenMP commands by adding -omp on the cc command line. Compiler directives allow the programmer to instruct the compiler on issues of thread creation, work load distribution, data management, and thread synchronization. The format for an OpenMP compiler directive is

```
#pragma omp directive_name [clause, · · · ]
                newline_character.
```

Notice that each directive could have a collection of clauses. Table 6.1 summarizes some of the OpenMP pragma directives

Listing 6.5 The following code fragment shows how #omp comp parallel compiler directive is sued to fork additional threads to execute the tasks specified by the affected code section:

Table 6.1   Some OpenMP Pragma Directives

OpenMP pragma directive	Description
#pragma omp atomic	Defines a memory location to be updated atomically
#pragma omp barrier	Synchronizes all the threads in a parallel region
#pragma omp critical	Defines the code section that follows the directive to be executed by a single thread at a time
#pragma omp flush	Synchronization directive to ensure all threads in a parallel region have the same view of specified objects in memory
#pragma omp for	Specifies that the for loop iterations should be run in parallel using multiple threads
#pragma omp parallel	Defines a parallel code region to be run by multiple threads; the original process will be the master thread
#pragma omp parallel do	Splits up the loop iterations among threads
#pragma omp parallel for	Similar to `parallel do` pragma

```
#pragma omp parallel default(shared) private(a, b)
{
  // The code between brackets will run in parallel
  statement 1;
  statement 2;
  statement 3;
    ⋮
}
```

6.4.2 Compiler Directive Clauses

Some of the compiler directives use one or more clauses. The order in which clauses are written is not important. Most clauses accept a comma-separated list of items. Clauses deal with different types of compiler directives: data sharing among the threads. Other clauses deal with data copying of a private variable value from a thread to a corresponding variable in another thread.

The following table shows some directives and their associated clauses.

Directive	Clause
Parallel	Copying, default, private, firstprivate, reduction, shared
Sections	Private, firstprivate, lastprivate, reduction, schedule
Section	Private, firstprivate, lastprivate, reduction
Critical	None
Barrier	None
Atomic	None
Flush (*list*)	None
Ordered	None
Threadadaptive (*list*)	None

The following table explains some of the directive clauses mentioned above. More clauses are explained in Section 6.4.4.

Clause	Description
default (*mode*)	Controls the default data sharing attributes of variables. Mode could be *private*, *shared*, and *none*.
shared (*list*)	Lists items to be shared by threads generated by parallel or task compiler directives, for example, #pragma omp parallel default(shared)
copyin (*list*)	Copies the values of the list items from the master thread to the other parallel worker threads
num_threads (*integer_expr*)	Requests the number of threads specified by the *integer expression*

6.4.3 OpenMP Work Sharing

The work sharing directives control which threads execute which statements. These directives do not fork new threads. The two directives are #pragma omp for and #pragma omp sections. We discuss these two directives in the following sections.

6.4.4 Loop Directive: for

Most parallel algorithms contain FOR loops, and we dedicate this section to discussing the compiler directive related to FOR loops. The format of the for compiler directive is

#pragma omp for [*clause* · · ·] *newline*.

There are several *clauses* associated with the for compiler directive as shown in Table 6.2.

When the schedule clause is schedule(static, 3), iterations are divided into pieces of size 3 and are assigned to threads in a round-robin fashion ordered by the thread number.

When the schedule clause is schedule(dynamic, 3), iterations are divided into pieces of size 3 and are assigned to next available thread. When a thread completes its task, it looks for the next available chunk.

The following is a code fragment showing a compiler directive to parallelize a for loop that adds two vectors, *a* and *b*, and produces the output vector *c*. Notice that the iterations within the loop body are independent and can be executed concurrently.

Table 6.2   OpenMP Loop Compiler Directive Clauses

#pragma omp for Clauses	Description
schedule (*type* [, chunk size])	Schedule type could be static or dynamic. It describes how the work is divided among the threads. Number of loop iterations done by each thread equals chunk size.
private (*list*)	List of variables private to each thread.
firstprivate (*list*)	Variables are initialized with the value before entering the block or region.
lastprivate (*list*)	Variables are updated going out of a block or region.
shared (*list*)	List of variables shared among the threads.
reduction(*operator: list*)	Perform a reduction on the variables specified by the *list* using the *operator*. The operator could be: +, *, -, &, |, ∧, &&, ||. Operator works on thread outputs when all of them finish execution.
collapse (*n*)	
nowait	Threads do not synchronize at the end of the parallel FOR-loop.

Listing 6.6   The `reduction` and `schedule` clauses are used [69]:

```
 1: #include <omp.h>
 2: #include <stdio.h>
 3: #include <stdlib.h>
 4:
 5: int main (int argc, char *argv[]){
 6:   int i, n;
 7:   float a[100], b[100], sum;
 8:   n = 100;
 9:   for (i=0; i < n; i++)
10:    a[i] = b[i] = i*1.0;
11:   sum = 0.0;
12:
13:   #pragma omp parallel for schedule(dynamic,16)
reduction(+:sum)
14:   for (i = 0; i < 64; i++)
15:     sum = sum + (a(i)* b(i));
16:   printf( "sum = %f\n", sum);
17: }
```

Line 13 is the compiler directive to parallelize the FOR loop that follows on line 14. Dynamic scheduling of threads is chosen and the chunk size for each iteration is set at 16 iterations of the loop. The reduction operator applies the addition operation to the sum variable. Figure 6.3 shows how the code above is broken into threads that execute in parallel.

Master
thread

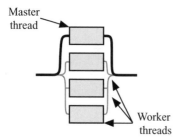

Worker
threads

Figure 6.3   Parallelizing a FOR loop into threads that execute in parallel.

Listing 6.7 The following example illustrates using the `parallel` and `parallel for` constructs to implement two finite impulse response (FIR) filters, both of length $n = 40$:

```
1: #pragma omp parallel default (none) \
2:    shared (x, m, n) private (i, j, h1, h2, y1, y2)
3: { // start of parallel region
4:    #pragma omp for nowait
5:    for (i = 0; i < m; i++) {
6:      for (j = 0; j < n; j++)
7:        y1(i) = y1(i) + h1(j) *x(i-j);
8:    }
9:    #pragma omp for nowait
10:   for (i = 0; i < m; i++) {
11:     for (j = 0; j < n; j++)
12:       y2(i) = y2(i) + h2(j) *x(i-j);
13:   }
14: } // end of parallel region
```

Notice the backslash (\) at the end of line 1. This is needed as a line continuation character to accommodate the clauses for the `parallel` directive.

Line 1 identifies to the compiler a parallel region of code as delineated by the curly brackets starting at line 3 and ending at line 14. The `default (none)` clause defines the default data scope of variables in each thread. There are two options with this clause: `none` and `shared`.

In line 2, the `shared (x, m, n)` clause declares the scope of the comma-separated data variables in the list to be shared across all threads. The `private (i, j, h1, h2, y1, y2)` clause declares the scope of the comma-separated data variables in the list to be private to each thread.

Line 4 is a compiler directive used to parallelize the FOR loop statement in Line 5. Notice that each iteration of the outer FOR loop is a nested FOR loop. This means that the outer loop will execute in parallel using several threads, and each thread will execute the inner loop in a serial fashion. The `nowait` clause indicate that the threads do not synchronize at end of the outer FOR loop. This avoids the implied barrier at the end of the `for` compiler directive. Nesting parallelism might or might not be supported. The programmer determines if nesting is supported by the `omp_get_nested()` library function. Enabling of nesting, when supported, can be accomplished by `omp_set nested()` library routing or by setting the OMP_ NESTED environment variable to TRUE.

Line 9 is similar to line 4.

6.4.5 Loop Directive: `sections`

Listing 6.8 Several blocks are executed in parallel using the `sections` directive:

```
 1: #pragma omp parallel
 2: {
 3:   #pragma omp sections [clause [ ···]] newline
 4:   {
 5:     #pragma omp section
 6:       {
 7:         structured block # 1 statements
 8:       }
 9:     #pragma omp section
10:       {
11:         structured block # 2 statements
12:       }
13:     #pragma omp section
14:       {
15:         structured block # 3 statements
16:       }
17:   }
18: }
```

Line 1 directs the compiler to parallelize the block enclosed by the curly brackets starting at line 2 and ending at line 18.

Line 3 directs the compiler to execute the sections that follow in separate threads. Line 5 defines the first section between lines 6 and 8 to be executed by one thread. Line 9 defines the first section between lines 10 and 12 to be executed by one thread. Line 13 defines the first section between lines 14 and 16 to be executed by one thread.

6.4.6 Runtime Library Routines

The header file <omp.h> contains the prototypes of the routines. Runtime library routines control the parallel execution environment, control and monitor threads, and control and monitor processors [70].

Execution environment routines include

```
void omp_set_num_threads (int num_threads);
```

which controls the number of threads used for the subsequent parallel regions that do not have a `num_threads` clause.

The library has lock routines to synchronize access to data. A type `omp_loc_t` is defined as an object type capable of representing a lock and of assigning the lock to a thread. OpenMP runtime library functions are

Library routine	Description
`double omp_get_wtime (void);`	Return elapsed wall clock time in seconds.
`double omp_get_wtick (void);`	Return the precision of the time used by the `omp_get_wtime` function.
`omp_set_num_threads`	Set the number of threads: `Omp_set_num_threads ( 4 ); // fork four parallel threads`
`omp_get_num_threads`	Get the number of threads.
`omp_get_num_procs`	Get the number of processors: `processors =omp_get_num_procs();`

6.4.7   Environment Variables

Environment variables are used to alter the execution of OpenMP applications. Some of the functions of environment variables include

- number of threads,
- type of scheduling policy,
- nested parallelism, and
- thread limit.

Environment variable names are upper case and the values assigned to them are case insensitive. Some environment variables are

#pragma omp for clauses	Description
OMP_NUM_THREADS *num*	Specifies the number of threads to be forked
OMP_DYNAMIC [*true—false*]	Dynamically adjusts the number of threads in a parallel region
OMP_THREAD_LIMIT *limit*	Controls the maximum number of threads in the OpenMP program

To specify a certain environment variable, the user includes lines in C/C++ code:

```
setenv OMP_NUM_THREADS 4.
```

This instructs the compiler to generate four threads when needed.

6.4.8   OpenMP Synchronization

Lock control routines synchronize the execution of threads to guarantee data read/write integrity among the parallel threads. OpenMP offers compiler directives to control the execution of threads through synchronization. The programmer must guard against synchronization deadlocks. OpenMP has five synchronization directives: `critical`, `ordered`, `atomic`, `flush`, and `barrier`.

There is an implicit barrier at the end of parallel constructs like omp for or omp parallel. This implicit synchronization can be removed with the nowait clause as we saw earlier. We can explicitly specify a synchronization barrier as explained in the following sections.

`critical` *Directive*

The `critical` directive instructs that the threads executing some parallel code halt execution upon reaching the directive. A thread will execute the code section following the `critical` directive when no other thread is executing it.

The code below is for the `critical` directive, which specifies a region of code that must be executed by one thread at a time. This ensures that a critical section is executed by one thread without interruptions from the other threads.

```
#pragma omp critical [name] newline
             structured block
```

The name in the above code allows for multiple critical sections to exist. Listing 6.9 illustrates multiple critical sections.

Listing 6.9   An example of use of critical section.

```
 1: #include <omp.h>
 2: main (){
 3:    int x = 0;
 4:    #pragma omp parallel
 5:    {
 6:       statements
 7:       :
 8:       #pragma omp critical
 9:       x = x+1;
10:       statements
11:       :
12:    }
13: }
```

Line 4 indicates that the following code section is to be done in parallel by all threads. This code spans lines 6–11. However, line 8 indicates that the statement on line 9 must be executed by exactly one thread at a time and all other threads that reach that line must wait.

`barrier` *Directive*

The `barrier` directive synchronizes all the threads. When a thread reaches the barrier, it will wait until all the other threads have reached their barrier, after which all threads resume executing the code following the barrier in parallel:

```
#pragma omp barrier newline.
```

When a barrier directive is reached by a thread, it will wait until all other threads have reached the barrier too. After that, all threads will start to process the parallel code that follows the barrier.

6.5 COMPUTE UNIFIED DEVICE ARCHITECTURE (CUDA)

CUDA is a software architecture that enables the graphics processing unit (GPU) to be programmed using high-level programming languages such as C and C++. The programmer writes a C program with CUDA extensions, very much like Cilk++ and OpenMP as previously discussed. CUDA requires an NVIDIA GPU like Fermi, GeForce 8XXX/Tesla/Quadro, and so on. Source files must be compiled with the CUDA C compiler *NVCC*.

A CUDA program uses *kernels* to operate on the *data streams*. Examples of data streams are vectors of floating point numbers or a group of frame pixels for video data processing. A kernel is executed in a GPU using parallel threads. CUDA provides three key mechanisms to parallelize programs [71]: thread group hierarchy, shared memories, and barrier synchronization. These mechanisms provide fine-grained parallelism nested within coarse-grained task parallelism.

The following definitions define the terms used in CUDA parlance:

Definition 6.1 The host or central processing unit (CPU) is the computer that interfaces with the user and controls the device used to execute the data-parallel, compute-intensive portion of an application. The host is responsible for executing the serial portion of the application.

Definition 6.2 The GPU is a general-purpose graphics processor unit capable of implementing parallel algorithms.

Definition 6.3 Device is the GPU connected to the host computer to execute the data-parallel, compute-intensive portion of an application. The device is responsible for executing the parallel portion of the application.

Definition 6.4 Kernel is a function callable from the host computer and executed in parallel on the CUDA device by many CUDA threads.

The kernel is executed simultaneously by many (thousands of) threads. An application or library function might consist of one or more kernels [72]. Fermi can run several kernels at a time provided the kernels belong to the same application context [73]. A kernel can be written in C language with additional key words to express parallelism.

The thread and memory hierarchies are shown in Fig. 6.4.

1. A thread at the lowest level of the hierarchy
2. A block composed of several concurrently executing threads

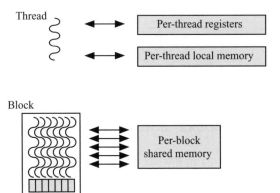

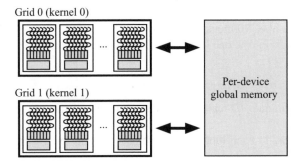

Grid 0 (kernel 0)

Grid 1 (kernel 1)

Per-device
global memory

Figure 6.4 Thread and
memory hierarchy.
© NVIDIA Corporation, 2008.

3. A grid composed of several concurrently executing thread blocks

4. Per-thread local memory visible only to a thread

5. Per-block shared memory visible only to threads in a given block

6. Per-device global memory

Notice that each thread has its own *local memory* as well as *registers*, as shown at the top of the diagram. The registers are on-chip and have small access time. The per-thread local memory and registers are shown by the shaded areas below each thread. The local memory is off-chip and is a bit slower than the registers.

A thread block in the middle of the diagram has its own off-chip *shared memory* for fast and scalable interthread communication. The shared memory is private to that block.

A grid is a set of thread blocks as shown at the bottom of the figure. A grid has its per-device *global memory*. This is in addition to the per-block and per-thread shared and local memories, respectively. The device global memory communicates with the host memory and is the means of communicating data between the host and the general-purpose graphics processor unit (GPGPU) device.

Block 0 Block 1   Block *k*-1

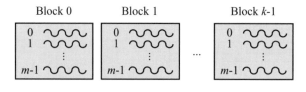

Figure 6.5 Arranging *m* threads in a block and *k* blocks in the grid. © NVIDIA Corporation, 2008.

6.5.1 Defining Threads, Blocks, and Grids in CUDA

The programmer must specify the number of threads in a block and the number of blocks in the grid. The number of blocks in the grid is specified by the variable gridDim. We can arrange our blocks into one-dimensional array and the number of blocks would be

$$\texttt{gridDim}.x \;=\; k.$$

For example, if $k = 10$, then we have 10 blocks in the grid.

We can arrange the threads into a one-dimensional array of *m* threads per block:

$$\texttt{blockDim}.x \;=\; m.$$

Each block is given a unique *ID* called *blockIdx* that spans the range $0 \;\leq\; \texttt{blockId} \;<\; \texttt{gridDim}$.

A picture of the thread array in each block and the block array in the grid is shown in Fig. 6.5.

To allocate a thread to the *i*th vector component, we need to specify which block the thread belongs to and the location of the thread within that block:

$$i \;=\; \texttt{blockIdx}.x \;\times\; \texttt{blockDim} \;+\; \texttt{threadIdx}.x.$$

The variables gridDim and blockIdx are automatically defined and are of type dim3. The blocks in the grid could be arranged in one, two, or three dimensions. Each dimension is accessed by the constructs blockIdx.x, blockId.y, and blockId.z. The following CUDA command specifies the number of blocks in the *x*, *y*, and z dimensions:

$$\texttt{dim3 dimGrid(4, 8, 1);}$$

Essentially, the above command defines 32 blocks arranged in a two-dimensional array with four rows and eight columns.

The number of threads in a block is specified by the variable blockDim. Each thread is given a unique *ID* called *threadIdx* that spans the range $0 \;\leq\; \texttt{threadIdx} \;<\; \texttt{blockDim}$. The variables blockDim and threadIdx are automatically defined and are of type dim3. The threads in a block could be arranged in one, two, or three dimensions.

Each dimension is accessed by the constructs threadIdx.x, threadIdx.y, and threadIdx.z. The following CUDA command specifies the number of threads in the *x*, *y*, and z dimensions:

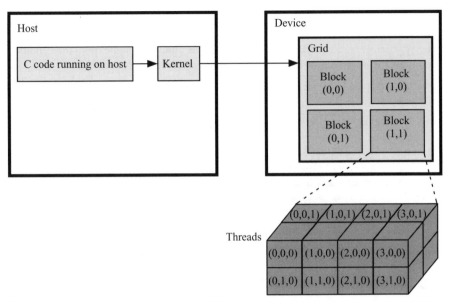

Figure 6.6   Relation between the kernel, grid, blocks, and threads. © NVIDIA Corporation, 2008.

dim3 dimBlock(100, 1, 1);

Essentially, the above command defines 100 threads arranged in an array with 100 components. Figure 6.6 shows the organization and relations between the kernel, grid, blocks, and threads. The figure indicates that each kernel is associated with a grid in the device. The choice of thread and block dimensionality is dictated by the nature of the application and the data it is dealing with. The objective is for the programmer to use natural means of simplifying access to data.

6.5.2 Assigning Functions for Execution by a Kernel in CUDA

To define a function that will be executed as a kernel, the programmer modifies the C code for the function prototype by placing the key word _global_ before the function prototype declaration:

```
1:   _global_    void    kernel_function_name(function_
     argument_list);
2:   {
3:      ⋮
4:   }
```

Note that the _global_ function qualifier must return void. The programmer now needs to instruct the NVCC to launch the kernel for execution on the device.

The programmer modifies the C code specifying the structure of the blocks in the grid and the structure of the threads in a block by placing the declaration <<<gridDim, blockDim>>> between the function name and the function argument list as shown in line 7 of the following listing:

```
 1:  int main()
 2:  {
 3:    :
 4:    // Serial portion of code
 5:    :
 6:    // Start of parallel portion of code
 7:    kernel_function_name<<< gridDim, blockDim >>>
      (function_argument_list);
 8:    // End of parallel portion of code
 9:    :
10:    // Serial portion of code
11:    :
12:  }
```

6.5.3 Communication between Host and CUDA Device

The host computer has its own memory hierarchy and the device has its own separate memory hierarchy also. Exchange of data between the host and the device is accomplished by copying data between the host dynamic random access memory (DRAM) and the device global DRAM memory. Similar to C programming, the user must allocate memory on the device global memory for the data in the device and free this memory after the application is finished. The CUDA runtime system calls summarized in Table 6.3 provide the function calls necessary to do these operations.

Figure 6.7 shows the memory interface between the device and the host [74, 75]. The global memory at the bottom of the figure is the means of communicating

Table 6.3   Some CUDA Runtime Functions

Function	Comment
cudaThreadSynchronize( )	Blocks until the device has completed all preceding requested tasks
cudaChooseDevice( )	Returns device matching specified properties
cudaGetDevice( )	Returns which device is currently being used
cudaGetDeviceCount( )	Returns number of devices with compute capability
cudaGetDeviceProperties( )	Returns information about the compute device
cudaMaloc( )	Allocates an object in the device global memory; requires two parameters: address of a pointer to the object and the size of the object
cudaFree( )	Free object from device global memory
cudaMemcpy( )	Copies data from host to device; requires four parameters: destination pointer, source pointer, number of bytes, and transfer type

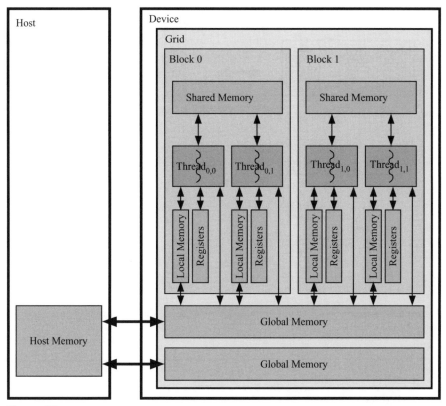

Figure 6.7   Memory interface between host and device. © NVIDIA Corporation, 2008.

data between the host and the device. The contents of the global memory are visible to all threads, as the figure shows. The per-block shared memory is visible to all threads in the block. Of course, the per-thread local memory is visible only to the associated thread.

The host launches a kernel function on the device as shown in Fig. 6.8. The kernel is executed on a grid of thread blocks. Several kernels can be processed by the device at any given time. Each thread block is executed on a streaming multi-processor (SM). The SM executes several thread blocks at a time. Copies of the kernel are executed on the streaming processors (SPs) or thread processors, which execute the threads that evaluate the function. Each thread is allocated to an SM.

6.5.4   Synchronization and Communication for CUDA Threads

When a parallel application is running in the device, synchronization and communication among the threads must be accomplished at different levels. Synchronization and communication can be accomplished at different levels:

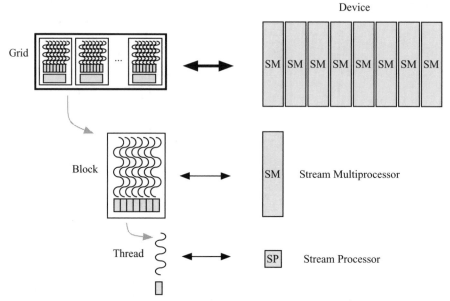

Figure 6.8 Execution of a CUDA kernel function on the device using blocks and threads courtesy of NVIDIA Corporation.

1. Kernels and grids
2. Blocks
3. Threads

6.5.5 Kernels and Grids

At any given time, several kernels are executing on the device. The following listing illustrates this point:

```
1: void main () {
2:    :
3: kernel_1<<<nblocks_1, blocksize_1>>>(function_
argument_list_1);
4: kernel_2<<<nblocks_2, blocksize_2>>>(function_
argument_list_2);
5:    :
```

Kernel_1 will run first on the device and will define a grid that contains dimGrid blocks, and each block will contain dimblock threads. All threads will run the same code specified by the kernel. When kernel_1 is completed, kernel_2 will be forwarded to the device for execution.

Communication between the different grids is indirect through leaving data in the host or device global memory to be used by the next kernel.

6.5.6   Blocks

At any given time, several blocks are executing on the device. All blocks in a grid execute independent of each other. There is no synchronization mechanism between blocks. When a grid is launched, the blocks are assigned to the SM in arbitrary order and the issue order of the blocks is undefined.

Communication among the threads within a block is accomplished through the per-block shared memory. A variable is declared to be shared by threads in the same blocks by preceding the variable declaration with the keyword _shared_. Such variable will be stored in the per-block shared memory. During kernel execution, a private version of this variable is created in the per-thread local memory.

The per-block shared memory is on the same chip as the cores executing the thread communication is relatively fast since the static random access memory (SRAM) is a faster than the off-chip DRAM memories. Each thread has a direct access to its own on-chip registers and its off-chip per-thread local memory. Registers are much faster than the local memory since they are essentially a DRAM. Each thread can also access the per-device global memory. Communication with the off-chip local and global memories suffers from the usual interchip communication penalties (e.g., delay, power, and bandwidth).

6.5.7   Threads

At any given time, a large number of threads are executing on the device. A block that is assigned to an SM is divided into 32-thread *warps*. Each SM can handle several warps simultaneously, and when some of the warps stall due to memory access, the SM schedules another warp. Threads in a block can be synchronized using the _synchthreads() synchronization barrier. A thread cannot proceed beyond this barrier until all other threads in the block have reached it.

Each thread uses its on-chip per-thread registers and on-chip per-thread local memory. Both of these use SRAM technology, which implies small memory size but fast, low-power communication. Each thread also uses the off-chip global memory, which is slow since it is DRAM based.

Table 6.4   Declaration Specifiers

Declaration	Comment
global void function($\cdots$);	Define kernel function to run on device
device int var;	Store variable in device global memory
shared int var;	Store variable in per-block shared memory
local int var;	Store variable in per-block shared memory
constant int const;	Store constant in per-block constant memory

6.5.8 CUDA C Language Extensions

A good place to explore the CUDA library is NVIDIA [76]. The following subsections illustrate some of the useful key words with example codes.

Declarations specify where things will live, as shown in Table 6.4.

The CUDA runtime application program interface (API) serves for management of threads, device, and memory. The runtime API also controls the execution of the threads. Some of the runtime functions to control the operation of CUDA were listed in Table 6.3. The CUDA library documentation can be found in NVIDIA [76].

Chapter 7

Ad Hoc Techniques for Parallel Algorithms

7.1 INTRODUCTION

This chapter discusses several ad hoc techniques used to implement parallel algorithms on parallel computers. Most of these techniques dealt with what is called embarrassingly parallel algorithms [2] or trivially parallel algorithms [29]. Parallel algorithms are expressed using loops. The simplest of these algorithms can be parallelized by assigning different iterations to different processors or even by assigning some of the operations in each iteration to different processors [29].

The techniques presented here do not deal efficiently with data dependencies. Unless the algorithm has no or very simple data dependence, it would be a challenge to correctly implement the algorithm in software using multithreading or in hardware using multiple processors. It will also be challenging to optimize interthread or interprocessor communications. In Chapters 9–11, we introduce formal techniques to deal with such algorithms. This chapter deals with what is termed "embarrassingly parallel" or "trivially parallel" algorithms. We should caution the reader, though, that some of these algorithms are far from trivial or embarrassingly simple. The full design space becomes apparent only by following the formal techniques discussed in Chapters 9–11. Take for example the algorithm for a one-dimensional (1-D) finite impulse response (FIR) digital filter given by the equation

$$y(i) = \sum_{j=0}^{I-1} a(j)x(i-j), \tag{7.1}$$

where $a(j)$ are the filter coefficients and I is the filter length. Such an equation is described by two nested loops as shown in Algorithm 7.1.

Algorithms and Parallel Computing, by Fayez Gebali
Copyright © 2011 John Wiley & Sons, Inc.

Algorithm 7.1   1-D FIR digital filter algorithm

Require: Input: filter coefficients $a(n)$ and input samples $x(n)$

1: $y(n) = 0$
2: **for** $i \geq 0$ **do**
3:    $y(i) = 0$
4:    **for** $j = 0 : I - 1$ **do**
5:       $y(i) = y(i) + a(j)x(i - j)$
6:    **end for**
7:    **RETURN** $y(i)$
8: **end for**

The iterations in the nested loops are independent, and it is fairly easy to apply the techniques discussed here. However, these techniques only give one design option compared to the techniques in Chapters 9–11.

Take another example for a 1-D infinite impulse response (IIR) digital filter given by the equation

$$y(i) = \sum_{j=0}^{I-1} [a(j)x(i - j) - b(j)y(i - j)], \tag{7.2}$$

where $a(j)$ and $b(j)$ are the filter coefficients and I is the filter length. Note that $b(0) = 0$ in the above equation. Such an equation is described by two nested loops as shown in Algorithm 7.2.

Algorithm 7.2   1-D IIR digital filter algorithm

Require: Input: filter coefficients $a(n)$ and $b(n)$ and input samples $x(n)$

1: $y(n) = 0$
2: **for** $i \geq 0$ **do**
3:    $y(i) = 0$
4:    **for** $j = 0 : I - 1$ **do**
5:       $y(i) = y(i) + a(j)x(i - j) - b(j)y(i - j)$
6:    **end for**
7:    **RETURN** $y(i)$
8: **end for**

Although this algorithm has two simple nested FOR loops, the data dependencies within the loop body dictate that the evaluation of $y(i)$ be serial. The techniques of this chapter will not be feasible here. However, the techniques of Chapters 9–11 will allow us to explore the possible parallelization techniques for this seemingly serial algorithm.

7.2 DEFINING ALGORITHM VARIABLES

We define three types of variables in an algorithm:

- Input variables
- Output variables
- Intermediate or input/output (*I/O*) variables

An input variable is one that has its instances appearing only on the right-hand side (RHS) of the equations of the algorithm. $a(j)$, $b(j)$, and $x(i-j)$ in Eq. 7.1 are examples of input variables. An output variable is one that has its instances appearing only on the left-hand side (LHS) of the algorithm. The IIR algorithm does not have output variables as such. An intermediate variable is one that has its instances appearing both on the LHS and on the RHS of the equations of the algorithm. Variable $y(i)$ in Eq. 7.2 is an example of an intermediate *I/O* variable. We consider an intermediate variable as being both an input or output variable with different index dependencies for each side of the iteration statement. This will be discussed in more detail in the next two sections. We will see in Chapter 12 how we are able to extract a parallel execution for any algorithm using the formal techniques we present in the following chapters.

7.3 INDEPENDENT LOOP SCHEDULING

An independent loop is one that does not contain intermediate or *I/O* variables. The iterations in an independent loop can be carried out in any order and can still produce the correct results. The FIR digital filter is an example of parallel algorithms that can be described by an independent loop. The following equations describe 1-D, two-dimensional (2-D), and three-dimensional (3-D) FIR filters used to process voice, image, and video data, respectively:

$$y(i) = \sum_{k=0}^{I-1} a(k)x(i-k) \tag{7.3}$$

$$y(i, j) = \sum_{w=0}^{W-1}\sum_{h=0}^{H-1} a(w, h)x(i-w, j-h) \tag{7.4}$$

$$y(i, j, k) = \sum_{w=0}^{W-1}\sum_{h=0}^{H-1}\sum_{f=0}^{F-1} a(w, h, f)x(i-w, j-h, k-f), \tag{7.5}$$

where I is the filter length, W is the width of the filter window, H is the height of the filter window, and F is the number of frames in the filter window. All the variables in the above equations are either an input or output type.

Another example of algorithms that result in independent loops is matrix–vector multiplication ($c = Ab$) and matrix–matrix multiplication ($C = AB$):

$$c(i) = \sum_{j=0}^{J-1} A(i, j)b(j) \qquad 0 \le i < I \tag{7.6}$$

$$C(i, j) = \sum_{k=0}^{K-1} A(i, k)B(k, j) \qquad 0 \le i < I, 0 \le j < J. \tag{7.7}$$

Consider for illustration the 1-D FIR in Eq. 7.1. If we had N processors and $I > N$, then we could assign $\lceil I/N \rceil$ loop iterations to each processor to ensure equal processor load balancing. Processor k is assigned to produce output variables $y(i)$, where i and k are related by

$$k = \lfloor i/N \rfloor \qquad 0 \le i < I. \tag{7.8}$$

The speedup of algorithm implementation on N parallel processors is estimated as

$$\text{Speedup}(I, N) = \frac{I}{\lceil I/N \rceil}. \tag{7.9}$$

7.4 DEPENDENT LOOPS

A dependent loop is one that contains intermediate or I/O variables such that the variable has different index dependences on both sides of the iteration statements. As an example, the loop in Listing 7.1 is a dependent loop, but the I/O variable has the same index independence on both sides. Each iteration of the loop can be done independently of the other iterations.

Listing 7.1   A dependent loop where its iterations are independent

```
1:  for  i  =  1:I  do
2:     a(i)  =  a(i)  +  b(i)
3:  end  for
```

On the other hand, the dependent loop in Listing 7.2 is a dependent loop, but the I/O variable has different index dependencies on both sides. Each iteration of the loop cannot be done independently of the other iterations.

Listing 7.2   A dependent loop where its iterations are dependent

```
1:  for  i  =  1:I  do
2:     a(i)  =  a(i  -  1)  +  b(i)
3:  end  for
```

Inherently, such loops would be executed serially on uniprocessor or multiprocessor systems. However, by using the formal techniques in Chapters 9–11, we will be able to explore a rich set of parallel implementations of such loops. There are some special and obvious cases where dependent loops can be parallelized. This is done through a technique called loop spreading [77] as explained in the next section.

7.5 LOOP SPREADING FOR SIMPLE DEPENDENT LOOPS

Consider the dependent loop shown in Listing 7.3, where $s(i, j)$ is some statement or task to be executed.

Listing 7.3   1-D IIR digital filter algorithm

```
1:  for i = 1:I do
2:     for j = 1:J do
3:        s(i, j) = f(s(i, j - 1))
4:     end for
5:  end for
```

where function evaluated by statement $s(i, j)$ depends on $s(i, j - 1)$. One way to distribute the tasks among the processors is to implement each iteration of the outer loop among I processors so that processor i implements all the iterations of the inner loop with its dependencies. We could increase the workload for each processor by allocating more than one iteration of the outer loop for each processor using a similar technique to the one explained in Section 7.3.

7.6 LOOP UNROLLING

Loop unrolling transforms a loop into a sequence of statements. It is a parallelizing and optimizing compiler technique [29] where loop unrolling us used to eliminate loop overhead to test loop control flow such as loop index values and termination conditions. The technique was also used to expose instruction-level parallelism [20]. Consider the loop shown in Listing 7.4 [20]:

Listing 7.4   Exposing potential parallelism by loop unrolling

```
1:  for i = 1:I do
2:     y(i) = y(i) + y(i - 5)
3:  end for
```

We note that the output version of the intermediate variable $y(i)$ depends on its current value $y(i)$ and a value that is distant 5, that is, $y(i - 5)$. The loop can be unrolled to execute five statements in parallel as shown in Listing 7.5 [20].

Listing 7.5   Exposing potential parallelism by loop unrolling.

```
1:  for i = 1:5:I do
2:     y(i)     = y(i)     + y(i - 5)
3:     y(i + 1) = y(i + 1) + y(i - 4)
4:     y(i + 2) = y(i + 2) + y(i - 3)
5:     y(i + 3) = y(i + 3) + y(i - 2)
6:     y(i + 4) = y(i + 4) + y(i - 1)
7:  end for
```

Now we can execute five statements of the loop at each iteration and gain a speedup ratio of 5.

7.7 PROBLEM PARTITIONING

Problem partitioning breaks up the computation task into smaller parts or subtasks that take less time to compute. Partitioning strives to generate subtasks that have the same size. Partitioning works best, of course, for trivially parallel algorithms. Otherwise, the subtasks will not execute in parallel. The challenge now shifts to how to combine the results of the subtasks to obtain the final result.

Take the simple example of adding K numbers using N processors:

$$b = \sum_{i=0}^{K-1} a_i. \tag{7.10}$$

Since addition is associative and distributive, we can break up the problem into N tasks where each task requires adding $s = |K/N|$ numbers on each processor:

$$c_i = \sum_{i=0}^{s-1} a_{j+ik} \qquad 0 \le i < N \tag{7.11}$$

$$c = \sum_{i=0}^{N-1} c_i. \tag{7.12}$$

Figure 7.1 shows a schematic representation of the partitioning technique. The original task or problem is partitioned into small equal portions that should execute faster. The number of partitions would typically equal the number of available processors.

After these additions are complete, we are faced with N partial sums that must be combined. One processor could be used to add those N partial sums. The task would be simple if the partial sums were stored in a shared memory. The task would take longer if the sums were stored in a distributed memory since N messages would have to be exchanged between the processors.

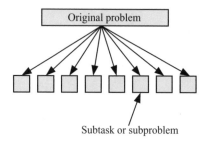

Figure 7.1   Problem partitioning divides the problem into N equal-sized subtasks. In this case, $N = 8$.

Let us attempt to find the time required to complete the computation using the partitioning technique. Assuming time to add two pairs of numbers is τ_a, the computation delay is given by

$$T_c = (s-1)\tau_a. \tag{7.13}$$

The communication delay T_m is the time required to send $N-1$ messages for the partial results to one processor:

$$T_m = (N-1)\tau_m, \tag{7.14}$$

where τ_m is the time to exchange a message between two processors. The total time to complete the task would be given by

$$T_{N,total} = (N-1)\tau_m + (s-1)\tau_a. \tag{7.15}$$

Typically, $\tau_a \ll \tau_m$ for multiprocessors, while $\tau_a \approx \tau_m$ for multicore processors and $s \gg N$. It would be worthwhile at this point to recall the results of Section 1.8 and, in particular, Fig. 1.7, which discusses parallel computer speedup and how it relates to the communication-to-computation ratio R. We saw that we reap the benefit of parallel computing when $R < 0.01$. Therefore, we must ensure the following inequality:

$$T_c \gg T_m \tag{7.16}$$

$$K \gg N^2 \frac{\tau_m}{\tau_a}. \tag{7.17}$$

For example, if the ratio $\tau_m/\tau_a = 1,000$ and $N = 8$, then we gain only for problem sizes of 10^7 numbers to be added.

7.8 DIVIDE-AND-CONQUER (RECURSIVE PARTITIONING) STRATEGIES

Divide-and-conquer techniques partition the problem into subtasks of the same size, but it iteratively keeps repeating this process to obtain yet smaller problems. In that sense, divide and conquer iteratively applies the problem partitioning technique as shown in Fig. 7.2. Divide and conquer is sometimes called recursive partitioning. Typically, the problem size N is an integer power of 2 and the divide-and-conquer technique halves the problem into two equal parts during each iteration.

Let us apply the divide-and-conquer technique to the problem of adding K numbers in Eq. 7.10. Assume that we have $N = 8$ processors. Since $N = 2^3$, the divide-and-conquer technique progresses through three iterations and the size of the subtask allocated to each processor is

$$s = \frac{K}{N}. \tag{7.18}$$

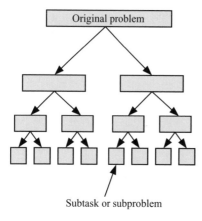

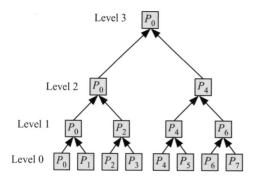

Figure 7.2 Divide-and-conquer technique iteratively partitions the problem into N equal-sized subtasks. In this case, $N = 8$.

Figure 7.3 Divide-and-conquer technique applied to the problem of adding $K = 128$ numbers using $N = 8$ processors.

Figure 7.3 shows how adding the K numbers progresses among the processors. The size of the smallest task allocated to each processor is $s = 128/8 = 16$. Thus, each processor has to add 16 numbers. This is shown at the bottom of the diagram at level 0. At the end of processing at level 0, $N = 8$ temporary results are produced. At level 1, these eight results are added by selecting four processors as shown to produce four partial results. Level 2 sums the four partial results to produce two partial results. Level 3 produces the desired output c.

Let us attempt to find the time required to complete the computation using the divide-and-conquer technique. Assuming the time to add two pairs of numbers is τ_a, the computation delay is given by

$$T_c = (s-1)\tau_a + \tau_a \log_2 N. \tag{7.19}$$

The first term on RHS represents delay due to adding s numbers by a processor at level 0. The second term on RHS represents addition delay due to adding a pair of numbers at the higher levels.

The communication delay T_m is the time required to send messages for the partial results between pairs of computers.

$$T_m = \tau_m \log_2 N, \tag{7.20}$$

where we assume that the interconnection network allows for a simultaneous exchange of messages between processors.

The total time to complete the task would be given by

$$T_{N,total} = T_m + T_c \tag{7.21}$$
$$= \tau_m \log_2 N + (s-1)\tau_a + \tau_a \log_2 N \tag{7.22}$$
$$\approx \tau_m \log_2 N + (s-1)\tau_a. \tag{7.23}$$

We saw that we reap the benefit of parallel computing when $R < 0.01$. Therefore, we must ensure the following inequality:

$$T_c \gg T_m \tag{7.24}$$

$$K \gg N \log_2 N \frac{\tau_m}{\tau_a}. \tag{7.25}$$

For example, if the ratio $\tau_m/\tau_a = 1,000$ and $N = 8$, then we gain only for problem sizes of 10^6 numbers to be added.

7.9 PIPELINING

We showed in Chapter 2 how pipelining enhanced the performance of uniprocessors. Pipelining was used in the arithmetic and logic unit (ALU) to increase the amount of computations to be performed per clock cycle. Pipelining was also used in the control unit to increase the number of instructions to be processed per clock cycle.

In general, pipelining is a very effective technique for improving system throughput, which is defined as the rate of task completion per unit time. This technique requires two conditions to be effective:

1. There should be many instances of the task and all of them must be completed at a high rate.
2. Each task should be divisible into several serial or parallel subtasks.

A pipeline executes a task in successive stages by breaking it up into smaller tasks. It is safe to assume that a smaller task will complete in a shorter time compared with the original task.

Examples of using pipelining to speed up the high-performance coordinate rotation digital computer (HCORDIC) algorithm, which is a very powerful algorithm for evaluating elementary functions such as trigonometric, hyperbolic, logarithmic, square root, and division operations [5–8]. Evaluating elementary functions is required in many engineering applications such as adaptive filters, telecommunications, scientific computing, and so on. Figure 7.4 shows a schematic of the data and

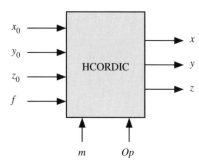

Figure 7.4 Schematic of the data and control inputs of the HCORDIC algorithm and the resulting outputs. x_0, initial x-coordinate of a point in the plane; y_0, initial y-coordinate of a point in the plane; z_0, initial value of an angle; f, final value of x, y, or z.

Table 7.1 HCORDIC Output in the Vectoring Operation $(y \rightarrow f)$

	x	z
$m = 1$	$K_1\sqrt{x_0^2 + y_0^2 - f^2}$	$z_0 + \tan^{-1}(y_0 - f/x_0)$
$m = 0$	$(y_0 - f)/x_0$	$z_0 + (y_0 - f)/x_0$
$m = -1$	$K_{-1}\sqrt{f^2 - x_0^2 + y_0^2}$	$z_0 + \tanh^{-1}(y_0 - f/x_0)$

x_0, y_0, and z_0 are the initial or input values to the HCORDIC algorithm.

Table 7.2 HCORDIC Output in the Rotation Operation $(z_0 \rightarrow f)$

	x_n	y_n
$m = 1$	$K_1(x_0\cos(f - z_0) + y_0\sin(f - z_0))$	$K_1(y_0\cos(f - z_0) - x_0\sin(f - z_0))$
$m = 0$	x_0	$y_0 - x_0(f - z_0)$
$m = -1$	$K_{-1}(x_0\cosh(f - z_0) - y_0\sinh(f - z_0))$	$K_{-1}(y_0\cosh(z_f - z_0) - x_0\sinh(z_f - z_0))$

x_0, y_0, and z_0 are the initial or input values to the coordinate rotation digital computer (CORDIC) algorithm.

control inputs of the HCORDIC algorithm and the resulting outputs. HCORDIC accepts four input data.

The control inputs for HCORDIC are

1. m, the mode (-1, 0, or 1), and

2. Op, the desired operation (vectoring or rotation).

The vectoring operation changes the value of y_0 to f at the output ($y_0 \rightarrow f$). The rotation operation changes the value of z_0 to 0 at the output ($z_0 \rightarrow f$).

Table 7.1 shows the HCORDIC output for the vectoring operation. Choosing the proper values of x_0, y_0, z_0, and f, we can obtain square root, division, tan^{-1}, or $tanh^{-1}$ functions.

Table 7.2 shows the HCORDIC output for the rotation operation. Choosing the proper values of x_0, y_0, z_0, and f, we can obtain sin, cos, sinh, or cosh functions.

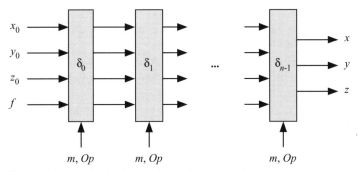

Figure 7.5   Pipeline implementation of HCORDIC algorithm.

HCORDIC is serial and must be done through successive iterations. At iteration i, the values of x, y, and z are updated according to the following equations:

$$x_{i+1} = x_i + m y_i \delta_i$$
$$y_{i+1} = y_i - x_i \delta_i \tag{7.26}$$
$$z_{i+1} = z_i + \theta_i,$$

where δ_i and θ_i are iteration constants that are stored in lookup tables. The algorithm performs other operations during each iteration, but we are not concerned about this here.

Now HCORDIC is amenable to pipelining since it satisfies pipelining requirements: HCORDIC is composed of iterative steps, and it is required to perform many HCORDIC operations on many input data streams. Figure 7.5 shows the pipeline implementation of HCORDIC to ensure that one result is produced per iteration cycle. In the figure, n is the number of pipeline stages, which equals the number of iterations required by HCORDIC to complete its calculations. Input data are delivered as a series of input vectors. Each input vector sample contains its own data and the associated control information

$$\text{Data} = \begin{bmatrix} x_0 & y_0 & z_0 & f_0 & m & \text{Op} \end{bmatrix}. \tag{7.27}$$

As each data set, x, y, z, and f travels through the pipeline stages, the associated control information m and Op also travel to control the operation at each pipeline stage. In this way, we could have a vectoring operation or rotation operation applied to adjacent data and we could have different values of m also to get different output functions for each input data sample.

7.10   PROBLEMS

7.1. Consider the MAX function that finds the maximum number from a list of n numbers where N is assumed to be an integer power of 2; that is, $n = \log_2 N$. Write down the serial algorithm for the MAX function then explain a binary algorithm to perform the MAX function in parallel.

7.2. Study the quicksort algorithm for sorting N numbers and show how the algorithm can be parallelized using the divide-and-conquer technique. What can you say about the number of parallel processors that could be employed?

7.3. One way to speed up quicksort is to use more than one pivot. Let us assume that at each invocation of quicksort, we choose m pivots. Describe how this algorithm might work and why it would be faster than the one pivot quicksort.

7.4. Find expressions for the worst and best times of the sequential m-pivot quicksort algorithm.

7.5. Explain how the bubble sort algorithm can be parallelized.

Chapter 8

Nonserial–Parallel Algorithms

8.1 INTRODUCTION

We discussed in Chapter 1 that algorithms can be classified broadly as

1. serial algorithms,
2. parallel algorithms,
3. serial–parallel algorithms (SPAs),
4. nonserial–parallel algorithms (NSPAs), and
5. regular iterative algorithms (RIAs).

This chapter discusses how to extract parallelism from NSPAs so we can implement them on parallel computer platforms. Serial, parallel, and SPAs are all relatively simple to implement on parallel computer platforms. Chapters 9–11 are all dedicated to the software and hardware implementations of RIAs. That leaves NSPA as an interesting problem that requires a formal technique to deal with them.

Chapter 1 mentioned that an NSPA can contain cycles or can be cycle free. NSPAs can be represented by its associated directed graph (DG) or its associated adjacency matrix $\mathbf{A}$. When the DG contains no cycles, we get what is called directed acyclic graph (DAG). When a cycle is present or detected in the NSPA, we have a directed cyclic graph (DCG). A DCG operates on a different principle compared to other algorithms.

8.2 COMPARING DAG AND DCG ALGORITHMS

Figure 8.1a is an example of a DAG algorithm and Fig. 8.1b is an example of a DCG algorithm. An algorithm represented with a DAG requires a certain time to complete its tasks and the data flow is unidirectional from the inputs to the outputs. Thus, each task in the graph is completed once for each instance of the algorithm.

Algorithms and Parallel Computing, by Fayez Gebali
Copyright © 2011 John Wiley & Sons, Inc.

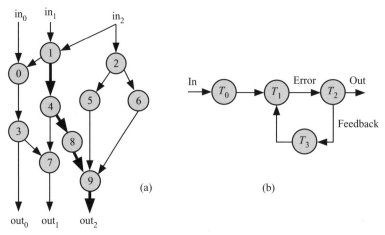

Figure 8.1 Example directed graphs for nonserial–parallel algorithms. (a) Directed acyclic graph (DAG). (b) Directed cyclic graph (DCG).

When all tasks have been completed, the algorithm is terminated or another instance of it is started with another set of input data.

The DCG is most commonly encountered in discrete time feedback control systems such as adaptive filters and digital controllers for plant control. An example of a feedback control systems is a car automatic speed control and the airplane autopilot. The input is supplied to task T_0 for prefiltering or for input signal conditioning. Task T_1 accepts the conditioned input signal and the conditioned feedback output signal. The output of task T_1 is usually referred to as the error signal, and this signal is fed to task T_2 to produce the output signal. An algorithm represented by a DCG usually operates on a set of input data streams and produces a set of output data streams. The time between samples is called the *sample time*, which is equal to the maximum delay exhibited by any of the tasks shown in Fig. 8.1:

$$\tau_{\text{sample}} = \max\left(\tau_0, \tau_1, \tau_2, \tau_3\right), \tag{8.1}$$

where τ_{sample} is the sample time and τ_i is the execution time of task T_i. This equation is similar to determining the pipeline period for a pipelined system as was discussed in Chapter 2. During each sample time, *all* the tasks must be evaluated. To shorten the sample time and to speed up the system data rate, we must shorten the execution times of each task individually. Table 8.1 compares the two main types of NSPAs: DAG and DCG. The techniques we use to accomplish this depend on the nature of the algorithms or functions implemented in each task. Thus, we can use techniques discussed in Chapters 2, 9–11, and 7 and in this chapter.

Table 8.1   Comparing the Two Main Types of NSPA Algorithms

DAG	DCG
Algorithm parallelization attempts to determine which of the algorithm tasks can be executed at the same time.	Algorithm parallelization attempts to parallelize each task *independently* of the other tasks.
An algorithm instance executes once only.	An algorithm instance executes one for each sample time and repeats for as long as we have input data or for as long as we desire output data.
Input data are available initially before the algorithm is started.	Input data are supplied in a stream or as long as the algorithm is executing.
Output data are obtained typically after the algorithm has finished executing.	Output data are obtained in a stream as long as the algorithm is running.
The characteristic time is the algorithm execution time, which depends on the critical path.	The characteristic time is the *sample time*.
The workload is the number of tasks to be executed (W).	The workload is W for *each* sample time; that is, all tasks execute for each time step and then all of them are evaluated again at the next time step.
The application domain is typically abstract data fairly detached from actual physical phenomena.	The application domain is typically applied to tangible physical phenomena to be controlled, such as speed, temperature, pressure, and fluid flow.

8.3   PARALLELIZING NSPA ALGORITHMS REPRESENTED BY A DAG

This chapter discusses techniques for extracting parallelism from DAG. Each task accepts input data and produces output results. We say a task, T_i, is dependent on task T_j if the output of T_j is used as its input to T_i. When the number of algorithm tasks is small, the algorithm can be described by a directed graph, which shows no regular patterns of interconnections among the tasks. Figure 8.1a shows an example of representing an NSPA by a DAG. The graph is characterized by two types of constructs: the *nodes*, which describe the tasks comprising the algorithm, and the *directed edges*, which describe the direction of data flow among the tasks. The edges exiting a node represent an output, and when they enter a node, they represent an input. Chapter 1 defined the types of nodes and edges in a DG: input node/edge, output node/edge, and intermediate node/edge.

Figure 8.1 shows the algorithm as drawn or sketched by the programmer or some graphing tool. Nodes 0, 1, and 2 are the only input nodes, and nodes 7 and 9 are the only output nodes. The algorithm has three *primary inputs*: in_0, in_1, and in_2, and three *primary outputs*: out_0, out_1, and out_2.

Example 8.1   A very popular series in computer science is the Fibonacci sequence:

$$0, 1, 1, 2, 3, 5, 8, 13, \ldots.$$

An algorithm to calculate the nth Fibonacci number is given by

$$N_n = N_{n-1} + N_{n-2},$$

where $N_0 = 0$ and $N_1 = 1$. Draw a DAG to show how the task T_n for calculating the nth Fibonacci number depends on the tasks for calculating the earlier numbers.

From the definition of the nth Fibonacci number, we can write

$$T_n = T_{n-1} + T_{n-2}.$$

Take the case when $n = 10$. Figure 8.2 shows the DAG associated with this algorithm. We see that the Fibonacci algorithm is a serial algorithm since no two tasks can be executed in parallel.

An algorithm has three important properties:

1. *Work (W)*, which equals the number of tasks describing the algorithm. These describe the amount of processing work to be done. For the algorithm in Fig. 8.1, we have $W = 10$.

2. *Depth (D)*, which is also known as the *critical path* and *span*. The depth is defined as the maximum path length between any input node and any output node. For the algorithm in Fig. 8.1, we have $S = 4$ since the longest path is path $1 \rightarrow 4 \rightarrow 8 \rightarrow 9$ as indicated by the bold arrows.

3. *Parallelism (P)*, which is also known as the *degree of parallelism* of the algorithm. Parallelism is defined as the maximum number of nodes that can be processed in parallel. The maximum number of parallel processors that could be active at any given time will not exceed P since anymore processors will not find any tasks to execute. At this stage, it is hard to figure out P for the algorithm in Fig. 8.1.

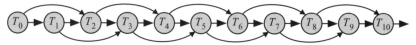

Figure 8.2   DAG associated with the algorithm for calculating the nth Fibonacci number when $n = 10$.

8.4 FORMAL TECHNIQUE FOR ANALYZING NSPAs

In this chapter, we will show that representing an algorithm by a DG is suitable only when the number of tasks comprising the algorithm is small. However, it is difficult to extract some of the algorithm properties from an inspection of the graph.

For example, it is simple to find W by counting the number of nodes in the graph. Estimating D is slightly more difficult since it involves path search, while estimating P is even more difficult by inspecting the graph.

We need to introduce a more formal technique to deal with the case when the number of tasks is large or when we want to automate the process of extracting the algorithm W, D, and P parameters. We will refer to the tasks of the algorithm as nodes since that was the term we used in the DG description. The technique we explain here converts the DAG of an NSPA into a DAG for an SPA.

Given W nodes/tasks, we define the 0-1 *adjacency matrix* $\mathbf{A}$, which is a square $W \times W$ matrix defined so that element $a(i, j) = 1$ indicates that node i depends on node j. The source node is j and the destination node is i. Of course, we must have $a(i, i) = 0$ for all values of $0 \le i < W$ since node i does not depend on itself (self-loop) and we assumed that we do not have any loops. As an example, the adjacency matrix for the algorithm in Fig. 8.1 is given by

$$\mathbf{A} = \begin{bmatrix} 0 & 0 & 0 & 0 & 0 & 0 & 0 & \mathbf{0} & \mathbf{0} & \mathbf{0} \\ 0 & 0 & 0 & 0 & 0 & 0 & 0 & \mathbf{0} & \mathbf{0} & \mathbf{0} \\ 0 & 0 & 0 & 0 & 0 & 0 & 0 & \mathbf{0} & \mathbf{0} & \mathbf{0} \\ 1 & 0 & 0 & 0 & 0 & 0 & 0 & \mathbf{0} & \mathbf{0} & \mathbf{0} \\ 0 & 1 & 0 & 0 & 0 & 0 & 0 & \mathbf{0} & \mathbf{0} & \mathbf{0} \\ 0 & 0 & 1 & 0 & 0 & 0 & 0 & \mathbf{0} & \mathbf{0} & \mathbf{0} \\ 0 & 0 & 1 & 0 & 0 & 0 & 0 & \mathbf{0} & \mathbf{0} & \mathbf{0} \\ 0 & 0 & 0 & 1 & 1 & 0 & 0 & \mathbf{0} & \mathbf{0} & \mathbf{0} \\ 0 & 0 & 0 & 0 & 1 & 0 & 0 & \mathbf{0} & \mathbf{0} & \mathbf{0} \\ 0 & 0 & 0 & 0 & 0 & 1 & 1 & \mathbf{0} & \mathbf{1} & \mathbf{0} \end{bmatrix}. \tag{8.2}$$

Matrix $\mathbf{A}$ has some interesting properties related to our topic. An input node i is associated with row i, whose elements are all zeros. An output node j is associated with column j, whose elements are all zeros. We can write

$$\text{Input node } i \Rightarrow \sum_{j=0}^{W-1} a(i, j) = 0 \tag{8.3}$$

$$\text{Output node } j \Rightarrow \sum_{i=0}^{W-1} a(i, j) = 0. \tag{8.4}$$

All other nodes are interior nodes. Note that all the elements in rows 0, 1, and 2 are all zeros since nodes 0, 1, and 2 are input nodes. This is indicated by the bold entries in these three rows. Note also that all elements in columns 7 and 9 are all zeros since nodes 7 and 9 are output nodes. This is indicated by the bold entries in these two columns. All other rows and columns have one or more nonzero elements to indicate interior nodes. If node i has element $a(i, j) = 1$, then we say that node j is a parent of node i.

Example 8.2 Derive the adjacency matrix for the generation of the 10th Fibonacci number based on the DAG discussed in Example 8.1.

From the DAG, we get the following adjacency matrix:

$$A(\text{Fibonacci}) = \begin{bmatrix} 0 & 0 & 0 & 0 & 0 & 0 & 0 & 0 & 0 & 0 \\ 0 & 0 & 0 & 0 & 0 & 0 & 0 & 0 & 0 & 0 \\ 1 & 1 & 0 & 0 & 0 & 0 & 0 & 0 & 0 & 0 \\ 0 & 1 & 1 & 0 & 0 & 0 & 0 & 0 & 0 & 0 \\ 0 & 0 & 1 & 1 & 0 & 0 & 0 & 0 & 0 & 0 \\ 0 & 0 & 0 & 1 & 1 & 0 & 0 & 0 & 0 & 0 \\ 0 & 0 & 0 & 0 & 1 & 1 & 0 & 0 & 0 & 0 \\ 0 & 0 & 0 & 0 & 0 & 1 & 1 & 0 & 0 & 0 \\ 0 & 0 & 0 & 0 & 0 & 0 & 1 & 1 & 0 & 0 \\ 0 & 0 & 0 & 0 & 0 & 0 & 0 & 1 & 1 & 0 \end{bmatrix}$$

8.4.1 Significance of Powers of A^i: The Connectivity Matrix

Let us see what happens if we raise the adjacency matrix in (8.2) to a higher power. We square the matrix to get matrix A_2 defined as the adjacency matrix raised to the power 2.

$$A_2 \equiv A^2 = \begin{bmatrix} 0 & 0 & 0 & 0 & 0 & 0 & 0 & 0 & 0 & 0 \\ 0 & 0 & 0 & 0 & 0 & 0 & 0 & 0 & 0 & 0 \\ 0 & 0 & 0 & 0 & 0 & 0 & 0 & 0 & 0 & 0 \\ 0 & 0 & 0 & 0 & 0 & 0 & 0 & 0 & 0 & 0 \\ 0 & 0 & 0 & 0 & 0 & 0 & 0 & 0 & 0 & 0 \\ 0 & 0 & 0 & 0 & 0 & 0 & 0 & 0 & 0 & 0 \\ 0 & 0 & 0 & 0 & 0 & 0 & 0 & 0 & 0 & 0 \\ 1 & 1 & 0 & 0 & 0 & 0 & 0 & 0 & 0 & 0 \\ 0 & 1 & 0 & 0 & 0 & 0 & 0 & 0 & 0 & 0 \\ 0 & 0 & 2 & 0 & 1 & 0 & 0 & 0 & 0 & 0 \end{bmatrix}. \tag{8.5}$$

There are few nonzero entries and some entries are not 1 anymore. Element a_2 (7, 0) is 1 to indicate that there is a two-hop path from node 0 to node 7. We call $\mathbf{A}_2$ the connectivity matrix of degree 2 to indicate that it shows all two-hop connections between nodes in the graph. Specifically, that path is $0 \rightarrow 3 \rightarrow 7$. Node 7 has another two-hop path as indicated by element a_2 (7, 1), which is path $1 \rightarrow 4 \rightarrow 7$. Element a_2 (9, 2) = 2, which indicates that there are two alternative two-hop paths to node 9 starting at node 2. These two paths are $2 \rightarrow 5 \rightarrow 9$ and $2 \rightarrow 6 \rightarrow 9$.

Now let us look at the connectivity matrix of order 3, that is, $\mathbf{A}^3$:

$$\mathbf{A}_3 \equiv \mathbf{A}^3 = \begin{bmatrix} 0 & 0 & 0 & 0 & 0 & 0 & 0 & 0 & 0 & 0 \\ 0 & 0 & 0 & 0 & 0 & 0 & 0 & 0 & 0 & 0 \\ 0 & 0 & 0 & 0 & 0 & 0 & 0 & 0 & 0 & 0 \\ 0 & 0 & 0 & 0 & 0 & 0 & 0 & 0 & 0 & 0 \\ 0 & 0 & 0 & 0 & 0 & 0 & 0 & 0 & 0 & 0 \\ 0 & 0 & 0 & 0 & 0 & 0 & 0 & 0 & 0 & 0 \\ 0 & 0 & 0 & 0 & 0 & 0 & 0 & 0 & 0 & 0 \\ 0 & 0 & 0 & 0 & 0 & 0 & 0 & 0 & 0 & 0 \\ 0 & 0 & 0 & 0 & 0 & 0 & 0 & 0 & 0 & 0 \\ 0 & 1 & 0 & 0 & 0 & 0 & 0 & 0 & 0 & 0 \end{bmatrix}. \tag{8.6}$$

Now all the elements of $\mathbf{A}^3$ are zero except for a_3 (9, 1). This indicates that there is only one three-hop path between nodes 1 and 9, specifically, $1 \rightarrow 4 \rightarrow 8 \rightarrow 9$. Let us now go one step further and see the value of $\mathbf{A}^4$:

$$\mathbf{A}_4 \equiv \mathbf{A}^4 = \begin{bmatrix} 0 & 0 & 0 & 0 & 0 & 0 & 0 & 0 & 0 & 0 \\ 0 & 0 & 0 & 0 & 0 & 0 & 0 & 0 & 0 & 0 \\ 0 & 0 & 0 & 0 & 0 & 0 & 0 & 0 & 0 & 0 \\ 0 & 0 & 0 & 0 & 0 & 0 & 0 & 0 & 0 & 0 \\ 0 & 0 & 0 & 0 & 0 & 0 & 0 & 0 & 0 & 0 \\ 0 & 0 & 0 & 0 & 0 & 0 & 0 & 0 & 0 & 0 \\ 0 & 0 & 0 & 0 & 0 & 0 & 0 & 0 & 0 & 0 \\ 0 & 0 & 0 & 0 & 0 & 0 & 0 & 0 & 0 & 0 \\ 0 & 0 & 0 & 0 & 0 & 0 & 0 & 0 & 0 & 0 \\ 0 & 0 & 0 & 0 & 0 & 0 & 0 & 0 & 0 & 0 \end{bmatrix} = \mathbf{0}. \tag{8.7}$$

The fact that all elements of $\mathbf{A}_4$ are zero indicates that there are no paths with a length of four hops. Of course, this implies that all powers of $\mathbf{A}^i$ for $i > 3$ will be zero also. Thus, we can determine the critical path or paths from the highest power of $\mathbf{A}$ for which the result is not the zero matrix.

8.5 DETECTING CYCLES IN THE ALGORITHM

This section explains how cycles could be detected in the algorithm using the adjacency matrix $\mathbf{A}$. Let us assume we modify the cycle-free algorithm in Fig. 8.1 to have an algorithm with a cycle in it like the one shown in Fig. 8.3. The dashed arrows indicate the extra links we added. Inspecting the figure indicates we have a cycle, $3 \rightarrow 7 \rightarrow 5 \rightarrow 8 \rightarrow 3$.

The corresponding adjacency matrix is given by

$$\mathbf{B} = \begin{bmatrix} 0 & 0 & 0 & 0 & 0 & 0 & 0 & 0 & 0 & 0 \\ 0 & 0 & 0 & 0 & 0 & 0 & 0 & 0 & 0 & 0 \\ 0 & 0 & 0 & 0 & 0 & 0 & 0 & 0 & 0 & 0 \\ 1 & 0 & 0 & 0 & 0 & 0 & 0 & 0 & 1 & 0 \\ 0 & 0 & 0 & 0 & 0 & 0 & 0 & 0 & 0 & 0 \\ 0 & 0 & 1 & 0 & 0 & 0 & 0 & 1 & 0 & 0 \\ 0 & 0 & 1 & 0 & 0 & 0 & 0 & 0 & 0 & 0 \\ 0 & 0 & 0 & 1 & 1 & 0 & 0 & 0 & 0 & 0 \\ 0 & 0 & 0 & 0 & 1 & 1 & 0 & 0 & 0 & 0 \\ 0 & 0 & 0 & 0 & 0 & 1 & 1 & 0 & 1 & 0 \end{bmatrix}. \tag{8.8}$$

An inspection of the matrix would not reveal the presence of any cycle. In fact, nothing too interesting happens for powers of $\mathbf{B}^2$ and $\mathbf{B}^3$. However, for $\mathbf{B}^4$, the matrix takes on a very interesting form:

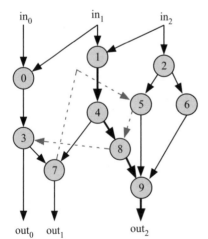

Figure 8.3 Modifying the algorithm of Fig. 8.1 to contain a cycle as indicated by the dashed arrows.

$$
\mathbf{B}^4 = \begin{bmatrix}
0 & 0 & 0 & 0 & 0 & 0 & 0 & 0 & 0 & 0 \\
0 & 0 & 0 & 0 & 0 & 0 & 0 & 0 & 0 & 0 \\
0 & 0 & 0 & 0 & 0 & 0 & 0 & 0 & 0 & 0 \\
0 & 0 & 0 & 1 & 1 & 0 & 0 & 0 & 1 & 0 \\
0 & 0 & 0 & 0 & 0 & 0 & 0 & 0 & 0 & 0 \\
0 & 0 & 0 & 0 & 1 & 1 & 0 & 0 & 0 & 0 \\
0 & 0 & 0 & 0 & 0 & 0 & 0 & 0 & 0 & 0 \\
0 & 1 & 1 & 0 & 0 & 0 & 0 & 1 & 0 & 0 \\
1 & 1 & 0 & 0 & 1 & 1 & 0 & 0 & 1 & 0 \\
1 & 1 & 0 & 1 & 1 & 0 & 0 & 0 & 1 & 0
\end{bmatrix}. \tag{8.9}
$$

We note that there are four nonzero diagonal elements: b_4 (3, 3), b_4 (5, 5), b_4 (7, 7), and b_4 (8, 8). This indicates that there is a four-hop loop between nodes 3, 5, 7, and 8. The order of the loop can be determined by examining the rows associated with these nodes. Starting with node 3, we see that it depends on node 8. So, the path of the loop is $8 \rightarrow 3$. Now we look at row 8 and see that it depends on node 5. So, the path of the loop is $5 \rightarrow 8 \rightarrow 3$. Continuing in this fashion, we see that our loop is $3 \rightarrow 7 \rightarrow 5 \rightarrow 8 \rightarrow 3$, which we have found by inspection of the graph. The advantage of this technique is that it is applicable to any number of nodes and can be automated.

Another interesting property of cyclic algorithms and cyclic graphs is that higher powers of the adjacency matrix will not produce a zero matrix. In fact, the adjacency matrix will show *cyclic* or *periodic* behavior:

$$
\mathbf{A}^4 = \mathbf{A}^8 = \mathbf{A}^{12} \cdots . \tag{8.10}
$$

8.6 EXTRACTING SERIAL AND PARALLEL ALGORITHM PERFORMANCE PARAMETERS

In order to extract the D and P properties of an algorithm, we construct a W component nonnegative *sequence vector* $\mathbf{S}$, such that the component of the vector at the ith location $S(i) \geq 0$ indicates the order or priority of execution assigned to node i. The value $S(i) = k$ indicates that node i belongs to the execution sequence k.

We outline some basic definitions that we will need in our technique.

Definition 8.1 Parents of a node n: the source nodes for the directed edges terminating at node n.

Definition 8.2 Sequence of a node n: when a node can be executed by the processors.

Definition 8.3 Parallel set T_s: the set of all nodes/tasks that can be executed at sequence s.

The process of evaluating the algorithm starts with all the nodes that have sequence value 0, then when all the processing is done, the nodes with sequence value 1 are executed, and so on. We populate the sequence vector according to the iterative procedure shown in Algorithm 8.1.

Algorithm 8.1   Algorithm to assign execution sequences or levels to the nodes

---

Require: Input: $W \times W$ adjacency matrix **A**

1: $\mathcal{P} = \phi$ // initialize parents set to empty set
2: $\mathcal{N} = \mathcal{W}$ // initialize nodes set to include all the nodes of the algorithm
3: $s = 0$ // Initial sequence has zero value (0).
4: $\mathcal{T}_0 = \phi$ // initialize set of concurrent tasks at level $s = 0$
5: **for** $node \in \mathcal{N}$ **do**
6:    **if** $node$ is input node **then**
7:       $S(node) = s$ // Components of **S** associated with each input node have value $s = 0$.
8:       insert $node$ in $\mathcal{P}$ // start defining the parents node set
9:       delete $node$ from $\mathcal{N}$ // leave unassigned nodes in $\mathcal{N}$
10:    **end if**
11: **end for**
12: **while** $\mathcal{N} \neq \phi$ **do**
13:    $s = s + 1$ // increment sequence value to be allocated to newly assigned nodes
14:    $\mathcal{T} = \phi$ // initialize temporary set to contain nodes in new level
15:    $\mathcal{T}_s = \phi$ // initialize set of concurrent tasks at level s
16:    **for** $node \in \mathcal{N}$ **do**
17:       **if** all parents of $node \in \mathcal{P}$ **then**
18:          insert $node$ in $\mathcal{T}$
19:          delete $node$ from $\mathcal{N}$
20:          $S(node) = s$
21:       **end if**
22:    **end for**
23:    append $\mathcal{T}$ to $\mathcal{P}$ // update nodes in $\mathcal{P}$ to include newly assigned nodes
24:    append $\mathcal{T}$ to $\mathcal{T}_s$
25: **end while**

After implementing Algorithm 8.1, all nodes will be assigned to an execution level. Figure 8.4 shows the levels of execution of the algorithm in Fig. 8.1 and the allocation of nodes to levels.

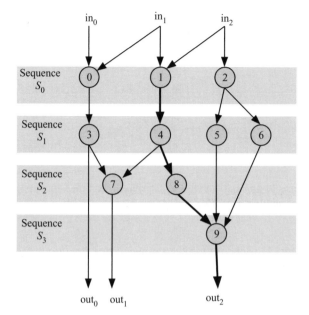

Figure 8.4 The assignment of the nodes in Fig. 8.1 according to the procedure in Algorithm 8.1.

8.7 USEFUL THEOREMS

We show in this section some useful theorems related to the formal technique we proposed in the previous section. The following theorem discusses how we can check if a given algorithm is cycle free or not.

Theorem 8.1 *An algorithm with* W *nodes/tasks is cycle free if and only if* $\mathbf{A}^k$ *has zeros in its main diagonal elements for* $1 \le k \le W$.

Proof:
Assume the algorithm is cycle free. In that case, we do not expect any diagonal element to be nonzero for $\mathbf{A}^k$ with $k \ge 1$. The worst case situation is when our algorithm has all the nodes connected in one long string of W nodes as shown in Fig. 8.5a. The highest power for $\mathbf{A}^k$ is when $k = W - 1$ since this is the maximum length of the path between W nodes. $\mathbf{A}^W = 0$ since there is no path of length W. Thus, a cycle-free algorithm will produce zero diagonal elements for all powers of $\mathbf{A}^k$ with $1 \le k \le W$.

Now assume that all powers of $\mathbf{A}^k$ for $1 \le k \le W$ are all zero diagonal elements. This proves that we do not have any cycles of length 1 to W in the algorithm. This proves that the algorithm does not have any cycles since for W nodes, we cannot have a cycle of length greater than W. Figure 8.5b shows the longest possible cycle in an algorithm of W nodes/tasks.

The following theorem gives us the performance parameter D.

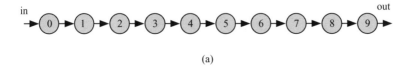

(a)

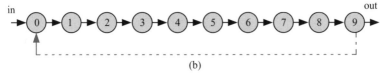

(b)

Figure 8.5 Worst case algorithm that has 10 nodes. (a) When the algorithm is cycle free. (b) The longest possible cycle in an algorithm with 10 nodes is 10.

Theorem 8.2 *A DAG has depth* D *if and only if the following two conditions are satisfied:*

$$\mathbf{A}^k \neq 0 \qquad 0 \leq k < D \tag{8.11}$$
$$\mathbf{A}^D = 0, \tag{8.12}$$

where $1 \leq D \leq W$.

Proof:
Assume the DAG has depth D. This indicates that the maximum possible path length is $D - 1$. This implies the following two equations:

$$\mathbf{A}^k \neq 0 \qquad 1 \leq k < D \tag{8.13}$$
$$\mathbf{A}^D = 0. \tag{8.14}$$

The condition $\mathbf{A}^D = 0$ above implies that there are no paths of length D or less in the algorithm and the longest path length is $D - 1$ according to Eq. 8.13. This is the length of the path that connects D nodes together. The first node is the input node and the last node is the output node.

Now assume the two conditions in (8.13) and (8.14) are true. Thus, the maximum path length is D for the algorithm.

The following theorem results as a consequence of the procedure for assigning execution order to the nodes according to Algorithm 8.1. It assures that the execution sequence assigned to each node is the smallest or earliest possible value.

Theorem 8.3 *A node is assigned to sequence* k *if and only if it depends on one or more nodes assigned to sequence* k − 1.

Proof:
Assume that node i is assigned sequence k. This implies that it must be executed after all the nodes in sequence $k - 1$. This implies that it depends on one or more nodes from that sequence. If that was not the case, the procedure of Algorithm 8.1 would have assigned a smaller sequence value to node i.

Now assume that node i depends on one or more nodes that belong to sequence $K-1$. This node can only execute after all these nodes complete their execution. This implies that the sequence to be assigned to node i should have the value k.

The following theorem assures us that we can execute all nodes having the execution sequence in parallel or simultaneously.

Theorem 8.4   *Nodes belong to the same sequence if and only if they are independent of each other and can be evaluated in parallel.*

Proof:
Assume two nodes, i and j, have the same sequence S_k. This implies that the two nodes can be evaluated simultaneously in parallel and that they are independent of each other.

Now assume that two nodes, i and j, are independent and can be evaluated in parallel at the same time. This implies that the two nodes belong to the same sequence value. These two nodes could be moved to the earliest sequence, S_k, where both nodes depend on one or more nodes from sequence S_{k-1}.

The following theorem is unique to DAGs. It indicates that the last nodes executed are all output nodes and their outputs are not used to supply other nodes.

Theorem 8.5   *A DAG has depth D if and only if all the nodes in sequence S_D are output nodes.*

Proof:
When the depth of the DAG is D, then nodes in sequence S_D cannot be interior nodes. If a node were interior, then it must send its output data to a node i at sequence $D+1$ since we do not have cycles. This would imply that node i will be evaluated at sequence S_{D+1} and the depth of the graph is at least $D+1$. This contradicts the requirement that the depth is D.

Now assume that all nodes in sequence S_D are output nodes. This implies that there are no more nodes that depend on them. Thus, the depth of the graph is D.

The following theorem is perhaps the most important theorem for DAGs. Essentially, it assures us that the sequence assigned to the nodes is the fastest possible schedule.

Theorem 8.6   *The task execution schedule constructed from Algorithm 8.1 is the optimal schedule possible for the given DAG assuming we have enough computing resources to execute all the tasks in a given sequence level.*

Theorems 8.3 and 8.5 indicate that we cannot reduce the depth of the graph by moving nodes from the given sequence to an earlier sequence. Hence, depth D cannot be reduced below its value.

Theorem 8.4 indicates that we have the maximum number of nodes in any given sequence level. So, we have the maximum number of nodes that could be assigned the same sequence order.

The above two paragraphs imply the following:

1. We have maximum parallelism at any sequence level.
2. We have the absolute minimum number of levels under the given assumptions.

Hence, the schedule obtained from Algorithm 8.1 is the optimal schedule.

The following theorem assures us that the execution order assigned to the nodes preserves the order dictated by the algorithm.

Theorem 8.7   *The procedure in Algorithm 8.1 for setting the execution order of the algorithm tasks preserves the correctness of the algorithm.*

Proof:

Two facts about the procedure assure us of the correctness of executing the algorithm:

1. The procedure in Algorithm 8.1 does not remove any parent from the parent set of any node and does not disturb the links between the tasks.
2. Theorem 8.3 assures us that any task will only be executed after all its parent tasks have been executed.

8.8 PERFORMANCE OF SERIAL AND PARALLEL ALGORITHMS ON PARALLEL COMPUTERS

The construction of Fig. 8.4 helps us identify all the algorithm parameters: W, D, and P.

The work parameter W is of course determined by counting all the nodes or tasks comprising the algorithm. From Fig. 8.4, we conclude that $W = 10$.

The parallelism of the algorithm is found by estimating the number of nodes assigned to each execution sequence.

$$P = \max \left(P_i \mid 0 \leq i < D \right). \tag{8.15}$$

From Fig. 8.1, we find that the parallelism of the algorithm is $P = 4$. Dedicating more than four processors will not result in any speedup of executing the algorithm.

From Fig. 8.4, we find the depth (D) as equal to the number of sequences required to complete the algorithm. From Fig. 8.4, we conclude that $D = 4$.

Using P parallel processors, the minimum algorithm latency is defined as the minimum time to execute the algorithm on P processors as given by

$$T_p(P) = D\tau_p, \tag{8.16}$$

where τ_p is the processor time required to execute one task or node in the dependence graph.

The time its takes a single processor (uniprocessor) to complete the algorithm would be

$$T_p(1) = W\tau_p. \tag{8.17}$$

The maximum speedup due to using parallel processing is estimated as

$$S(P) = \frac{T_p(1)}{T_p(P)} = \frac{W}{D}.$$ (8.18)

8.9 PROBLEMS

8.1. Suppose that the adjacency matrix $\mathbf{A}$ has row $i = 0$ and column $i = 0$. What does that say about task i?

8.2. Assume an ASA with $W = 5$ nodes or tasks and its depth is the maximum possible value.

(1) What is the maximum value of depth D?

(2) What is the structure of the adjacency matrix under this condition?

(3) What type of matrix is this adjacency matrix?

(4) What kind of matrix results if you raise the adjacency matrix to higher powers?

(5) Comment on the structure of $\mathbf{A}^k$.

(6) What is the maximum power of the adjacency matrix at which the matrix is zero?

8.3. Assume a cyclic sequential algorithm with $W = 5$ nodes or tasks and it has a maximum-length cycle.

(1) What is the maximum value of depth D?

(2) What is the structure of the adjacency matrix under this condition?

(3) What kind of matrix results if you raise the adjacency matrix to higher powers?

(4) What is the maximum power of the adjacency matrix at which the matrix is zero?

8.4. An NSPA algorithm consists of nine tasks that depend on each other as follows:

Task	Depends on tasks
1	NA
2	NA
3	NA
4	NA
5	NA
6	1, 2, 3, 4
7	5
8	1, 4
	6, 7, 8

(1) Draw the DAG for this algorithm.

(2) Assign tasks to the sequences.

(3) Identify the algorithm parameters D, P, and W.

Chapter 9

z-Transform Analysis

9.1 INTRODUCTION

Many digital signal processing (DSP) algorithms are studied using the z-transform where the signals being considered are discrete time signals. A discrete time signal is denoted by $x(n)$, where the variable n assumes nonnegative integer values 0, 1, … . The samples of a right-sided signal x are represented by the time sequence

$$x(n) = x(0) \quad x(1) \quad x(2) \quad \cdots. \tag{9.1}$$

The most common examples of these algorithms are found in digital filters such as one-dimensional (1-D) and multidimensional finite impulse response (FIR) filters and infinite impulse response (IIR) filters. We see examples of such algorithms also in multirate systems such as decimators, interpolators, and filter banks. z-Domain is used here to obtain different ways to implement a given algorithm using pipelines. The analysis in this chapter will proceed using as a working example the case of a 1-D FIR filter.

9.2 DEFINITION OF z-TRANSFORM

The one-sided z-transform of a discrete time signal $x(n)$ is given by the relation [78, 79]

$$X(z) = \sum_{n=0}^{\infty} x(n) z^{-n}, \tag{9.2}$$

where z is a complex number. We can write the z-transform in polynomial form:

$$X(z) = x(0) + x(1)z^{-1} + x(2)(z^{-1})^2 + \cdots. \tag{9.3}$$

We say that the signal $x(n)$ in the time domain has an equivalent representation, $X(z)$, in the z-domain.

The z-transform $X(z)$ of the sequence $x(n)$ is a polynomial of the different powers of z^{-1}, such that $x(i)$ is the coefficient of the ith power of z^{-1}.

Algorithms and Parallel Computing, by Fayez Gebali
Copyright © 2011 John Wiley & Sons, Inc.

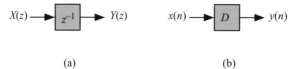

(a)   (b)

Figure 9.1   Schematic for introducing unit delay to a signal. (a) z-domain notation. (b) Time domain notation.

An important property of the z-transform is that the quantity z^{-1} in the z-domain corresponds to a time shift of 1 in the time domain. To prove this, we multiply $X(z)$ by z^{-1} to obtain a new signal, $Y(z)$:

$$
\begin{aligned}
Y(z) &= z^{-1}X(z) \\
&= 0z^0 + x(0)z^{-1} + x(1)z^{-2} + x(2)z^{-3} + \cdots.
\end{aligned}
\tag{9.4}
$$

The time domain representation $y(n)$ is found by using the coefficients of the above polynomial. At time i, we find that

$$
y(i) = x(i-1).
\tag{9.5}
$$

In effect, the term z^{-1} delayed each sample by one time step. We can write the relation between $x(n)$ and $y(n)$ as follows:

n	0	1	2	3	4	...
$x(n)$	$x(0)$	$x(1)$	$x(2)$	$x(3)$	$x(4)$	...
$y(n)$	0	$x(0)$	$x(1)$	$x(2)$	$x(3)$	...

Multiplication by z^{-1} has the effect of delaying the signal by one time step. We consider the term z^{-1} as a *unit delay operator*, and the relation between the signal $x(n)$ and $y(n)$ could be graphically shown in Fig. 9.1, where the box labeled z^{-1} denotes the unit delay. In real signals, the unit delay block is implemented by an edge-triggered D-type flip-flop when signal x is single-bit data or it could be a register if the signal x has multiple bits.

9.3   THE 1-D FIR DIGITAL FILTER ALGORITHM

We are now ready to illustrate how to use the z-transform to obtain systolic structures. We use 1-D FIR. The 1-D FIR digital filter algorithm can be expressed as the set of difference equations

$$
y(n) = \sum_{k=0}^{N-1} a(k)x(n-k),
\tag{9.6}
$$

where $a(k)$ is the filter coefficient and N is the filter length, which is the number of filter coefficients. Such an algorithm is a set of computations that is performed on input variables to produce output variables. The variables we might encounter are of three types: input, output, and intermediate or input/output (I/O) variables.

An input variable is one that has its instances appearing only on the right-hand side (RHS) of the equations of the algorithm. An output variable is one that has its instances appearing only on the left-hand side (LHS) of the algorithm. An intermediate variable is one that has its instances appearing on the right-hand side and left-hand side of the equations. In Eq. 9.6, the variable *y* is an output variable, and variables *x* and *a* are input variables.

We study this algorithm using the *z*-transform of each side of the above equation to obtain

$$Y = \sum_{i=0}^{N-1} a(i)z^{-i}X, \tag{9.7}$$

where *X* and *Y* are the *z*-transform of the signals *x*(*n*) and *y*(*n*), respectively. We can think of Eq. 9.7 as a polynomial expression in the different powers of z^{-1}.

9.4 SOFTWARE AND HARDWARE IMPLEMENTATIONS OF THE *z*-TRANSFORM

By using different polynomial evaluation techniques, the filter expression is converted to a set of recursive expressions that can be evaluated using multithreads or hardware systolic arrays. The *z*-domain technique is used for mapping the IIR filter algorithm onto tasks. These tasks, in turn, can be implemented by concurrent threads in software or by systolic arrays in hardware. The identification of tasks is described using the following steps:

1. The *z*-domain expression for the algorithm is converted to a set of recursive expressions. The data type in the recursive expressions determines the algorithm granularity. This will ultimately determine the computation load of the software tasks or the hardware complexity of the systolic array processing elements (PEs).

2. Each iteration in the recursive expression is assigned a task or a thread. In the case of hardware implementation, each iteration is assigned a PE.

3. The RHS of each expression defines the operations to be performed by each PE on the input variables.

4. The LHS of each expression defines the corresponding processor output.

5. The delay operators attached to each variable dictate the size of the buffers (amount of delay) within each processor.

6. The number of tasks, threads, or PEs is determined by the number of iterations required to produce the final result.

7. By ordering the shift and functional operators in the filter equations, different recursive expressions and, consequently, different structures are derived.

In the following sections, we illustrate how different FIR structures are obtained through the use of different techniques to evaluate the expression in Eq. 9.7.

9.5 DESIGN 1: USING HORNER'S RULE FOR BROADCAST INPUT AND PIPELINED OUTPUT

Suppose we want to evaluate the polynomial for a certain value of x:

$$p(x) = 2x^4 + 4x^3 + 5x^2 + 3x + 9. \tag{9.8}$$

We can rewrite the polynomial using Horner's scheme as

$$p(x) = (((2x + 4)x + 5)x + 3)x + 9. \tag{9.9}$$

Now the polynomial is recursively evaluated through the following steps:

1. Evaluate the innermost term $y_0 = 2x + 4$.
2. Evaluate the next innermost term $y_1 = y_0 x + 5$.
3. Evaluate the term $y_2 = y_1 x + 3$.
4. Evaluate the term $y_3 = y_2 x + 9$.
5. Evaluate $p(x)$ to y_3.

Now we apply Horner's' scheme to Eq. 9.7 to obtain the recursive expression

$$Y = a(0)X + z^{-1}[a(1)X + \cdots + z^{-1}[a(N-1)X]]\cdots]. \tag{9.10}$$

The above equation can be written as

$$Y_i = a(i)X + z^{-1}[Y_{i+1}] \qquad 0 < i < N \tag{9.11}$$
$$Y_0 = a(0)X + z^{-1}Y_1 \tag{9.12}$$
$$Y_N = 0 \tag{9.13}$$
$$Y = Y_0. \tag{9.14}$$

Based on the above iterative expression, task $T(i)$ computes Y_i in Eq. 9.11 using one multiplication and one addition:

$$Y_i = a(i)X + z^{-1}Y_{i+1}. \tag{9.15}$$

The output of $T(i)$ is saved then forwarded to $T(i-1)$ and the input to $T(N-1)$ is initialized to 0. Figure 9.2a shows the resulting directed acyclic graph (DAG) for an output sample, y. The figure can be replicated to show the different DAGs for other output samples. When these tasks are implemented in hardware, this DAG becomes the systolic array structure that implements the FIR filter. This structure is actually one of the classical canonic realizations of Eq. 9.7. Figure 9.2b shows the details of a processor element in case of hardware implementation of the DAG. Note that the input signal is broadcast to all tasks and the output is pipelined between the tasks.

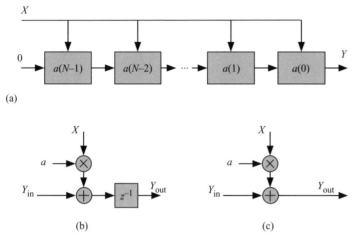

Figure 9.2   FIR digital filter software/hardware implementation with pipelined outputs.
(a) DAG for FIR digital filter. (b) Processor element details.

9.6 DESIGN 2: PIPELINED INPUT AND BROADCAST OUTPUT

In this design, we apply the delay operator to the input data samples to obtain delayed input data that we use to obtain our output:

$$Y = a(0)X + \left[a(1)z^{-1}(X)\right] + \left[a(2)z^{-1}\left(z^{-1}X\right)\right] +$$
$$\left[a(3)z^{-1}\left(z^{-2}X\right)\right] + \cdots + \left[a(N-1)z^{-1}\left(z^{-(N-2)}X\right)\right]. \tag{9.16}$$

The above equation can be converted to the iterative expressions

$$Y = \sum_{i=0}^{N-1} a(i)X_i$$
$$X_i = z^{-1}X_{i-1} \tag{9.17}$$
$$X_0 = X.$$

Figure 9.3a shows the resulting DAG for an output sample y. The figure can be replicated to show the different DAGs for other output samples. When these tasks are implemented in hardware, this DAG becomes the systolic array structure that implements the FIR filter. This structure is actually one of the classical canonic realizations of Eq. 9.7. Figure 9.3b shows the details of a processor element in case of hardware implementation of the DAG. Note that only the input is pipelined between the PE stages and the output is pipelined between the tasks. A problem with this design is that the output is not stored in a register between the PE stages. For a large filter order, the design slows down since the adders evaluating the outputs are all working in parallel.

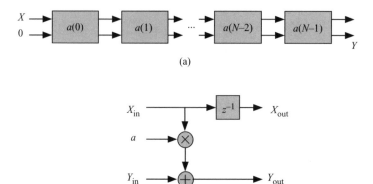

(a)

(b)

Figure 9.3   FIR digital filter software/hardware implementation with pipelined inputs.
(a) DAG for FIR digital filter. (b) Processor element details.

9.7   DESIGN 3: PIPELINED INPUT AND OUTPUT

A possible attractive implementation would be when both the input and output of each PE are stored in a register. This implies a fully pipelined design, which is potentially the fastest design possible. Assume without loss of generality that N is even. We can write Eq. 9.7 as

$$
\begin{aligned}
Y &= \left[a(0)X + a(1)z^{-1}X\right] + z^{-1}\left[a(2)z^{-1}X + a(3)z^{-2}X\right] + \cdots \\
&\quad z^{-(N/2-1)}\left[a(N-2)z^{-(N/2-1)}X + a(N-1)z^{-N/2}X\right] \\
&= \sum_{i=0}^{N/2-1} z^{-i}\left[a(2i)z^{-i}X + a(2i+1)z^{-(i+1)}X\right].
\end{aligned}
\tag{9.18}
$$

We perform an iteration on the inputs X in the above equation:

$$
X_i = z^{-1}X_{i-1} \qquad 1 \le i \le N/2
\tag{9.19}
$$

$$
X_0 = X,
\tag{9.20}
$$

and the output is given by

$$
Y = \sum_{i=0}^{N/2-1} z^{-i}\left[a(2i)X_i + a(2i+1)X_{i+1}\right].
\tag{9.21}
$$

The above equation can be written as the iteration

$$
Y_i = z^{-1}\left[a(2i)X_i + a(2i+1)X_{i+1} + Y_{i+1}\right] \qquad 0 < i < N/2
\tag{9.22}
$$

$$
Y_{N/2} = 0
\tag{9.23}
$$

$$
Y_0 = a(0)X_0 + a(1)X_1 + Y_1
\tag{9.24}
$$

$$
Y = Y_0.
\tag{9.25}
$$

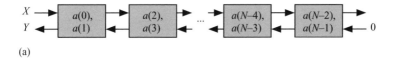

(a)

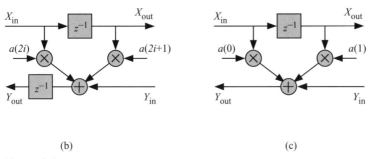

(b) (c)

Figure 9.4 FIR digital filter software/hardware implementation with pipelined inputs and outputs. (a) DAG for FIR digital filter. (b) Processor element details. (c) Leftmost processor element details.

Figure 9.4a shows the resulting DAG for an output sample, y. The figure can be replicated to show the different DAGs for other output samples. This is a new structure that has been reported in the literature by Sunder et al. [23]. Figure 9.4b shows the details of a processor element. Note that both the input and output are pipelined between the PE stages. Figure 9.4c shows the details of the first PE storing the filter coefficient $a(0)$ and $a(1)$. Note that the output is not stored in a register.

9.8 PROBLEMS

9.1. A recursive IIR filter is described by the set of difference equations

$$y(n) = \sum_{k=0}^{N-1} [a(k)x(n-k) - b(k)y(n-k)] \qquad n \le 0,$$

where $b(0) = 0$ and N is the filter length.

    (1) Derive the z-transform expression for the IIR filter.

    (2) Obtain different designs using the different methods used in this chapter.

9.2. Apply the z-domain technique to the 1-D correlation algorithm.

9.3. Apply the z-domain technique to the two-dimensional correlation algorithm.

9.4. Apply the z-domain technique to the three-dimensional correlation algorithm.

9.5. Apply the z-domain technique to the 1-D convolution algorithm.

9.6. Apply the z-domain technique to the two-dimensional convolution algorithm.

9.7. Apply the z-domain technique to the three-dimensional convolution algorithm.

Chapter 10

Dependence Graph Analysis

10.1 INTRODUCTION

The dependence graph technique is a very simple yet powerful approach for the design space exploration of regular iterative algorithms (RIAs). One restriction on this approach is that the algorithm must be two-dimensional (2-D) or three-dimensional (3-D) at the most so that the designer could visualize the resulting structures. Chapter 11 will extend this approach to algorithms having higher dimensions by replacing the dependence graph with a *convex hull* in the integer $\mathcal{Z}^n$ space. Many parallel algorithms have 2-D or 3-D dimensions such as one-dimensional (1-D) digital filters, 1-D decimators and interpolators, matrix–vector multiplication, and pattern matching algorithms. Furthermore, many types of higher-dimensional algorithms can be recursively broken down into lower-dimensional problems. For example, we can hierarchically decompose 2-D or 3-D digital filters into modules of 1-D filters. In this chapter, we illustrate how to obtain different multithreading and systolic structures for a given algorithm. We are going to use the 1-D finite impulse response (FIR) digital filter as a running example.

10.2 THE 1-D FIR DIGITAL FILTER ALGORITHM

The 1-D FIR digital filter algorithm is an example of a RIA that can be expressed as the set of difference equations

$$y(i) = \sum_{j=0}^{N-1} a(j)x(i-j) \qquad i \geq 0, \tag{10.1}$$

where $a(j)$ is the filter coefficient and N is the filter length. $y(i)$ is our output variable, which depends on the i index only. On the other hand, $a(i)$ is an input variable that depends on the j index only and $x(i-j)$ is another input variable that depends on both the i and j indices. The above equation describes two iterations. One iteration is over the index i and the other iteration is over the index j, which is to be repeated N times. The data type in the above equation determines the algorithm granularity. This will ultimately determine the computation load of each task, which

Algorithms and Parallel Computing, by Fayez Gebali
Copyright © 2011 John Wiley & Sons, Inc.

will translate to software threads or hardware systolic array processing elements (PEs).

10.3 THE DEPENDENCE GRAPH OF AN ALGORITHM

Traditionally, a RIA is represented as a directed acyclic graph (DAG) as was discussed in Chapters 1 and 8. The graph is composed of a set of nodes representing the tasks to be performed by the algorithm, and the directed edges represent the data flowing between the tasks from the task producing the data to the task that uses the data. In this chapter, we start our analysis not from the DAG but by constructing a dependence graph in an integer space Z^n, where n denotes the number of indices of the algorithm. Once we develop a dependence graph, we will derive several DAGs based on our scheduling techniques as we shall discuss here and in Section 10.5 and in Chapter 11. Stated more explicitly, an RIA can be represented by one dependence graph. The same algorithm could result in several DAGs.

Definition 10.1   A dependence graph is a set of nodes and edges in the integer domain Z^n. A node is a point $\mathbf{p} \in Z$ and represents the tasks to be performed at the given values of the indices. The edges show how the algorithm variables depend on the algorithm indices. The points lying on an edge indicate that the operations performed by nodes use the data carried by the edge.

Notice the definition of edges in the dependence graph. A dependence graph is not a DAG since the edges are not directed. Further, an edge in the dependence graph could be associated with an input, output, or input/output intermediate values depending on the variable.

Table 10.1   Comparing the Dependence Graph and the Directed Acyclic Graph (DAG)

Dependence graph	Directed acyclic graph (DAG)
The graph is really a *convex hull* ($\mathcal{D}$) in the integer space Z^n.	The graph is a 2-D drawing on a sheet of paper or on the computer screen.
Undirected edges.	Directed edges.
Edge represents how a variable depends on the algorithm indices.	The edge represents data flowing from the output of a task to the input of another task.
An edge covers many nodes and spans the entire computation domain $\mathcal{D}$.	An edge is confined between two tasks (nodes).
The node represents a task done by the algorithm.	The node represents a task done by the algorithm.
The node is located at a specific coordinate point in Z^n.	There is no significance as to where a node is located on the graph.
The execution sequence cannot be determined from inspecting the dependence graph.	The execution sequence can be determined by inspecting the DAG. The task producing a datum must be executed before the task consuming that datum.

Lemma 10.1 The dependence graph of an algorithm is unique to each algorithm since there is only one way to describe how the variables depend on the indices.

The advantage of this approach will become apparent in the following discussion and in Chapter 11 where we will be able to study the algorithm in terms of powerful linear algebra and computational geometry concepts. Table 10.1 compares the dependence graph defined above and the DAG defined in Chapter 1.

10.4 DERIVING THE DEPENDENCE GRAPH FOR AN ALGORITHM

We use Eq. 10.1 to study the dependence of the algorithm variables. Variable y is an output variable, and variables x and a are input variables. We note that the algorithm gives rise to a 2-D graph $\mathcal{D}$ since we have two indices, i and j. Since the dimensionality of $\mathcal{D}$ is low, it is best to visualize $\mathcal{D}$ using a dependence graph since this is easier for humans to analyze. We refer to any point in $\mathcal{D}$ as a vector $\mathbf{p}$

$$\mathbf{p} = \begin{bmatrix} i & j \end{bmatrix}^t. \tag{10.2}$$

For given values of the indices, the vector corresponds to a point in the $\mathcal{Z}^2$ space. The graph $\mathcal{D}$ covers the points $\mathbf{p}(i, j) \in \mathcal{D}$ where the range of the indices defines the boundaries of $\mathcal{D}$ as

$$0 \le i \quad \text{and} \quad 0 \le j < N. \tag{10.3}$$

Note that $\mathcal{D}$ extends to ∞ in the i direction, which defines an *extremal ray*.

10.4.1 Defining the Algorithm Variables in $\mathcal{D}$

We study in this section how to define the dependence of a variable in $\mathcal{D}$. Figure 10.1 shows the dependence graph of the 1-D FIR filter for the case $N = 4$. Let us consider the input variable a in Eq. 10.1. A specific instance of that variable such as $a(2)$, for example, implies that we have set the index j equal to 2. We can formally write this substitution as

$$j = 2. \tag{10.4}$$

The above equation is a straight line equation in $\mathcal{D}$ where $a(2)$ is represented by a horizontal line. Figure 10.1 shows the dependence graph of the three variables y, a, and x. The horizontal straight line actually defines a set of points in $e_a \in \mathcal{D}$, where all the points use the same instant of a to do their operations. Equation 10.4 can be written in matrix form as $\mathbf{Ap} = 2$ where $\mathbf{A}$ is the dependence matrix of variable e_a and $\mathbf{p}$ is any point. For our 2-D case, $\mathbf{A}$ becomes a row vector given by [0 1]. We call e_a the *subdomain* of variable a. This subdomain e_a is described by the *basis vector*

$$\mathbf{b}_a = \begin{bmatrix} 0 & 1 \end{bmatrix}^t. \tag{10.5}$$

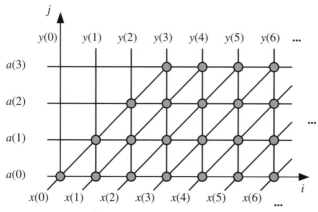

Figure 10.1   Dependence graph for the 1-D FIR filter for the case $N = 4$.

Chapter 11 will explain why this vector is a basis vector of the dependence matrix for a variable. We will need later to define the *nullvector* **b** associated with the basis vector of a variable. Variable a has the associated nullvector

$$\mathbf{e}_a = \begin{bmatrix} 1 & 0 \end{bmatrix}^t. \tag{10.6}$$

The two vectors $\mathbf{e}_a$ and $\mathbf{b}_a$ satisfy the equation:

$$\mathbf{e}_a^t \mathbf{b}_a = 0. \tag{10.7}$$

A specific value for variable $x(3)$ can similarly be described by the straight line equation

$$i - j = 3. \tag{10.8}$$

The associated nullvector $\mathbf{e}_x$ is

$$\mathbf{e}_x = \begin{bmatrix} 1 & 1 \end{bmatrix}^t. \tag{10.9}$$

This is represented by the diagonal lines in Fig. 10.1. The associated basis vector $\mathbf{b}_x$ is given by

$$\mathbf{b}_x = \begin{bmatrix} 1 & -1 \end{bmatrix}^t. \tag{10.10}$$

For output $y(5)$, the index dependence is given by the equation

$$i = 5, \tag{10.11}$$

and the nullvector $\mathbf{e}_y$ is given by

$$\mathbf{e}_y = \begin{bmatrix} 0 & 1 \end{bmatrix}^t. \tag{10.12}$$

The basis vector $\mathbf{b}_y$ encompasses all the points in $\mathcal{D}$ that produce results to be used to calculate a specific instance of y. The associated basis vector is given by

$$\mathbf{b}_y = \begin{bmatrix} 1 & 0 \end{bmatrix}^t. \tag{10.13}$$

A node in $\mathcal{D}$ represents the operations to be performed by each iteration. In our example, only one operation is to be performed by an iteration:

$$y_{\text{temp}}(i, j) = y_{\text{temp}}(i, j-1) + a(j)x(i-j). \tag{10.14}$$

Since the addition operation is associative, we could have written the above iterative step as

$$y_{\text{temp}}(i, j) = y_{\text{temp}}(i, j+1) + a(j)x(i-j). \tag{10.15}$$

Having derived the dependence graph for the given algorithm, we now need to synchronize the operation of each node. We need to know how to assign time values to each node dictating when the operation in each node is to be performed. This is called *node scheduling*. We also need to assign each node to a unique hardware processor or thread in a multicore, multithreaded implementation. This is called *node projection*.

10.5 THE SCHEDULING FUNCTION FOR THE 1-D FIR FILTER

This section discusses how to execute the tasks in the dependence graph in stages of execution. At each stage, a group of the tasks gets executed followed by tasks in the next stage and so on. We use an affine scheduling function such that any point $\mathbf{p} = [i\ j]^t \in \mathcal{D}$ is associated with the time value

$$t(\mathbf{p}) = \mathbf{s}\,\mathbf{p} - s \tag{10.16}$$
$$= i\,s_1 + j\,s_2 - s, \tag{10.17}$$

where $\mathbf{s} = [s_1\ s_2]$ is the scheduling vector and s is a scalar constant. Typically, the constant $s = 0$ since the domain $\mathcal{D}$ is typically in the first quadrant, the point at the origin $\mathbf{p}(0, 0) \in \mathcal{D}$ and $\mathbf{s}$ usually has positive components.

The main purpose of the scheduling function is to divide the tasks in the dependence graph into stages that are executed sequentially. Several tasks will be executed in parallel at each stage. Effectively, the scheduling function will convert the dependence graph into a DAG, and more specifically, it will convert it into a serial–parallel algorithm (SPA) as Theorems 11.2 and 11.3 will prove in Chapter 11. The parallel tasks could be implemented using concurrent threads or parallel processors for software or hardware implementations, respectively. The different stages of the SPA are accomplished using barriers or clocks for software or hardware implementations, respectively.

The scheduling function determines the computational load to be performed by the computing system at each stage of execution. This is a subtle but very important by-product. Also, we shall see that the linear or affine scheduling function affords us little control on the amount of that work. We will introduce nonlinear scheduling techniques that will allow us to control the total work assigned to the system during each time step. Another effect of the scheduling function is the fact that dependencies between tasks will be created and that interthread and interprocessor communication can thus be determined.

10.5.1   From Dependence Graph to DAG/SPA

The scheduling function will convert the dependence graph to a DAG or SPA since it will give an order of executing the nodes/tasks of the graph by assigning to each node a unique time index value. Nodes with equal time index values are said to belong to the same equitemporal zone. Figure 10.1 illustrates the dependence graph of the 1-D FIR filter. Figure 10.2 shows how this graph is transformed to a DAG using the affine scheduling function.

The scheduling function will also assign a direction to the algorithm variables, and the graph edges will become directed edges. An edge connecting two nodes in adjacent equitemporal zones will become directed from the zone with a lower time index to the zone with a higher time index. In that sense, this data will become *pipelined* data.

If the edge connects two nodes in the same equitemporal zone, then there is no direction associated with the edge since the data are available to all nodes at the same time. In that sense, this data will become *broadcast* data. Data broadcast could be accomplished in hardware using a system-wide bus or an interconnection network capable of broadcasting a single data item to all the PEs. In software, data broadcast could be accomplished by using a broadcast message to all threads or by using a shared memory.

An affine scheduling function should satisfy several conditions in order to be a valid scheduling function:

$$\mathbf{s}\,\mathbf{p} \geq s \quad \mathbf{p} \in D \quad \text{positive time values} \tag{10.18}$$

$$\mathbf{s}\,\mathbf{e} = 0 \quad \text{broadcast restriction} \tag{10.19}$$

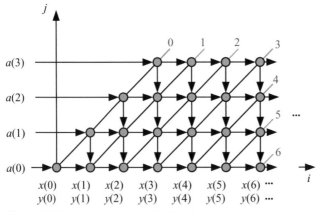

Figure 10.2   DAG for the 1-D FIR filter for the case $N = 4$.

$$\mathbf{s\,f} \neq 0 \quad \text{pipelining restriction} \qquad (10.20)$$
$$\mathbf{s\,d} \neq 0 \quad \text{projection restriction} \qquad (10.21)$$
$$\mathbf{s\,R} > 0 \quad \text{causality,} \qquad (10.22)$$

where

e   broadcast nullvector
f   pipelining nullvector
d   projection direction (discussed later)
R   any extremal ray in our domain

10.5.2 Broadcasting a Variable

Definition 10.2   A variable is broadcast when all the nodes in $\mathcal{D}$ that belong to its subdomain are assigned the same time value.

Assume two points, $\mathbf{p}_1$ and $\mathbf{p}_2$, lie in the subdomain of a variable. We can write

$$\mathbf{p}_2 = \mathbf{p}_1 + \alpha\mathbf{e}_v, \qquad (10.23)$$

where $\alpha \neq 0$ is some integer constant and $\mathbf{e}_v$ is the nullvector for the subdomain of the variable. If the two points are to be assigned the same time value, we must have

$$t(\mathbf{p}_1) = t(\mathbf{p}_2) \qquad (10.24)$$
$$\mathbf{sp}_1 - s = \mathbf{sp}_2 - s \qquad (10.25)$$
$$\mathbf{s}(\mathbf{p}_1 - \mathbf{p}_2) = 0. \qquad (10.26)$$

From Eqs. 10.23 and 10.26, we can write

$$\mathbf{se}_v = 0. \qquad (10.27)$$

Thus, to broadcast a variable, we must ensure that the scheduling vector is orthogonal to the nullvector of the variable. And we have as a condition for broadcasting a variable

$$\mathbf{s}^t \propto \mathbf{b}_v, \qquad (10.28)$$

where $\mathbf{b}_v$ is the basis vector for the broadcast subdomain of the variable. In other words, a variable is broadcast when the scheduling vector is parallel to the basis vector and is orthogonal to the nullvector associated with the variable in question.

10.5.3 Pipelining a Variable

Pipelining is the opposite of broadcasting, as can be checked out by comparing Definition 10.2 with the following definition:

Definition 10.3   A variable is pipelined when all the nodes in $\mathcal{D}$ that belong to its subdomain are assigned different time values.

Assume two points, $\mathbf{p}_1$ and $\mathbf{p}_2$, lie in the subdomain of a variable. The times associated with each point are expressed as

$$t(\mathbf{p}_1) \neq t(\mathbf{p}_2) \tag{10.29}$$
$$\mathbf{sp}_1 - s = \mathbf{sp}_2 - s \tag{10.30}$$
$$s(\mathbf{p}_1 - \mathbf{p}_2) \neq 0. \tag{10.31}$$

Thus, to pipeline a variable, we must ensure that the scheduling vector is not orthogonal to the nullvector of the variable.

From Eqs. 10.23 and 10.31, we can write

$$\mathbf{se}_v \neq 0, \tag{10.32}$$

where $\mathbf{e}_v$ is the nullvector for the subdomain of the variable. And we have as a condition for broadcasting a variable

$$\mathbf{sb}_v = 0, \tag{10.33}$$

where $\mathbf{b}_v$ is the basis vector for the broadcast subdomain of the variable. In other words, a variable is pipelined when the scheduling vector is not orthogonal to the null vector and is orthogonal to the basis vector associated with the variable in question.

10.5.4 Determining the Scheduling Function

In order to determine the components of $\mathbf{s}$, we turn our attention to the filter inputs x. The input data are assumed to be supplied to our array at consecutive time steps. From the dependence graph, we see that samples $x(i)$ and $x(i + 1)$ could be supplied at points $\mathbf{p}_1 = [i\ 0]^t$ and $\mathbf{p}_2 = [i + 1\ 0]^t$, respectively. The time steps associated with these two input samples are given from Eq. 10.17 by

$$t(\mathbf{p}_1) = i\, s_1 \tag{10.34}$$
$$t(\mathbf{p}_2) = (i+1)\, s_1. \tag{10.35}$$

Assuming that the consecutive inputs arrive at each time step, we have $t(\mathbf{p}_2) - t(\mathbf{p}_1) = 1$, and we must have

$$\mathbf{s} = [1\quad s_2]. \tag{10.36}$$

So now we know one component of the scheduling vector based on input data timing requirements. Possible valid scheduling functions could be

$$\mathbf{s} = \begin{cases} [1 & -1] \\ [1 & 0] \\ [1 & 1]. \end{cases} \tag{10.37}$$

All the above timing schedules are valid and have different implications on the timing of the output and partial results. The first scheduling vector results in broadcast input and pipelined output. The second scheduling vector results in the broadcast of the output variable y and could produce design 2, which was discussed in Chapter 9. The third scheduling vector results in pipelined input and output and could produce design 3, which was discussed in Chapter 9.

Let us investigate the scheduling vector $\mathbf{s} = [1 \ -1]$. This choice implies that

$$\mathbf{s}\,\mathbf{e}_x = 0, \tag{10.38}$$

which results in broadcast x samples. Based on our choice for this time function, we obtain the DAG/SPA shown in Fig. 10.2. The gray lines indicate *equitemporal* planes, or they could be thought of as representing the different stages of the SPA. All nodes lying on the same gray line execute their operations at the time indicated beside the line. The gray numbers indicate the times associated with each stage. Notice from the figure that all the input and output signals are pipelined as indicated by the arrows connecting the graph nodes. At this stage, we know the timing of the operations to be performed by each node. In other words, we know the *total computation load* to be performed by our system at any given time step or stage of execution. We do not know how many threads or PEs are required to do this work. This is the subject of Section 10.6. Of course, inspection of the DAG could give us an idea as to how many threads/tasks should be executed at each stage or equitemporal plane. We could also figure out the input and output data required at each stage.

10.5.5 Limitations of Linear Thread/Task Scheduling

The scheduling function of the previous section is simple but not too flexible. We do not have control over how much calculations could be performed globally by the parallel computing system at a given time step by the multiprocessing system. The workload might be light or it might exceed the processing capabilities of the system.

Figure 10.3 shows the node scheduling based on different choices for the scheduling function $\boldsymbol{\sigma}$. Gray lines indicate order of execution of the operations. The figure only shows the calculations performed by the FIR algorithm at any given time step. Each column in the figure corresponds to the nodes required to produce one output sample.

Figure 10.3a shows the equitemporal planes for $\mathbf{s} = [1 \ 0]$. In that case, point (i, j) in $\mathcal{D}$ will be associated with the time value i. Thus, all the calculations required to produce an output sample are performed in the same time, which is desirable. However, we note that the different output samples are executed serially at different time steps. We might as well have implemented the filter on one processor. The maximum workload done at each time step is equal to $N = 4$, the filter length where the unit of workload is a simple multiply accumulate operation.

Figure 10.3b shows the equitemporal planes for $\mathbf{s} = [0 \ 1]$. In that case, point (i, j) in $\mathcal{D}$ will be associated with the time value j. At any time step, the partial results

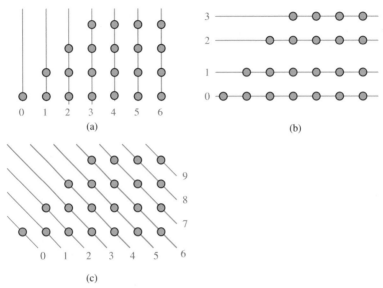

Figure 10.3 Scheduling options for the 1-D FIR filter for the case $N = 4$. Gray lines indicate order of execution of the operations. (a) When the scheduling function is $\mathbf{s} = [1\ 0]$. (b) When the scheduling function is $\mathbf{s} = [0\ 1]$. (c) When the scheduling function is $\mathbf{s} = [1\ 1]$.

of all the output samples are produced. The workload now is equal to the number of desired output samples, which could be very large. Further, all the input samples must be available for the calculations. This scheduling option is the least desirable or practical.

Figure 10.3c shows the equitemporal planes for $\mathbf{s} = [1\ 1]$. In that case, point (i, j) in $\mathcal{D}$ will be associated with the time value $i + j$. At most, only N threads can operate simultaneously, but each thread only performs a simple operation. We do not have means to match the threads to the available cores since the function schedules N threads, which depends on the parameters of the filter used. The maximum workload done at each time step is equal to $N = 4$, the filter length. At any time step, partial results of N output samples are produced and one complete output result is produced.

10.5.6 Nonlinear Scheduling Operation

The scheduling vector $\mathbf{s}_1$ of Fig. 10.3a produces one output sample at a time. We modify the scheduling function to a nonlinear schedule as follows:

$$t(\mathbf{p}) = \mathrm{floor}\left(\frac{\mathbf{sp}}{n}\right), \tag{10.39}$$

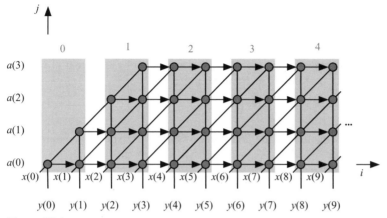

Figure 10.4 Allocation of nodes to different equitemporal domains using nonlinear scheduling. The shaded areas indicate the different domains and the grayed numbers indicate the order of execution of the nodes for the case $N = 4$ and $n = 2$.

where the floor(.) function finds the largest integer smaller than the division operation and n is the level of data aggregation. When $n = 2$, we have two input or output data being fed or extracted from our system at each time step.

Now we can schedule as many nodes as we want to execute at the same time. Figure 10.4 shows the scheduling of nodes using Eq. 10.39 with $n = 2$. The gray areas indicate the different equitemporal regions and the gray numbers indicate the order of execution of the nodes. The global computation workload w_{total} at any time step is given by

$$w_{\text{total}} = nN. \tag{10.40}$$

10.6 NODE PROJECTION OPERATION

In Section 10.5, we discussed how we can associate a time step value to each point in the computation domain $\mathcal{D}$. In this section, we discuss how we can assign a processor or a thread to each point in the DAG. The combination of node scheduling and node projection will result in determination of the work done by each task at any given time step. The choice of the projection operation will impact the interthread or interprocessor communication, which is a very crucial factor in determining the speed of the execution of the algorithm.

The projection operation transforms our DAG in $\mathcal{Z}^n$ to a projected DAG in an integer space of reduced dimensionality $\mathcal{Z}^k$ where $k < n$. We label the new projected acyclic graph $\overline{\text{DAG}}$. Central to the projection operation is the *projection matrix* **P** and the *projection direction* **d**.

A subtle point to be noticed in the projection operation is that it controls the amount of workload assigned to each software thread for a multithreaded implementation or the workload assigned to each PE for a systolic array implementation. Just like affine scheduling, affine projection affords us little control over the workload assigned to a thread or a PE. However, nonlinear projection operations will give us very good control over the workload assigned to each thread or PE.

Definition 10.4   A projection matrix $\mathbf{P}$ is a $k \times n$ matrix of rank k that provides a many-to-one projection of points in $\mathcal{Z}^n$ to points in $\mathcal{Z}^k$

$$\bar{\mathbf{p}} = \mathbf{Pp}. \tag{10.41}$$

For our case, the *DAG* lies in the 2-D integer space $\mathcal{Z}^2$. The projection matrix becomes a row vector

$$\mathbf{P} = \begin{bmatrix} P_1 & P_2 \end{bmatrix}, \tag{10.42}$$

and a point $\mathbf{p} = [i\ j]^t$ will map to the point

$$\bar{p} = iP_1 + jP_2.$$

Definition 10.5   A projection direction d is a nullvector of the projection matrix $\mathbf{P}$.

Proof of the above definition is found in Chapter 11. For our case, the nullvector associated with the projection matrix is given by

$$\mathbf{d} = \begin{bmatrix} P_2 & -P_1 \end{bmatrix}^t. \tag{10.43}$$

Conversely, if we start by selecting a certain projection direction $\mathbf{d} = [d_1\ d_2]^t$, the associated projection matrix becomes $\mathbf{P} = [d_2\ -d_1]$.

Points or nodes lying along the projection direction will be mapped onto the same point in the new projected DAG ($\overline{\text{DAG}}$). A restriction on the projection direction $\mathbf{d}$ is that two points that lie on an equitemporal plane should not map to the same point in $\overline{\text{DAG}}$. This can be expressed as

$$\mathbf{s}\,\mathbf{d} \neq 0. \tag{10.44}$$

The projection direction should not be orthogonal to the scheduling vector since this is contradictory to the requirements of parallelism—namely, all nodes executing simultaneously are assigned to the same thread or PE.

As a result of the above equation, choosing a particular scheduling vector restricts our options for valid projection directions. Let us work with our choice for the scheduling vector of $\mathbf{s} = [1\ -1]$. Therefore, we have three possible choices for projection directions:

$$\mathbf{d}_1 = \begin{bmatrix} 1 & 0 \end{bmatrix}^t \tag{10.45}$$
$$\mathbf{d}_2 = \begin{bmatrix} 0 & 1 \end{bmatrix}^t \tag{10.46}$$
$$\mathbf{d}_3 = \begin{bmatrix} 1 & -1 \end{bmatrix}^t. \tag{10.47}$$

All these projection directions are not orthogonal to our scheduling vector.

10.7 NONLINEAR PROJECTION OPERATION

The linear projection operation in combination with the scheduling function determines the workload assigned to each thread or PE at any given time step. The linear projection operation is simple but not too flexible. We do not have control over how much calculations could be performed by each thread or PE at a given time step.

We modify the linear projection operation as follows:

$$\tilde{\mathbf{p}} = \text{floor}\left(\frac{\mathbf{Pp}}{m}\right),$$

(10.48)

where m is the desired number of points in $\overline{\text{DAG}}$ that will be allocated to one thread or PE. The floor(.) function finds the largest integer smaller than the division operation. We can therefore control the workload allocated to each thread or PE per time step as

$$w_{\text{thread}} = m.$$

(10.49)

For a concrete example, assume that our scheduling vector and projection direction are given by

$$\mathbf{s} = [1 \quad 0]$$

(10.50)

$$\mathbf{d} = [1 \quad 0]^t.$$

(10.51)

We also assume that $N = 1,024$, $n = 2$, and $m = 8$. In that case, the global workload per time step to be done by all threads is equal to $nN = 2,048$, and in that case, the output samples will be allocated to threads according to Table 10.2.

10.7.1 Using Concurrency Platforms

At this stage, the programmer is able to determine the execution order of the threads and the timing of the algorithm variables by inspecting the DAG. With this knowledge, the programmer can determine the locations of required locks and barriers in the program. By counting the number of nodes that belong to each equitemporal zone, the programmer can determine the required number of threads to be created. The speedup of the algorithm, and other performance parameters can also be

Table 10.2 Allocation of 1-D FIR Filter Output Samples to Threads Using a Nonlinear Projection Operation When $m = 8$ Output Samples Are Allocated to One Thread

Thread ID	Output samples produced by each thread	Input data required by each thread
0	$y(0)\ldots y(7)$	$x(0)\ldots x(8-N)$
1	$y(8)\ldots y(15)$	$x(8)\ldots x(16-N)$
3	$y(16)\ldots y(23)$	$x(16)\ldots x(24-N)$
4	$y(24)\ldots y(31)$	$x(24)\ldots x(32-N)$

determined. The following section illustrates how this information can be *automatically* obtained instead of inspecting the DAG of the algorithm.

10.8 SOFTWARE AND HARDWARE IMPLEMENTATIONS OF THE DAG TECHNIQUE

By using different scheduling functions and projection directions, the DAG is converted to a set of tasks that can be executed concurrently in software threads or in hardware systolic arrays. The technique maps the DAG of the algorithm to simultaneous multithreaded (SMT) tasks or single instruction multiple data stream (SIMD)/systolic hardware. In the following section, we shall refer to the computations at each node as *tasks*, knowing that tasks translate to threads in software or PEs in hardware. In all cases discussed in this section we choose the scheduling function $\mathbf{s} = [1 \ {-}1]$.

10.8.1 Design 1: Projection Direction $\mathbf{d}_1 = [1 \ 0]^t$

Since the chosen projection direction is along the extremal ray direction, the number of concurrent tasks will be finite. A point $\mathbf{p} = [i \ j]^t \in \mathrm{DAG}$ maps to the point $\tilde{\mathbf{p}} = j$. The pipeline is shown in Fig. 10.5. Task $T(i)$ stores the filter coefficient $a(i)$. The filter output is obtained from the rightmost PE. Notice that both inputs x and y are pipelined between the PEs. Some explanation of notation in the $\overline{\mathrm{DAG}}$ is in order. An arrow connecting tasks $T(i)$ to task $T(j)$ indicates that the output data of $T(i)$ is stored in memory and is made available to $T(j)$ at the *next* time step. An arrow exiting a task indicates calculations or data to be completed by the task at

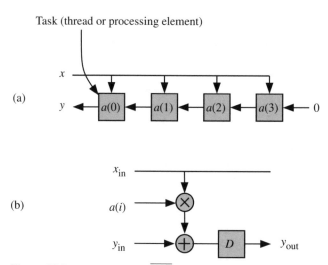

Figure 10.5 Projected DAG ($\overline{\mathrm{DAG}}$) for the 1-D FIR filter for the case $N = 4$, $\mathbf{s} = [1 \ {-}1]$, and $\mathbf{d}_1 = [1 \ 0]^t$. (a) The resulting $\overline{\mathrm{DAG}}$. (b) The task processing details.

the end of the time step. An arrow entering a task indicates data read at the start of the time step.

10.8.2   Design 2: Projection Direction $d_2 = [0\ -1]^t$

A point $\mathbf{p} = [i\ j]^t \in D$ maps to the point $\tilde{\mathbf{p}} = i$. The pipeline is shown in Fig. 10.6. Each task stores all the filter coefficients locally to reduce intertask communication requirements. $T(i)$ accepts input samples $x(i - N + 1)$ to $x(i)$ from the shared memory or input data bus at time step i. $T(i)$ produces the output $y_{out}(i)$ at time step i and stores that data in memory or sends that signal onto the output data bus. The number of tasks is infinite since our projection direction did not coincide with the ray direction. However, each task is active for the duration of N time steps. The task activities at different time steps are shown in Fig. 10.7. The timing diagram thus indicates that

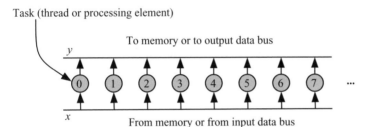

Figure 10.6   Projected DAG ($\overline{\text{DAG}}$) for the 1-D FIR filter for the case $N = 4$, $\mathbf{s} = [1\ -1]$, and $\mathbf{d}_2 = [0\ -1]^t$.

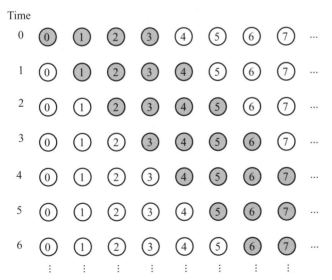

Figure 10.7   Task activity for the 1-D FIR filter for the case $N = 4$, $\mathbf{s} = [1\ -1]$, and $\mathbf{d}_2 = [0\ -1]^t$.

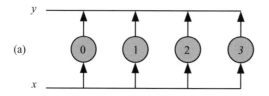

(a)

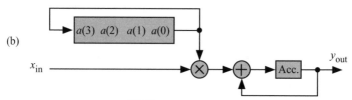

(b)

Figure 10.8 The reduced $\overline{\text{DAG}}$ for the 1-D FIR filter for $N = 4$, $\mathbf{s} = [1\ -1]$, and $\mathbf{d}_2 = [0\ -1]'$. (a) The $\overline{\text{DAG}}$. (b) The task processing details.

we could merge the tasks. Therefore, we relabel the task indices such that $T(i)$ maps to $T(j)$, such that

$$j = i \quad \text{mod } N. \tag{10.52}$$

The reduced $\overline{\text{DAG}}$ is shown in Fig. 10.8.

10.9 PROBLEMS

10.1. Given are two causal signals $h(n)$ and $x(n)$, which are N samples each. Their cross-correlation is given by the equation

$$r_{hx}(n) = \frac{1}{N} \sum_{k=0}^{N-1} h(k)x(k+n),$$

where $n = 0, 1, \ldots, N-1$. Assuming $N = 5$:

    (1) Draw the dependence graph for the algorithm where the index n is to be drawn on the horizontal axis and the index k is to be drawn on the vertical axis.

    (2) Write down nullvectors and basis vectors for the algorithm variables.

    (3) Find possible simple scheduling functions for this algorithm and discuss the implication of each function on the pipelining and broadcasting of the variables.

    (4) Choose one scheduling function and draw the associated DAG for the algorithm.

    (5) Show possible nonlinear scheduling options for the scheduling function you chose in part 4.

    (6) Find possible projection directions corresponding to the scheduling function you chose in part 4.

(7) Choose one projection direction and draw the resulting $\overline{\text{DAG}}$ and the PE details for systolic array implementation.

(8) Show possible nonlinear projection options for the projection direction you chose in part 7.

10.2. The autocorrelation is obtained when, in the problem, we replace signal $h(n)$ with $x(n)$. Study the problem for this situation.

10.3. Apply the dependence graph technique to the sparse matrix–vector multiplication algorithm.

10.4. Apply the dependence graph technique to the sparse matrix–matrix multiplication algorithm.

10.5. Draw the dependence graph of the discrete Hilber transform (DHT) and design multithreaded and systolic processor structures.

10.6. Draw the dependence graph of the inverse discrete Hilber transform (IDHT) and design multithreaded and systolic processor structures.

Chapter 11

Computational Geometry Analysis

11.1 INTRODUCTION

The techniques we have discussed so far for regular iterative algorithms (RIAs) are based on the availability of the dependence graph [80, 81]. At best, a dependence graph can handle algorithms that can be represented by computational domains of dimension 3 at most. In the case of attempting to implement a three-dimensional (3-D) filter on parallel hardware or using multithreading, the resulting dependence graph would be representable in a six-dimensional space. Such a dependence graph becomes very complex.

In this chapter, we study the RIA by studying each variable in the algorithm *separately* using concepts in computational geometry and matrix algebra. The variables we might encounter are of three types: input, output, and intermediate or input/output variables. An input variable is one that has its instances appearing only on the right-hand side (RHS) of the equations of the algorithm. An output variable is one that has its instances appearing only on the left-hand side (LHS) of the algorithm. An intermediate variable is one that has its instances appearing both on the LHS and on the RHS of the equations of the algorithm such that the variable has different index dependences on both sides of the iteration statements. We consider an intermediate variable as being both an input or output variable with different index dependencies for each instance. Using this artifact, we reduce our set of variables to input and output variables only.

The analysis in this chapter will proceed using as a working example the case of matrix multiplication.

11.2 MATRIX MULTIPLICATION ALGORITHM

Assume we are given two compatible matrices $\mathbf{M}_2$ and $\mathbf{M}_3$ of dimensions $I \times K$ and $K \times J$, respectively. Their product is matrix $\mathbf{M}_1$ of dimension $I \times J$. The matrix multiplication algorithm can be expressed as

Algorithms and Parallel Computing, by Fayez Gebali
Copyright © 2011 John Wiley & Sons, Inc.

$$\mathbf{M}_1(i,j) = \sum_{k=0}^{K-1} \mathbf{M}_2(i,k)\, \mathbf{M}_3(k,j) \qquad 0 \le i < I, \quad 0 \le j < J. \tag{11.1}$$

This equation can be expressed in any *serial algorithm* (i.e., any computer code) as three nested loops. An outer loop iterates over the index i; the next inner loop iterates over the index j. The innermost loop iterates over the index k.

Variable $\mathbf{M}_1$ in the above equation is an output variable, while variables $\mathbf{M}_2$ and $\mathbf{M}_3$ are input variables. The above matrix multiplication algorithm has three indices: i, j, and k, and we can think of these indices as coordinates of a point in a 3-D volume. We organize our indices in the form of a vector:

$$\mathbf{p} = [i \quad j \quad k]^t; \tag{11.2}$$

for given values of the indices, the vector corresponds to a point in the Z^3 space [9].

11.3 THE 3-D DEPENDENCE GRAPH AND COMPUTATION DOMAIN $\mathcal{D}$

As we mentioned above, this chapter starts by studying a multidimensional computation domain $\mathcal{D}$ rather than a dependence graph. We shift our focus from graphs, nodes, and edges to *convex hulls* in Z^3 as will be explained below.

The recursive algorithm in Eq. 11.1 is an equation involving the indexed variables $v_i(\mathbf{p})$, where $i = 1, 2, 3$ to account for one output variable, M_1, and two input variables, M_2 and M_3, in Eq. 11.1. The boundaries of the Z^3 space describing our algorithm are defined by the restrictions imposed on the values of the indices as will be discussed in the following subsection. The collection of points within imposed boundaries defines the *computation domain* $\mathcal{D}$. The dimension of $\mathcal{D}$ is $n = 3$, which is the number of indices in the algorithm.

11.3.1 3-D Domain Boundaries

The 3-D computation domain extends in the index space over a volume defined by the limits imposed on the index vector $\mathbf{p}$. We define the computation domain $\mathcal{D}$ as the set of points in the 3-D space that satisfies certain criteria [82]:

$$\mathcal{D} = \{\mathbf{p} \in Z^n : \Psi_i \mathbf{p} \le \psi_i, \Lambda_j \mathbf{p} \ge \lambda_j\}, \tag{11.3}$$

with $i = 1, 2, 3$ and $j = 1, 2, 3$.

The row vectors Ψ_i and ψ_i define the upper hull of $\mathcal{D}$ [82–85]. Similarly, the row vectors Λ_j and λ_j define the lower hull of $\mathcal{D}$. These two hulls describe the *surfaces* defining $\mathcal{D}$. To give a tasty example, consider $\mathcal{D}$ as an ice cream cone. In that case, the upper hull represents the chocolate coating on top. The lower hull represents the cone or wafer. The points of the computational domain correspond to the ice cream.

From Eq. 11.1, the upper hull of our matrix algorithm is described by the equations of several planes in the 3-D space:

$$[1 \quad 0 \quad 0]\mathbf{p} \le I-1 \tag{11.4}$$
$$[0 \quad 1 \quad 0]\mathbf{p} \le J-1 \tag{11.5}$$
$$[0 \quad 0 \quad 1]\mathbf{p} \le K-1. \tag{11.6}$$

The above three inequalities simply state that the upper bound on points in $\mathcal{D}$ is described by the equations of planes defining the top surfaces of $\mathcal{D}$:

$$i \le I-1 \tag{11.7}$$
$$j \le J-1 \tag{11.8}$$
$$k \le K-1. \tag{11.9}$$

The first inequality describes a plane perpendicular to the i-axis and so on for the other two equations.

From Eq. 11.1, the lower hull of our matrix algorithm is described by the equations of several planes in the 3-D space:

$$[1 \quad 0 \quad 0]\mathbf{p} \ge 0 \tag{11.10}$$
$$[0 \quad 1 \quad 0]\mathbf{p} \ge 0 \tag{11.11}$$
$$[0 \quad 0 \quad 1]\mathbf{p} \ge 0. \tag{11.12}$$

The above three inequalities simply state that the lower bound on points in $\mathcal{D}$ is described by the equations of planes defining the bottom surfaces of $\mathcal{D}$:

$$i \ge 0 \tag{11.13}$$
$$j \ge 0 \tag{11.14}$$
$$k \ge 0. \tag{11.15}$$

Figure 11.1 shows the computation domain $\mathcal{D}$ for the matrix multiplication algorithm. $\mathcal{D}$ is a convex hull, which is another way of saying it is a volume in the 3-D space that has upper and lower bounds on its index values.

Note that the limits imposed on the algorithm indices define the computation domain $\mathcal{D}$ in a direct and simple manner. Earlier approaches used the domain vertices and "extremal rays" to define $\mathcal{D}$. However, in most cases, these quantities are simply not directly available.

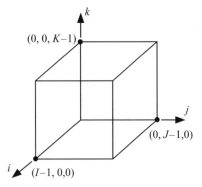

Figure 11.1   The 3-D computation domain $\mathcal{D}$ for the matrix multiplication algorithm.

In the design of multiprocessors or multithreaded applications, it is important to determine the regions where and when data will be fed or extracted. This is related to the study of the facets and vertices of $\mathcal{D}$ as explained in the following two sections.

11.4   THE FACETS AND VERTICES OF $\mathcal{D}$

A point $\mathbf{p} \in \mathcal{D}$ lies on the kth facet (or surface) of the upper hull if it satisfies the equation

$$\Psi_k \mathbf{p} = \psi_k. \tag{11.16}$$

This facet is of dimension 2 (i.e., $n - 1$). We can generalize by saying that multiplying the point $\mathbf{p}$ by a matrix of rank 1 results in the set of points that lies on a facet of dimension 1 less than n, the dimension of $\mathcal{D}$. Similarly, a point $\mathbf{p} \in \mathcal{D}$ lies on the kth facet of the lower hull if it satisfies the equation

$$\Lambda_k \mathbf{p} = \lambda_k. \tag{11.17}$$

We can extend the above argument and find all the points that satisfy two upper hull boundary conditions. Let us choose the two boundary conditions Ψ_1 and Ψ_2. Point $\mathbf{p} \in \mathcal{D}$ lies on the 1-2 facet of the upper hull when it satisfies the equation

$$\begin{bmatrix} \Psi_1 \\ \Psi_2 \end{bmatrix} \mathbf{p} = \begin{bmatrix} \psi_1 \\ \psi_2 \end{bmatrix}. \tag{11.18}$$

This facet is of dimension 1 (i.e., $n - 2$) since $\Psi_1 \neq \Psi_2$ by choice, which produces a matrix of rank 2. Since this facet is of dimension 1, it is actually a straight line describing the intersection of face 1 with face 2 of $\mathcal{D}$. This is an edge of the cubic volume.

Similarly, a domain point $\mathbf{p} \in \mathcal{D}$ lies on the 1-2 facet of the lower hull satisfies the equation

$$\begin{bmatrix} \Lambda_1 \\ \Lambda_2 \end{bmatrix} \mathbf{p} = \begin{bmatrix} \lambda_1 \\ \lambda_2 \end{bmatrix}. \tag{11.19}$$

This facet is of dimension 1 (i.e., $n - 2$) since $\Lambda_1 \neq \Lambda_2$ by choice. It is also possible to find the i–jth facets of $\mathcal{D}$ that result due to the intersection of the upper and lower hulls by picking a Ψ_i and a Λ_j in the above constructions. The above procedure could be extended to construct 3×3 matrices of rank 3 to obtain the vertices of $\mathcal{D}$.

11.5   THE DEPENDENCE MATRICES OF THE ALGORITHM VARIABLES

Previous works on parallel algorithms and parallel processing attempted to study data dependencies by studying how the output variables depend on the input variables. We do not follow this approach here. Instead, we study how each variable depends on the indices of the algorithm.

Assume a variable v in the algorithm described by Eq. 11.1 depends on m out of the n indices describing the algorithm. The index dependence of the variable v could be written as a function of its indices in the *affine* form

$$v = v(\mathbf{Ap} - \mathbf{a}), \qquad (11.20)$$

where $\mathbf{A}$ is the dependence matrix, which is an integer $m \times n$ matrix ($m \leq n$), and $\mathbf{a}$ is an integer m-vector. We call $\mathbf{A}$ the dependence matrix and $\mathbf{a}$ the dependence vector. The dependence matrix relates the variable to the domain indices and does not describe the dependence of the output variable on the input variables.

Typically, indexed variables have $\mathbf{a} = 0$, where 0 is an m-vector whose components are all zeros.

Assume we have a specific instance of a variable v given by $v(\mathbf{c})$, where $\mathbf{c}$ is a constant vector. From the definition of the dependence matrix in Eq. 11.20, we can write

$$\mathbf{A}\,\mathbf{p} = \mathbf{c} + \mathbf{a}. \qquad (11.21)$$

The above is a system of m linear equations in n unknowns. When $m < n$, we have many solutions for the unknown index values. When $n = m$, we have one unique solution. These concepts are elaborated upon in the next section in terms of the nullspace and nullvector of $\mathbf{A}$.

11.6 NULLSPACE OF DEPENDENCE MATRIX: THE BROADCAST SUBDOMAIN *B*

We will see in this section that the nullvector of the dependence matrix $\mathbf{A}$ of some variable v describes a subdomain $B \subset \mathcal{D}$. We will prove that all points in B contain the same instance of v.

11.6.1 The Nullspace of A

If the dependence matrix $\mathbf{A}$ is rank deficient, then the number of independent nullvectors associated with $\mathbf{A}$ is given by

$$\text{Number of nullvectors} = n - \text{rank}(\mathbf{A}), \qquad (11.22)$$

where n is the number of indices of the algorithm. These nullvectors define the *nullspace* of matrix $\mathbf{A}$.

Now assume a specific instance for the variable $v(\mathbf{c})$. The following theorem identifies the points in $\mathcal{D}$ that use that variable.

Theorem 11.1 *Consider a particular nullvector* e *associated with a variable* v. *If two distinct points* $\mathbf{p}_1$ *and* $\mathbf{p}_2$ *use the same instance* $v(\mathbf{c})$, *then the vector connecting the two points is a nullvector of* $\mathbf{A}$.

Proof:

Assume the two points use the same instance $v(\mathbf{c})$. Substitute the two points into Eq. 11.21 to get

$$\mathbf{A}\,\mathbf{p}_1 = \mathbf{c} + \mathbf{a} \tag{11.23}$$

$$\mathbf{A}\,\mathbf{p}_2 = \mathbf{c} + \mathbf{a}. \tag{11.24}$$

Subtracting the two equations, we get

$$\mathbf{A}(\mathbf{p}_1 - \mathbf{p}_2) = \mathbf{0}. \tag{11.25}$$

We can write above equation as

$$\mathbf{A}(\mathbf{p}_1 - \mathbf{p}_2) = \alpha\mathbf{A}\,\mathbf{e}, \tag{11.26}$$

where $\alpha \neq 0$. Therefore, the vector connecting the two points is a nullvector of $\mathbf{A}$. Now assume the two points lie along the nullvector $\mathbf{e}$. We can write

$$\mathbf{p}_1 - \mathbf{p}_2 = \alpha\mathbf{e}, \tag{11.27}$$

where $\alpha \neq 0$ since the two points are distinct. We can write

$$\mathbf{A}(\mathbf{p}_1 - \mathbf{p}_2) = \alpha\mathbf{A}\,\mathbf{e} = 0. \tag{11.28}$$

Thus, the vector connecting the two points is a nullvector.

Now assume that $\mathbf{p}_1$ is associated with the variable instance $v(\mathbf{c}_1)$ and $\mathbf{p}_2$ is associated with the variable instance $v(\mathbf{c}_2)$, but the vector connecting the two points is a nullvector of $\mathbf{A}$. We can use Eq. 11.21 to get

$$\mathbf{A}\,\mathbf{p}_1 = \mathbf{c}_1 + a \tag{11.29}$$

$$\mathbf{A}\,\mathbf{p}_2 = \mathbf{c}_2 + a. \tag{11.30}$$

Subtracting the above two equations, we get

$$\mathbf{A}(\mathbf{p}_1 - \mathbf{p}_2) = \mathbf{c}_1 - \mathbf{c}_2. \tag{11.31}$$

From Eqs. 11.28 and 11.31, we have

$$\mathbf{c}_1 - \mathbf{c}_2 = \mathbf{0}. \tag{11.32}$$

This implies that $\mathbf{c}_1 = c_2$. This proves the theorem.

We conclude from the above theorem that if the rank of the dependence matrix $\mathbf{A}$ associated with variable v is less than n, then there is a set of nullvectors of $\mathbf{A}$ associated with the variable v. This set defines a subdomain B. An instance of v is defined over a subdomain $B \subset \mathcal{D}$, which we call the *broadcast subdomain*. Every point in B sees the same instance of v.

Every variable v of the algorithm, indexed by the pair $[\mathbf{A}, \mathbf{a}]$, is associated with a broadcast subdomain B whose basis vectors are the nullspace of $\mathbf{A}$. The basis vectors will prove useful to pipeline the variable v and eliminate broadcasting.

The dimension of the broadcast subdomain B is given by [85]

$$\text{Dimension of } B = n - \text{rank}(\mathbf{A}), \tag{11.33}$$

where n is the dimension of the computation domain $\mathcal{D}$.

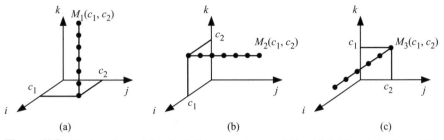

Figure 11.2   The broadcast subdomain for input and output variables. (a) Subdomain B_1 for variable $M_1(c_1, c_2)$. (b) Subdomain B_2 for variable $M_2(c_1, c_2)$. (c) Subdomain B_3 for variable $M_3(c_1, c_2)$.

From Eq. 11.1, the index dependence of the input variable $M_1(i, j)$ is given by

$$\mathbf{A}_1 = \begin{bmatrix} 1 & 0 & 0 \\ 0 & 1 & 0 \end{bmatrix} \quad \text{and} \quad \mathbf{a}_1 = 0. \tag{11.34}$$

The rank of $\mathbf{A}_1$ is two. This implies that its nullspace basis vector space is only one-dimensional (1-D), corresponding to one vector only. That nullspace basis vector could be given by

$$\mathbf{e}_1 = [0 \quad 0 \quad 1]^t. \tag{11.35}$$

We note that the broadcast domain for $M_1(i, j)$ is 1-D and coincides with the k-axis. Figure 11.2a shows the broadcast domain B_1 for the output variable instance $M_1(c_1, c_2)$. This output is calculated using all the points in $\mathcal{D}$ whose indices are $(c_1 \ c_2 \ k)$, where $0 \le k < K$.

From Eq. 11.1, the index dependence of the input variable $M_2(i, k)$ is given by

$$\mathbf{A}_2 = \begin{bmatrix} 1 & 0 & 0 \\ 0 & 0 & 1 \end{bmatrix} \quad \text{and} \quad \mathbf{a}_2 = 0. \tag{11.36}$$

The rank of $\mathbf{A}_2$ is two. This implies that its nullspace basis vectors space is only 1-D, corresponding to one vector only. That basis vector of its nullspace could be given by

$$\mathbf{e}_2 = [0 \quad 1 \quad 0]^t. \tag{11.37}$$

Figure 11.2b shows the broadcast domain B_2 for the input variable instance $M_2(c_1, c_2)$. This input is supplied to all the points in $\mathcal{D}$ whose indices are $(c_1 \ j \ c_2)$, where $0 \le j < J$.

From Eq. 11.1, the index dependence of the input variables $M_3(k, j)$ is given by

$$\mathbf{A}_3 = \begin{bmatrix} 0 & 0 & 1 \\ 0 & 1 & 0 \end{bmatrix} \quad \text{and} \quad \mathbf{a}_3 = 0. \tag{11.38}$$

The rank of $\mathbf{A}_3$ is two. This implies that its nullspace basis vectors space is only 1-D, corresponding to one vector only. That basis vector of its nullspace could be given by

$$\mathbf{e}_3 = [1 \quad 0 \quad 0]^t. \tag{11.39}$$

Figure 11.2c shows the broadcast domain B_3 for the input variable instance $M_3(c_1, c_2)$. This input is supplied to all the points in $\mathcal{D}$ whose indices are $(i\ c_2\ c_1)$, where $0 \le i < I$. Note that for this variable in particular, the first index c_1 maps to the k-axis and the second index c_2 maps to the j-axis. This stems from the fact that we indexed this input variable using the notation $M_3(k, j)$ in our original algorithm in Eq. 11.1.

11.7 DESIGN SPACE EXPLORATION: CHOICE OF BROADCASTING VERSUS PIPELINING VARIABLES

At this point, we know we have three variables, M_1, M_2, and M_3, for our matrix multiplication algorithm. We have a choice whether to broadcast or to pipeline each variable. Thus, we have eight different possible design choices for the implementation of our algorithm. Some of these choices might not be feasible though. In what follows, we show only one of those choices, but the reader can explore the other choices following the same techniques we provide here.

Broadcasting an output variable means performing all the calculations necessary to produce it at the same time. It is not recommended to broadcast output variables since this would result in a slower system that requires gathering all the partial outputs and somehow using them to produce the output value. To summarize, if v is an input variable, all points in B potentially use the same value of v. If v is an output variable, all points in B are potentially used to produce v.

Broadcasting an input variable means making a copy available to all processors at the same time. This usually results in the algorithm completing sooner. It is always preferable to broadcast input variables since this only costs using buses to distribute the variables. Data broadcast could be accomplished in hardware using a system-wide bus or an interconnection network capable of broadcasting a single data item to all the processing elements (PEs). In software, data broadcast could be accomplished using a broadcast message to all threads or using a shared memory.

11.7.1 Feeding/Extraction Point of a Broadcast Variable

The problem we address in this section is as follows. Assume we are given a particular instance $M_2(c_1, c_2)$ of the input variable M_2. We want to determine a point in $\mathcal{D}$ to feed this input instance. We choose this point at the boundaries of $\mathcal{D}$. To find such a point, we find the intersection of the broadcast subdomain of M_2 with $\mathcal{D}$. The intersection point is found by augmenting the dependence matrix $\mathbf{A}_2$ to make it full rank. We use one of the three candidate facets from the lower or upper hull. We choose to feed the variable from the lower hull facets described by Eqs. 11.13, 11.14, or 11.15. Only the facet described by Eq. 11.14 increases the rank of A_2 as it is linearly independent for all its rows. Now our augmented matrix will be

$$A_{2,aug} = \begin{bmatrix} 1 & 0 & 0 \\ 0 & 0 & 1 \\ 0 & 1 & 0 \end{bmatrix}. \tag{11.40}$$

The intersection point is specified by the equation

$$M_{2,aug} \; p = \begin{bmatrix} c \\ 0 \end{bmatrix}, \tag{11.41}$$

where c is the intersection point in the domain $\mathcal{D}$. Specifically, we can write

$$\begin{bmatrix} 1 & 0 & 0 \\ 0 & 0 & 1 \\ 0 & 1 & 0 \end{bmatrix} \begin{bmatrix} i \\ j \\ k \end{bmatrix} = \begin{bmatrix} c_1 \\ c_2 \\ 0 \end{bmatrix}. \tag{11.42}$$

Solving the above three simultaneous equations in the three unknowns i, j, and k, we get the intersection point for variable $M_2(c_1, c_2)$ as

$$p = [c_1 \quad 0 \quad c_2]^t. \tag{11.43}$$

Thus, instance $M_2(c_1, c_2)$ is fed to the system at the point with coordinates given by the above equation. Figure 11.3 shows the feeding point for supplying variable instance $M_2(c_1, c_2)$ to the 3-D computation domain $\mathcal{D}$ for the matrix multiplication algorithm.

Let us now find the feeding point for input variable instance $M_3(c_1, c_2)$. We also choose to augment the dependence matrix A_3 from one of the facets of the lower hull. Only the facet described by Eq. 11.13 increases the rank of M_3 as it is linearly independent for all its rows. We should not spend too much time worrying about

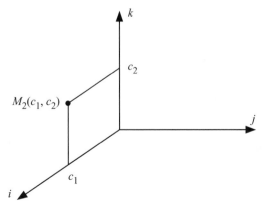

Figure 11.3   The feeding point for supplying variable instance $M_2(c_1, c_2)$ to the 3-D computation domain $\mathcal{D}$ for the matrix multiplication algorithm.

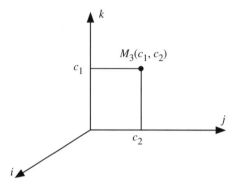

Figure 11.4   The feeding point for supplying variable instance $M_3(c_1, c_2)$ to the 3-D computation domain $\mathcal{D}$ for the matrix multiplication algorithm.

whether to choose the augmenting facet from the lower or upper hulls since broadcasting does not really care where the bus is fed from as long as all processors receive the data. Now our augmented matrix will be

$$\mathbf{A}_{3,\text{aug}} = \begin{bmatrix} 0 & 0 & 1 \\ 0 & 1 & 0 \\ 1 & 0 & 0 \end{bmatrix}. \tag{11.44}$$

The intersection point is specified by the equation

$$\mathbf{M}_{3,\text{aug}}\, \mathbf{p} = \begin{bmatrix} \mathbf{c} \\ 0 \end{bmatrix}, \tag{11.45}$$

where $\mathbf{c}$ is the intersection point in the domain $\mathcal{D}$. Specifically, we can write

$$\begin{bmatrix} 0 & 0 & 1 \\ 0 & 1 & 0 \\ 1 & 0 & 0 \end{bmatrix} \begin{bmatrix} i \\ j \\ k \end{bmatrix} = \begin{bmatrix} c_1 \\ c_2 \\ 0 \end{bmatrix}. \tag{11.46}$$

Solving the above three simultaneous equations in the three unknowns we get the intersection point for variable $M_3(c_1, c_2)$ as

$$\mathbf{p} = \begin{bmatrix} 0 & c_2 & c_1 \end{bmatrix}^t. \tag{11.47}$$

Thus, instance $M_3(c_1, c_2)$ is fed to the system at the point with coordinates given by the above equation. Figure 11.4 shows the feeding point for supplying variable instance $M_3(c_1, c_2)$ to the 3-D computation domain $\mathcal{D}$ for the matrix multiplication algorithm.

11.7.2 Pipelining of a Variable

We can introduce pipelining to the broadcast subdomain B of variable v by dedicating some of the basis vectors of B as data pipeline directions. The remaining basis vectors will remain broadcast directions. When we assign some basis vectors to describe our pipelining, the remaining basis vectors define a reduced broadcast subdomain over which variable v is still broadcast. In this way, we can mix pipelining and broadcasting strategies to propagate (or evaluate) the same input (or output) variable.

For our matrix multiplication algorithm, we choose to pipeline our output data samples $M_1(c_1, c_2)$. Now pipelined data travels from one point in $\mathcal{D}$ to another along a given direction. We need to determine the directions of data pipelining, which are the nullspace of the dependence matrix for M_1, that is, along the direction given by the vector given by $\mathbf{e} = [0\ 0\ 1]^t$. We need to determine two distinct intersection points of B with $\mathcal{D}$. One point is used to initialize the pipeline. The other point is used to extract the pipeline output. To find the intersection points, we augment the dependence matrix $\mathbf{A}_1$ using lower and upper hull facets. The only possible candidates for augmenting $\mathbf{A}_1$ are given by Eqs. 11.9 and 11.15.

Now our augmented matrix will be

$$\mathbf{A}_{1,\text{aug}} = \begin{bmatrix} 1 & 0 & 0 \\ 0 & 1 & 0 \\ 0 & 0 & 1 \end{bmatrix}. \tag{11.48}$$

We can write the two augmented matrices using the expression

$$\mathbf{M}_{1,\text{aug}}\ \mathbf{p} = \begin{bmatrix} \mathbf{c} \\ 0 \end{bmatrix} \quad \text{and} \quad \mathbf{M}_{1,\text{aug}}\ \mathbf{p} = \begin{bmatrix} \mathbf{c} \\ K-1 \end{bmatrix}. \tag{11.49}$$

We can explicitly write the above two equations as

$$\begin{bmatrix} 1 & 0 & 0 \\ 0 & 1 & 0 \\ 0 & 0 & 1 \end{bmatrix} \mathbf{p} = \begin{bmatrix} c_1 \\ c_2 \\ 0 \end{bmatrix} \quad \text{and} \quad \begin{bmatrix} 1 & 0 & 0 \\ 0 & 1 & 0 \\ 0 & 0 & 1 \end{bmatrix} \mathbf{p} = \begin{bmatrix} c_1 \\ c_2 \\ K-1 \end{bmatrix}. \tag{11.50}$$

The solution for the above two equations gives

$$\mathbf{p} = [c_1\ \ c_2\ \ 0]^t \quad \text{and} \quad \mathbf{p} = [c_1\ \ c_2\ \ K-1]^t. \tag{11.51}$$

Thus, we know the possible locations of initializing or extracting the pipeline data in the computation domain. The detailed method to obtain the extraction points and the feeding points at the projected domain will be discussed later in this chapter.

11.8 DATA SCHEDULING

We discuss in this section how to divide the tasks in the algorithm into stages such that at each stage a group of tasks gets executed in parallel while preserving the correctness of the results. The section will also determine the stages when data are to be fed or extracted from a processor or thread. We need to find a function that will take the coordinates of a point $\mathbf{p}$ in the computation domain $\mathcal{D}$ and to assign a time value to it. We use an affine scheduling function to specify the scheduling of the algorithm tasks. The affine scheduling functions are of the form [86]

$$t(\mathbf{p}) = \mathbf{sp} - s, \tag{11.52}$$

where $\mathbf{s}$ is a row vector of length n, which is called scheduling vector, and s is an integer that biases the ordering to ensure non-negative stage index values.

The main purpose of the scheduling function is to assign an execution time to several nodes in $\mathcal{D}$. Consequently, this function determines the computational load to be performed by the computing system at each time step or execution sequence. This is a subtle but very important by-product. As we shall see, the linear or affine scheduling function affords us little control on the amount of that work. However, we still need it to correctly perform the algorithm tasks. Nonlinear scheduling techniques will allows us to control the total work assigned to the system during each time step. Another effect of the scheduling function is the fact that dependencies between tasks will be created, and interthread and interprocessor communication can thus be determined.

Assigning time values to the nodes of $\mathcal{D}$ transforms it to a serial–parallel algorithm (SPA) where the parallel tasks could be implemented using a thread pool or parallel processors for software or hardware implementations, respectively. The different stages of the SPA are accomplished using barriers or clocks for software or hardware implementations, respectively.

The following theorem will prove that the scheduling function will convert the dependence graph into a DAG.

Theorem 11.2   *The affine scheduling function changes a dependence graph into a DAG even if the dependence graph contained cycles.*

Proof:
Given a dependence graph, we define a k-hop cycle as one involving k-nodes as shown in Fig. 11.5. We exclude one-hop loops since they represent local computations and are absorbed within a node. Without loss of generality, we assume a 1-D dependence graph where the nodes lie on a straight line with index i. Now assume that there are one or more k-hops involving nodes whose indices are $0, 1, \ldots, k - 1$ where $k > 1$. The presence of a loop in the dependence graph implies that there are undirected links between the following pairs of nodes:

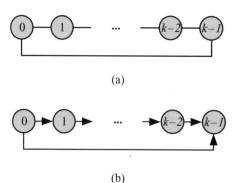

(a)

(b)

Figure 11.5   Illustration of the presence of cycles in a dependence graph and a DAG. (a) Undirected links and cycles in the dependence graph. (b) Directed links only to produce a DAG.

$$(0 \leftrightarrow 1), (1 \leftrightarrow 2), \ldots, (k-2 \leftrightarrow k-1), (k-1 \leftrightarrow 0).$$

For our 1-D situation, the affine timing function is given by $t(\mathbf{p}) = i$; the times associated with these points become

$$0, 1, 2, \ldots, k-1.$$

The execution time associated with each point imparts an ordering on the times and a direction to the unidirectional links. We can write

$$t(0) < t(1) < t(2) \ldots < t(k-1).$$

The above inequalities give direction to the undirected edges of the dependence graph. We thus have the following directional links:

$$(1 \rightarrow 1), (1 \rightarrow 2), \ldots, (k-2 \rightarrow k-1), (0 \rightarrow k-1).$$

The dependence graph has now become a DAG and the loopback edge between the first and last nodes 0 and $k-1$ has now become directed from node 0 to node $k-1$. Thus, our undirected dependence graph, which included cycles, is transformed into a DAG.

The following theorem will prove that the affine scheduling function will convert the dependence graph to a SPA.

Theorem 11.3 *The affine scheduling function changes a dependence graph into a SPA.*

Proof:
Assume without loss of generality a two-dimensional (2-D) dependence graph. A node in the dependence graph is described by the coordinates i, j:

$$\mathbf{p} = [i \quad j]^t. \tag{11.53}$$

The scheduling function assigns an order of execution to each node given by the expression

$$t(\mathbf{p}) = \mathbf{s}\mathbf{p} = s_1 i + s_2 j + s. \tag{11.54}$$

For given values of s_1, s_2, and s, we get

$$s_1 i + s_2 j + s = c, \tag{11.55}$$

where c is some constant.

The algorithm computation domain $\mathcal{D}$ is defined in the integer space $\mathcal{Z}^2$ by the inequalities

$$0 \leq i \leq I \tag{11.56}$$
$$0 \leq j \leq J, \tag{11.57}$$

where we assumed that the indices in our 2-D case fall in the limits indicated above. The scheduling function imposes another restriction as given by Eq. 11.55. All nodes satisfying the above two inequality and satisfying Eq. 11.55 will describe a subset of $\mathcal{D}$. All these nodes are assigned stage c.

Changing the value of c to k identifies a new set of nodes that will be executed at stage k. Thus, we have divided the nodes in our computation domain $\mathcal{D}$ to a set of sequential stages, and each stage executes a set of nodes in parallel. This is the definition of a SPA

The affine scheduling function should satisfy five conditions in order to be a valid scheduling function:

$$\mathbf{s\,p} \geq s \quad \mathbf{p} \in D \quad \text{positive time values} \tag{11.58}$$
$$\mathbf{s\,e} = 0 \quad \text{broadcast restriction} \tag{11.59}$$
$$\mathbf{s\,f} \neq 0 \quad \text{pipelining restriction} \tag{11.60}$$
$$\mathbf{s\,d} \neq 0 \quad \text{projection restriction} \tag{11.61}$$
$$\mathbf{s\,R} > 0 \quad \text{causality} \tag{11.62}$$

where

- **e** broadcast nullvector,
- **f** pipelining nullvector,
- **d** projection direction (discussed later), and
- **R** any extremal ray in our domain.

It is important to mention here that the restrictions implied by Eq. 11.59 preclude any broadcast directions that coincide with the projection directions, defined in Section 11.9. The above conditions provide the minimum constraints that must be satisfied for a possible valid scheduling function. Further restrictions are imposed to narrow our choices as will be explained in Section 11.8.1.

Since the point $[0\ 0\ 0]^t \in \mathcal{D}$, we have $s = 0$. Thus, our scheduling function is simply given by

$$t(\mathbf{p}) = \mathbf{sp}, \tag{11.63}$$

or more explicitly, we can write above Equation as

$$t(\mathbf{p}) = s_1 i + s_2 j + s_3 k. \tag{11.64}$$

We need to come up with values for the variables s_1, s_2, and s_3, which are based on the restrictions given by Eqs. 11.58–11.62.

To start, let us assume that we want to pipeline output variable $\mathbf{M}_1$ since this leads to faster and simpler hardware. For this, we need to know the nullvector associated with $\mathbf{M}_1$. The nullspace for output variable $\mathbf{M}_1$ is given in Eq. 11.35 as

$$\mathbf{e}_1 = [0 \quad 0 \quad 1]^t. \tag{11.65}$$

From restriction (Eq. 11.60), we can write

$$[s_1 \quad s_2 \quad s_3][0 \quad 0 \quad 1]^t \neq 0, \tag{11.66}$$

which implies $s_3 \neq 0$. Let us choose $s_3 = 1$. Thus, our scheduling function so far is given by

$$\mathbf{s} = [s_1 \quad s_2 \quad 1]. \tag{11.67}$$

Next, let us assume that we want to broadcast input variable $\mathbf{M}_2$. For this, we need to know the nullvector associated with $\mathbf{M}_2$. The nullspace for input variable $\mathbf{M}_2$ is given in Eq. 11.37 as

$$\mathbf{e}_2 = [0 \quad 1 \quad 0]^t. \tag{11.68}$$

From restriction (Eq. 11.59), we can write

$$[s_1 \quad s_2 \quad 1][0 \quad 1 \quad 0]^t = 0, \tag{11.69}$$

which implies $s_2 = 0$. Thus, our scheduling function so far is given by

$$\mathbf{s} = [s_1 \quad 0 \quad 1]. \tag{11.70}$$

To find the component s_1, we consider the third variable, $\mathbf{M}_3$. Let us pipeline that variable. For this, we need to know the nullvector associated with $\mathbf{M}_3$. The nullspace for output variable $\mathbf{M}_3$ is given in Eq. 11.35 as

$$\mathbf{e}_3 = [1 \quad 0 \quad 0]^t. \tag{11.71}$$

From restriction (Eq. 11.60), we can write

$$[s_1 \quad 0 \quad 1][1 \quad 0 \quad 0]^t \neq 0, \tag{11.72}$$

which implies $s_1 \neq 0$. Let us choose $s_1 = 1$. Thus, our scheduling function is finally given by

$$\mathbf{s} = [1 \quad 0 \quad 1]. \tag{11.73}$$

Equation 11.73 defines the valid scheduling function for our matrix multiplication algorithm given our choices for data broadcast and pipelining.

11.8.1 Impact of Scheduling Function on Data Timing

The restrictions on our choice for a valid scheduling function were developed in the previous section.

The timing function so far that we developed in Eq. 11.73 imposes certain restrictions on the timing of the output variable. The output data samples are indexed using two indices, for example,

$$M_1(i, j) = \text{output matrix element} \tag{11.74}$$
$$i = \text{row index} \tag{11.75}$$
$$j = \text{column index.} \tag{11.76}$$

The feeding and extraction for this variable were found in Eq. 11.51. These two points can be used to determine the timing of the variable. Consider the output sample $M_1(i, j)$. According to Eq. 11.51, the extraction point for this instance is given by

$$\mathbf{p} = [i \quad j \quad K - 1]^t. \tag{11.77}$$

We can write the following time value for this element:

$$t(\mathbf{p}) = \begin{bmatrix} 1 & 0 & 1 \end{bmatrix} \times \begin{bmatrix} i \\ j \\ K-1 \end{bmatrix} = i + K - 1. \tag{11.78}$$

This Equation states that output elements in the same column of $\mathbf{M}_1$ are obtained from the processors or the threads at the same time. The first row with $i = 0$ is obtained in time instance $K - 1$; the second row is obtained at time K, and so on.

The reader can verify that input variable sample $\mathbf{M}_2(i, k)$ is supplied to the array at time

$$t[\mathbf{M}_2(i,k)] = i + k. \tag{11.79}$$

Thus, the inputs for this variable are supplied such that all elements whose row and column index sum is equal to the same value are supplied simultaneously. Element $M_2(0, 0)$ is supplied at time 0. Elements $M_2(1, 0)$ and $M_2(0, 1)$ are supplied at time 1, and so on.

Similarly, input variable sample $\mathbf{M}_3(k, j)$ is supplied to the array at time

$$t[\mathbf{M}_3(k,j)] = k. \tag{11.80}$$

All elements on the same row are supplied to the system at the same time. Element $M_3(0, j)$ is supplied at time 0. Element $M_3(1, j)$ is supplied at time 1, and so on.

11.9 PROJECTION OPERATION USING THE LINEAR PROJECTION OPERATOR

In Section 11.8, we discussed how we can associate a time step value to each point in the computation domain $\mathcal{D}$. In this section, we discuss how we can assign a task to each point in the computation domain $\mathcal{D}$. This task could later be assigned to a thread for the case of multithreaded software implementation, or the task could be assigned to a PE for the case of hardware systolic implementation. It is a waste of resources (number of processors or number of threads) to associate a unique processor or thread to each point in the computation domain $\mathcal{D}$. The main reason is that each point is active only for *one time instant and is idle the rest of the time*. The basic idea then is to allocate one processor or thread to several points of $\mathcal{D}$. There are basically three ways of doing this:

1. Use linear projection operator matrix $\mathbf{P}$ to reduce the *dimensions* of $\mathcal{D}$ to produce a new computation domain $\bar{\mathcal{D}}$ whose dimensions $k < n$. Matrix $\mathbf{P}$ has dimensions $k \times n$ and its rank is k. For our matrix multiplication example, $\mathcal{D}$ was 3-D. The linear projection operation would produce a computation domain $\bar{\mathcal{D}}$ that is 2-D or 1-D.

2. Use a nonlinear operator to reduce the *size* of the computation domain $\mathcal{D}$, but keep its dimension n fixed. For our matrix multiplication example, the size of $\mathcal{D}$ is a $I \times J \times K$ cube in 3-D space. The nonlinear operator would produce a new 3-D cube, $\bar{\mathcal{D}}$, whose size is now $I' \times J' \times K'$, where $I' < I, J' < J$ and $K' < K$.

3. Use both linear and nonlinear operators to reduce both the size and dimension of the computation domain.

We explain here the first approach since it is the one most used to for design space exploration.

A subtle point to be noticed in the projection operation is that it controls the amount of workload assigned to each software thread for a multithreaded implementation or the workload assigned to each PE for a systolic array implementation. Just like affine scheduling, affine projection affords us little control over the workload assigned to a thread or a PE. However, nonlinear projection operations will give us very good control over the workload assigned to each thread or PE.

11.9.1 The Projection Matrix P

We define a linear projection operation for multithreading as the projection matrix **P** that maps a point in domain $\mathcal{D}$ (of dimension n) to point $\bar{\mathbf{p}}$ in the k-dimensional computational domain $\bar{\mathcal{D}}$ according to the equation

$$\bar{\mathbf{p}} = \mathbf{P}\,\mathbf{p}. \tag{11.81}$$

The following theorem places a value on the rank of the projection matrix in relation to the dimension of the projected domain.

Theorem 11.4   *Given the dimension of $\mathcal{D}$ is* n *and the dimension of $\bar{\mathcal{D}}$ is* k *and rank(P) is* r. *Then we must have* r = k, *that is rank(P) = k, if* **P** *is to be a valid projection matrix.*

Proof:
P has dimension $k \times n$ with $k < n$. The definition of the rank of a matrix indicates that the rank could not exceed the smaller of n or k. Thus we conclude that $r \leq k$.

Now assume that the rank of **P** is smaller than k. If $r < k$, then we have r linearly independent rows and $k - r$ rows that are a linear combination of the r rows. Thus, the linear equation given by

$$\bar{\mathbf{p}} = \mathbf{P} \times \mathbf{p} \tag{11.82}$$

is a system of linear equations in k unknowns, and the number of equations is less than the unknowns. Thus, we have an infinity of solutions. This contradicts our assertion that the mapping matrix maps any point in $\mathcal{D}$ to a unique point in $\bar{\mathcal{D}}$.

Therefore, we conclude that we must have the rank of **P** equal to k; that is, $r = k$.

Now the projection matrix **P** maps two points $\mathbf{p}_1$ and $\mathbf{p}_2$ in $\mathcal{D}$ associated with a particular output variable instance $v(\mathbf{c})$ to the point $\bar{\mathbf{p}}$. Thus, we can write

$$\mathbf{P}(\mathbf{p}_1 - \mathbf{p}_2) = 0. \tag{11.83}$$

But from Theorem 11.1 and Eq. 11.27, we can write the expression

$$\mathbf{P}(\mathbf{p}_1 - \mathbf{p}_2) = \alpha \mathbf{P}\,\mathbf{e} = 0, \tag{11.84}$$

where **e** is a nullvector associated with the output variable. We conclude therefore that the nullvectors of the projection matrix **P** are also the nullvectors associated with the output variable v. The following theorem relates the rank of the projection matrix to

Theorem 11.5   *Assume the dimension of $\mathcal{D}$ is* n. *If output variable* v *has* r *orthogonal nullvectors, then the dimension of $\bar{\mathcal{D}}$ is* k = n − r *and the rank of the projection matrix* **P** *is* k.

Proof:
The nullvectors of **P** are the r nullvectors. Thus, the rank of **P** is given by

$$\text{Rank}(\mathbf{P}) = n - r. \tag{11.85}$$

But we proved in Theorem 11.4 that the rank of **P** is equal to k. Thus, we must have

$$k = n - r. \tag{11.86}$$

Based on this theorem, if our variable had only one nullvector, then the dimension of $\bar{\mathcal{D}}$ will be $n - 1$. If the variable had two nullvectors, then the dimension of $\bar{\mathcal{D}}$ would be $n - 2$, and so on.

11.9.2   The Projection Direction

A projection matrix is required to effect the projection operation described by Eq. 11.81. However, the projection operation is typically defined in terms of a *projection direction*, or directions, **d**. Knowing the desired projection directions helps in finding the corresponding projection matrix **P**.

Definition 11.1   The projection direction is defined such that any two distinct points, $\mathbf{p}_1$ and $\mathbf{p}_2$, in $\mathcal{D}$ will be projected to the same point in $\bar{\mathcal{D}}$ if it satisfies the relation

$$\mathbf{p}_2 - \mathbf{p}_1 = \alpha \, \mathbf{d}, \tag{11.87}$$

where $\alpha \neq 0$ is some constant. In other words, the vector connecting $\mathbf{p}_1$ and $\mathbf{p}_2$ is parallel to **d**.

Theorem 11.6   *The projection direction* **d** *is in the nullspace of the projection matrix* **P**.

Proof:
From Definition 11.1, we can write

$$\bar{\mathbf{p}} = \mathbf{P}\mathbf{p}_1 \tag{11.88}$$
$$\bar{\mathbf{p}} = \mathbf{P}\mathbf{p}_2. \tag{11.89}$$

Subtracting the above two equations, we get

$$\alpha \mathbf{P}\mathbf{d} = 0. \tag{11.90}$$

11.9.3   Choosing Projection Direction d

One guideline for choosing a projection direction is the presence of extremal ray r in domain $\mathcal{D}$. An extremal ray is a direction vector in $\mathcal{D}$ where the domain extends to infinity or a large value of the indices. The projection matrix should have those rays in its nullspace; that is,

$$\mathbf{P\,r} = 0. \tag{11.91}$$

This is just a *recommendation* to ensure that the dimension of the projected domain $\mathcal{D}$ is finite. However, the projection directions do not necessarily have to include the extremal ray directions to ensure a valid multiprocessor. Our 3-D matrix multiplication algorithm deals with matrices of finite dimensions. As such, there are no extremal ray directions. However, we impose two requirements on our multiprocessor.

A valid scheduling function cannot be orthogonal to any of the projection directions, a condition of Eq. 11.61. Therefore, the projection directions impose restrictions on valid scheduling functions or vice versa. For our matrix multiplication algorithm, we obtained a scheduling function in Eq. 11.73 as

$$\mathbf{s} = [1 \quad 0 \quad 1]. \tag{11.92}$$

Possible projection directions that are not orthogonal to $\mathbf{s}$ are

$$\mathbf{d}_1 = [1 \quad 0 \quad 0]^t \tag{11.93}$$
$$\mathbf{d}_2 = [0 \quad 0 \quad 1]^t \tag{11.94}$$
$$\mathbf{d}_3 = [1 \quad 0 \quad 1]^t. \tag{11.95}$$

In the next section, we will show how matrix $\mathbf{P}$ is determined once the projection vectors are chosen.

11.9.4   Finding Matrix P Given Projection Direction d

We present here an algorithm to get the projection matrix assuming we know our projection directions. We start first with the simple case when we have chosen only one projection direction $\mathbf{d}$.

Step 1
Choose the projection directions. In our case, we choose only one projection direction with the value

$$\mathbf{d} = [1 \quad 0 \quad 0]^t. \tag{11.96}$$

This choice will ensure that all points along the i-axis will map to one point in $\bar{\mathcal{D}}$.

Step 2
Here we determine the basis vectors for $\mathcal{D}$, such that one of the basis vectors is along $\mathbf{d}$ and the other two basis vectors are orthogonal to it. In our case, we have three basis vectors:

$$\mathbf{b}_0 = [1 \quad 0 \quad 0]^t = \mathbf{d} \tag{11.97}$$

$$\mathbf{b}_1 = [0 \quad 1 \quad 0]^t \tag{11.98}$$

$$\mathbf{b}_2 = [0 \quad 0 \quad 1]^t. \tag{11.99}$$

Equation 11.97 implies that the i-axis will be eliminated after the projection operation since our choice implies that $\mathbf{Pb}_0 = 0$.

Step 3
Choose the basis vectors for $\bar{\mathcal{D}}$. In this case, we have two basis vectors since the dimension of $\bar{\mathcal{D}}$ is two. We choose the basis vectors as

$$\bar{\mathbf{b}}_1 = [1 \quad 0]^t \tag{11.100}$$

$$\bar{\mathbf{b}}_2 = [0 \quad 1]^t. \tag{11.101}$$

The above two equations imply that the j-axis will map to $\bar{\mathbf{b}}_1$ and the k-axis will map to $\bar{\mathbf{b}}_2$. These become the $\bar{j}$- and $\bar{k}$-axes for $\bar{\mathcal{D}}$, respectively.

Step 4
Associate each basis vector $\bar{\mathbf{b}}$ with a basis vector $\mathbf{b}$. Based on that, we can write

$$\mathbf{Pb}_i = \bar{\mathbf{b}}_i \qquad i = 1, 2. \tag{11.102}$$

Step 5
We now have a sufficient number of equations to find all the elements of the 2×3 projection matrix $\mathbf{P}$:

$$\mathbf{Pb}_0 = \mathbf{0} \tag{11.103}$$

$$\mathbf{Pb}_i = \bar{\mathbf{b}}_i \qquad i = 1, 2. \tag{11.104}$$

The first Equation is a set of two equations. The second Equation is a set of 2×2 equations. In all, we have a set of 2×3 equations in 2×3 unknowns, which are the elements of the projection matrix $\mathbf{P}$.

For our case, we can write the above equations in a compact form as

$$\mathbf{P}[\mathbf{b}_0 \quad \mathbf{b}_1 \quad \mathbf{b}_2] = [\mathbf{0} \quad \bar{\mathbf{b}}_1 \quad \bar{\mathbf{b}}_2]. \tag{11.105}$$

Explicitly, we can write

$$\begin{bmatrix} P_{0,0} & P_{0,1} & P_{0,2} \\ P_{1,0} & P_{1,1} & P_{1,2} \end{bmatrix} \times \begin{bmatrix} 1 & 0 & 0 \\ 0 & 1 & 0 \\ 0 & 0 & 1 \end{bmatrix} = \begin{bmatrix} 0 & 1 & 0 \\ 0 & 0 & 1 \end{bmatrix}. \tag{11.106}$$

The solution to the above Equation is simple and is given by

$$\begin{bmatrix} P_{0,0} & P_{0,1} & P_{0,2} \\ P_{1,0} & P_{1,1} & P_{1,2} \end{bmatrix} = \begin{bmatrix} 0 & 1 & 0 \\ 0 & 0 & 1 \end{bmatrix}. \tag{11.107}$$

Thus, a point $\mathbf{p} = [i \quad j \quad k]^t \in D$ maps to point $\bar{\mathbf{p}} = [j \quad k]^t \in \bar{D}$.

11.10 EFFECT OF PROJECTION OPERATION ON DATA

Now that we know both the projection and scheduling functions, we are able to study how the input and output variables map to the projected domain $\bar{\mathcal{D}}$.

11.10.1 Output Data M_1

The pipeline direction for the output data is mapped to the vector $\bar{e}_1$ given by

$$\bar{e}_1 = Pe_1 = \bar{b}_2. \tag{11.108}$$

Therefore, the output data will map to pipelining arrows along the k-axis (vertical lines) in the resulting multiprocessor architecture shown in Fig. 11.6.

The initialization and extraction points for the output data are found in Eq. 11.51. The initialization point for input $M_1(c_1, c_2)$ map in $\bar{\mathcal{D}}$ to the point $\bar{p}$.

$$\bar{p} = P \begin{bmatrix} c_1 \\ c_2 \\ 0 \end{bmatrix} = \begin{bmatrix} c_2 \\ 0 \end{bmatrix}. \tag{11.109}$$

Similarly, the extraction point for input $M_1(c_1, c_2)$ map in $\bar{\mathcal{D}}$ to the point $\bar{p}$.

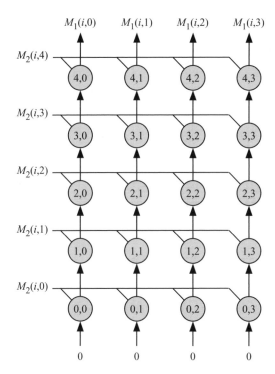

Figure 11.6 The projected or reduced computation domain $\bar{\mathcal{D}}$ for the matrix multiplication algorithm when the dimensions of the matrices are $I = 3$, $J = 4$, and $K = 5$.

$$\bar{\mathbf{p}} = \mathbf{P} \begin{bmatrix} c_1 \\ c_2 \\ K-1 \end{bmatrix} = \begin{bmatrix} c_2 \\ K-1 \end{bmatrix}. \tag{11.110}$$

11.10.2   Input Data $\mathbf{M}_2$

The broadcast direction for input data is mapped to the vector $\bar{\mathbf{e}}_2$ given by

$$\bar{\mathbf{e}}_2 = \mathbf{P}\mathbf{e}_2 = \bar{\mathbf{b}}_1. \tag{11.111}$$

Therefore, the input data for $\mathbf{M}_2$ will map to lines along the j-axis (horizontal lines) in the resulting multiprocessor architecture shown in Fig. 11.6.

The input sample $\mathbf{M}_2(c_1, c_2)$ is fed to our multiprocessor using its intersection point from Eq. 11.43.

$$\bar{\mathbf{p}} = \mathbf{P} \begin{bmatrix} c_1 \\ 0 \\ c_2 \end{bmatrix} = \begin{bmatrix} 0 \\ c_2 \end{bmatrix}. \tag{11.112}$$

11.10.3   Input Data $\mathbf{M}_3$

The broadcast direction for the input data is mapped to the vector $\bar{\mathbf{e}}_3$ given by

$$\bar{\mathbf{e}}_3 = \mathbf{P}\mathbf{e}_3 = \mathbf{0}. \tag{11.113}$$

This means that the input $\mathbf{M}_3$ is *localized* and is neither pipelined nor broadcast.

The input sample $\mathbf{M}_3(c_1, c_2)$ is fed to our multiprocessor using its intersection point from Eq. 11.47.

$$\bar{\mathbf{p}} = \mathbf{P} \begin{bmatrix} 0 \\ c_2 \\ c_1 \end{bmatrix} = \begin{bmatrix} c_2 \\ c_1 \end{bmatrix}. \tag{11.114}$$

11.11   THE RESULTING MULTITHREADED/ MULTIPROCESSOR ARCHITECTURE

At this stage, we have the following:

1. We have chosen a certain affine scheduling function (Eq. 11.73),

$$\mathbf{s} = [1 \quad 0 \quad 1].$$

2. We have chosen a certain projection direction (Eq. 11.96),

$$\mathbf{d} = [1 \quad 0 \quad 0]^t,$$

which produced the projection matrix (Eq. 11.107)

$$\begin{bmatrix} P_{0,0} & P_{0,1} & P_{0,2} \\ P_{1,0} & P_{1,1} & P_{1,2} \end{bmatrix} = \begin{bmatrix} 0 & 1 & 0 \\ 0 & 0 & 1 \end{bmatrix}.$$

From all the above results, we are able to construct our reduced or projected computation domain ($\bar{\mathcal{D}}$) as shown in Fig. 11.6 for the case when $I = 3$, $J = 4$, and $K = 5$. Each node in the $\bar{\mathcal{D}}$ represents a task to be performed by a software thread or a PE in a systolic array at a given time step. The input data $M_2(i, j)$ represent broadcast data coming from memory. The output data $M_1(i, j)$ represent the output of each task that is being used as input to adjacent tasks at the next time step.

11.12 SUMMARY OF WORK DONE IN THIS CHAPTER

At this stage, we were able to completely specify the reduced computation domain $\bar{\mathcal{D}}$ associated with the matrix–matrix multiplication algorithm. This $\bar{\mathcal{D}}$ could represent the required concurrent threads for a software implementation or the required PEs needed for a systolic array hardware implementation. Below we summarize what we have done and why:

1. We started by expressing the matrix multiplication as an iterative Equation (Eq. 11.1).
2. The indices of the iterative Equation defined the multidimensional computation domain $\mathcal{D}$. The facets and vertices of this domain were studied in Sections 11.3 and 11.4.
3. We identified the dependence matrix **A** associated with each variable of the algorithm in Section 11.5. Based on this matrix, we identified its nullvectors, which represent the broadcast subdomain B of the variable. We were also able to identify the intersection points of B with $\mathcal{D}$. These intersection points help in supplying input variables or extracting output results. At this stage, we can decide whether to broadcast or to pipeline our variables.
4. Scheduling of data was discussed in Section 11.8 using affine scheduling functions.
5. The projection of domain $\mathcal{D}$ onto another domain $\bar{\mathcal{D}}$ was discussed in Section 11.9. Three different projection operations were discussed, but only one was studied in more detail.

11.13 PROBLEMS

To get a feel for the formal computational geometry analysis technique, it is helpful to apply it to simple 2-D or 3-D algorithms. Some of the following problems are intended for that purpose. In order to analyze the problem, the following steps are required:

1. Determine the computation domain $\mathcal{D}$ and its facets and vertices.

2. Obtain the dependence matrix of each variable then determine the basis vectors and nullvectors of the matrix.

3. Obtain the feeding or extraction points of the variables, which lie on some of the f acets of $\mathcal{D}$.

4. Determine the projection matrix.

5. Determine the scheduling function.

11.1. Apply the computational geometry technique to the 1-D finite impulse response (FIR) digital filter algorithm.

11.2. Apply the computational geometry technique to the 2-D FIR digital filter algorithm.

11.3. Apply the computational geometry technique to the 1-D infinite impulse response (IIR) digital filter algorithm.

11.4. Apply the computational geometry technique to the 2-D IIR digital filter algorithm.

11.5. Apply the computational geometry technique to the matrix–vector multiplication algorithm.

11.6. Apply the computational geometry technique to the 1-D convolution algorithm.

11.7. Apply the computational geometry technique to the 2-D convolution algorithm.

11.8. Apply the computational geometry technique to the 1-D autocorrelation algorithm.

11.9. Apply the computational geometry technique to the 1-D cross-correlation algorithm.

11.10. Apply the computational geometry technique to the 2-D autocorrelation algorithm.

11.11. Apply the computational geometry technique to the 2-D cross-correlation algorithm.

11.12. Apply the computational geometry technique to the 3-D autocorrelation algorithm.

11.13. Apply the computational geometry technique to the 3-D cross-correlation algorithm.

Chapter 12

Case Study: One-Dimensional IIR Digital Filters

12.1 INTRODUCTION

In this chapter, we illustrate how to obtain different multithreaded or systolic array structures for the one-dimensional (1-D) infinite impulse response (IIR) digital filters. The IIR algorithm is an essentially a serial algorithm since each FOR loop iteration depends on $N - 1$ previous iterations where N is the filter length. Therefore, the programmer and the concurrency platforms would not be able to parallelize the algorithm. The techniques discussed in this book would help the programmer extract and explore the inherent parallelism in this seemingly serial algorithm.

We use the dependence graph technique introduced in Chapter 10 and the computational geometry technique discussed in Chapter 11. At the end of the chapter, we will also use the z-domain approach discussed in Chapter 9.

12.2 THE 1-D IIR DIGITAL FILTER ALGORITHM

The 1-D IIR digital filter algorithm can be expressed as the set of difference equations

$$y(i) = \sum_{j=0}^{N-1} [a(j)x(i-j) - b(j)y(i-j)], \qquad (12.1)$$

where $a(j)$ and $b(j)$ are the filter coefficients and N is the filter length. Note that $b(0) = 0$ in the above equation.

12.3 THE IIR FILTER DEPENDENCE GRAPH

We use Eq. 12.1 to study the index dependencies of the algorithm variables. Variable y is an input/output or intermediate variable, and variables x, a, and b are all input variables. An input/output variable is one that is present on the right-hand side

Algorithms and Parallel Computing, by Fayez Gebali
Copyright © 2011 John Wiley & Sons, Inc.

(RHS) and left-hand side (LHS) of the algorithm equations with different index dependencies for each side.

We note that the algorithm gives rise to a two-dimensional (2-D) computation domain $\mathcal{D}$ since we have two indices, i and j. Since the dimensionality of $\mathcal{D}$ is low, it is best to visualize $\mathcal{D}$ using a dependence graph since this is easier for humans to visualize and analyze.

We organize our indices in the form of a vector:

$$\mathbf{p} = \begin{bmatrix} i & j \end{bmatrix}^t ; \tag{12.2}$$

for given values of the indices, the vector corresponds to a point in the $\mathcal{Z}^2$ space.

12.3.1   The 2-D Dependence Graph

The dimension of a dependence graph is two, which is the number of indices in the algorithm. The graph covers the points $\mathbf{p}(i, j) \in \mathcal{D}$, where the range of the indices defines the boundaries of the dependence graph as

$$0 \le i \qquad \text{and} \qquad 0 \le j < N. \tag{12.3}$$

Note that $\mathcal{D}$ extends to ∞ in the i direction, which defines an *extremal ray* in that direction.

The dependence matrices for the variables will help us plot them in the filter dependence graph. We prefer to use the concept of dependence graph here because of the low dimensionality of a dependence graph, which facilitates visualization.

Figure 12.1 shows the dependence graph of the 1-D IIR filter for the case $N = 4$. The following paragraphs describe how the dependence graph was obtained. The missing circles near the j-axis indicate that there are no operations to be performed at these locations since the input to our filter does not have negative indices.

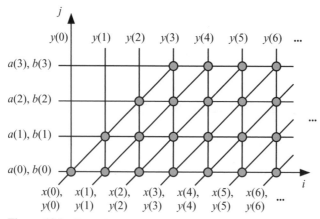

Figure 12.1   Dependence graph for the 1-D IIR filter for the case $N = 4$.

The output variable y has a dependence matrix given by

$$\mathbf{A}_{y,\text{output}} = [1 \quad 0]. \tag{12.4}$$

The null vector associated with this matrix is

$$\mathbf{e}_{y,\text{output}} = [0 \quad 1]^t. \tag{12.5}$$

Therefore, the broadcast domains for this variable are vertical lines in $\mathcal{D}$. This is shown in Fig. 12.1 for the case $N = 4$.

The input variables a and b have a dependence matrix given by

$$\mathbf{A}_{a,b} = [0 \quad 1]. \tag{12.6}$$

The null vector associated with this matrix is

$$\mathbf{e}_{a,b} = [1 \quad 0]^t. \tag{12.7}$$

Therefore, the broadcast domains for these two variables are the horizontal lines in $\mathcal{D}$. The input variable x has a dependence matrix given by

$$\mathbf{A}_x = [1 \quad -1]. \tag{12.8}$$

The null vector associated with this matrix is

$$\mathbf{e}_x = [1 \quad 1]^t. \tag{12.9}$$

Therefore, the broadcast domains for this variable are the diagonal lines in $\mathcal{D}$.

The input variable y has a dependence matrix given by

$$\mathbf{A}_{y,\text{input}} = [1 \quad -1]. \tag{12.10}$$

The null vector associated with this matrix is

$$\mathbf{e}_{y,\text{input}} = [1 \quad 1]^t. \tag{12.11}$$

Therefore, the broadcast domains for this variable are the diagonal lines in $\mathcal{D}$ also.

12.3.2 The Scheduling Function for the 1-D IIR Filter

We start by using an affine scheduling function given by

$$\mathbf{s} = [s_1 \quad s_2] - s, \tag{12.12}$$

where the constant $s = 0$ since the point at the origin $\mathbf{p}(0, 0) \in \mathcal{D}$. Any point $\mathbf{p} = [i \ j]^t \in \mathcal{D}$ is associated with the time value

$$t(\mathbf{p}) = \mathbf{s} \, \mathbf{p} = i \, s_1 + j \, s_2. \tag{12.13}$$

Assigning time values to the nodes of the dependence graph transforms the dependence graph to a directed acyclic graph (DAG) as was discussed in Chapters 10 and 11. More specifically, the DAG can be thought of as a serial–parallel algorithm (SPA) where the parallel tasks could be implemented using a thread pool or parallel processors for software or hardware implementations, respectively. The different stages of the SPA are accomplished using barriers or clocks for software or hardware implementations, respectively.

In order to determine the components of **s**, we turn our attention to the filter inputs x. The input data are assumed to be supplied to our array at consecutive time steps. From the dependence graph, we see that samples $x(i)$ and $x(i + 1)$ could be supplied at points $\mathbf{p}_1 = [i\ 0]^t$ and $\mathbf{p}_2 = [i + 1\ 0]^t$, respectively. The time steps associated with these two input samples are given from Eq. 10.17 by

$$t(\mathbf{p}_1) = i\, s_1 \tag{12.14}$$
$$t(\mathbf{p}_2) = (i+1)\, s_1. \tag{12.15}$$

Assuming that the consecutive inputs arrive at each time step, we have $t(\mathbf{p}_2) - t(\mathbf{p}_1) = 1$, and we must have

$$\mathbf{s} = [1\quad s_2]. \tag{12.16}$$

So now we know one component of the scheduling vector based on input data timing requirements. Possible valid scheduling functions could be

$$\mathbf{s} = \begin{cases} [1\ -1] \\ [1\ \ \ 0] \\ [1\ \ \ 1]. \end{cases} \tag{12.17}$$

All the above timing schedules are valid and have different implications on the timing of the output and partial results. The first scheduling vector results in broadcast input and pipelined output. The second scheduling vector results in broadcast of the output variable y and could produce Design 2, discussed in Chapter 9. The third scheduling vector results in pipelined input and output and could produce Design 3, discussed in Chapter 9. Let us investigate the scheduling vector $\mathbf{s} = [1\ -1]$. This choice implies that

$$\mathbf{s}\, \mathbf{e}_{y,in} = 0, \tag{12.18}$$

which results in broadcast x and y_{in} samples. Based on our choice for this time function, we obtain the DAG shown in Fig. 12.2. The gray lines indicate *equitemporal*

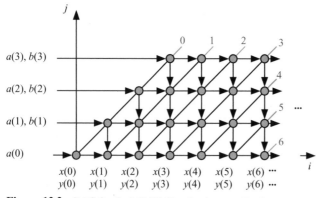

Figure 12.2 DAG for the 1-D IIR filter for the case $N = 4$.

planes. All nodes lying on the same gray line execute their operations at the time indicated beside the line. The gray numbers indicate the times associated with each equitemporal plane. Notice from the figure that all the input signals x and y_{in} are broadcast to all nodes in an equitemporal plane and output signals y_{out} are pipelined as indicated by the arrows connecting the graph nodes. At this stage, we know the timing of the operations to be performed by each node. We do not know yet which processing element each node is destined to. This is the subject of the next subsection.

12.3.3 Choice of Projection Direction and Projection Matrix

Chapters 10 and 11 explained that the projection operation assigns a node or a group of nodes in the DAG to a thread or processor. The number of assigned nodes determines the workload associated with each task. The operation also indicates the input and output data involved in the calculations. The projection operation controls the workload assigned to each thread/processor at each stage of the execution of the SPA.

From Chapter 11, a restriction on the projection direction $\mathbf{d}$ is that

$$\mathbf{s}\,\mathbf{d} \neq 0. \tag{12.19}$$

Therefore, we have three possible choices for projection directions:

$$\mathbf{d}_1 = [1 \quad 0]^t \tag{12.20}$$

$$\mathbf{d}_2 = [0 \quad 1]^t \tag{12.21}$$

$$\mathbf{d}_3 = [1 \quad -1]^t. \tag{12.22}$$

The projection matrices associated with each projection direction are given by

$$\mathbf{P}_1 = [0 \quad 1]^t \tag{12.23}$$

$$\mathbf{P}_2 = [1 \quad 0]^t \tag{12.24}$$

$$\mathbf{P}_3 = [1 \quad 1]^t. \tag{12.25}$$

12.3.4 Design 1: Projection Direction $\mathbf{d}_1 = [1 \ 0]^t$

Since the chosen projection direction is along the extremal ray direction, the number of tasks will be finite. A point $\mathbf{p} = [i\,j]^t \in \mathcal{D}$ maps to the point $\bar{\mathbf{p}}$, which is given by

$$\bar{\mathbf{p}} = \mathbf{P}_1\,\mathbf{p} = j. \tag{12.26}$$

The reduced or projected DAG ($\overline{\text{DAG}}$) is shown in Fig. 12.3. Task $T(i)$ stores the two filter coefficients $a(i)$ and $b(i)$. The filter output is obtained from the top tasks and is fed back to the first task at the next time step. Notice that both inputs x and y are pipelined between the tasks.

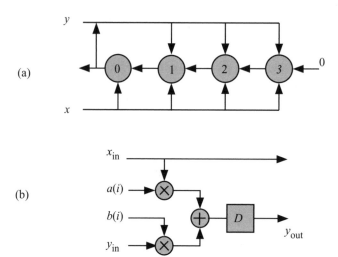

Figure 12.3 $\overline{\text{DAG}}$ for the 1-D IIR filter for the case $N = 4$ and $\mathbf{d}_1 = [1\ 0]^t$. (a) The $\overline{\text{DAG}}$ for the tasks. (b) Task processing details and array implementation.

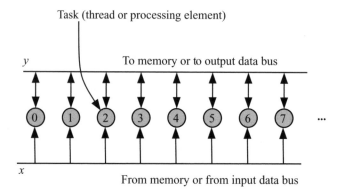

Figure 12.4 $\overline{\text{DAG}}$ for the 1-D IIR filter for the case $N = 4$ and $\mathbf{d}_2 = [0\ 1]^t$.

12.3.5   Design 2: Projection Direction $d_2 = [0\ 1]^t$

A point $\mathbf{p} = [i\ j]^t \in \mathcal{D}$ maps to the point $\bar{\mathbf{p}} = i$. The pipeline is shown in Fig. 12.4. Each task stores all the filter coefficients and is responsible for producing an output sample, which reduces intertask communication requirements. Task $T(i)$ accepts input samples $x(i - N + 1)$ to $x(i)$ from the memory or input data bus at time steps $i - N + 1$ to i. Task $T(i)$ also reads the memory or the output data bus for samples $y_{in}(i - N + 1)$ to $y_{in}(i - 1)$ at time steps $i - N + 1$ to $i - 1$. Task $T(i)$ produces the output $y_{out}(i)$ at time step i and stores that signal in the shared memory or places the signal on the output data bus for the case of hardware implementation. The number of tasks is infinite since our projection direction did not coincide with the ray direction. However, each task is active for the duration of N time steps. The task activities at different time steps are shown in Fig. 12.5. The timing diagram thus indicates that we could merge the tasks. Therefore, we relabel the task indices such that $T(i)$ maps to $T(j)$, such that

$$j = i \quad mod \ N. \tag{12.27}$$

The reduced DAG is shown is in Fig. 12.6.

Time

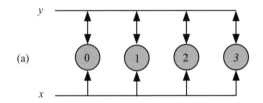

Figure 12.5   Task activities for the 1-D FIR filter for the case $N = 4$ and $\mathbf{d}_2 = [0\ 1]^t$.

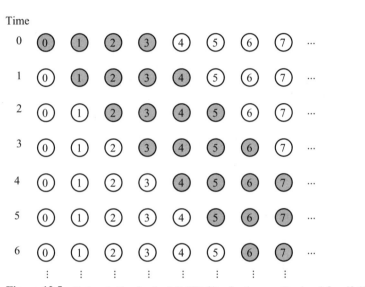

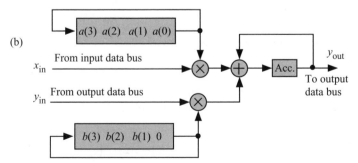

Figure 12.6   The reduced $\overline{\text{DAG}}$ for the 1-D FIR filter for $N = 4$ and $\mathbf{d}_2 = [0\ 1]^t$. (a) The $\overline{\text{DAG}}$ (b) Task processing details.

12.4 z-DOMAIN ANALYSIS OF 1-D IIR DIGITAL FILTER ALGORITHM

The z-domain 1-D IIR digital filter algorithm is obtained from Eq. 12.1 as

$$Y = \sum_{i=0}^{N-1} a(i)z^{-i}X - \sum_{i=0}^{N-1} b(i)z^{-i}Y, \tag{12.28}$$

where X and Y are the z-transform of the signals $x(n)$ and $y(n)$, respectively, and $b(0) = 0$. We can think of Eq. 12.28 as a polynomial expression in the different powers of z^{-1}. By using different polynomial evaluation techniques, the filter expression is converted to a set of recursive expressions that can be evaluated using a processor array or multiple software threads.

12.4.1 Design 3: Broadcast Inputs and Pipelined Output

Apply Horner's' scheme to Eq. 12.28 to obtain the recursive expression

$$Y = a(0)X + z^{-1}[a(1)X - b(1)Y + \cdots + z^{-1}[a(N-1)X - b(N-1)Y]]\cdots]. \tag{12.29}$$

The above equation can be written as

$$Y_i = a(i)X - b(i)Y + z^{-1}[Y_{i+1}] \qquad 0 < i < N \tag{12.30}$$

$$Y_0 = a(0)X + z^{-1}Y_1 \tag{12.31}$$

$$Y_N = 0 \tag{12.32}$$

$$Y = Y_0. \tag{12.33}$$

Based on the above iterative expression, task $T(i)$ computes Y_i in Eq. 12.30 using one multiplication and one addition:

$$Y_i = a(i)X - b(i)Y + z^{-1}Y_{i+1}. \tag{12.34}$$

The output of $T(i)$ is buffered then forwarded to $T(i-1)$ and the input to $T(N-1)$ is initialized to 0. The above equations produce Design 1 in Fig. 12.3.

12.4.2 Design 4: Pipelined Inputs and Broadcast Output

In this design, we apply the delay operator to the input data samples to obtain delayed input data that we use to obtain our output. We start by applying our delay operators to the input samples X and Y:

$$Y = a(0)X + \left[a(1)z^{-1}(X) - b(1)z^{-1}(Y)\right] + \left[a(2)z^{-1}\left(z^{-1}X\right) - b(2)z^{-1}\left(z^{-1}X\right)\right]$$
$$+ \cdots + \left[a(N-1)z^{-1}\left(z^{-(N-2)}X\right) - b(N-1)z^{-1}\left(z^{-(N-2)}Y\right)\right]. \tag{12.35}$$

The above equation can be converted to the iterative expressions

$$Y = \sum_{i=0}^{N-1} a(i)X_i - \sum_{i=0}^{N-1} b(i)Y_i$$

(12.36)

$$X_i = z^{-1}X_{i-1} \quad \text{and} \quad Y_i = z^{-1}Y_{i-1}$$

$$X_0 = X \quad \text{and} \quad Y_0 = Y.$$

The resulting DAG is identical to that shown in Fig. 12.6.

12.4.3 Design 5: Pipelined Input and Output

A possible attractive implementation would be when both the input and output of each task are stored in a register. This implies a fully pipelined design, which is potentially the fastest design possible. Assume without loss of generality that N is even. We can write Eq. 12.28 as

$$Y = [a(0)X + a(1)z^{-1}X - b(1)z^{-1}Y] +$$
$$z^{-1}[a(2)z^{-1}X - b(2)z^{-1}Y + a(3)z^{-2}X - b(3)z^{-2}Y] +$$
$$\cdots + z^{-(N/2-1)}[a(N-2)z^{-(N/2-1)}X - b(N-2)z^{-(N/2-1)}Y +$$
$$a(N-1)z^{-N/2}X - b(N-1)z^{-N/2}Y].$$

(12.37)

We write the above expression in the succinct form

$$Y = \sum_{i=0}^{N/2-1} z^{-i}[a(2i)z^{-i}X + a(2i+1)z^{-(i+1)}X - b(2i)z^{-i}Y - b(2i+1)z^{-(i+1)}Y],$$

(12.38)

We perform an iteration on the input X in the above equation:

$$X_i = z^{-1}X_{i-1} \quad 1 \le i \le N/2$$

(12.39)

$$Y_i = z^{-1}Y_{i-1} \quad 1 \le i \le N/2$$

(12.40)

$$X_0 = X$$

(12.41)

$$Y_0 = Y,$$

(12.42)

and the output is given by

$$Y = \sum_{i=0}^{N/2-1} z^{-i}[a(2i)X_i + a(2i+1)X_{i+1}].$$

(12.43)

The above equation can be written as the iteration

$$Y_i = z^{-1}[a(2i)X_i + a(2i+1)X_{i+1} - b(2i)Y_i - b(2i+1)Y_i + Y_{i+1}] \quad 0 < i < N/2$$ (12.44)

$$Y_{N/2} = 0$$

(12.45)

$$Y_0 = [a(0)X_0 + a(1)X_1 - b(1)Y_1] + Y_1$$

(12.46)

$$Y = Y_0.$$

(12.47)

Figure 12.7a shows the resulting $\overline{\text{DAG}}$. This is a new structure that has been reported in the literature by the author [23]. Figure 12.7b shows the details of a

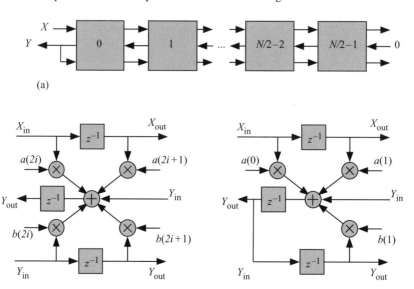

Figure 12.7   IIR digital filter $\overline{\text{DAG}}$ with pipelined input and output. (a) The $\overline{\text{DAG}}$. (b) Task processing details. (c) Leftmost task processing details.

processor element. Note that both the input and output are pipelined between the task stages. Figure 12.7c shows the details of the first task storing the filter coefficient $a(0)$, $a(1)$, and $b(1)$. Note that the output is not stored in a register.

12.5 PROBLEMS

12.1. Study the 1-D digital correlation operation using the z-transform technique.

12.2. Study the 2-D digital correlation operation using the z-transform technique.

12.3. Study the three-dimensional digital correlation operation using the z-transform technique.

12.4. Study the three-dimensional finite impulse response (FIR) filter using the z-transform technique.

12.5. Study the three-dimensional IIR filter using the z-transform technique.

Chapter 13

Case Study: Two- and Three-Dimensional Digital Filters

13.1 INTRODUCTION

Multidimensional digital filters are used in several areas of digital signal processing. Two-dimensional (2-D) digital filters are used for image processing applications such as image enhancement and noise removal. Three-dimensional (3-D) digital filters are used to process consecutive frames of images such as video data and medical imaging, such as computerized tomography (CT) and magnetic resonance imaging (MRI) scans. Another interesting example of 3-D filters is velocity filters. Velocity filters can be used to detect the speed of an object in a video sequence. Velocity filters are used also in the processing of seismic data sets or signal streams from microphone arrays to separate different signal components.

13.2 LINE AND FRAME WRAPAROUND PROBLEMS

There is an inherent problem in processing raster-scanned images: line and frame wraparound. Consider 2-D filters for an image. Figure 13.1 shows the main system parameters for a 2-D first-quadrant digital filter. The image being processed has a width of W pixels and a height of H pixels. The 2-D filter window width is w pixels and the height is h pixels. The axes are as shown since typically, lines are numbered starting from the top. The output sample at location (i, j) is indicated by the dark circle and is obtained by processing all the pixels in the dark gray area shown.

Figure 13.2 shows the different locations of the filter window as it scans the image to produce the processed image as an output. Output pixel a in Fig. 13.2 shows the case when the output sample lies in the first row. The window buffer of the filter is mostly empty except for the input data shown as the shaded region in the window area. Output pixel b in Fig. 13.2 shows the case when the output sample

Algorithms and Parallel Computing, by Fayez Gebali
Copyright © 2011 John Wiley & Sons, Inc.

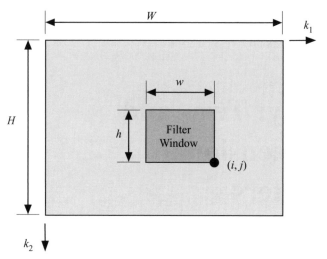

Figure 13.1   System parameters for a 2-D digital filter.

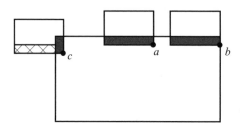

Figure 13.2   Illustrating the line wraparound problem in 2-D filters.

is the last pixel in the first row. Now the filter moves to produce the first pixel in the second row as shown in the figure by point c. The valid input data are shown by the dark shaded area. The stipple pattern shows the data remaining in the filter due to scanning output b. The correct output c should have been obtained by clearing the filter buffer storing that stipple region. In general, the first $w - 1$ pixels of each line will contain contributions from the last $w - 1$ pixels of the previous line. This phenomenon is known as line wraparound. Because of this problem, early hardware structure produced $H(w - 1)$ erroneous pixels in each image. Measures should be taken to clear the filter buffer of all extraneous data.

For 3-D filters, the first $h - 1$ lines of each frame will contain contributions from the last $h - 1$ lines of the previous frame. This phenomenon is known as frame wraparound. Again, earlier hardware designs produced $W(h - 1)$ incorrect pixels, which are produced at the start of a new frame before the first correct results appear. Thus, for a continuous processing of raster-scanned images, the total number of erroneous pixels produced per frame is equal to $H(w - 1) + W(h - 1) - (w - 1)(h - 1)$. In this chapter, we discuss how to eliminate both line and frame wraparound problems in the resulting implementations.

13.3   2-D RECURSIVE FILTERS

A first-quadrant 2-D recursive filter can be represented by the equation

$$Y = \sum_{k_2=0}^{h-1} \sum_{k_1=0}^{w-1} a(k_1,k_2) X z_1^{-k_1} z_2^{-k_2} - \sum_{k_2=0}^{h-1} \sum_{k_1=0}^{w-1} b(k_1,k_2) Y z_1^{-k_1} z_2^{-k_2}, \tag{13.1}$$

where $X \equiv X(z_1, z_2)$, $Y \equiv Y(z_1, z_2)$, and $b(0, 0) = 0$. The term z_1^{-1} represents one time step delay along a line. This delay could be implemented as memory address locators for use by the software threads or it could be implemented as actual hardware buffer for use by the software systolic array processing elements. The term z_2^{-1} represents one sample delay along a column. For progressive raster-scanned images, this is equivalent to W time-step delays where W is the image width. The above equation can also be written in a hierarchical way as

$$Y = \sum_{k_2=1}^{h-1} \left[F(k_2) z_2^{-k_2} X - G(k_2) z_2^{-k_2} Y \right], \tag{13.2}$$

where the terms $F(k_2)$ and $G(k_2)$ are two one-dimensional (1-D) infinite impulse response (IIR) filter operators given by

$$F(k_2) = \sum_{k_1=0}^{w-1} a(k_1,k_2) z_1^{-k_1} \tag{13.3}$$

$$G(k_2) = \sum_{k_1=0}^{w-1} b(k_1,k_2) z_1^{-k_1}. \tag{13.4}$$

From Eq. 13.2, it can be seen that a 2-D recursive filter can be treated as a combination of 1-D recursive filters. In the following sections, we derive different hierarchical 2-D recursive structures in terms of 1-D recursive structures.

13.3.1   2-D IIR Design 1: Broadcast *X* and *Y* Inputs and Pipelined Output

In this design, we broadcast the X and Y inputs to each 1-D filter section and pipeline their outputs to obtain the 2-D filter output. Using Horner's rule on Eq. 13.2 in the form

$$Y = F(0)X - G(0)Y + z_2^{-1}[F(1)X - G(1)Y + z_2^{-1}[F(2)X - G(2)Y + \cdots \\ z_2^{-1}[F(h-1)X - G(h-1)Y]] \cdots], \tag{13.5}$$

the above Equation can be written in iterative form as

$$S_i = F(i)X - G(i)Y + z_2^{-1} S_{i+1} \qquad 0 \le i < h \tag{13.6}$$

$$S_h = 0 \tag{13.7}$$

$$Y = S_0. \tag{13.8}$$

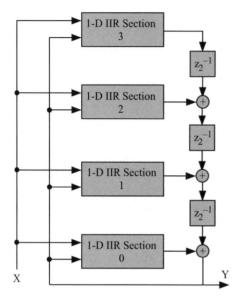

Figure 13.3   DAG of a 2-D recursive filter using Design 1 for a filter window height of $h = 4$.

Using the results of Chapter 9, we obtain the directed acyclic graph (DAG) shown in Fig. 13.3. This design was previously developed by the author's group in References 23 and 87. The DAG could be implemented by multithreads in software or by using systolic arrays in hardware.

Line wraparound can be eliminated by clearing all the storage elements *within* the 1-D filters. This should be done after the reception of the last pixel of a given line and before the reception of the first pixel of the next line by any 1-D filter structure.

Frame wraparound can be eliminated by clearing all the storage elements within the tasks of each 1-D filter as well as all the z^{-1} elements between adjacent 1-D filters. This should be done after the reception of the last pixel in the last line of a given frame and before the reception of the first pixel of the following frame.

13.3.2 2-D IIR Design 2: Pipelined *X* and *Y* Inputs and Broadcast Output

Equation 13.2 is modified by associating the z^{-1} delay operators with the input samples. In effect, we are introducing the delays to the input signals X and Y.

$$Y = \sum_{k_2=0}^{h-1} \left[F(k_2)\left(z_2^{-k_2} X\right) - G(k_2)\left(z_2^{-k_2} Y\right) \right]. \tag{13.9}$$

We develop the iterative equations for the input signals as

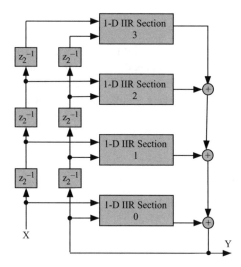

Figure 13.4   DAG of a 2-D recursive filter using Design 2 for a filter window height of $h = 4$.

$$X_i = z_2^{-1} X_{i-1} \qquad 0 < i < h \tag{13.10}$$

$$Y_i = z_2^{-1} Y_{i-1} \qquad 0 < i < h \tag{13.11}$$

$$X_0 = X \tag{13.12}$$

$$Y_0 = Y. \tag{13.13}$$

Finally, we have the filter output given by

$$Y = \sum_{i=0}^{h-1} Y_i. \tag{13.14}$$

The resulting DAG is shown in Fig. 13.4. This DAG can be implemented using software multithreading or hardware systolic arrays. The systolic array of the 2-D recursive structure is similar to the one reported in References 23, 87, and 88. Line and frame wraparound can be eliminated by using the approach described in the previous section.

13.4 3-D DIGITAL FILTERS

A first-quadrant 3-D recursive filter can be represented by the equation

$$Y = \sum_{k_3=0}^{f-1} \sum_{k_2=0}^{h-1} \sum_{k_1=0}^{w-1} a(k_1, k_2, k_3) X z_1^{-k_1} z_2^{-k_2} z_3^{-k_3} - \sum_{k_3=0}^{f-1} \sum_{k_2=0}^{h-1} \sum_{k_1=0}^{w-1} b(k_1, k_2, k_3) Y z_1^{-k_1} z_2^{-k_2} z_3^{-k_3}, \tag{13.15}$$

where $X \equiv X(z_1, z_2, z_3)$, $Y \equiv Y(z_1, z_2, z_3)$, and $b(0, 0, 0) = 0$. In the above equation, h is the height of the filter window, w is the width of the filter window, and f is the depth of the filter window, which is the number of frames used to collect the filter input samples.

Assuming progressive raster-scanned data, the term z_1^{-1} represents one time-step delay through the use of a single register as a storage element. The term z_2^{-1} represents W time-step delays where W is the frame width. The term z_3^{-1} represents HW time-step delays where H is the frame height. These delays could be implemented as memory address locators for use by the software threads, or they could be implemented as actual hardware buffers for use by the software systolic array processing elements.

The above equation can be written in a hierarchical way as

$$Y = \sum_{k_3=1}^{f-1} \left[F_2(k_3)z_3^{-k_3}X - G_2(k_3)z_3^{-k_3}Y \right], \tag{13.16}$$

where the terms $F_2(k_3)$ and $G_2(k_3)$ are two 2-D IIR filter operators given by

$$F_2(k_3) = \sum_{k_2=0}^{h-1} \sum_{k_1=0}^{w-1} a(k_1,k_2)z_1^{-k_1}z_2^{-k_1} \tag{13.17}$$

$$G_2(k_3) = \sum_{k_2=0}^{h-1} \sum_{k_1=0}^{w-1} b(k_1,k_2)z_1^{-k_1}z_2^{-k_1}. \tag{13.18}$$

From Eq. 13.16, it can be seen that a 3-D recursive filter can be treated as a combination of 2-D recursive filters. In the following sections, we derive different hierarchical 3-D recursive DAG structures in terms of 2-D recursive DAG structures.

13.4.1   3-D IIR Design 1: Broadcast X and Y Inputs and Pipelined Output

In this design, we broadcast the X and Y inputs to each 2-D filter section and pipeline their outputs to obtain the 3-D filter output. Using Horner's rule on Eq. 13.16 in the form

$$Y = F_2(0)X - G_2(0)Y + z_3^{-1}[F_2(1)X - G_2(1)Y + z_3^{-1}[F_2(2)X - G_2(3)Y + \cdots$$
$$z_3^{-1}[F_2(f-1)X - G_2(f-1)Y]]\cdots], \tag{13.19}$$

the above Equation can be written in iterative form as

$$S_i = F_2(i)X - G_2(i)Y + z_2^{-1}S_{i+1} \qquad 0 \le i < f \tag{13.20}$$

$$S_f = 0 \tag{13.21}$$

$$Y = S_0. \tag{13.22}$$

Using the results of Chapter 9, we obtain the DAG shown in Fig. 13.5. The DAG implementations of 1-D discussed in the previous chapters and 2-D IIR filters discussed in the previous sections can be used to implement the 3-D DAG task in the figure. Frame wraparound can be eliminated by clearing all the storage elements *within* the 2-D filters. This should be done after the reception of the last pixel of a given frame and before the reception of the first pixel of the next frame by any 2-D filter structure.

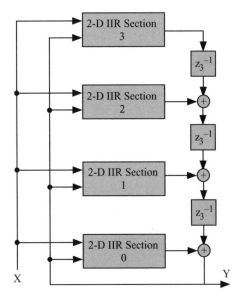

Figure 13.5 DAG of a 3-D recursive filter using Scheme 1 for a filter window depth of $f = 4$.

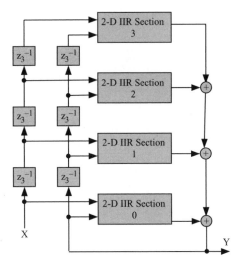

Figure 13.6 DAG of a 3-D recursive filter using Scheme 2 for a filter window depth of $f = 4$.

13.4.2 3-D IIR Design 2: Pipelined *X* and *Y* Inputs and Broadcast Output

Equation 13.16 is modified by associating the z_3^{-1} delay operators with the input samples. In effect, we are introducing the delays to the input signals X and Y:

$$Y = \sum_{k_2=0}^{h-1} \left[F_2(k_3)\left(z_3^{-k_3}X\right) - G_2(k_3)\left(z_3^{-k_3}Y\right) \right]. \tag{13.23}$$

We develop the iterative equations for the input signals as

$$X_i = z_3^{-1} X_{i-1} \qquad 0 < i < h \tag{13.24}$$
$$Y_i = z_3^{-1} Y_{i-1} \qquad 0 < i < h \tag{13.25}$$
$$X_0 = X \tag{13.26}$$
$$Y_0 = Y. \tag{13.27}$$

Finally, we have the filter output given by

$$Y = \sum_{i=0}^{f-1} Y_i. \tag{13.28}$$

The resulting DAG structure is shown in Fig. 13.6. The different DAGs of 1-D discussed in the previous chapters and 2-D IIR filters discussed in the previous sections can be used to implement the 2-D tasks in the figure. Line and frame wrap-around can be eliminated by using the approach described in the previous section.

Chapter 14

Case Study: Multirate Decimators and Interpolators

14.1 INTRODUCTION

Multirate digital processing systems are important due to the numerous applications in which efficient translations among various sampling frequencies are needed. An important application of multirate digital filters is to implement the discrete wavelet transform. Decimators and interpolators are the most basic elements of such systems. They have also found applications in sub-band coding and analog-to-digital (A/D) conversion [89–93]. Particular interest is nowadays focused on the implementation of multirate filters for real-time applications.

Multirate systems rely on the use of *decimators* and *interpolators*. A decimator accepts a high-rate input signal and produces a low-rate output signal. An interpolator accepts a low-rate input signal and produces a high-rate output signal. We discuss in this chapter how to design multithreaded systems that implement decimators and interpolators.

14.2 DECIMATOR STRUCTURES

A decimator is a device that passes a high-rate input signal through a low-pass filter then picks out some of the filter outputs to get a low-rate output. The low-pass filter is sometimes referred to as an anti-aliasing filter. Decimation is usually used for signals whose Nyquist rate is much higher than the highest frequency of the signal. In this way, computations and memory savings can result by reducing the data rate without loss of information.

The model of an M-to-1 decimator is shown in Fig. 14.1 [94, 95]. The operating frequencies of the different components are indicated above the input and output lines. The sample periods are indicated below the input and output lines. The block on the left is an N-tap finite impulse response (FIR) digital filter with impulse response $h(nT)$, where T is the high-rate sampling period, which operates at the high sampling rate F. $M - 1$ out of every M output samples are discarded by the M-to-1

Algorithms and Parallel Computing, by Fayez Gebali
Copyright © 2011 John Wiley & Sons, Inc.

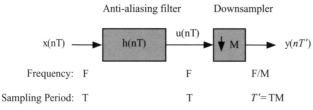

Figure 14.1 General M-to-1 decimator system.

sampling rate compressor, or downsampler, shown as the block on the right in Fig. 14.1. The low-pass filter generates the signal $u(nT)$ and the downsampler generates the signal $y(nT')$. The system in Fig. 14.1 implies a serial algorithm where input data samples are first filtered then downsampled. The techniques we discuss here merge the two operations and extract different parallelization options.

We can write the following equations for the two output signals

$$u(n) = \sum_{k=0}^{N-1} h(k)\, x(n-k) \qquad (14.1)$$

$$y(n) = u(nM). \qquad (14.2)$$

In this chapter, we assume that the filter length is an integer multiple of M. If it is not, we augment it with zero-valued coefficients to simplify the analysis.

14.3 DECIMATOR DEPENDENCE GRAPH

The author and his group provided a z-transform technique for obtaining several decimator structures [96–98]. However, for the case of multirate systems, this approach was not able to provide the rich set of design space exploration that the dependence graph approach could provide. Figure 14.2 shows the dependence graph of the decimator, which was obtained for the two signals in Eqs. 14.1 and 14.2. The horizontal axis is the n-axis and vertical axis is the k-axis. The figure shows the dependence graph of the filter whose output samples are $u(n)$. At the top of the figure, we indicate the decimator output $y(n)$. Note that sample $y(n)$ corresponds to the sample $u(M\,n)$. In order to conserve space, we used subscripts in the figure to indicate index values for the different samples.

The thick vertical lines indicate the decimator output $y(n)$. The solid circles in the figure indicate useful filtering operations that result in the generation of the output samples $u(nM)$ and $y(n)$, while the empty circles indicate filtering operations that will result in no useful output samples. In a sense, these are wasted operations that consume unnecessary resources. Essentially, the decimator uses a regular low-pass filter to produce some output samples at the high input data rate. Then, we selectively pick the Mth sample to represent the desired decimator outputs.

Figure 14.3 shows the dependence graph of the decimator where only the useful operations and outputs are indicated.

This figure is a bit less cluttered compared with Fig. 14.2. We removed the empty circles and only retained the shaded circles that give the desired outputs.

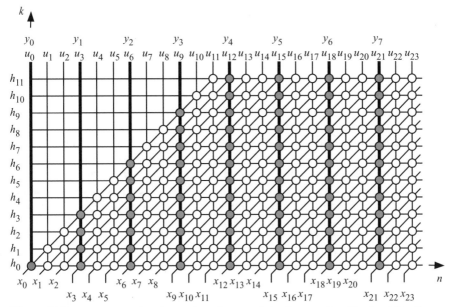

Figure 14.2   General M-to-1 decimator dependence graph for the case when $M = 3$ and $N = 12$.

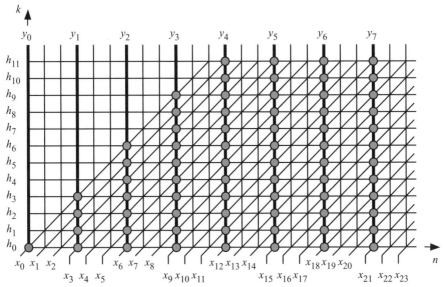

Figure 14.3 M-to-1 decimator dependence graph for the case when $M = 3$ and $N = 12$. Unnecessary operations and output samples have been removed from the figure.

14.4 DECIMATOR SCHEDULING

As usual, we employ an affine timing function

$$t(\mathbf{p}) = \mathbf{sp}, \tag{14.3}$$

where the row vector $\mathbf{s} = [s_1 \; s_2]$ is the scheduling vector and the column vector $\mathbf{p} = [n \; k]^t$ is any point in the dependence graph. The first component refers to the horizontal axis and the second component refers to the vertical axis.

Assigning time values to the nodes of the dependence graph transforms the dependence graph to a directed acyclic graph (DAG) as discussed in Chapters 10 and 11. More specifically, the DAG can be thought of as a serial–parallel algorithm (SPA) where the parallel tasks could be implemented using a thread pool or parallel processors for software or hardware implementations, respectively. The different stages of the SPA are accomplished using barriers or clocks for software or hardware implementations, respectively.

The restrictions on our timing function were discussed in Chapters 10 and 11. We assume that the input data $x(n)$ arrive at consecutive times. Let us study the times associated with the points at the bottom of the graph, $\mathbf{p} = [n \; 0]^t$. Two input samples, $x(n)$ and $x(n + 1)$, arrive at the two points, $\mathbf{p}_1 = [n \; 0]^t$ and $\mathbf{p}_2 = [n + 1 \; 0]^t$, respectively. Applying the scheduling function in Eq. 14.3, we get

$$t(\mathbf{p}_1) = s_1 n \tag{14.4}$$

$$t(\mathbf{p}_2) = s_1(n+1). \tag{14.5}$$

Since the difference $t(\mathbf{p}_2) - t(\mathbf{p}_1) = 1$, we must have $s_1 = 1$. A valid scheduling vector that satisfies input data timing must be specified as

$$\mathbf{s} = \begin{bmatrix} 1 & s_2 \end{bmatrix}. \tag{14.6}$$

The value of s_2 will be determined by our choice of whether we need to pipeline or broadcast the output sample $y(n)$. Choosing $s_2 = 0$ would result in broadcast of $y(n)$. Choosing $s_2 = \pm 1$ would result in pipelining $y(n)$. We have three possible valid scheduling functions that we can employ:

$$\mathbf{s}_1 = \begin{bmatrix} 1 & 0 \end{bmatrix} \tag{14.7}$$

$$\mathbf{s}_2 = \begin{bmatrix} 1 & -1 \end{bmatrix} \tag{14.8}$$

$$\mathbf{s}_3 = \begin{bmatrix} 1 & 1 \end{bmatrix}. \tag{14.9}$$

Scheduling vector $\mathbf{s}_1$ results in pipelined input $x(n)$ and broadcast output $y(n)$. Scheduling vector $\mathbf{s}_2$ results in broadcast input $x(n)$ and pipelined output $y(n)$. Scheduling vector $\mathbf{s}_3$ results in pipelined input $x(n)$ and pipelined output $y(n)$.

In the following subsections, we explore the possible designs afforded by the above scheduling vectors. We should point out that the advantage of using the approach in this section is reduction in the number of processing tasks. This comes, however, at the price of task processing speed that matches the input data rate and increases task complexity. Later in this chapter, we will explore *polyphase* designs that do not suffer from these disadvantages.

14.5 DECIMATOR DAG FOR $s_1 = [1\ \ 0]$

The DAG corresponding to $\mathbf{s}_1$ is shown in Fig. 14.4. The equitemporal planes are indicated by the gray lines, and the time index values are indicated by the grayed numbers associated with the equitemporal planes. We note from the figure that a maximum of 12 tasks or nodes is active at any time step, which corresponds to the anti-aliasing filter length N. It should also be noted that the time values are associated with the high data rate of the decimator input.

We have three possible valid projection vectors:

$$\text{Design 1a: } \mathbf{d}_{1a} = \begin{bmatrix} 1 & 0 \end{bmatrix}^t \tag{14.10}$$

$$\text{Design 1b: } \mathbf{d}_{1b} = \begin{bmatrix} 1 & 1 \end{bmatrix}^t \tag{14.11}$$

$$\text{Design 1c: } \mathbf{d}_{1c} = \begin{bmatrix} 1 & -1 \end{bmatrix}^t. \tag{14.12}$$

These projection directions correspond to the projection matrices

$$\text{Design 1a: } \mathbf{P}_{1a} = \begin{bmatrix} 0 & 1 \end{bmatrix}^t \tag{14.13}$$

$$\text{Design 1b: } \mathbf{P}_{1b} = \begin{bmatrix} 1 & -1 \end{bmatrix}^t \tag{14.14}$$

$$\text{Design 1c: } \mathbf{P}_{1c} = \begin{bmatrix} 1 & 1 \end{bmatrix}^t. \tag{14.15}$$

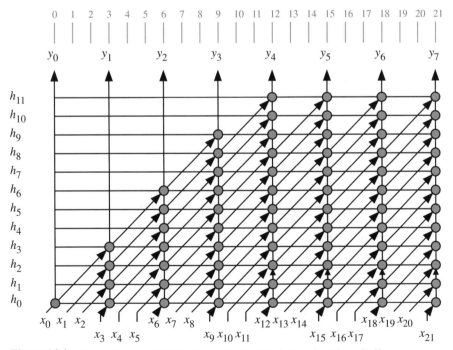

Figure 14.4 M-to-1 decimator DAG for the case when $M = 3$, $N = 12$, and $\mathbf{s}_1 = [1\ 0]$.

We consider only the design corresponding to $\mathbf{d}_{1a}$ since the other two designs will be more complex and will not lead to a better task workload. A point in the DAG given by the coordinates $\mathbf{p} = [n\ k]'$ will be mapped into the point in $\overline{\text{DAG}}$ given by

$$\overline{\mathbf{p}} = \mathbf{P}_{1a}\mathbf{p} = k. \tag{14.16}$$

Output sample calculations are all performed at the same time step. In that sense, the input samples are pipelined and the output samples are broadcast. We note, however, that each task is active once every M time steps. In order to reduce the number of threads or processors, we modify the linear projection operation above to employ a *nonlinear* projection operation

$$\overline{\mathbf{p}} = \left\lfloor \frac{\mathbf{P}_{1a}\mathbf{p}}{M} \right\rfloor = \left\lfloor \frac{k}{M} \right\rfloor. \tag{14.17}$$

Figure 14.5 shows the reduced or projected $\overline{\text{DAG}}$ architecture for Design 1a. Figure 14.5a shows the $\overline{\text{DAG}}$ where input samples are pipelined between the tasks and the partial results for the output samples are broadcast among the tasks. Note that the number of tasks required is N/M. Figure 14.5b shows the task detail. Each task has a simple processing and control structure. Each task accepts input samples and forwards the inputs to the next task after a delay of M time steps. During each M time step, each task accumulates the partial results then loads the accumulated data to the parallel adder using a software barrier or hardware tristate buffer as shown

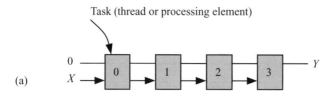

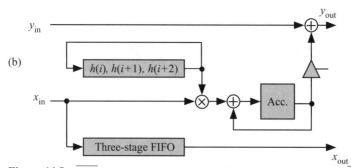

Figure 14.5 $\overline{\text{DAG}}$ for Design 1a for $\mathbf{s}_1$, $\mathbf{d}_{1a}$, $N = 12$, and $M = 3$. (a) Resulting $\overline{\text{DAG}}$. (b) Task processing detail.

on the left of the figure. All tasks pipeline the incoming data $x(n)$ at the high data rate T and perform the filtering operation at the high data rate T also. The output is obtained from the rightmost task at time iMT.

14.6 DECIMATOR DAG FOR $s_2 = [1 -1]$

The DAG corresponding to s_2 is shown in Fig. 14.6. The equitemporal planes are indicated by the gray lines and the time index values are indicated by the grayed numbers associated with the equitemporal planes. We note from the figure that a maximum of 12 tasks or nodes is active at any time step, which corresponds to the anti-aliasing filter length N. It should also be noted that the time values are associated with the high data rate of the decimator input.

Chapters 10 and 11 explained that the projection operation assigns a node or a group of nodes in the DAG to a thread or processor. The number of assigned nodes determines the workload associated with each task. The operation also indicates the input and output data involved in the calculations. The projection operation controls the workload assigned to each thread/processor at each stage of the execution of the SPA. We have three possible valid projection vectors:

$$\text{Design 1a: } \mathbf{d}_{2a} = \begin{bmatrix} 1 & 0 \end{bmatrix}^t \tag{14.18}$$

$$\text{Design 1b: } \mathbf{d}_{2b} = \begin{bmatrix} 1 & -1 \end{bmatrix}^t \tag{14.19}$$

$$\text{Design 1c: } \mathbf{d}_{2c} = \begin{bmatrix} 0 & 1 \end{bmatrix}^t. \tag{14.20}$$

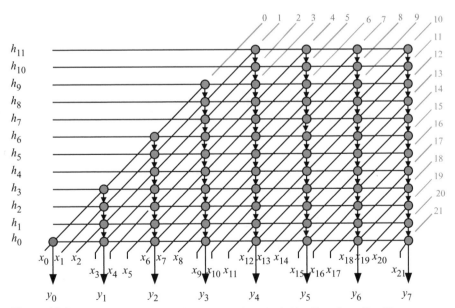

Figure 14.6 M-to-1 decimator DAG for the case when $M = 3$, $N = 12$, and $s_2 = [1 - 1]$.

These projection directions correspond to the projection matrices

$$\text{Design 1a: } \mathbf{P}_{2a} = \begin{bmatrix} 0 & 1 \end{bmatrix}^t \tag{14.21}$$

$$\text{Design 1b: } \mathbf{P}_{2b} = \begin{bmatrix} 1 & 1 \end{bmatrix}^t \tag{14.22}$$

$$\text{Design 1c: } \mathbf{P}_{2c} = \begin{bmatrix} 1 & 0 \end{bmatrix}^t. \tag{14.23}$$

We consider only the design corresponding to $\mathbf{d}_{2a}$ since the other two designs will be more complex and will not lead to a better task workload. A point in the DAG given by the coordinates $\mathbf{p} = \begin{bmatrix} n & k \end{bmatrix}^t$ will be mapped into a point in $\overline{\text{DAG}}$ given by

$$\bar{\mathbf{p}} = \mathbf{P}_{1a}\mathbf{p} = k. \tag{14.24}$$

Input samples are supplied to the nodes at the same time step. In that sense, the input samples are broadcast and the output samples are pipelined. We note, however, that each node is active once every M time steps. In order to reduce the number of nodes, we modify the linear projection operation above to employ a nonlinear projection operation:

$$\bar{\mathbf{p}} = \lfloor \frac{\mathbf{P}_{1a}\mathbf{p}}{M} \rfloor = \lfloor \frac{k}{M} \rfloor. \tag{14.25}$$

Figure 14.7 shows the $\overline{\text{DAG}}$ architecture for Design 2a. Figure 14.7a shows the $\overline{\text{DAG}}$ where input samples are broadcast between the tasks and the partial results for the output samples are pipelined among the tasks. Note that the number of tasks required is N/M. Figure 14.7b shows the task detail. The workload of each task is simple in processing and control structures. Each task accepts input samples and

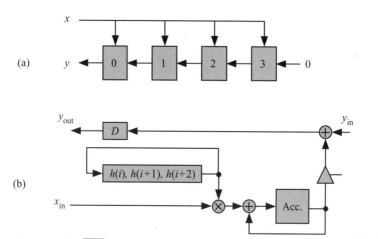

Figure 14.7 $\overline{\text{DAG}}$ for Design 2a for $\mathbf{s}_2$, $\mathbf{d}_{2a}$, $N = 12$, and $M = 3$. (a) Resulting $\overline{\text{DAG}}$. (b) Task detail when the $\overline{\text{DAG}}$ is implemented in hardware systolic arrays.

forwards the inputs to the next task after a delay of M time steps. During each M time step, each task accumulates the partial results then loads the accumulated data to the parallel adder using a software barrier or a tristate buffer as shown on the left of the figure. All tasks pipeline the incoming data $x(n)$ at the high data rate T and perform the filtering operation at the high data rate T also. The output is obtained from the rightmost task at times iMT.

14.7 DECIMATOR DAG FOR $s_3 = [1\ 1]$

This choice of a scheduling function would produce a decimator $\overline{\text{DAG}}$ similar to the the decimator $\overline{\text{DAG}}$ of the previous two sections. We will leave this to the reader to explore.

14.8 POLYPHASE DECIMATOR IMPLEMENTATIONS

A polyphase decimator splits the high-rate input signals into M low-rate nonoverlapped streams such that each stream is applied to a filter with length N/M. Figure 14.8 shows the splitting of the input data stream into M nonoverlapped streams, and each stream is fed to a low-pass FIR filter. Each filter has the following characteristics:

1. It operates at the longer sample time $T' = MT$.
2. The number of filter coefficients is reduced to N/M.
3. Every Mth input sample is used.

In order to get a dependence graph for a polyphase filter, we break up the dependence graph of Fig. 14.1 into $M = 3$ dependence graphs. Figure 14.9 shows the dependence graph corresponding to the stream feeding the filter $h_0(nT')$. Each dependence graph corresponds to one branch of the polyphase filter structure of Fig. 14.8. Table 14.1 shows the filter coefficients associated with the filter whose impulse transfer function

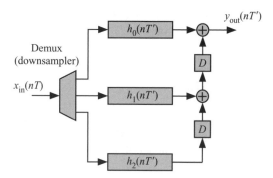

Figure 14.8 Polyphase implementation of a decimator for the case $M = 3$.

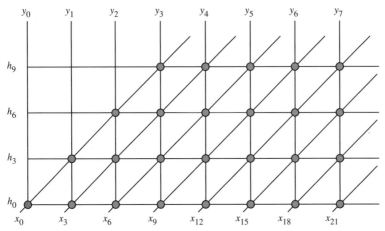

Figure 14.9 Dependence graph for polyphase filter $h_0(nT')$ for an M-to-1 decimator for the case when $M = 3$ and $N = 12$.

Table 14.1 Filter Coefficients and Input Samples Associated with Each Polyphase Filter for the Case $M = 3$ and $N = 12$

Polyphase filter	Filter coefficients				Input samples				
$h_0 (nT')$	h_0	h_3	h_6	h_9	x_0	x_3	x_6	x_9	$\ldots$
$h_1 (nT')$	h_2	h_5	h_8	h_{11}	x_1	x_4	x_7	x_{10}	$\ldots$
$h_2 (nT')$	h_1	h_4	h_7	h_{10}	x_2	x_5	x_8	x_{11}	$\ldots$

is $h_i(nT)$ and also shows the stream of input data samples allocated to it. In general, polyphase filter $h_i(nT)$ ($0 \leq i < M$) is fed the ith downsampled stream and uses the filter coefficient h_{k+jM} where $0 \leq j < N/M$ and is given by

$$k = (-i) \bmod M \qquad 0 \leq i < M. \qquad (14.26)$$

The advantages of polyphase filters are that each filter operates at the slower rate of MT and its length is N/M. We can use the different 1-D FIR filter structures discussed previously to realize the polyphase decimator.

14.9 INTERPOLATOR STRUCTURES

An interpolator is a device that passes a low-rate input signal through a low-pass filter then inserts the filter outputs to get a high-rate output. The low-pass filter is sometimes referred to as an anti-imaging filter. The model of a 1-to-L interpolator

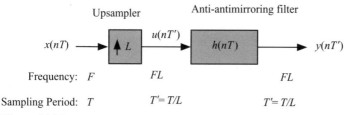

Upsampler   Anti-antimirroring filter

Figure 14.10   General 1-to-L interpolator system.

is shown in Fig. 14.10 [94, 95]. The operating frequencies of the different components are indicated above the input and output lines. The sample periods are
indicated below the input and output lines. The block on the left is an N-tap FIR
digital filter with impulse response $h(nT')$, where T is the high-rate sampling period,
and operates at the high sampling rate F. The 1-to-M upsampler, or sample rate
expander, inserts $M - 1$ zeros between the input sample $x(nT)$, shown as the block
on the left of Fig. 14.10. The upsampler generates the signal $u(nT')$ and the low-pass
filter generates the signal $y(nT')$. The upsampler simply inserts $L - 1$ zeros between
the input sample $x(n)$ to produce a signal at L times the data rate. This process is
sometimes called "zero-stuffing." We can write the following equations for the two
output signals:

$$u(nL) = x(n) \tag{14.27}$$

$$y(n) = \sum_{k=0}^{N-1} h(k)\, u(n-k). \tag{14.28}$$

14.10 INTERPOLATOR DEPENDENCE GRAPH

The author and his group provided a z-transform technique for obtaining several
decimator structures [96–98]. However, for the case of multirate systems, this
approach was not able to provide the rich set of design space exploration that the
dependence graph approach could provide. Fig. 14.11 shows the dependence graph
of the interpolator. The horizontal axis is the n-axis and vertical axis is the k-axis.
The figure shows the dependence graph of the filter whose input samples are $u(nL)$.
At the top of the figure, we indicate the interpolator output $y(n)$. In order to conserve
space, we used subscripts in the figure to indicate index values for the different
samples. The gray circles correspond to the samples $x(n)$ and the empty circles correspond to the stuffed zero-valued samples. In a sense, this is wasted operations.
Figure 14.12 shows the dependence graph of the interpolator where only the useful
operations and outputs are indicated. This figure is a bit less cluttered compared to
Fig. 14.11. We removed the empty circles and only retained the shaded circles that
give the desired outputs.

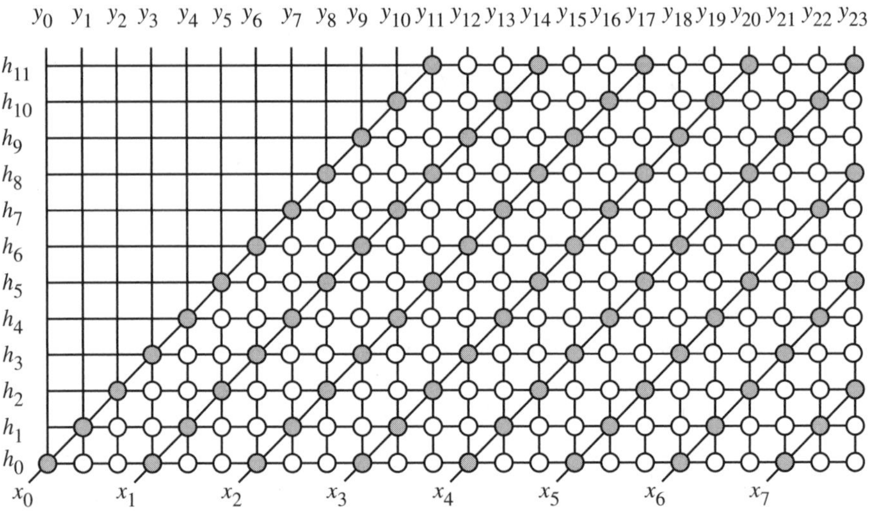

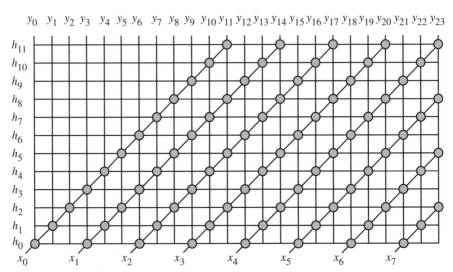

y_0 y_1 y_2 y_3 y_4 y_5 y_6 y_7 y_8 y_9 y_{10} y_{11} y_{12} y_{13} y_{14} y_{15} y_{16} y_{17} y_{18} y_{19} y_{20} y_{21} y_{22} y_{23}
h_{11} h_{10} h_9 h_8 h_7 h_6 h_5 h_4 h_3 h_2 h_1 h_0
x_0 x_1 x_2 x_3 x_4 x_5 x_6 x_7

Figure 14.11 General 1-to-L interpolator dependence graph for the case when $L = 3$ and $N = 12$.

y_0 y_1 y_2 y_3 y_4 y_5 y_6 y_7 y_8 y_9 y_{10} y_{11} y_{12} y_{13} y_{14} y_{15} y_{16} y_{17} y_{18} y_{19} y_{20} y_{21} y_{22} y_{23}
h_{11} h_{10} h_9 h_8 h_7 h_6 h_5 h_4 h_3 h_2 h_1 h_0
x_0 x_1 x_2 x_3 x_4 x_5 x_6 x_7

Figure 14.12 1-to-L interpolator dependence graph for the case when $L = 3$ and $N = 12$. Unnecessary operations and output samples have been removed from the figure.

14.11 INTERPOLATOR SCHEDULING

As usual, we employ an affine timing function:

$$t(\mathbf{p}) = \mathbf{sp}, \tag{14.29}$$

where the row vector $\mathbf{s} = [s_1 \; s_2]$ is the scheduling vector and the column vector $\mathbf{p} = [n \; \mathrm{k}]^t$ is any point in the dependence graph. The first component refers to the horizontal axis and the second component refers to the vertical axis. The restrictions on our timing function were discussed in Chapters 10 and 11. We assume that the input data $x(n)$ arrive at consecutive times. Let us study the times associated with the points at the bottom of the graph $\mathbf{p} = [n\ 0]^t$. Two input samples, $x(n)$ and $x(n+1)$, arrive at the two points, $\mathbf{p}_1 = [n\ 0]^t$ and $\mathbf{p}_2 = [nL + 1\ 0]^t$, respectively. Applying the scheduling function in Eq. 14.3, we get

$$t(\mathbf{p}_1) = s_1 n \tag{14.30}$$

$$t(\mathbf{p}_2) = s_1(n+1). \tag{14.31}$$

Since the difference $t(\mathbf{p}_2) - t(\mathbf{p}_1) = L$, we must have $s_1 = 1$. A valid scheduling vector that satisfies input data timing must be specified as

$$\mathbf{s} = [1\ \ s_2]. \tag{14.32}$$

The value of s_2 will be determined by our choice of whether we need to pipeline or broadcast the output sample $y(n)$. Choosing $s_2 = 0$ would result in the broadcast of $y(n)$. Choosing $s_2 = \pm 1$ would result in pipelining of $y(n)$. We have three possible valid scheduling functions that we can employ:

$$\mathbf{s}_1 = [1\ \ 0] \tag{14.33}$$

$$\mathbf{s}_2 = [1\ \ -1] \tag{14.34}$$

$$\mathbf{s}_3 = [1\ \ 1]. \tag{14.35}$$

Scheduling vector $\mathbf{s}_1$ results in pipelined input $x(n)$ and broadcast output $y(n)$. Scheduling vector $\mathbf{s}_2$ results in broadcast input $x(n)$ and pipelined output $y(n)$. Scheduling vector $\mathbf{s}_3$ results in pipelined input $x(n)$ and pipelined output $y(n)$.

In the following subsections, we explore the possible designs afforded by the above scheduling vectors. We should point out that the advantages of using the approach in this section are reduction in the number of nodes. This comes, however, at the price of processing speed that matches the input data rate and increased task complexity. Later in this chapter, we will explore *polyphase* designs that do not suffer from these disadvantages.

14.12 INTERPOLATOR DAG FOR $s_1 = [1\ 0]$

The DAG corresponding to $\mathbf{s}_1$ is shown in Fig. 14.13. The equitemporal planes are indicated by the gray lines and the time index values are indicated by the grayed numbers associated with the equitemporal planes. We note from the figure that a maximum of four tasks or nodes is active at any time step. It should also be noted that the time values are associated with the high data rate of the interpolator output. We have three possible valid projection vectors:

$$\text{Design 1a: } \mathbf{d}_{1a} = [1\ \ 0]^t \tag{14.36}$$

$$\text{Design 1b: } \mathbf{d}_{1b} = [1\ \ 1]^t \tag{14.37}$$

$$\text{Design 1c: } \mathbf{d}_{1c} = [1\ \ -1]^t. \tag{14.38}$$

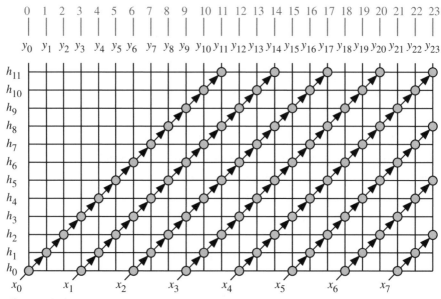

Figure 14.13 1-to-L interpolator DAG for the case when $L = 3$, $N = 12$, and $\mathbf{s}_1 = [1\ 0]$.

These projection directions correspond to the projection matrices

$$\text{Design 1a: } \mathbf{P}_{1a} = \begin{bmatrix} 0 & 1 \end{bmatrix}^t \quad (14.39)$$

$$\text{Design 1b: } \mathbf{P}_{1b} = \begin{bmatrix} 1 & -1 \end{bmatrix}^t \quad (14.40)$$

$$\text{Design 1c: } \mathbf{P}_{1c} = \begin{bmatrix} 1 & 1 \end{bmatrix}^t. \quad (14.41)$$

We consider only the design corresponding to $\mathbf{d}_{1a}$ since the other two designs will be more complex and will not lead to a better task workload. A point in the DAG given by the coordinate $\mathbf{p} = [n\ k]^t$ will be mapped into the point in the reduced or projected DAG given by

$$\bar{\mathbf{p}} = \mathbf{P}_{1a}\mathbf{p} = k. \quad (14.42)$$

Output sample calculations are all performed at the same time step. In that sense, the input samples are pipelined and output samples are broadcast. We note however, that each task is active once every L time steps. In order to reduce the number of nodes, we modify the linear projection operation above to employ a nonlinear projection operation:

$$\bar{\mathbf{p}} = \left\lfloor \frac{\mathbf{P}_{1a}\mathbf{p}}{L} \right\rfloor = \left\lfloor \frac{k}{L} \right\rfloor. \quad (14.43)$$

Figure 14.14 shows the implementation of Design 1a. Figure 14.14a shows the DAG, where input samples are pipelined between the tasks and the partial results

Task (thread or processing element)

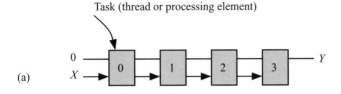

(a)

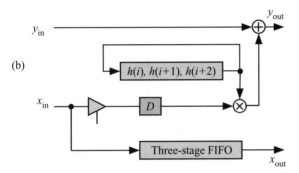

(b)

Figure 14.14   Interpolator Design 1a for s_1, d_{1a}, $N = 12$, and $L = 3$. (a) Resulting $\overline{\text{DAG}}$. (b) Task processing detail. In the figure FIFO is first-in-first-out buffer.

for the output samples are broadcast among the tasks. Note that the number of tasks required is N/L. Figure 14.14b shows the task detail. Each task is simple in hardware and in control structure. Each task accepts an input sample every L time steps and forwards the input to the next task after a delay of L time steps. All tasks pipeline the incoming data $x(n)$ at the low data rate and perform the filtering operation at the high data rate. The output is obtained from the rightmost task at each time step.

14.13 INTERPOLATOR DAG FOR $s_2 = [1\ -1]$

The DAG corresponding to s_2 is shown in Fig. 14.15. The equitemporal planes are indicated by the gray lines and the time index values are indicated by the grayed numbers associated with the equitemporal planes. We note from the figure that a maximum of four nodes is active at any time step. It should also be noted that the time values are associated with the high data rate of the interpolator input. We have three possible valid projection vectors:

$$\text{Design 1a: } \mathbf{d}_{2a} = \begin{bmatrix} 1 & 0 \end{bmatrix}^t \tag{14.44}$$

$$\text{Design 1b: } \mathbf{d}_{2b} = \begin{bmatrix} 1 & -1 \end{bmatrix}^t \tag{14.45}$$

$$\text{Design 1c: } \mathbf{d}_{2c} = \begin{bmatrix} 0 & 1 \end{bmatrix}^t. \tag{14.46}$$

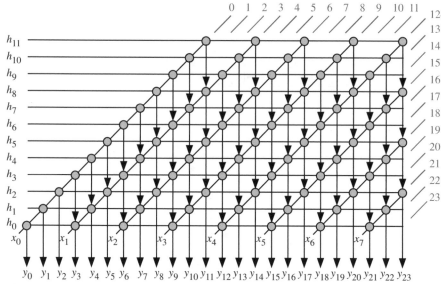

Figure 14.15 1-to-L interpolator DAG for the case when $L = 3$, $N = 12$, and $\mathbf{s}_2 = [1\,-1]$.

These projection directions correspond to the projection matrices

$$\text{Design 1a: } \mathbf{P}_{2a} = \begin{bmatrix} 0 & 1 \end{bmatrix}^t \tag{14.47}$$

$$\text{Design 1b: } \mathbf{P}_{2b} = \begin{bmatrix} 1 & 1 \end{bmatrix}^t \tag{14.48}$$

$$\text{Design 1c: } \mathbf{P}_{2c} = \begin{bmatrix} 1 & 0 \end{bmatrix}^t. \tag{14.49}$$

We consider only the design corresponding to $\mathbf{d}_{2a}$ since the other two designs will be more complex and will not lead to better processing element (task) designs. A point in the DAG given by the coordinate $\mathbf{p} = [n\ k]^t$ will be mapped into the point

$$\bar{\mathbf{p}} = \mathbf{P}_{1a}\mathbf{p} = k. \tag{14.50}$$

Input samples are supplied to the array at the same time step. In that sense, the input samples are broadcast and output samples are pipelined. We note, however, that each task is active once every L time steps. In order to reduce the number of nodes, we modify the linear projection operation above to employ a nonlinear projection operation:

$$\bar{\mathbf{p}} = \left\lfloor \frac{\mathbf{P}_{1a}\mathbf{p}}{L} \right\rfloor = \left\lfloor \frac{k}{L} \right\rfloor. \tag{14.51}$$

Figure 14.16 shows the hardware architecture for Design 2a. Figure 14.16a shows the pipeline where input samples are broadcast between the tasks and the partial results for the output samples are pipelined among the nodes. Note that the

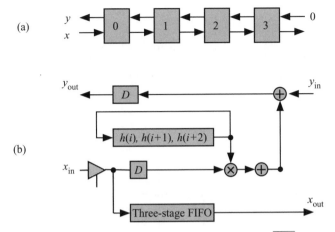

Figure 14.16   Design 2a for s_2, d_{2a}, $N = 12$, and $L = 3$. (a) $\overline{\text{DAG}}$. (b) Task detail for hardware systolic array implementation.

number of tasks required is N/L. Figure 14.16b shows the task detail. Each task is simple in hardware and in control structure. Each task accepts an input sample every L time steps and forwards the input to the next task after a delay of L time steps. All tasks pipeline the incoming data $x(n)$ at the low data rate and perform the filtering operation at the high data rate. The output is obtained from the leftmost task at each time step.

14.14   INTERPOLATOR DAG FOR s_3 = [1 1]

This choice of a scheduling function would produce systolic decimator hardware similar to the decimator structures of the previous two sections. We will leave this to the reader to explore.

14.15   POLYPHASE INTERPOLATOR IMPLEMENTATIONS

A polyphase decimator splits the high-rate input signals into M low-rate nonstreams such that each stream is applied to a filter with length N/M. Figure 14.17 shows the splitting of the input data stream into M nonoverlapped streams. Each filter has the following characteristics:

1. It operates at the longer sample time $T' = T/L$.
2. The number of filter coefficients is reduced to N/L.
3. Every Lth input sample is used.

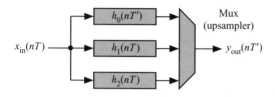

Figure 14.17   Dependence graph for polyphase filter $h_0(nT')$ for a 1-to-L interpolator for the case when $L = 3$ and $N = 12$.

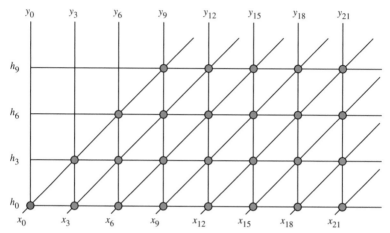

Figure 14.18   Polyphase 1-to-L interpolator dependence graph for the case when $L = 3$ and $N = 12$.

Table 14.2   Filter Coefficients and Input Samples Associated with Each Polyphase Filter for the Case $M = 3$ and $N = 12$

Polyphase filter	Filter coefficients				Output samples				
$h_0\ (nT)$	h_0	h_3	h_6	h_9	y_0	y_3	y_6	y_9	$\ldots$
$h_1\ (nT)$	h_1	h_4	h_7	h_{10}	y_1	y_4	y_7	y_{10}	$\ldots$
$h_2\ (nT)$	h_2	h_5	h_8	h_{11}	y_2	y_5	y_8	y_{11}	$\ldots$

In order to get a dependence graph for a polyphase filter, we break up the dependence graph of Fig. 14.1 into $M = 3$ DAGs as shown in Fig. 14.18. Each dependence graph corresponds to one branch of the polyphase filter structure of Fig. 14.17. Table 14.2 shows the filter coefficients associated with the filter whose impulse transfer function is $h_i(nT)$ and also shows the stream of input data samples allocated to it. In general, polyphase filter $h_i(nT)$ ($0 \leq i < L$) produces the ith upsampled stream and uses the filter coefficients h_{i+jM} where $0 \leq j < N/L$. The advantages of polyphase filters is that each filter operates at the slower rate of LT and its length is N/L. We can use the different 1-D FIR filter structures discussed previously to realize the polyphase decimator.

Chapter 15

Case Study: Pattern Matching

15.1 INTRODUCTION

String matching is employed in several applications, such as packet classification, computational biology, spam blocking, and information retrieval. String search operates on a given alphabet set Σ of size $|\Sigma|$, a pattern $P = p_0 p_1 \ldots p_{m-1}$ of length m, and a text string $T = t_0 t_1 \ldots t_{n-1}$ of length n, with $m \leq n$. The problem is to find all occurrences of the pattern P in the text string T. The average time complexity for implementing the string search problem on a single processor was proven to be $O(n)$ [99]. We refer the reader to Reference 100 for a comprehensive review of the different hardware implementations of the string matching problem.

A hardware implementation for the search engine can be assumed to have the following characteristics:

- The text length n is typically big and variable.
- The pattern length m varies from a word of few characters to hundreds of characters (e.g., a URL address).
- The word length w is determined by the data storage organization and datapath bus width.
- Typically, the search engine is looking for the existence of the pattern P in the text T; that is, the search engine only locates the first occurrence of the P in T.
- The text string T is supplied to the hardware in word serial format.

15.2 EXPRESSING THE ALGORITHM AS A REGULAR ITERATIVE ALGORITHM (RIA)

To develop a multithreaded or systolic array implementation, we must first be able to describe the string matching algorithm using recursions that convert the algorithm into a RIA. We can write the basic string search algorithm as in Algorithm 15.1:

Algorithms and Parallel Computing, by Fayez Gebali
Copyright © 2011 John Wiley & Sons, Inc.

Algorithm 15.1 Basic string search algorithm

1: input T and P
2: **for** i = 0:n-m **do**
3:   $j = 0$
4:   **while** $j < m$ AND $t_{i+j} = p_j$ **do**
5:     $j = j + 1$
6:   **end while**
7:   **if** $j = m$ **then**
8:     mathc_flag = TRUE
9:     match_location = i
10: **end if**
11: **end for**

This algorithm can also be expressed in the form of an iteration using two indices, i and j:

$$y_i = \bigwedge_{j=0}^{m-1} \text{Match}(t_{i+j}, p_j) \qquad 0 \le i \le n-m, \tag{15.1}$$

where y_i is a Boolean-type output variable. If y_i = true, then there is a match at position t_i; that is, $t_{i:i+m+1} = p_{0:m-1}$. Match(a, b) is a function that is true when character a matches character b. $\wedge$ represents an m-input AND function.

15.3 OBTAINING THE ALGORITHM DEPENDENCE GRAPH

The string matching algorithm of Eq. 15.1 is defined on a two-dimensional (2-D) domain since there are two indices (i, j). Therefore, a data dependence graph can be easily drawn as shown in Fig. 15.1. The *computation domain* is the convex hull in

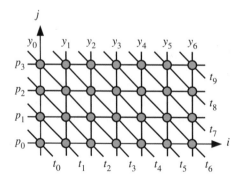

Figure 15.1 Dependence graph for $m = 4$ and $n = 10$.

the 2-D space where the algorithm operations are defined as indicated by the grayed circles in the 2-D plane [86]. The output variable y is represented by vertical lines so that each vertical line corresponds to a particular instance of y. For instance, the line described by the equation $i = 3$ represents the output variable instance y_3. The input variable t is represented by the slanted lines. Again, as an example, the line represented by the equation

$$i + j = 3 \qquad (15.2)$$

represents the input variable instance t_3. Similarly, the input variable p is represented by the horizontal lines.

15.4 DATA SCHEDULING

The timing function assigns a time value to each node in the dependence graph. The algorithm dependence graph becomes transformed into a directed acyclic graph (DAG), which will help us determine multithreaded or systolic array implementations. A simple but very useful timing function is an affine scheduling function of the form [86]

$$t(\mathbf{p}) = \mathbf{s}^t \mathbf{p} - s, \qquad (15.3)$$

where the function $t(\mathbf{p})$ associates a time value t to a point $\mathbf{p}$ in the dependence graph. The column vector $\mathbf{s} = [s_1, s_2]$ is the scheduling vector and s is an integer.

A valid scheduling function uniquely maps any point $\mathbf{p}$ to a corresponding time index value. Such affine scheduling function must satisfy several conditions in order to be a valid scheduling function as explained below.

Assigning time values to the nodes of the dependence graph transforms the dependence graph to a DAG as discussed in Chapters 10 and 11. More specifically, the DAG can be thought of as a serial–parallel algorithm (SPA) where the parallel tasks could be implemented using a thread pool or parallel processors for software or hardware implementations, respectively. The different stages of the SPA are accomplished using barriers or clocks for software or hardware implementations, respectively.

Input data timing restricts the space of valid scheduling functions. We assume the input text $T = t_0 \, t_1 \, \dots \, t_{n-1}$ arrives in word serial format where the index of each word corresponds to the time index. This implies that the time difference between adjacent words is one time step. Take the text instances at the bottom row nodes in Fig. 15.1 characterized by the line whose equation is $j = 0$. Two adjacent words, t_i and t_{i+1}, at points $\mathbf{p}_1 = (i, 0)$ and $\mathbf{p}_2 = (i + 1, 0)$ arrive at the time index values i and $i + 1$, respectively. Applying our scheduling function in Eq. 15.3 to these two points, we get

$$t(\mathbf{p}_1) = js_1 - s \qquad (15.4)$$
$$t(\mathbf{p}_2) = (j + 1)s_1 - s. \qquad (15.5)$$

Since the time difference $t(\mathbf{p}_2) - t(\mathbf{p}_1) = 1$, we must have $s_1 = 1$. Therefore, a scheduling vector that satisfies input data timing must be specified as

$$\mathbf{s} = \begin{bmatrix} 1 & s_2 \end{bmatrix}. \tag{15.6}$$

This leaves two unknowns in the possible timing functions, mainly the component s_1 and the integer s. If we decide to pipeline a certain variable whose null vector is $\mathbf{e}$, we must satisfy the following inequality [86]:

$$\mathbf{s}^t \mathbf{e} \neq 1. \tag{15.7}$$

We have only one output variable, Y, whose null vector is $\mathbf{e}_y = [0\ 1]$. If we want to pipeline y, then the simplest valid scheduling vectors are described by

$$\mathbf{s}_1 = \begin{bmatrix} 1 & 1 \end{bmatrix} \tag{15.8}$$
$$\mathbf{s}_2 = \begin{bmatrix} 1 & -1 \end{bmatrix}. \tag{15.9}$$

On the other hand, to broadcast a variable whose null vector is $\mathbf{e}$, we must have [86]

$$\mathbf{s}^t \mathbf{e} = 0. \tag{15.10}$$

If we want to broadcast Y, then from Eqs. 15.6 and 15.10, we must have

$$\mathbf{s}_3 = \begin{bmatrix} 1 & 0 \end{bmatrix}. \tag{15.11}$$

Broadcasting an output variable simply implies that all computations involved in computing an instance of Y must be done in the same time step. Another restriction on system timing is imposed by our choice of the projection operator as explained in the next section.

15.5   DAG NODE PROJECTION

The projection operation is a many-to-one function that maps several nodes of the DAG onto a single node in a reduced DAG, which we refer to as $\overline{\text{DAG}}$. Thus, several tasks in the DAG are mapped to a single task in $\overline{\text{DAG}}$. The projection operation allows for a better task workload and control design by multiplexing several nodes in the DAG to a single node in the $\overline{\text{DAG}}$. We explained in Chapters 10 and 11 how to perform the projection operation using a projection matrix P. To obtain the projection matrix, we require to define a desired projection direction $\mathbf{d}$. The vector d belongs to the null space of P. Since we are dealing with a 2-D DAG, matrix P is a row vector and $\mathbf{d}$ is a column vector.

A valid projection direction must satisfy the inequality

$$\mathbf{s}^t \mathbf{d} \neq 0. \tag{15.12}$$

In the following sections, we will discuss design space explorations for the three values of **s** obtained in Eqs. 15.8–15.11.

15.6 DESIGN 1: DESIGN SPACE EXPLORATION WHEN s = [1 1]^t

The feeding point of input sample t_0 is easily determined from Fig. 15.1 to be p = $[0\ 0]^t$. The time value associated with this point is $t(\mathbf{p}) = 0$. Using Eq. 15.3, we get $s = 0$. Applying the scheduling function in Eq. 15.8 to $\mathbf{e}_P$ and $\mathbf{e}_T$, we get

$$[1\quad 1]\mathbf{e}_P = 1 \tag{15.13}$$
$$[1\quad 1]\mathbf{e}_Y = 2. \tag{15.14}$$

This choice for the timing function implies that both input variables P and Y will be pipelined. The pipeline direction for the input T flows in a southeast direction in Fig. 15.1. The pipeline for T is initialized from the top row in the figure defined by the line $j = m - 1$. Thus, the feeding point of t_0 is located at the point $\mathbf{p} = [-m\ m]^t$. The time value associated with this point is given by

$$t(\mathbf{p}) = -2m - s = 0. \tag{15.15}$$

Thus, the scalar s should be $s = -2m$. The tasks at each stage of the SPA derived in this section will have a latency of $2m$ time steps compared to Design 1.a.

Figure 15.2 shows how the dependence graph of Fig. 15.1 is transformed to the DAG associated with $\mathbf{s} = [1\ 1]^t$. The equitemporal planes are shown by the gray lines and the execution order is indicated by the gray numbers. We note that the variables P and Y are pipelined between tasks, while variable T is broadcast among tasks lying in the same equitemporal planes. Pipelining means that a value produced by a source task at the end of a time step is used by a destination task at the start of the next time step. Broadcasting means that a value is made available to all tasks at the start of a time step.

There are three simple projection vectors such that all of them satisfy Eq. 15.12 for the scheduling function in Eq. 15.8.

The three projection vectors will produce three designs:

$$\text{Design 1.a: } \mathbf{d}_a = [1\quad 0]^t \tag{15.16}$$
$$\text{Design 1.b: } \mathbf{d}_b = [0\quad 1]^t \tag{15.17}$$
$$\text{Design 1.c: } \mathbf{d}_c = [1\quad 1]^t. \tag{15.18}$$

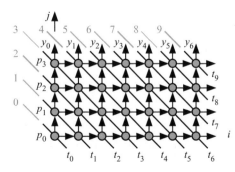

Figure 15.2   DAG for Design 1 when $n = 10$ and $m = 4$.

The corresponding projection matrices could be given by

$$\mathbf{P}_a = [0 \quad 1]^t \tag{15.19}$$
$$\mathbf{P}_b = [1 \quad 0]^t \tag{15.20}$$
$$\mathbf{P}_c = [1 \quad -1]^t. \tag{15.21}$$

Our task design space now allows for three configurations for each projection vector for the chosen timing function. In the following sections, we study the multithreaded implementations associated with each design option.

15.6.1 Design 1.a: Using s = [1 1]^t and d$_a$ = [1 0]^t

A point in the DAG given by the coordinate $\mathbf{p} = [i \, j]^t$ will be mapped by the projection matrix P_a into the point

$$\overline{\mathbf{p}} = \mathbf{P}_a \, \mathbf{p} = j. \tag{15.22}$$

A $\overline{\text{DAG}}$ corresponding to Design 1.a is shown in Fig. 15.3. Input T is broadcast to all nodes or tasks in the graph and word p_j of the pattern P is allocated to task T_j. The intermediate output of each task is pipelined to the next task with a higher index such that the output sample y_i is obtained from the rightmost task T_{m-1}. $\overline{\text{DAG}}$ consists of m tasks and each task is active for n time steps.

15.6.2 Design 1.b: Using s = [1 1]^t and d$_b$ = [0 1]^t

A point in the DAG given by the coordinate $\mathbf{p} = [i \, j]^t$ will be mapped by the projection matrix P_b into the point

$$\overline{\mathbf{p}} = \mathbf{P}_b \, \mathbf{p} = i. \tag{15.23}$$

The projected $\overline{\text{DAG}}$ is shown in Fig. 15.4. $\overline{\text{DAG}}$ consists of $n - m + 1$ tasks. Word p_i of the pattern P is fed to task T_0 and from there, it is pipelined to the other tasks. The text words t_i are broadcast to all tasks. Output y_i is obtained from task t_i at time step i and is broadcast to other tasks. Each task is active for m time steps only. Thus,

Figure 15.3 $\overline{\text{DAG}}$ for Design 1.a when $m = 4$.

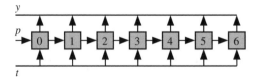

Figure 15.4 $\overline{\text{DAG}}$ for Design 1.b when $n = 10$ and $m = 4$.

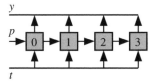

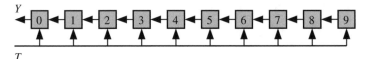

Figure 15.5   Reduced $\overline{\text{DAG}}$ for Design 1.b when $n = 10$ and $m = 4$.

Figure 15.6   Tasks at each SPA stage for Design 1.c.

the tasks are not well utilized as in Design 1.a. However, we note from the DAG of Fig. 15.4 that task T_0 is active for the time step 0 to $m - 1$, and T_m is active for the time period m to $2m - 1$. Thus, these two tasks could be mapped to a single task without causing any timing conflicts. In fact, all tasks whose index is expressed as

$$i' = i \bmod m \qquad (15.24)$$

can all be mapped to the same node without any timing conflicts. The resulting $\overline{\text{DAG}}$ after applying the above modulo operations on the array in Fig. 15.4 is shown in Fig. 15.5. The $\overline{\text{DAG}}$ now consists of m tasks. The pattern P could be chosen to be stored in each task or it could circulate among the tasks where initially T_i stores the pattern word p_i. We prefer the former option since memory is cheap, while communications between tasks will always be expensive in terms of area, power, and delay. The text word t_i is broadcast on the input bus to all tasks. T_i produces outputs $i, i + m, i + 2m, \ldots$ at times $i, i + m, i + 2m$, and so on.

15.6.3   Design 1.c: Using s = [1 1]^t and d$_c$ = [1 1]^t

A point in the DAG given by the coordinate $\mathbf{p} = [i\,j]^t$ will be mapped by the projection matrix $\mathbf{P}_c$ into the point

$$\bar{\mathbf{p}} = \mathbf{P}_c\,\mathbf{p} = i - j. \qquad (15.25)$$

The resulting tasks are shown in Fig. 15.6 for the case when $n = 10$ and $m = 4$, after adding a fixed increment to all task indices to ensure nonnegative task index values. The DAG consists of n tasks where only m of the tasks are active at a given time step as shown in Fig. 15.7. At time step i, input text t_i is broadcast to all tasks in DAG. We notice from Fig. 15.7 that at any time step, only m out of the n tasks are active. To improve task utilization, we need to reduce the number of tasks. An obvious task allocation scheme could be derived from Fig. 15.7. In that scheme, operations involving the pattern word p_i are allocated to task T_i. In that case, the DAG in Fig. 15.3 will result.

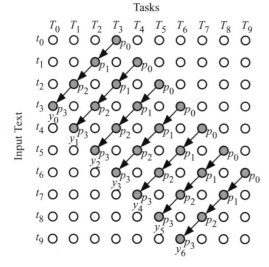

Figure 15.7 Task activity at the different time steps for Design 1.c.

15.7 DESIGN 2: DESIGN SPACE EXPLORATION WHEN s = [1 −1]^t

Figure 15.8 shows how the dependence of Fig. 15.1 is transformed to the DAG associated with $\mathbf{s} = [1\ 1]^t$. The equitemporal planes are shown by the gray lines and the execution order is indicated by the gray numbers. We note that the variables P, T, and Y are pipelined between tasks.

There are three simple projection vectors such that all of them satisfy Eq. 15.12 for the scheduling function. The three projection vectors are

$$\text{Design 2.a: } \mathbf{d}_a = \begin{bmatrix} 1 & 0 \end{bmatrix}^t \tag{15.26}$$

$$\text{Design 2.b: } \mathbf{d}_b = \begin{bmatrix} 0 & 1 \end{bmatrix}^t \tag{15.27}$$

$$\text{Design 2.c: } \mathbf{d}_c = \begin{bmatrix} 1 & -1 \end{bmatrix}^t. \tag{15.28}$$

Our multithreading design space now allows for three configurations for each projection vector for the chosen timing function.

15.7.1 Design 2.a: Using s = [1 −1]^t and d$_a$ = [1 0]^t

The resulting $\overline{\text{DAG}}$ is shown in Fig. 15.9 for the case when $n = 10$ and $m = 4$. Input T is pipelined between the tasks and task T_i is allocated pattern p_i. The partial results for Y are pipelined such that the outputs are obtained from task T_0.

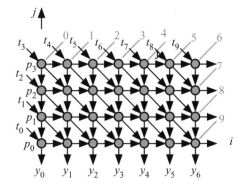

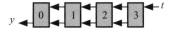

Figure 15.8   DAG for Design 2 when $n = 10$ and $m = 4$.

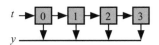

Figure 15.9 $\overline{\text{DAG}}$ for Design 2.a. when $n = 10$ and $m = 4$.

Figure 15.10   Tasks for Design 2.b.

15.7.2   Design 2.b: Using s = [1 −1]^t and d$_b$ = [0 1]^t

Using the same treatment as in Design 1.b, the resulting tasks are shown in Fig. 15.10 for the case when $n = 10$ and $m = 4$.

15.7.3   Design 2.c: Using s = [1 −1]^t and d$_c$ = [1 −1]^t

The tasks are similar to Design 1.c, which, in turn, is similar to Design 1.a.

15.8   DESIGN 3: DESIGN SPACE EXPLORATION WHEN s = [1 0]^t

The dependence graph of Fig. 15.1 is transformed to the DAG in Fig. 15.11, which is associated with $\mathbf{s} = [1\ 0]^t$. The equitemporal planes are shown by the gray lines and the execution order is indicated by the gray numbers. We note that the variables P and T are pipelined between tasks, while variable Y is broadcast among tasks lying in the same equitemporal planes.

There are three simple projection vectors such that all of them satisfy Eq. 15.12 for the scheduling function. The three projection vectors are

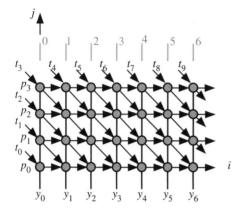

Figure 15.11 DAG for Design 3 when $n = 10$ and $m = 4$.

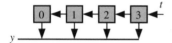

Figure 15.12 $\overline{\text{DAG}}$ for Design 3.a.

$$\text{Design 3.a: } \mathbf{d}_a = \begin{bmatrix} 1 & 0 \end{bmatrix}^t \qquad (15.29)$$

$$\text{Design 3.b: } \mathbf{d}_b = \begin{bmatrix} 1 & 1 \end{bmatrix}^t \qquad (15.30)$$

$$\text{Design 3.c: } \mathbf{d}_c = \begin{bmatrix} 1 & -1 \end{bmatrix}^t. \qquad (15.31)$$

Our multithreading design space now allows for three configurations for each projection vector for the chosen timing function.

15.8.1 Design 3.a: Using s = [1 0]^t and d$_a$ = [1 0]^t

The $\overline{\text{DAG}}$ corresponding to Design 3.a is drawn in Fig. 15.12 for the case when $n = 10$ and $m = 4$. Task T_j stores only the value p_j, which can be stored in a register similar to Design 1.a. The outputs of all the tasks must be combined using a reduce operation.

These two projection vectors produce the same configuration as Design 3.a. However, unlike Design 3.a, each task stores the entire pattern P in the on-chip memory.

Chapter 16

Case Study: Motion Estimation for Video Compression

16.1 INTRODUCTION

Motion estimation plays a key role in several applications such as video on demand, high-definition TV (HDTV), and multimedia communications. Motion estimation is used to remove temporal data redundancy between successive video frames. Video data compression rate can be improved by estimating the offset information of objects from one frame to another (motion estimation) and then by encoding only frame differences with respect to that offset (motion compensation).

There are several types of motion estimation: pixel based, block based, and region based, where motion estimation can be done pixel by pixel, block by block, or region by region, respectively. Block-based motion estimation is the most popular method due to its simplicity and suitability for hardware implementation. Block-based motion estimation is used in MPEG, H.263, H.264/AVC, and other video compression standards that aim at achieving high video compression ratios at real-time speeds, which requires a huge amount of computations. As a result, any efficient hardware would require the use of single instruction multiple data stream (SIMD) processors, which are special-purpose very large-scale integration (VLSI) circuitry employing a high degree of parallelism while requiring little input/output (I/O) communications. The main design challenge focuses on how to arrive at SIMD processor architectures that satisfy system-level requirements for a given complex algorithm with maximum processor utilization and minimum hardware cost.

There are several block matching algorithms that can be used for motion estimation. Full-search block matching algorithms (FBMAs) are preferred due to their relative simplicity and low-control overhead. However, the amount of calculations to be performed per second is prohibitive unless parallel hardware is used. In this chapter, we discuss a hierarchical design methodology for deriving hierarchical

Algorithms and Parallel Computing, by Fayez Gebali
Copyright © 2011 John Wiley & Sons, Inc.

SIMD processor architectures for FBMA, which possess adaptable sampling rates, adaptable processor complexity, low-memory bandwidth, low I/O pin count, and high throughput. The hierarchical design allows for trading processor complexity for data rate and vice versa to match system-level performance requirements. Our design methodology identifies the impact of the algorithm parameters on the system area and time complexities at each level of the design hierarchy. Thus, a designer is able to judge the effect of each parameter on the area–time complexity for any hierarchy level.

16.2 FBMAs

Figure 16.1 shows the main aspects of motion estimation. An intermediate image frame is divided into $B \times B$ macroblocks. Usually, $B = 8$ or 16. We choose a system of coordinates such that the i-axis points to the right and gives the pixel position in a line, and the j-axis points downward and gives the position of the line in the video

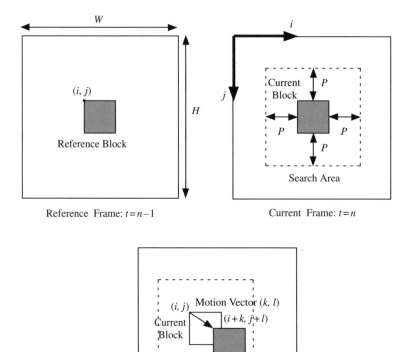

Figure 16.1 The reference block (gray) and the current block (white) in the current frame. The extent of the search area and the motion vector is indicated.

frame. In a sequence of frames, the current frame is predicted from a previous frame, known as the reference frame. The block to be matched in the current frame is referred to as the current block. The current block is compared with other reference blocks in the reference frame using a search area (window) with size $(2P + B) \times (2P + B)$, where typically, $P = 8$ or 16 pixels. Once a good match is found, the difference information is coded along with a motion vector that describes the offset of the best match with respect to the block being encoded.

The full-search algorithm is generally preferred for motion estimation since it is simple, although it requires a prohibitive amount of computations. The required number of operations per second can be calculated as follows: (1) the number of blocks per frame is $(W/B) \times (H/B)$, where W and H are the frame width and height in pixels, respectively; (2) the number of match operations to be performed for each block is $(2P + 1)^2$; (3) the number of point operations per match operation is B^2; and (4) frame rate is f frames per second. Thus, the number of operations per second is $(W/B) \times (H/B) \times (2P + 1)^2 \times B^2 \times f = W \times H \times (2P + 1)^2 \times f$. For example, consider a video transmission with parameters: $W = 720$ pixels, $H = 576$ pixels, $B = 16$, $P = 8$, and $f = 30$ frames/second. Such moderate settings require 3.6 billion operations each second.

16.3 DATA BUFFERING REQUIREMENTS

Due to the raster scan nature of the arriving frames, buffering will always be required whether to store incoming lines or to store intermediate results. Thus, no matter which approach is taken, output latency will always be encountered. We choose to buffer incoming data since this will result in separation of major buffer and hardware processing space. This will also limit the amount of chip I/O since all intermediate data will be fed directly to neighboring processing elements (PEs) without having to access distant memory modules. Figure 16.2 shows a shift-register buffer arrangement to simultaneously access all the $2P + 1$ pixels of the search area that lie in one column (fixed i). Each shift-register buffer accepts incoming data through a tristate

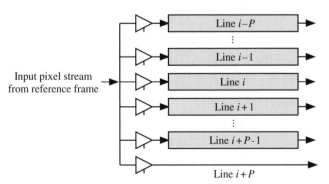

Figure 16.2   Shift-register buffer arrangement to simultaneously access all $2P + 1$ pixels of the search area that lie on one column.

buffer that is controlled by the select signal from the system controller. The number of shift-register buffers required will be $2P$ only. The length of each shift register is equal to the frame width W.

A similar arrangement could be employed for the current frame to simultaneously obtain all the pixels of the current block that lie on one column. The number of shift-register buffers required in that case will be $B - 1$ only.

16.4 FORMULATION OF THE FBMA

The motion vector $\mathbf{v}$ associated with the current block $c(i, j)$ is the displacement vector $\mathbf{v}(i, j) = [k^*\ l^*]^t$, which minimizes the sum of absolute differences, SAD (i, j, k, l), given by

$$SAD(i,j,k,l) = \sum_{m=0}^{B-1} \sum_{n=0}^{B-1} |c(i+m, j+n) - r(i+k+m, j+l+n)|, \qquad (16.1)$$

where $c(i + m, j + n)$ is the pixel intensity (luminance value) in the current block with coordinates (i, j); $r(i + k + m, j + l + n)$ is the pixel intensity in the reference block with coordinates $(i + k, j + l).(k, l)$ is a relative displacement between the reference block and the current block in the search area (as shown in Fig. 16.1), and (k^*, l^*) is the optimum relative displacement. The ranges of the indices i, j, k, and l are

$$i = 0, B, 2B, \cdots, (W/B - 1)B$$
$$j = 0, B, 2B, \cdots, (H/B - 1)B$$
$$k = k_{min}, k_{min+1}, \cdots, k_{max}$$
$$l = l_{min}, l_{min+1}, \cdots, l_{max},$$

where

$$k_{min} = \max(0, i - P)$$
$$k_{max} = \min(i + P, W - B)$$
$$l_{min} = \max(0, j - P)$$
$$l_{max} = \min(j + P, H - B).$$

The expressions above ensure valid bounds near the edges of the frame. Thus, the displacement vector $\mathbf{v}(i, j)$ can be expressed by

$$\mathbf{v}(i, j) = [k^*\ l^*]^t$$
$$= \min_{k,l}[SAD(i, j, k, l)]. \qquad (16.2)$$

Full-search motion estimation is a highly regular iterative algorithm with several embedded loops to reflect a hierarchical structure. We will make use of the embedded loop structure in what follows to illustrate a SIMD processor architecture that could be developed for each level of the hierarchy.

16.5 HIERARCHICAL FORMULATION OF MOTION ESTIMATION

There are several complications associated with motion estimation. First, the algorithm operations are not homogeneous, viz, subtraction, absolute value calculation, and minimum search. Second, a pixel is used more than once for several adjacent reference blocks. Third, a current block requires data from adjacent blocks around it. All these complications indicate that a hierarchical design methodology must be employed; hardware control must be considered during the design process; and extensive buffering must be used. Our strategy is to express Eq. 16.1 by a progressive set of hierarchical descriptions of the operations to be performed. The goal is to explore efficient parallel hardware architectures for each description at each hierarchy level. Figure 16.3 shows the $(2P + 1)2$ SAD values associated with a particular current block for a certain search area. Each SAD value is obtained at a different relative shift pair (k, l) between blocks c and r. The figure assumes $P = 3$ for simplicity, and the black circles indicate the minimum SAD value of each row. Figure 16.4 is a block diagram for the hierarchical decomposition of the full-search motion estimation hardware. The functions of each hierarchy level are described in the following sections.

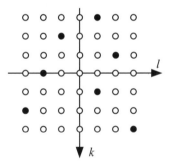

Figure 16.3 Different SAD values obtained due to the different k, l relative shifts between blocks c and r for $P = 3$.

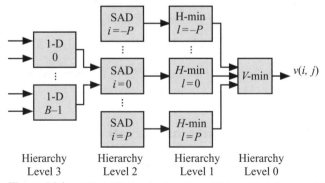

Figure 16.4 A block diagram for the proposed hierarchical decomposition of the full-search motion estimation hardware. The thick output arrows from the blocks at hierarchy level 3 indicate $2P + 1$ outputs.

16.5.1   Hierarchy Level 3 (Leftmost Level)

Referring to Fig. 16.4, blocks in hierarchy level 3 are divided into $2P + 1$ groups. Each group contains B one-dimensional (1-D) blocks as shown. All outputs from one group are fed to one block of the next level in the hierarchy. Each group is associated with a particular relative vertical shift l between blocks c and r. Each 1-D block of a group corresponds to one row of blocks c and r and produces $2P + 1$ SAD values (one at a time). The output of each 1-D block is given by the expression

$$D(i,j,k,l,n) = \sum_{m=0}^{B-1} |c(i+m,j+n) - r(i+k+m,j+l+n)|. \qquad (16.3)$$

16.5.2   Hierarchy Level 2

Referring to Fig. 16.4, each block at hierarchy level 2 produces $2P + 1$ SAD values (at different time instances but on a single output line) that are associated with a particular relative vertical shift l between blocks c and r. Each output corresponds to a particular relative horizontal shift k between blocks c and r and is represented by one circle in Fig. 16.3. The output from a SAD block associated with a particular relative shift pair (k, l) can be written as

$$SAD(i,j,k,l) = \sum_{n=0}^{B-1} D(i,j,k,l,n), \qquad (16.4)$$

where $D(i, j, k, l, m)$ represents an output of a 1-D block from hierarchy level 3.

16.5.3   Hierarchy Level 1

Referring to Fig. 16.4, each block at hierarchy level 1 produces the minimum SAD value H-min(i, j, l) for one row in Fig. 16.3 corresponding to a relative vertical shift l between blocks c and r. The output of each H-min block can be written as

$$H - \min(i,j,l) = \min_{k}[SAD(i,j,k,l)], \qquad (16.5)$$

where min is the function that selects the minimum of $2P + 1$ values and SAD (i, j, k, l) represents an output of a SAD block from hierarchy level 2.

16.5.4   Hierarchy Level 0 (Rightmost Level)

Referring to Fig. 16.4, level 0 of the hierarchy produces the motion vector $\mathbf{v}(i, j)$ by selecting the minimum SAD value from among a set of minimum values, H-min (i, j, l), which are indicated by the black circles in Fig. 16.3. The output of the V-min block corresponds to the output in Eq. 16.1 and can be written as

$$\mathbf{v}(i,j) = V - \min_l[H - \min(i,j,l)], \tag{16.6}$$

where V-min is the function that selects the minimum of $2P + 1$ values and H-min (i, j, l) represents an output of an H-min block from hierarchy level 1.

16.6 HARDWARE DESIGN OF THE HIERARCHY BLOCKS

In this section, we derive the hardware required to implement the different functional blocks in the hierarchical description of the algorithm shown in Fig. 16.4. We start with the leftmost level since the timing of the outputs of this level dictates the input timing of the blocks at the next higher level.

16.6.1 Hierarchy Level 3 Hardware Design

Level 3 of the hierarchy is probably the most important one since the hardware that implements it will have the most impact on the timing and hardware resource requirements. The blocks at this level implement 1-D SAD operations as described by Eq. 16.3. To study the data dependency in this equation, we write a 1-D SAD calculation equation in the general form

$$D(x) = \sum_{y=0}^{B-1} |c(y) - r(x+y)|, \tag{16.7}$$

where $D(x)$ represents the absolute difference calculation when the 1-D current block c is being compared to a reference 1-D block r that is shifted by x positions. The dependence graph of the above equation is shown in Fig. 16.5 for $B = 3$, $P = 3$, and $W = 15$.

Output variable $D(x)$ is represented by vertical lines so that each vertical line corresponds to a particular instance of D. As an example, output variable instance D_1 is represented by the line $x = 1$. Similarly, input variable $c(y)$ is represented by horizontal lines. Again, as an example, input variable instance c_3 is represented by the line $y = 3$. Also, input variable $r(x, y)$ is represented by diagonal lines. As an example, input variable instance r_3 is represented by the line $x + y = 3$.

Data Scheduling

Assigning time values to the nodes of the dependence graph in Fig. 16.5 transforms the dependence graph to a directed acyclic graph (DAG) as discussed in Chapters 10 and 11. More specifically, the DAG can be thought of as a serial–parallel algorithm (SPA) where the parallel tasks could be implemented using a thread pool or parallel processors for software or hardware implementations, respectively. The different stages of the SPA are accomplished using barriers or clocks for software or hardware implementations, respectively. There are several possible DAGs that could be obtained from the same dependence graph. This carries implications as which variables to pipeline and which to broadcast among the threads or processors. The

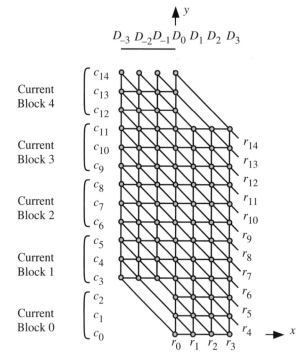

Figure 16.5 Dependence graph for the 1-D absolute difference calculation for $B = 3$, $P = 3$, and $W = 15$. Circles represent operations to be performed.

assignment of time values must take into consideration any input or output data timing restrictions. A simple but very useful timing function is an affine scheduling function of the form

$$t(\mathbf{p}) = \mathbf{s}\mathbf{p} - s, \qquad (16.8)$$

where the function $t(\mathbf{p})$ associates a time value t to a point $\mathbf{p}$ in the dependence graph. The row vector $\mathbf{s}$ is the scheduling vector and s is an integer. A valid scheduling function assigns a time index value to a point $\mathbf{p}$. Such affine scheduling function must satisfy several conditions in order to be a valid scheduling function as explained below. Since all points in the DAG must have nonnegative time index values, we must have

$$s = 0. \qquad (16.9)$$

Furthermore, since the extreme point $\mathbf{p} = (-3, 3)$ is in the DAG, we must have

$$s_2 \geq s_1, \qquad (16.10)$$

where s_1 and s_2 are the two components of the scheduling vector $\mathbf{s}$.

If we decide to broadcast a certain variable whose nullvector in the DAG is $\mathbf{e}$, then we must have

$$\mathbf{s}\mathbf{e} = 0. \qquad (16.11)$$

On the other hand, to pipeline a certain variable whose nullvector in the DAG is **e**, we must ensure the following inequality:

$$\mathbf{se} \neq 0. \tag{16.12}$$

It is a good idea to pipeline the algorithm's output variables since this speeds up the system timing. We have one output variable D whose nullvector is $\mathbf{e} = [0\ 1]'$. Equation 16.12 indicates that we must have

$$s_2 \neq 0. \tag{16.13}$$

Input data timing impacts our choice for a valid scheduling function. We assume the input data for blocks c and r arrive in a serial fashion; that is, $c = c_0 c_1 \ldots c_{W-1}$ and $r = r_0 r_1 \ldots r_{W-1}$, where the index of each pixel corresponds to the time index. This implies that the time difference between adjacent pixels is one time step. Take the c instances at the x-axis in Fig. 16.5 characterized by the line whose equation is $y = 0$. Two adjacent pixels, c_x and c_{x+1}, at points $\mathbf{p}_1 = (x, 0)$ and $\mathbf{p}_2 = (x + 1, 0)$ arrive at the time index values x and $x + 1$, respectively. Applying our scheduling function to these two points we get

$$t(\mathbf{p}_1) = s_1 x \tag{16.14}$$
$$t(\mathbf{p}_2) = s_1(x+1). \tag{16.15}$$

Since the time difference $t(\mathbf{p}_2) - t(\mathbf{p}_1) = 1$, we must have $s_1 = 1$. Applying the same reasoning for the input variable r results in the restriction $s_2 = 1$. Therefore, our timing function is now specified as

$$t(\mathbf{p}) = [1\ \ 1]^t. \tag{16.16}$$

The resulting DAG is shown in Fig. 16.6. The arrows indicate the directions of the flow of pipelined data. The equitemporal planes are shown by solid diagonal lines and the values of the time index are shown by gray numbers. White circles represent partial results of the SAD operations and black circles represent valid 1-D SAD outputs.

Note that inputs c are pipelined horizontally between computation nodes; inputs r are broadcasted along the diagonal lines; and outputs D are pipelined vertically between the computation nodes. It should be noted that in this case, for any valid scheduling function, a maximum of three valid 1-D SAD outputs is available at the same time. In general, the maximum number of simultaneous valid outputs is $\lceil (2P + 1)/B \rceil$, where $\lceil . \rceil$ represents the ceiling function.

Node Projection

The projection operation is a many-to-one function that projects several nodes of the DAG onto a single node in a new DAG. The new DAG is actually a description of the number of threads or PEs active at each stage of the SPA and it also gives information as to the required inputs and the resulting outputs of the stage.

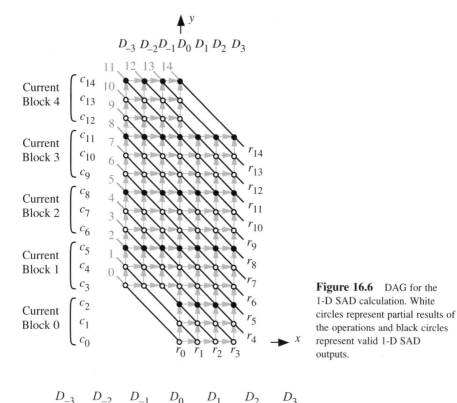

Figure 16.6 DAG for the 1-D SAD calculation. White circles represent partial results of the operations and black circles represent valid 1-D SAD outputs.

Figure 16.7 Task processing workload details at each SPA stage for implementing 1-D SAD calculation for $B = 3$, $P = 3$, and $W = 15$.

The projection operation could be implemented using a projection matrix. The null space of the projection matrix describes the projection vectors associated with that matrix. We choose a projection vector,

$$\mathbf{d} = [0 \quad 1]^t, \tag{16.17}$$

since this choice leads to the minimum number of tasks while maintaining maximum speed performance. The resulting tasks associated with each stage of the SPA are shown in Fig. 16.7, where each task calculates a 1-D SAD operation and accumulates the result.

The task activities in Fig. 16.7 are shown in Table 16.1. Notice that the 1-D SAD outputs associated with a given block are obtained consecutively and require $2P + 1$ time steps. We also observe that the maximum number of 1-D SAD outputs associated with different blocks is $(2P + 1)/B$.

Table 16.1   Task Activities for the 1-DSAD Vector Processing for $B = 3$, $P = 3$, and $W = 15$

Clock 0	$T(0)$	$T(1)$	$T(2)$	$T(3)$	$T(4)$	$T(5)$	$T(6)$
1							
2	$D(-3)$			$D(0)$			
3		$D(-2)$			$D(1)$		
4			$D(-1)$			$D(2)$	
5	$D(-3)$			$D(0)$			$D(3)$
6		$D(-2)$			$D(1)$		
7			$D(-1)$			$D(2)$	
8	$D(-3)$			$D(0)$			$D(3)$
9		$D(-2)$			$D(1)$		
10			$D(-1)$			$D(2)$	
11	$D(-3)$			$D(0)$			$D(3)$
12		$D(-2)$			$D(1)$		
13			$D(-1)$			$D(2)$	
14				$D(0)$			$D(3)$

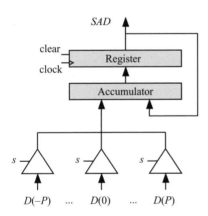

Figure 16.8   Task processing workload details at each SPA stage of the SAD blocks at hierarchy level 2 in Fig. 16.4.

16.6.2   Hierarchy Level 2 Hardware Design

The blocks at this level of the hierarchy implement a sum operation as described by Eq. 16.4. We write a SAD calculation equation in the general form

$$\text{SAD} = \sum_{x=0}^{B-1} D(x), \tag{16.18}$$

where SAD represents the sum of B 1-D SAD values that were obtained from the processor hardware at hierarchy level 3. Since the inputs are obtained at consecutive time index values, the hardware implementation of such a block is a simple accumulator as shown in Fig. 16.8,

16.6.3 Hierarchy Level 1 Hardware Design

Referring to Fig. 16.4, each block at this level of the hierarchy produces the minimum SAD value H-min(i, j, l) corresponding to one row in Fig. 16.3 for a relative vertical shift of value l between blocks c and r. Each row has $2P + 1$ SAD values, and the minimum value is indicated by a black circle.

16.6.4 Hierarchy Level 0 Hardware Design

Referring to Fig. 16.4, block V-min at this level of the hierarchy produces the motion vector estimation value $v(i, j)$, which is the minimum value of the black circles in Fig. 16.3. As all the H-min output values are produced at the same time, the V-min block must select the minimum value of the $2P + 1$ results in one time step. If this is not feasible, the outputs of the H-min blocks could be retimed using retiming buffers.

Chapter 17

Case Study: Multiplication over GF(2^m)

17.1 INTRODUCTION

There are many excellent books on applied cryptography that explain the ideas discussed in this chapter such as finite Galois fields and the basic mathematical operations performed in them [101, 102]. It is assumed that the reader of this chapter is already familiar with these concepts and wants to know how the algorithms could be implemented in parallel hardware. A number of cryptographic algorithms (e.g., the Advanced Encryption Standard [AES], elliptic curve cryptography [ECC]) rely heavily on GF(2^m) multiplication [103]. All these algorithms require fast, inexpensive, and secure implementation of multiplication over GF(2^m). Therefore, the design of efficient high-speed algorithms and hardware architectures for computing GF(2^m) multiplication are highly required and considered. Hardware implementation techniques for GF(2^m) multiplier include traditional techniques [104, 105] and processor array (PA) techniques [106–108]. Traditional multipliers are not attractive since their hardware structures are irregular and could be quite different for different m values. Moreover, as m gets larger, the propagation delay increases, which causes unavoidable performance deterioration. On the contrary, PA multipliers do not suffer from the above problems. They have regular structures consisting of a number of replicated basic cells. Furthermore, since each basic cell is only connected to its neighboring cells, signals propagate at a high clock speed [107]. In 1984, Yeh et al. [109] proposed a parallel-in parallel-out PA architecture to calculate AB + C in a general field GF(2^m). Since then, many PA multipliers have been proposed [106–108]. The main idea of this chapter is the PA design space exploration for GF(2^m)-based multipliers. This exploration results in different PA configurations. Among these configurations, we choose the fastest one to suit real-time applications. We made use of National Institute for Standards and Technology (NIST)-recommended irreducible polynomials, which makes our design secure and more suitable for cryptographic applications.

Algorithms and Parallel Computing, by Fayez Gebali
Copyright © 2011 John Wiley & Sons, Inc.

17.2   THE MULTIPLICATION ALGORITHM IN GF(2^m)

Let $A(x)$ and $B(x)$ be two field elements in the finite field GF(2^m), where m is an integer that typically has the values 163, 233, 283, 409, or 571. The two elements $A(x)$ and $B(x)$ can be written as the order $m - 1$ polynomials

$$A(x) = \sum_{i=0}^{m-1} a(i)x^i \tag{17.1}$$

$$B(x) = \sum_{i=0}^{m-1} b(i)x^i, \tag{17.2}$$

where $a(i)$ and $b(i)$ could have the values 0 or 1.

The elements of the finite field are generated by a primitive polynomial $R(x)$ of order m,

$$R(x) = \sum_{i=0}^{m} r(i)x^i, \tag{17.3}$$

where $r(m)$ must have the value $r(m) = 1$, and we can express the above equation as the sum

$$R(x) = x^m + \sum_{i=0}^{m-1} r(i)x^i = x^m + f(x), \tag{17.4}$$

where $f(x)$ is a polynomial of order $m - 1$.

The product of the field elements $A(x)$ and $B(x)$ is written as

$$C(x) = A(x)B(x) \mod R(x)$$
$$= \sum_{i=0}^{m-1} \sum_{j=0}^{m-1} a(i)b(j)x^{i+j} \mod R(x). \tag{17.5}$$

We can evaluate the above double summation as

$$C(x) = b(m-1)x^{m-1}A(x) + b(m-2)x^{m-2}A(x) \cdots$$
$$+ b(1)xA(x) + b(0)A(x) \mod R(x)$$
$$= [[\cdots[b(m-1)A(x)]x + b(m-2)A(x)]x + \cdots$$
$$+ b(1)A(x)]x + b(0)A(x) \mod R(x). \tag{17.6}$$

The above equation can be evaluated using the so-called "left-to-right shift-and-add" field multiplication method [110]. This algorithm is shown as follows:

Algorithm =17.1 Left-to-right shift-and-add field multiplication

Require: Input: Binary polynomials $A(x)$ and $B(x)$ of degree at most $m - 1$ and R(x) of degree m

1: $C(x) = 0$
2: **for** $i = m - 1 : 0$ **do**
3:   $C(x) = xC(x)$ mod $R(x)$
4:   $C(x) = C(x) + b_i A(x)$
5: **end for**
6: **RETURN** $C(x) // = A(x)B(x)$ mod $R(x)$

A few things must be noted in Algorithm 17.1:

1. The left shift operation $xC(x)$ in line 3 could result in a polynomial larger than $R(x)$, and hence the modulo operation in that step might be necessary. Specifically, if the coefficient $c(m - 1) = 1$, then we must subtract $R(x)$ from the polynomial $xC(x)$.
2. Bitwise add or subtract in GF(2) is equivalent to a bitwise exclusive OR (XOR) operation.
3. The addition operation in line 4 is a bitwise XOR operation over the m terms of the polynomials.
4. From Eq. 17.4, we can write line 3 as

$$xC(x) \mod R(x) = c(m-1) + \sum_{i=0}^{m-1} c(i)x^i \mod R(x)$$

$$= c(m-1)f(x) + \sum_{i=0}^{m-1} r(i)x^i. \qquad (17.7)$$

The above equation ensures that the modulo operation, which is accomplished by adding $f(x)$, only takes place when $c(m - 1) = 1$.

Algorithm 17.1 can be modified to express it as a regular iterative algorithm (RIA). This is done by explicitly writing the iterations required at the bit level. Algorithm 17.2 is the bit-level implementation of Algorithm 17.1.

Algorithm 17.2 Bit-level left-to-right shift-and-add field multiplication. $\wedge$ represents logical AND operation and $\oplus$ represents logical XOR operation

Require:

1: Binary polynomials $A(x)$ and $B(x)$ of degree at most $m - 1$ and $R(x)$ of degree m
2: **for** $j = 0 : m - 1$ **do**
3:   $c(0, j) = 0$

4: **end for**

5: **for** $i = 1 : m - 1$ **do**

6:      $c(i, 0) = [a(0) \wedge b(m - i)] \oplus c(i - 1, m - 1)$

7:      **for** $j = 1 : m - 1$ **do**

8:          $c(i, j) = [a(j) \wedge b(m - 1 - i)] \oplus c(i - 1, j - 1) \oplus [c(i - 1, m - 1) \wedge r(j)]$

9:      **end for**

10: **end for**

11: **RETURN** $C(x) // = A(x)B(x) \bmod R(x)$

Note that the index values of iterations in line 5 are increasing, while in Algorithm 17.1 the index in line 2 is decreasing. However, in both algorithms, the order of the operations is still preserved.

17.3 EXPRESSING FIELD MULTIPLICATION AS AN RIA

The basic operation in Algorithm 17.2 is the iterative expression

$$c(i, j) = [a(j) \wedge b(m - i)] \oplus c(i - 1, j - 1) \oplus [c(i - 1, m - 1) \wedge r(j)], \qquad (17.8)$$

with $0 \le i < m$ and $0 \le j < m$. The initial conditions for the above iterations are

$$c(0, j) = 0 \qquad 0 \le j < m \qquad (17.9)$$
$$c(i, 0) = [a(0) \wedge b(m - i)] \oplus c(i - 1, m - 1). \qquad (17.10)$$

The final result is given by

$$C(x) = \sum_{j=0}^{m-1} c(m, j)x^j. \qquad (17.11)$$

17.4 FIELD MULTIPLICATION DEPENDENCE GRAPH

The iterations in Eq. 17.8 are defined over a two-dimensional (2-D) computation domain $\mathcal{D}$ with the two indices i and j with the boundaries defined in Eq. 17.8. Since the dimensionality of $\mathcal{D}$ is low, it is preferable to draw a dependence graph for the data and use the graphic and combinational geometric analysis tools discussed in Chapters 10 and 11. Figure 17.1 shows the dependence graph for the left-to-right shift-and-add field multiplication algorithm for $m = 5$. The algorithm has three input variables a, b and r and one output variable c.

Input variables $a(j)$ and $r(j)$ will both map to horizontal lines. For example, input sample $a(3)$ is associated with the line whose equation is $i = 3$. Also, $a(j)$ or $r(j)$ are fed to the system at one of two points $(0, j)$ or $(m - 1, j)$. We choose to feed the variable at the former point.

Input variable $b(m - i)$ maps to vertical lines such that input instance $b(3)$ maps to the line equation $i = m - 3$. Since in our case $m = 5$, instance $b(3)$ maps to the

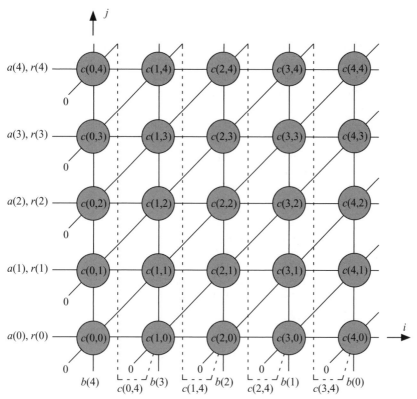

Figure 17.1 Dependence graph for the left-to-right shift-and-add field multiplication algorithm for $m = 5$.

line whose equation is $i = 2$ as shown in the figure. Also, $b(m - i)$ is fed to the system at one of two points $(i, 0)$ or $(i, m - 1)$. We choose to feed the variable at the former point.

Output variable $c(i, j)$ is represented by point $\mathbf{p} = [i\ j]^t$ in $\mathcal{D}$. Notice that output instances $c(i - 1, j - 1)$ are used as inputs to calculate outputs $c(i, j)$. This is indicated by the diagonal lines connecting each node to its southwest neighbor.

17.5 DATA SCHEDULING

Pipelining or broadcasting the variables of an algorithm is determined by the choice of a timing function that assigns a time value to each node in the dependence graph. A simple but useful timing function is an affine scheduling function of the form

$$t(\mathbf{p}) = \mathbf{s}\mathbf{p} - s, \tag{17.12}$$

where the function $t(\mathbf{p})$ associates a time value t to a point $\mathbf{p}$ in the dependence graph. The row vector $s = [s_1\ s_2]$ is the scheduling vector and s is an integer. Since all points in $\mathcal{D}$ have nonnegative indices, the value of scalar s must be 0.

Assigning time values to the nodes of the dependence graph in transforms the dependence graph to a directed acyclic graph (DAG) as was discussed in Chapters 10 and 11. More specifically, the DAG can be thought of as a serial–parallel algorithm (SPA) where the parallel tasks could be implemented using a thread pool or parallel processors for software or hardware implementations, respectively. The different stages of the SPA are accomplished using barriers or clocks for software or hardware implementations, respectively.

Input data timing restricts the space of valid scheduling functions. Let us assume that input variable $b(i)$ arrives at different adjacent time steps. Referring to Eq. 17.8, if $b(m - i)$ arrives at iteration i corresponding to time t, then $b(m - i - 1)$ arrives at iteration $i + 1$ corresponding to time $t + 1$. The bits $b(m - i)$ and $b(m - i - 1)$ arrive at points $\mathbf{p}_1 = (i, 0)$ and $\mathbf{p}_2 = (i + 1, 0)$ at the time steps $t(\mathbf{p}_1)$ and $t(\mathbf{p}_2)$, respectively. By applying our scheduling function in Eq. 17.12 to these two points, we get

$$t(\mathbf{p}_1) = \begin{bmatrix} s_1 & s_2 \end{bmatrix} \begin{bmatrix} i \\ 0 \end{bmatrix} = is_1 \tag{17.13}$$

$$t(\mathbf{p}_2) = \begin{bmatrix} s_1 & s_2 \end{bmatrix} \begin{bmatrix} i+1 \\ 0 \end{bmatrix} = (i+1)s_1. \tag{17.14}$$

As the time difference $t(\mathbf{p}_2) - t(\mathbf{p}_2) = 1$, we must have $s_1 = 1$. Thus, our timing function is given by

$$\mathbf{s} = \begin{bmatrix} 1 & s_2 \end{bmatrix}. \tag{17.15}$$

This leaves s_2 unknown and we need another restriction or specification for the timing function.

Equation 17.8 indicates that the output $c(i, j)$ depends on the previous output value $c(i - 1, j - 1)$. These two output samples are associated with points $\mathbf{p}_2 = (i, j)$ and $\mathbf{p}_1 = (i - 1, j - 1)$. Thus, our timing function must ensure the following inequality

$$t(\mathbf{p}_1) < t(\mathbf{p}_2). \tag{17.16}$$

Thus, we get the following inequality:

$$s_2 > -1. \tag{17.17}$$

Similarly from Eq. 17.8, we observe that the output $c(i, j)$ depends on the previous output value $c(i - 1, m - 1)$. That previous value is obtained at from the point $\mathbf{p} = (i - 1, m - 1)$. Thus, we can write the following inequality:

$$t[\mathbf{p}(i-1, m-1)] < t[\mathbf{p}(i, j)]. \tag{17.18}$$

The above inequality becomes

$$(m-1-j)s_2 < 1. \tag{17.19}$$

Hence, Eqs. 17.17 and 17.19 could be merged as

$$-1 < s_2 < \frac{1}{m-1-j} \qquad 0 \le j < m. \tag{17.20}$$

The worst case in the above inequality is when $j = 0$; thus, we can write

$$-1 < s_2 < \frac{1}{m-1}. \tag{17.21}$$

The above inequality can be written as

$$-\frac{\alpha}{\beta} \le s_2 \le \frac{1}{m}, \tag{17.22}$$

where α and β are positive integers and $\alpha < \beta$.

From the above inequality, we have three reasonable solutions to **s**:

$$\mathbf{s}_1 = [1 \quad 0] \tag{17.23}$$
$$\mathbf{s}_2 = [1 \quad \tfrac{1}{m}] \tag{17.24}$$
$$\mathbf{s}_3 = [1 \quad -\tfrac{\alpha}{\beta}]. \tag{17.25}$$

Timing function $\mathbf{s}_1$ implies that all inputs $a(j)$ and $r(j)$ must be supplied simultaneously.

The timing functions $\mathbf{s}_2$ and $\mathbf{s}_3$ result in only one thread operating at a given time. To prove this, suppose that we have two points (i, j) and (i', j') mapped to the same time value. Using the scheduling function in Eq. 17.24, we can write

$$i + \frac{j}{m} = i' + \frac{j'}{m} \qquad 0 \le j < m. \tag{17.26}$$

The only solution to for arbitrary values of i, j and i', j' is when $i = i'$ and $j = j'$, which proves that only one node is active at the same time step. A similar argument is also valid for Eq. 17.25.

As a consequence of the above discussion, we consider only the timing function $\mathbf{s}_1$. Figure 17.2 is the DAG for the left-to-right shift-and-add field multiplication algorithm. The arrows indicate pipelined signals that move from the source node to the destination node every time step. The lines without arrows indicate broadcast signals that are distributed to all the nodes within the same time step. Note the time step values indicated by the bold numbers at the top of the diagrams. All nodes indexed $(0, j)$ perform their operations at time step 0 and so on.

17.6 DAG NODE PROJECTION

The projection operation is a many-to-one function that maps several nodes of the DAG onto a single node, which constitutes the resulting $\overline{\text{DAG}}$. Thus, several operations in the DAG are mapped to a single thread. The projection operation allows thread or hardware economy by multiplexing several operations in the DAG on a single node in $\overline{\text{DAG}}$. Chapters 10 and 11 explained how to perform the projection operation using a projection matrix P. To obtain the projection matrix, we need to define a desired projection direction **d**. The vector **d** belongs to the null-space of P. Since we are dealing with a 2-D DAG, matrix P is a row vector and **d** is a column vector. A valid projection direction **d** must satisfy the inequality

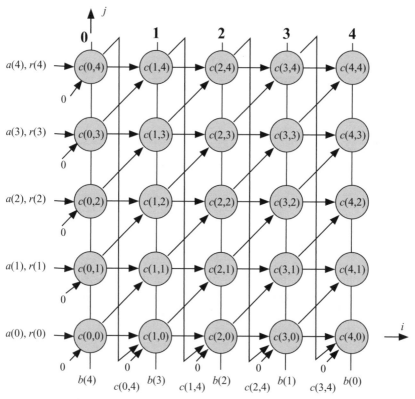

Figure 17.2   Directed acyclic graph (DAG) for the left-to-right shift-and-add field multiplication algorithm for $m = 5$ and $\mathbf{s}_1 = [1\ 0]$.

$$\mathbf{sd} = 0. \tag{17.27}$$

There are many projection vectors that satisfy Eq. 17.27 for the scheduling function $\mathbf{s}_1$. For simplicity, we choose three of them:

$$\mathbf{d}_1 = [1\quad 0]^t \tag{17.28}$$

$$\mathbf{d}_2 = [1\quad 1]^t \tag{17.29}$$

$$\mathbf{d}_3 = [1\quad -1]^t. \tag{17.30}$$

The corresponding projection matrices are given by

$$\mathbf{P}_1 = [0\quad 1] \tag{17.31}$$

$$\mathbf{P}_2 = [1\quad -1] \tag{17.32}$$

$$\mathbf{P}_3 = [1\quad 1]. \tag{17.33}$$

Our multithreading design space now allows for three configurations, one for each projection vector.

17.7 DESIGN 1: USING $d_1 = [1\ 0]^t$

A point in the dependence graph $\mathbf{p} = [i\ j]^t$ will be mapped by the projection matrix $\mathbf{P}_1 = [0\ 1]$ onto the point

$$\tilde{\mathbf{p}} = \mathbf{P}_1\mathbf{p} = j. \tag{17.34}$$

The $\overline{\text{DAG}}$ corresponding to the projection matrix $\mathbf{P}_1$ is shown in Fig. 17.3. DAG consists of m nodes or tasks, and each task is active for m time steps. The algorithm requires $m = 5$ clock cycles to complete. Notice that signal $b(m - 1 - i)$ is broadcast to all nodes as indicated by the line to the left of the processor array. Notice also that the output of $c(i, j)$ associated with task T_j is sent to the next task T_{j+1} at the end of time step i. At the end of time step i, all outputs $c(i, 0), c(i, 1), \ldots, c(i, m - 1)$ are obtained from tasks $T_0, T_1, \ldots T_{m-1}$, respectively.

17.8 DESIGN 2: USING $d_2 = [1\ 1]^t$

A point in the DAG $\mathbf{p} = [i\ j]^t$ will be mapped by the projection matrix $\mathbf{P}_2 = [1\ -1]$ onto the point

$$\tilde{\mathbf{p}} = \mathbf{P}_2\mathbf{p} = i - j. \tag{17.35}$$

To ensure that the index of the points in $\tilde{D}$ is nonnegative, we will add a fixed value $m - 1$ to all the points. Thus, a point in the dependence graph $\mathbf{p} = [i\ j]^t$ will be mapped by the projection matrix $\mathbf{P}_2 = [1\ -1]$ onto the point

$$\tilde{\mathbf{p}} = \mathbf{P}_2\mathbf{p} + m - 1 = i - j + m - 1. \tag{17.36}$$

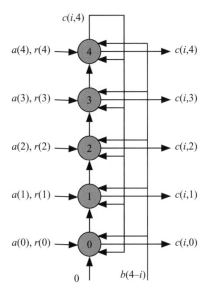

Figure 17.3 Task processing workload details at each SPA stage for the left-to-right shift-and-add field multiplication algorithm for $m = 5$ and $d_1 = [1\ 0]^t$. The signals $c(i, 4 - i)$ and $b(4 - i)$ are shown at time step i, where $0 \leq i < 5$.

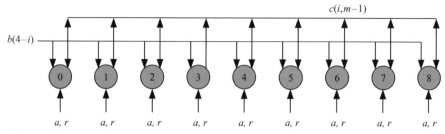

Figure 17.4 Task processing workload details at each SPA stage for the left-to-right shift-and-add field multiplication algorithm for $m = 5$ and $\mathbf{d}_2 = [1\ 1]'$.

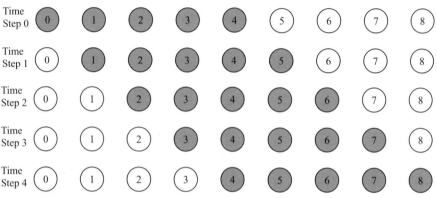

Figure 17.5 Task activity for the left-to-right shift-and-add field multiplication algorithm for $m = 5$ and $\mathbf{d}_2 = [1\ 1]'$.

The DAG corresponding to the projection matrix $\mathbf{P}_2$ is shown in Fig. 17.4. The DAG consists of $2m - 1$ nodes.

Although the DAG consists of $2m - 1$ nodes, most of them are not active all the time. For example, task T_0 and T_8 are active for one time step only. T_1 and T_7 are active for two time steps only. Figure 17.5 shows the node activities at the different time steps. In general, we note that T_i and T_{m+i} are active at nonoverlapping time steps. Therefore, we could map tasks T_i and T_j to T_k if the indices satisfy the equation

$$k = i - j \mod m. \tag{17.37}$$

Through this artifact, we are able to reduce the number of nodes and ensure that each task is active all the time. The reduced DAG is shown in Fig. 17.6. Notice that signal $b(m - 1 - i)$ is broadcast to all tasks. Notice also that the output of $c(i, j)$ is obtained at the end of the ith time step and is obtained from T_k, where k is given by

$$k = i - j + m - 1 \mod m. \tag{17.38}$$

At the end of time step i, all outputs $c(i, 0)$, $c(i, 1)$, ... $c(i, m - 1)$ are obtained from tasks T_0, T_1, ... T_{m-1}, respectively.

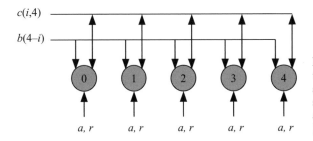

Figure 17.6 Task processing workload details at each SPA stage for the left-to-right shift-and-add field multiplication algorithm for $m = 5$ and $\mathbf{d}_2 = [1\ 1]^t$.

17.9 DESIGN 3: USING $\mathbf{d}_3 = [1\ -1]^t$

A point $\mathbf{p} = [i\ j]^t$ in DAG will be mapped to a point $\tilde{\mathbf{p}}$ in DAG given by

$$\tilde{\mathbf{p}} = \mathbf{P}_3 \mathbf{p} = i + j. \tag{17.39}$$

The resulting $\overline{\text{DAG}}$ corresponding to the projection matrix $\mathbf{P}_3$ will consist of $2m - 1$ nodes or tasks. Similar to design 2, each task is only active for m time steps at most. Therefore, we could map task T_i and T_j to T_k if the indices satisfy the equation

$$k = i + j \quad \text{mod } m. \tag{17.40}$$

Through this artifact, we are able to reduce the number of nodes and ensure that each node is active all the time. Before we proceed further, we need to observe more closely the diagonal lines transferring the output of $T_{i-1,j-1}$ to $T_{i,\,j}$. After mapping, we see that communication is accomplished between tasks according to the relations

$$T_0 \rightarrow T_2 \rightarrow T_4 \rightarrow T_1 \rightarrow T_3 \rightarrow T_0 \rightarrow \cdots.$$

17.10 APPLICATIONS OF FINITE FIELD MULTIPLIERS

The finite field multipliers we developed in the previous sections can be used to an advantage in cryptography. For example, elliptic curve encryption techniques require the following finite field operations:

1. Addition, which is simply performed by a bank of XOR gates;.

2. Multiplication, which was discussed before.

3. Squaring is a special case of multiplication.

$$C(x) = A(x)\,A(x) \tag{17.41}$$

   Specialized and fast hardware structures for field squaring were developed by the author's research group [111].

4. Inversion method based on Fermat's theorem requires $m - 1$ squaring operations and $m - 2$ multiplication operations [112]. Performance can be improved by using the method proposed by Itoh and Tsujii [112].

Chapter 18

Case Study: Polynomial Division over GF(2)

18.1 INTRODUCTION

Finite field polynomial division is an operation that is widely used to detect errors and encode data in digital communication systems [113], as well as detect errors in integrated circuits [114, 115]. In digital communications, detecting errors is called cyclic redundancy check (CRC), which appends bits to the message stream before transmission. These redundant bits are obtained from the message bits using finite field polynomial division. In digital integrated circuits, detecting errors is known as built-in self-test (BIST) where a generator produces a pseudorandom vector to be applied to a circuit under test. A compactor reduces the response of the circuit to a signature having a small number of bits. Both the generator and the compactor employ finite field polynomial division. The generation of pseudorandom numbers and polynomial division is usually done using a linear feedback shift register (LSFR). The operations performed by the LFSR can be done in software or hardware. We shall explore the different LFSR structures in this chapter.

Assume the information bits to be processed are represented by a dividend polynomial A. A divisor polynomial B is used to effect the finite field polynomial division. In the following section, we study polynomial division algorithm in more detail.

18.2 THE POLYNOMIAL DIVISION ALGORITHM

Assume that the dividend polynomial A of degree n is given by

$$A = \sum_{i=0}^{n} a_i x^i. \tag{18.1}$$

The divisor polynomial of degree m is given by

$$B = \sum_{i=0}^{m} b_i x^i. \tag{18.2}$$

Algorithms and Parallel Computing, by Fayez Gebali
Copyright © 2011 John Wiley & Sons, Inc.

The polynomial division operation produces the quotient and remainder polynomials Q and R

$$Q = \sum_{i=0}^{n-m} q_i x^i \qquad (18.3)$$

$$R = \sum_{i=0}^{m-1} r_i x^i, \qquad (18.4)$$

where

$$A = Q\,B + R. \qquad (18.5)$$

The division operation is a series of multiply/subtract iterations such that after each iteration one coefficient of the quotient polynomial is obtained, in descending order. Also, a partial remainder polynomial having m terms is obtained after each iteration. At the end of the iterations, all the coefficients of Q are determined as well as the final remainder polynomial R.

The notation we use in this chapter for the partial remainder polynomials is as follows:

- $R(i)$: input partial remainder polynomial at iteration i
- $R(i + 1)$: resulting partial remainder polynomial at iteration i
- $r_j(i)$: jth coefficient of $R(i)$, $0 \leq j < m$

According to the above definitions, can express $R(i)$ explicitly as

$$R(i) = \sum_{j=0}^{m-1} r_j(i) x^{n-m-i+j} \qquad 0 \leq i \leq n-m. \qquad (18.6)$$

We can express the long-division algorithm for polynomials as an iteration using an LFSR as indicated in Algorithm 18.1.

Algorithm 18.1   Linear feedback shift register (LFSR) polynomial division algorithm

---

1: // Initialization of partial remainder R and q
2: $q_{n-m} = a_n$
3: **for** $j = 0 : m - 1$ **do**
4:     $r_j(0) = a_{n-m+j}$
5: **end for**
6: // Start Iterations
7: **for** $i = 0 : n - m$ **do**
8:     **for** $j = 1 : m - 1$ **do**
9:         $r_j(i + 1) = r_{j-1}(i) + q_{n-m-i}b_{j-1}$
10: **end for**
11: $q_{n-m-i-1} = r_{m-1}(i)$

12: $r_0(i + 1) = a_{n-m-i}$

13: **end for**

14: // Final remainder

15: **for** $j = 0 : m - 1$ **do**

16:    $r_j = r_j(n - m + 1)$

17: **end for**

Note from the algorithm that the most significant coefficient of the divisor polynomial B is not used. Instead we use our knowledge of the $r_{m-1}(i)$ to directly estimate the quotient coefficient q_{m-n-i} for ensuring that $r_m(i) = 0$.

18.3 THE LFSR DEPENDENCE GRAPH

Based on Algorithm 18.1, the dependence graph of Fig. 18.1 is obtained. The gray circles indicate valid operations such as indicated in line 9 of Algorithm 18.1. The white circles have zero q inputs, and hence only transfer the northeast input to the southwest output. In that sense, we note that the inputs a_9 to a_4 become effective

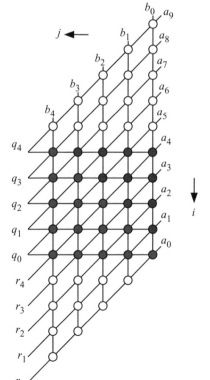

Figure 18.1 Dependence graph of the LFSR polynomial division algorithm for the case $n = 9$ and $m = 5$.

only when they arrive at the top line with gray circles. Likewise, the desired outputs r_4 to r_0 could be obtained as the outputs of the bottom row with gray circles.

Detailed explanations of how a dependence graph could be obtained were presented in Chapters 10 and 11 and by the author elsewhere [86, 100, 116–118]. The dependence graph is two-dimensional (2-D) since we have two indices, i and j. If we consider only the gray circles, then the bounds on the indices are $0 \leq i \leq n - m = 4$ and $0 \leq j < m = 5$. Each node in the algorithm performs the operations indicated in line 9 of Algorithm 18.1. If we extended the algorithm such that the inputs are fed from the same side and the outputs are obtained from the same side, then the bounds of the algorithm indices would be $0 \leq i \leq n + m$ and $0 \leq j < m$.

Coefficient q_{n-m-i} of Q, on line 11 of Algorithm 18.1, is obtained at iteration i. Hence, this coefficient is represented by the horizontal lnes in the figure. For example, the horizontal line $i = 3$ represents the coefficient $q_{n-m-i} = q_1$. Similarly, the line at $i = 0$ represents q_4.

Coefficient b_j of B, on line 9 of Algorithm 18.1, has an index dependency

$$j = c, \tag{18.7}$$

where c is a specific value of the index. For example, b_1 would be represented by the vertical line $j = 1$ as shown in the figure.

The partial remainder coefficient $r_j(i + 1)$, on line 9 of Algorithm 18.1, is obtained from b_j, q_{n-m-i} and $r_{j-1}(i)$. This explains the diagonal lines representing the inputs and outputs for each node.

18.4 DATA SCHEDULING

Data scheduling assigns a time index value to any point in the dependence graph of Fig. 18.1. We use an affine scheduling function to specify the scheduling of the algorithm tasks. The affine scheduling functions are of the form [86]

$$t(\mathbf{p}) = \mathbf{sp} - s, \tag{18.8}$$

where $\mathbf{s} = [s_1 \ s_2]$ is the scheduling vector and s is an integer.

Assigning time values to the nodes of the dependence graph transforms the dependence graph to a directed acyclic graph (DAG) as was discussed in Chapters 10 and 11. More specifically, the DAG can be thought of as a serial–parallel algorithm (SPA) where the parallel tasks could be implemented using a thread pool or parallel processors for software or hardware implementations, respectively. The different stages of the SPA are accomplished using barriers or clocks for software or hardware implementations, respectively.

Our choice for the scheduling vector is determined by any data input/output (I/O) requirements. Since the divisor polynomial is typically of low order, we can store its coefficients in memory and only treat A as an input polynomial supplied by the system generating the data to be compressed. From the figure, it appears that coefficient a_i of A is supplied to the dependence graph at the rightmost edge at point

$$\mathbf{p}_{a_i} = [n - i \quad 0]. \tag{18.9}$$

From Eqs. 18.8 and 18.9, the time index value associated with such point is given by

$$t(a_i) = (n - i) s_1 + s \qquad 0 \le i \le n. \tag{18.10}$$

Since the time of arrival difference between a_{i-1} and a_i is 1, we can write

$$t(a_{i-1}) - t(a_i) = 1$$
$$= s_1. \tag{18.11}$$

Thus, we must have $s_1 = 1$ in our scheduling function.

We can explore the possible values of s_2 by observing that the q input, shown by horizontal lines, is obtained at the left and is used by all the points on the horizontal line. Therefore, time associated with point (i, j) must be larger than or equal to the time value associated with point $(i, j + 1)$. We can write this as

$$\begin{bmatrix} 1 & s_2 \end{bmatrix} \begin{bmatrix} i \\ j \end{bmatrix} \ge \begin{bmatrix} 1 & s_2 \end{bmatrix} \begin{bmatrix} i \\ j+1 \end{bmatrix}. \tag{18.12}$$

The above equation yields the inequality

$$s_2 \le 0. \tag{18.13}$$

We have another restriction on the value of s_2. The source of data for points on any diagonal lines is the a coefficients that are supplied at the right. Therefore, time associated with point (i, j) must be smaller than or equal to the time value associated with point $(i + 1, j + 1)$. We can write this as

$$\begin{bmatrix} 1 & s_2 \end{bmatrix} \begin{bmatrix} i \\ j \end{bmatrix} \le \begin{bmatrix} 1 & s_2 \end{bmatrix} \begin{bmatrix} i \\ j+1 \end{bmatrix}. \tag{18.14}$$

The above equation yields the inequality

$$s_2 \ge -1. \tag{18.15}$$

From the above two inequalities, we deduce that the range for s_2 is

$$-1 \le s_2 \le 0. \tag{18.16}$$

There are three possible choices for our scheduling function:

$$\mathbf{s}_1 = \begin{bmatrix} 1 & -1 \end{bmatrix} \tag{18.17}$$
$$\mathbf{s}_2 = \begin{bmatrix} 1 & 0 \end{bmatrix} \tag{18.18}$$
$$\mathbf{s}_3 = \begin{bmatrix} 1 & -0.5 \end{bmatrix}. \tag{18.19}$$

18.5 DAG NODE PROJECTION

The projection operation is a many-to-one function that maps several nodes of the DAG onto a single node. Thus, several operations in the DAG are mapped to a single node or task. The projection operation allows for software thread economy or hardware economy by multiplexing several operations in the DAG on a single thread or processing element, respectively. For a 2-D DAG we are able to achieve node projection by choosing proper projection direction d. The author provided an extensive treatment of the projection operation in [86] and in Chapters 10 and 11.

The projection direction **d** projects a point **p** in the 2-D DAG to a point $\bar{\mathbf{p}}$ on a line such that

$$\bar{\mathbf{p}} = \mathbf{P}\mathbf{p}, \tag{18.20}$$

where P is a the projection matrix of dimension 1×2, which is in our case a vector normal to **d**. A valid projection direction must satisfy the inequality [86, 100, 116–118]

$$\mathbf{sd} \neq 0. \tag{18.21}$$

In the following three sections, we will discuss design space explorations for the three values of **s** obtained in Eqs. 18.17–18.19.

18.6 DESIGN 1: DESIGN SPACE EXPLORATION WHEN $s_1 = [1\ -1]$

Figure 18.2 shows the DAG for the polynomial division algorithm based on our timing function choice $\mathbf{s}_1$. The equitemporal planes are the diagonal lines shown as gray lines on the right of the diagram. The associated time index values are shown at the right of the diagram. We note from the figure that the signals corresponding to the coefficients of B and the estimated q output are all pipelined, as indicated by the arrows connecting the nodes. However, the estimated partial results for Q and R are broadcast, as indicated by the diagonal lines without arrows. There are three simple projection vectors such that all of them satisfy Eq. 18.21 for the scheduling function in Eq. 18.17. The three projection vectors will produce three designs:

$$\text{Design 1:a :} \mathbf{d}_{1a} = [1 \quad 0]^t \tag{18.22}$$
$$\text{Design 1:b :} \mathbf{d}_{1b} = [1 \quad -1]^t \tag{18.23}$$
$$\text{Design 1:c :} \mathbf{d}_{1c} = [0 \quad -1]^t. \tag{18.24}$$

The corresponding projection matrices are

$$\text{Design 1:a :} \mathbf{P}_{1a} = [0 \quad 1] \tag{18.25}$$
$$\text{Design 1:b :} \mathbf{P}_{1b} = [1 \quad 1] \tag{18.26}$$
$$\text{Design 1:c :} \mathbf{P}_{1c} = [1 \quad 0]. \tag{18.27}$$

Our design space now allows for three configurations for each projection vector for the chosen timing function. As it turns out, the choice of d_{1b} or d_{1c} would produce n nodes or tasks but only m of them are active at any time step. Through proper relabeling of the tasks, we would obtain the design corresponding to $\mathbf{d}_{1a}$. Therefore, we consider only the case when $\mathbf{s}_1$ and $\mathbf{d}_{1a}$. There will be m tasks that are all active at each time step. The design will result in the well-known Fibonacci (Type 1) LFSR. A point in the DAG given by the coordinates $\underline{\mathbf{p} = [i\ j]^t}$ will be mapped by the projection matrix $\mathbf{P}_{1a}$ into the point $\bar{\mathbf{p}} = \mathbf{P}_{1a}\mathbf{p}$. The DAG corresponding to design 1 is shown

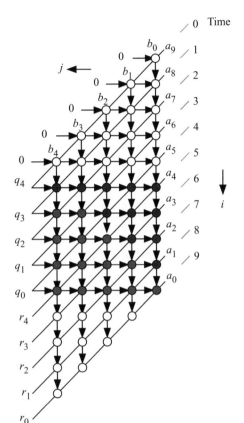

Figure 18.2 Directed acyclic graph (DAG) for polynomial division algorithm when $s_1 = [1\ -1]$, $n = 9$, and $m = 5$.

in Fig. 18.3. There will be m tasks where input coefficients of A are fed from the right and the partial remainders are pipelined among the processors. Coefficient b_j of divisor polynomial B is stored in task T_j. The task processing details are shown in Fig. 18.3b for hardware systolic implementation where D denotes a 1-bit register to store the partial output. The input to the LFSR is obtained from a multiplexer (MUX) so that in the first m time steps the q inputs are all zero.

Let q_i, $0 \le i < m$, be the present output of task T_i. The next state output q_i^+ is given by

$$q_i^+ = q_{i+1} \qquad 0 \le i < m. \tag{18.28}$$

The above expression is represented by the angled arrows at the top left of Fig. 18.2. And we identify the two outputs Q and R and inputs q of the Fibonacci (Type 1) LFSR as

$$Q, R = a \oplus (b_0 q_0) \oplus \cdots \oplus (b_{m-1} q_{m-1}) \tag{18.29}$$

$$q_m = \begin{cases} Q, R & \text{when} \quad select = 1 \\ 0 & \text{when} \quad select = 0. \end{cases} \tag{18.30}$$

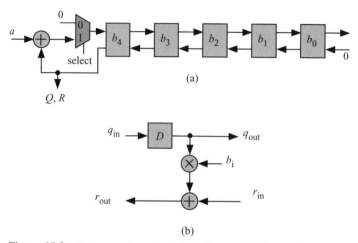

(a)

(b)

Figure 18.3   Task processing workload details at each SPA stage for Fibonacci (Type 1) LFSR when $s_1 = [1\ -1]$, $d_{1a} = [1\ 0]^t$, $n = 9$, and $m = 5$. (a) The resulting tasks at each SPA stage. (b) The task workload details.

The above equations determine the operation of the Fibonacci (Type 1) LFSR as follows:

1. Clear all the registers.

2. At time step 0, coefficient q_4 is calculated, which is simply a copy of a_9, which is the first bit of the input divisor polynomial.

3. At time step 1, only one node is active which calculates q_3.

4. At time step 2, two nodes are active which calculate q_2.

5. This sequence of operations is continued up to time step 5.

6. At time step 5, coefficient r_4 of the remainder polynomial R is obtained.

7. At time step 6, the *select* signal is set to 0 to ensure that register D_4 is cleared. In effect, r_3 is obtained and feedback path from coefficient b_4 in node T_4 is broken.

8. At time step 7, r_2 is obtained and feedback paths from coefficients b_3 and b_4 are broken.

9. This pattern continues till the end of iterations at time step 9.

18.7 DESIGN 2: DESIGN SPACE EXPLORATION WHEN $s_2 = [1\ 0]$

Figure 18.4 shows the DAG for the polynomial division algorithm based on our timing function choice s_2. We note from the figure that the signals corresponding to the coefficients of B and the intermediate partial remainders corresponding to R and Q are all pipelined, as indicated by the arrows connecting the nodes. However, the estimated q output is broadcast among the nodes, as indicated by the horizontal lines

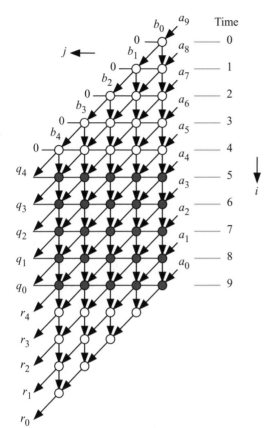

Figure 18.4 DAG for polynomial division algorithm when $\mathbf{s}_2 = [1\ 0]$, $n = 9$, and $m = 5$.

without arrows. There are three simple projection vectors such that all of them satisfy Eq. 18.21 for the scheduling function in Eq. 18.18. The three projection vectors will produce three designs:

$$\text{Design 2:a} : \mathbf{d}_{2a} = [1\quad 0]^t \tag{18.31}$$
$$\text{Design 2:b} : \mathbf{d}_{2b} = [1\quad 1]^t \tag{18.32}$$
$$\text{Design 2:c} : \mathbf{d}_{2c} = [1\quad -1]^t. \tag{18.33}$$

The corresponding projection matrices are

$$\text{Design 2:a} : \mathbf{P}_{2a} = [0\quad 1] \tag{18.34}$$
$$\text{Design 2:b} : \mathbf{P}_{2b} = [1\quad -1] \tag{18.35}$$
$$\text{Design 2:c} : \mathbf{P}_{2c} = [1\quad 1]. \tag{18.36}$$

Our multithreaded design space now allows for three configurations for each projection vector for the chosen timing function.

The different projection directions will produce identical designs through proper relabeling of the nodes. The resulting $\overline{\text{DAG}}$ will consist of m tasks that are all active

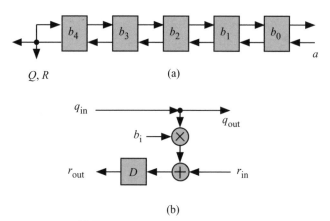

(a)

(b)

Figure 18.5 $\overline{\text{DAG}}$ for Galois (Type 2) LFSR when $\mathbf{s}_1 = [1\ 0]$, $\mathbf{d}_{2a} = [1\ 0]^t$, $n = 9$, and $m = 5$. (a) The resulting tasks at each SPA stage. (b) The task workload details.

at each time step. The design will result in the well-known Galois (Type 2) LFSR. A point in the DAG given by the coordinates $\mathbf{p} = [i\ j]^t$ will be mapped by the projection matrix $\mathbf{P}_{2a}$ into the point $\bar{\mathbf{p}} = \mathbf{P}_{2a}\mathbf{p}$. The $\overline{\text{DAG}}$ corresponding to design 2 is shown in Fig. 18.5. The $\overline{\text{DAG}}$ consists of $m - 1$ nodes. Input coefficients of A are fed from the right and the partial remainders are pipelined to all nodes. Coefficient b_j of B is stored in node T_j. The task details for hardware systolic implementation are shown in Fig. 18.5b, where D denotes a 1-bit register to store the partial output.

Let $r_i,\ 0 \le i < m$, be the present output of task T_i. The next state output r_i^+ is given by

$$r_i^+ = r_{i-1} \oplus (b_i r_{m-1}) \qquad 0 \le i < m. \tag{18.37}$$

And we identify the output and input of the Galois LFSR as

$$Q, R = r_{m-1} \tag{18.38}$$

$$r_{-1} = a. \tag{18.39}$$

The above equations determine the operation of the Galois (Type 2) LFSR as follows:

1. Clear all the registers.
2. For time steps 0–4, the LFSR is working as a simple shift register moving the coefficients a_9 to a_5 between the stages.
3. At time step 4, the first quotient coefficient q_4 is obtained and is available at the next time step to the leftmost node.
4. The coefficients of Q are obtained from the leftmost node at time steps 4–9.
5. At the end of time step 9, all the remainder polynomial R coefficients are stored in the shift register stages. They could be read off the LFSR in parallel if desired.
6. If it is desired to shift the R coefficients out, then the feedback path must be broken to selectively disable the LFSR action.

18.8 DESIGN 3: DESIGN SPACE EXPLORATION WHEN $s_3 = [1\ -0.5]$

Figure 18.6 shows the DAG for the polynomial division algorithm based on our timing function choice s_3. We note from the figure that all signals are now pipelined, as indicated by the arrows connecting the nodes. However, we note that there are nodes that do not lie on any equitemporal planes. We have several choices for the timing of nodes that lie between two temporal planes. Alternatively, we could assign a time value equal to either of the temporal planes surrounding the node. In addition, we could assign this node to operate on the negative edge of the clock. The former choice leads to nodes that do not have registers. The latter choice leads to nodes that have registers triggered by the negative edge of the clock. This is the option we follow here.

Similar to the two previous designs, we choose a projection vector given by

$$\text{Design 3:} \mathbf{d}_3 = [1\quad 0]^t. \tag{18.40}$$

The corresponding projection matrix $\mathbf{P}_3$ is given by

$$P_3 = [0\quad 1] \tag{18.41}$$

A point in the DAG given by the coordinates $\mathbf{p} = [i\ j]^t$ will be mapped by the projection matrix $\mathbf{P}_3$ into the point $\bar{\mathbf{p}} = \mathbf{P}_3\mathbf{p}$. The $\overline{\text{DAG}}$ corresponding to Design 3 is

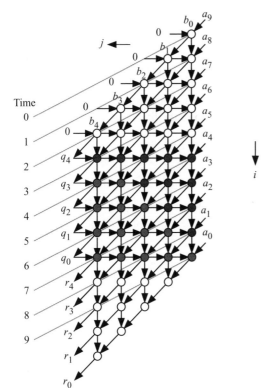

Figure 18.6 DAG for polynomial division algorithm when $s_3 = [1\ -0.5]$, $n = 9$, and $m = 5$.

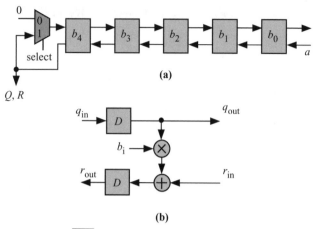

(a)

(b)

Figure 18.7 $\overline{\text{DAG}}$ or linear cellular automaton (LCA) processor array when $\mathbf{s}_3 = [1\ -0.5]$, $\mathbf{d}_3 = [1\ 0]^t$, $n = 9$, and $m = 5$. (a) The resulting tasks at each SPA stage. (b) The task workload details.

shown in Fig. 18.7. The $\overline{\text{DAG}}$ consists of $m - 1$ tasks. Input coefficients of A are fed from the right and the partial remainders are pipelined to all nodes. Coefficient b_j of B is stored in task T_j. The task details for hardware systolic array implementation are shown in Fig. 18.7b, where D denotes a 1-bit register to store the intermediate results. The even-numbered tasks contain two positive edge-triggered flip-flops. On the other hand, the odd-numbered tasks contain two negative edge-triggered flip-flops.

This design is usually called a linear cellular automaton (LCA) [119]. The design shown here differs from LCAs discussed in the literature in several aspects:

1. Even tasks are clocked using the clock rising-edge.

2. Odd tasks are clocked using the clock rising-edge.

3. One of the inputs is fed from a MUX.

Let q_i and r_i, $0 \le i < m$, be the present outputs of task T_i. The next state outputs q_i^+ and r_i^+ are given by

$$q_i^+ = q_{i+1} \qquad 0 \le i < m \tag{18.42}$$
$$r_i^+ = r_{i-1} \oplus (b_i q_{i+1}) \qquad 0 \le i < m. \tag{18.43}$$

And we identify the output and input of the LCA as

$$Q, R = r_{m-1} \tag{18.44}$$
$$q_m = \begin{cases} r_{m-1} & \text{when} \quad select = 1 \\ 0 & \text{when} \quad select = 0 \end{cases} \tag{18.45}$$
$$r_{-1} = a. \tag{18.46}$$

The above equations determine the operation of the LCA as follows:

1. Clear all the registers.
2. For time steps 0 and 2, the LFSR is working as a simple shift register moving the coefficients a_9 to a_5 between the stages.
3. At time step 4, the first quotient coefficient q_4 is obtained and is available at the next time step to the leftmost node.
4. The coefficients of Q are obtained from the leftmost node at time steps 4–9.
5. At the end of time step 9, all the remainder polynomial R coefficients are stored in the shift register stages.
6. If it is desired to shift the R coefficients out, then the feedback path must be broken to selectively disable the feedback action.

18.9 COMPARING THE THREE DESIGNS

The hardware structure for all three types of design above show similarities and differences. All designs have tasks that contain storage registers and have two inputs and two outputs. Designs 1 and 2 contain one register in each task, while design 3 contains three tasks. All the registers in designs 1 and 2 are clocked on the same edge of the clock, while design 3 has the even tasks clocked on the rising edge and the odd tasks clocked on the falling edge.

The click period of design 1 could be the longest since the input to the mux when *select* = 1 will propagate through m XOR gates in each clock cycle. The architectures of the three designs dictate respective clock periods given by

$$T_1 = \tau_D + m\tau_{XOR} + \tau_{mux} + \tau_{setup} \tag{18.47}$$

$$T_2 = \tau_D + \tau_p + \tau_{XOR} + \tau_{AND} + \tau_{setup} \tag{18.48}$$

$$T_3 = 2\tau_D + \tau_{XOR} + \tau_{mux} + 2\tau_{setup}, \tag{18.49}$$

where τ_{setup} is the setup time for the registers, τ_D is the register delay, τ_{XOR} is the XOR gate delay, τ_{AND} is the AND gate delay, and τ_p is the propagation time for a signal through all the tasks. This last delay component is due to the top signal in design 2, which is merely passed between the tasks perhaps through a long bus. More accurate predictions of system speeds are obtained for actual implementations.

Chapter 19

The Fast Fourier Transform

19.1 INTRODUCTION

The discrete Fourier transform (DFT) is a very important algorithm that finds use in many applications such as telecommunications, speech processing, image processing, medical imaging such as in computer assisted tomography (CAT), radar (synthetic aperture radar), sonar, and antenna array (phased arrays) [120, 121]. A very important application nowadays is the use of DFT techniques in orthogonal frequency division multiplexing (OFDM) as an efficient data modulation scheme. This technique is also extended for use in multiple-input multiple-output (MIMO) systems where each transmitter/receiver has multiple antennas to simultaneously transmit/receive multiple data streams in what is known as OFDM-MIMO systems [122]. This is not the forum to discuss what is OFDM and how it differs from the classic frequency division multiplexing (FDM). Excellent textbooks on digital communication cover such topics [113]

The DFT algorithm finds the spectrum of a periodic discrete-time signal with period N. The spectral component $X(k)$ is obtained by the equation

$$X(k) = \sum_{n=0}^{N-1} x(n) W_N^{nk} \qquad 0 \le k < N, \tag{19.1}$$

where W_N is the twiddle factor, which equals the Nth root of unity and is given by

$$W_N = e^{-2j\pi/N} \qquad j = \sqrt{-1}. \tag{19.2}$$

The dependence graph of the eight-point DFT algorithm is shown in Fig. 19.1. Input samples $x(n)$ are represented by the vertical lines and output samples $X(k)$ are represented by the horizontal lines. Input sample W_N^{nk} is represented by the point at location (n, k). The DFT algorithm is essentially a matrix–vector multiplication problem. For the case $N = 8$ we have

$$\mathbf{X} = \mathbf{W}\mathbf{x}, \tag{19.3}$$

Algorithms and Parallel Computing, by Fayez Gebali
Copyright © 2011 John Wiley & Sons, Inc.

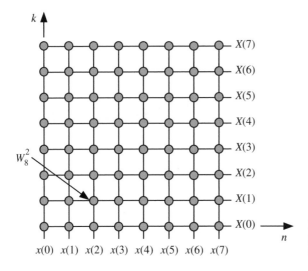

Figure 19.1 Dependence graph of an eight-point DFT algorithm.

where

$$\mathbf{X} = \begin{bmatrix} X(0) & X(1) & X(2) & X(3) & X(4) & X(5) & X(6) & X(7) \end{bmatrix}^t \tag{19.4}$$

$$\mathbf{x} = \begin{bmatrix} x(0) & x(1) & x(2) & x(3) & x(4) & x(5) & x(6) & x(7) \end{bmatrix}^t \tag{19.5}$$

$$\mathbf{W} = \begin{bmatrix} 1 & 1 & 1 & 1 & 1 & 1 & 1 & 1 \\ 1 & W & W^2 & W^3 & W^4 & W^5 & W^6 & W^7 \\ 1 & W^2 & W^4 & W^6 & 1 & W^2 & W^4 & W^6 \\ 1 & W^3 & W^6 & W & W^4 & W^7 & W^2 & W^5 \\ 1 & W^4 & 1 & W^4 & 1 & W^4 & 1 & W^4 \\ 1 & W^5 & W^2 & W^7 & W^4 & W & W^6 & W^3 \\ 1 & W^6 & W^4 & W^2 & 1 & W^6 & W^4 & W^2 \\ 1 & W^7 & W^6 & W^5 & W^4 & W^3 & W^2 & W \end{bmatrix}. \tag{19.6}$$

We removed the subscript from the twiddle factor to reduce clutter. We note that the powers of W are between 0 and 7.

Figure 19.2 shows the values of the different powers of W^i when $0 \le i < 8$. We see that the twiddle factor powers are uniformly distributed around the unit circle. The angle between successive values is $2\pi/N = 45°$ for the case $N = 8$. Notice that the complex number W^i has simple values when its angle is $0°$, $90°$, $180°$, and $270°$. Multiplying $x(n)$ by these values in Eq. 19.1 becomes a trivial operation. Direct evaluation of Eq. 19.1 requires $(N-1)^2$ complex number multiplications and $N(N-1)$ complex number additions. When $N = 1,024$, the number of operations becomes large. Very efficient techniques have been proposed for evaluating the DFT using much fewer operations than would be required by the original algorithm.

Fast Fourier transform (FFT) was developed to reduce the number of operations required to obtain the DFT. The main concept in FFT is to break the original DFT

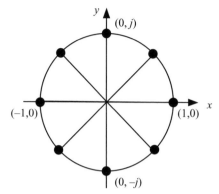

Figure 19.2   The values of twiddle powers W^i when $0 \le i < 8$.

sequence into two shorter sequences. The DFT of the shortened sequences are then recombined to give the DFT of the original sequence [123]. Assuming N is even, each of the $N/2$-point DFTs would require $(N/2)^2$ complex multiplications. A total of $N^2/2$ complex multiplication would be required. Assuming N to be an integer power of two, the splitting process can be repeated until a series of simple two-point DFTs are required.

19.2   DECIMATION-IN-TIME FFT

In the decimation-in-time FFT, the splitting algorithm breaks up the sum in Eq. 19.1 into even- and odd-numbered parts. The even and odd sequences x_0 and x_1 are given by McKinney [124]

$$x_0(n) = x(2n) \qquad n = 0, 1, \cdots N/2 - 1 \tag{19.7}$$
$$x_1(n) = x(2n+1) \qquad n = 0, 1, \cdots N/2 - 1 \tag{19.8}$$

The original sum in Eq. 19.1 is now split as

$$X(k) = \sum_{n=0}^{N/2-1} x(2n)W_N^{2nk} + \sum_{n=0}^{N/2-1} x(2n+1)W_N^{2(n+1)k} \qquad 0 \le k < N. \tag{19.9}$$

We notice that W_N^2 can be written as

$$W_N^2 = \left(e^{-2j\pi/N} \right)^2 = e^{-2j\pi/(N/2)} = W_{N/2}. \tag{19.10}$$

We can write Eq. 19.9 as

$$X(k) = \sum_{n=0}^{N/2-1} x_0(n)W_{N/2}^{nk} + W_N^k \sum_{n=0}^{N/2-1} x_1(n)W_{N/2}^{nk} \tag{19.11}$$

$$= X_0(k) + W_N^k X_1(k) \qquad 0 \le k < N/2, \tag{19.12}$$

where $X_0(k)$ and $X_1(k)$ are the $N/2$-point DFTs of $x_0(n)$ and $x_1(n)$, respectively. Notice, however, that $X(k)$ is defined for $0 \le k < N$, while $X_0(k)$ and $X_1(k)$ are defined for

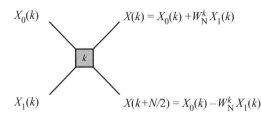

$X_0(k)$

$X(k) = X_0(k) + W_N^k X_1(k)$

k

$X_1(k)$

$X(k+N/2) = X_0(k) - W_N^k X_1(k)$

Figure 19.3   The butterfly signal flow graph for a decimation-in-time FFT algorithm.

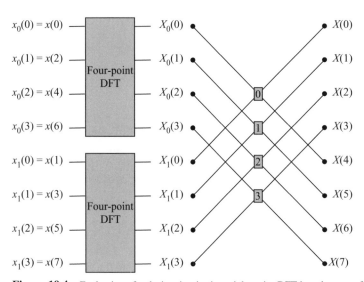

$x_0(0) = x(0)$ — $X_0(0)$ • • $X(0)$

$x_0(1) = x(2)$ — $X_0(1)$ • • $X(1)$

Four-point DFT

$x_0(2) = x(4)$ — $X_0(2)$ • • $X(2)$

$x_0(3) = x(6)$ — $X_0(3)$ • • $X(3)$

$x_1(0) = x(1)$ — $X_1(0)$ • • $X(4)$

$x_1(1) = x(3)$ — $X_1(1)$ • • $X(5)$

Four-point DFT

$x_1(2) = x(5)$ — $X_1(2)$ • • $X(6)$

$x_1(3) = x(7)$ — $X_1(3)$ • • $X(7)$

Figure 19.4   Evaluation of a decimation-in-time eight-point DFT based on two four-point DFTs.

$0 \leq k < N/2$. A way must be determined then to evaluate Eq. 19.12 for values of $k > N/2$. Since $X_0(k)$ and $X_1(k)$ are each periodic with a period $N/2$, we can express Eq. 19.12 as

$$X(k + N/2) = X_0(k) - W_N^k X_1(k) \qquad 0 \leq k < N/2. \qquad (19.13)$$

Equations 19.12 and 19.13 are referred to as the butterfly operations. Figure 19.3 shows the flow graph of the basic decimation-in-time butterfly operation. The results of the butterfly operation are indicated on right-hand side of the figure. We used the symbol k inside the gray box to indicate that the lower input is to be multiplied by W^k. Based on Eqs. 19.12 and 19.13, we can schematically show the evaluation of a decimation-in-time eight-point DFT in terms of two four-point DFTs as in Fig. 19.4.

We indicated in the previous section that when N is an integer power of two, then the FFT can be evaluated by successively splitting the input data sequence in even and odd parts. Table 19.1 shows the successive splitting of a 16-point input data sequence. Each splitting divides the input into even and odd parts. The first column of the table shows the binary address or order of the input data samples. The

Table 19.1 Successive Splitting of Input Data in Even and Odd Parts

Binary representation	Input sample natural order	First splitting length 4 DFT	Second splitting length 2 DFT	Binary representation
000	$x(0)$	$x(0)$	$x(0)$	000
001	$x(1)$	$x(2)$	$x(4)$	100
010	$x(2)$	$x(4)$	$x(2)$	010
011	$x(3)$	$x(6)$	$x(6)$	110
100	$x(4)$	$x(1)$	$x(1)$	001
101	$x(5)$	$x(3)$	$x(5)$	101
110	$x(6)$	$x(5)$	$x(3)$	011
111	$x(7)$	$x(7)$	$x(7)$	111

second column shows the data assuming it arrives, or stored, in the natural order in sequence. The third column is the data after the first splitting into even and odd data of length $N/2 = 4$. The fourth column shows the data after the second splitting. Note that at this stage, each sequence contains only two data samples where we can simply do a two-point DFT using additions and subtractions since $W_2^0 = 1$ and $W_2^1 = -1$. The fifth column shows the binary representation of the data index. This could be considered as their memory location, for example.

Compare the first and the last columns of the table. It shows what is known as bit reversal. The two-point DFTs need input data that is the bit reverse of the natural order; therefore, location 1, which is 001 in binary, will be bit reversed to 100, which corresponds to input sample $x(4)$. The eight-point FFT will use the information in Table 19.1 for its operation. We start with the two-point DFTs, whose input data correspond to the data in the fourth column (second splitting). The outputs will be fed to four-point DFTs, whose input data correspond to the data in the third column (first splitting). The reader can try constructing a similar table for a 16-point DFT.

Now we are ready to construct the DG for the eight-point decimation-in-time FFT algorithm, which is shown in Fig. 19.5. The eight-point FFT consists of three stages since $\log_2 8 = 3$. Each stage contains $N/2 = 4$ butterfly operations. *Stage* 2 performs two-point DFT processes and the butterflies at that stage operate on data whose indices are 2^2 apart. *Stage* 1 performs two-point DFT processes and the butterflies at that stage operate on data whose indices are 2^1 apart. *Stage* 0 performs two-point DFT processes and the butterflies at that stage operate on data whose indices are 2^0 apart. The sequence of operations is from left to right; therefore, all operations in *stage* 2 must be completed before operations in *stage* 1 can start.

The FFT algorithm we described here applied to the case when N is an integer power of two, that is, $N = 2^r$. This is called radix-2 FFT algorithm because the input samples are divided into two parts and the butterfly operations involve two inputs and produce two outputs. Higher radix FFTs are possible. For example, radix-4 FFT assumes $N = 4^r$ and divides the input data into four parts and the butterflies operate

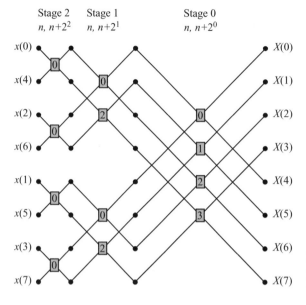

Figure 19.5 DG for an eight-point decimation-in-time FFT algorithm.

on four input samples and produce four output samples. The outputs of the butterfly would be related to the inputs according to the expressions

$$X_0 = x_0 + x_1 + x_2 + x_3 \tag{19.14}$$
$$X_1 = x_0 - jx_1 - x_2 + jx_3 \tag{19.15}$$
$$X_2 = x_0 - x_1 + x_2 - x_3 \tag{19.16}$$
$$X_3 = x_0 + jx_1 - x_2 - jx_3. \tag{19.17}$$

19.3 PIPELINE RADIX-2 DECIMATION-IN-TIME FFT PROCESSOR

Wold and Despain [121] proposed a pipeline FFT processor that is based on decimation-in-time FFT DG of Fig. 19.6. Their design is usually referred to as a radix-2 single-path delay feedback (R2SDF) processor. The structure assumes that input data $x(n)$ are available in word-serial format in natural order. This is why the processor at *stage* 2 delays the input sample by the four-word shift register (SR) buffer. For the first $N/2 = 4$ data words, the processor in *stage* 2 simply accepts the data words and moves them into the shift register buffer. After $N/2 = 4$ data samples have been shifted, the processor starts performing the butterfly operations on the input data and the data coming from the shift register buffer. The processor in *stage* 1 repeats the same actions for a period of $N/4 = 2$ delay and so on. A pipeline design for the radix-4 decimation-in-time FFT processor has been proposed by Despain [125]. The design is usually called a radix-4 single-path delay feedback (R4SDF) processor and is shown in Fig. 19.7 for a 64-point FFT. Other efficient designs are possible such as the ones given in References [126–128].

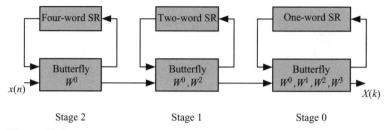

Figure 19.6 Cascade pipeline architecture for an eight-point decimation-in-time FFT algorithm using a R2SDF processor.

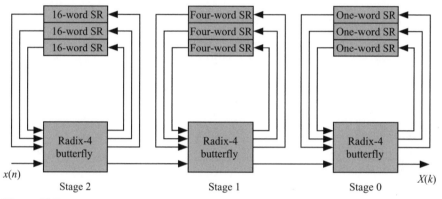

Figure 19.7   Cascade pipeline architecture for a 64-point FFT algorithm using an R4SDF processor.

19.4 DECIMATION-IN-FREQUENCY FFT

In the decimation-in-frequency FFT, the splitting algorithm breaks up the sum in Eq. 19.1 into the first $N/2$ points and the last $N/2$ points. This is equivalent to considering the even and odd parts of $X(k)$. By contrast, in decimation-in-time, we considered the even and odd parts of $x(n)$. The first and second part sequences x_0 and x_1 of $x(n)$ are given by McKinney [124]

$$x_0(n) = x(n) \qquad n = 0, 1, \cdots N/2 - 1 \tag{19.18}$$

$$x_1(n) = x(n + N/2) \qquad n = 0, 1, \cdots N/2 - 1. \tag{19.19}$$

The original sum in Eq. 19.1 is now split as

$$X(k) = \sum_{n=0}^{N/2-1} x(n) W_N^{nk} + \sum_{n=N/2}^{N-1} x(n) W_N^{nk} \qquad 0 \le k < N. \tag{19.20}$$

We can express the above equation in terms of $x_0(n)$ and $x_1(n)$ as

$$X(k) = \sum_{n=0}^{N/2-1} x_0(n)W_N^{nk} + \sum_{n=0}^{N/2-1} x_1(n)W_N^{(n+N/2)k} \qquad 0 \le k < N$$

$$= \sum_{n=0}^{N/2-1} \left[x_0(n) + e^{-j\pi k} x_1(n) \right] W_N^{nk} \qquad 0 \le k < N. \tag{19.21}$$

Consider the even samples of $X(k)$ in the above equation:

$$X(2k) = \sum_{n=0}^{N/2-1} \left[x_0(n) + x_1(n) \right] W_N^{2nk}$$

$$= \sum_{n=0}^{N/2-1} \left[x_0(n) + x_1(n) \right] W_{N/2}^{nk}, \tag{19.22}$$

where $e^{-j\pi k} = 1$ when k is even. On the other hand, the odd part of $X(k)$ is given by

$$X(2k+1) = \sum_{n=0}^{N/2-1} \left[x_0(n) - x_1(n) \right] W_N^{n(2k+1)}$$

$$= \sum_{n=0}^{N/2-1} \left[x_0(n) - x_1(n) \right] W_N^n W_{N/2}^{nk}, \tag{19.23}$$

where $e^{-j\pi k} = -1$ when k is odd.

In summary, the even and the odd terms of the DFT can be obtained from the $N/2$-DFTs:

$$X(2k) = \sum_{n=0}^{N/2-1} a(n)W_{N/2}^{nk} \qquad 0 \le k < N/2 \tag{19.24}$$

$$X(2k+1) = \sum_{n=0}^{N/2-1} b(n)W_{N/2}^{nk} \qquad 0 \le k < N/2, \tag{19.25}$$

where the input sequences $a(n)$ and $b(n)$ are

$$a(n) = x_0(n) + x_1(n) \qquad 0 \le n < N/2 \tag{19.26}$$

$$b(n) = \left[x_0(n) - x_1(n) \right] W_N^n \qquad 0 \le n < N/2. \tag{19.27}$$

The above two operations define the decimation-in-frequency butterfly operations. Figure 19.8 shows the flow graph of the basic decimation-in-frequency butterfly operation. The results of the butterfly operation are indicated on right-hand side of the figure. We used the symbol n inside the gray box to indicate that the lower input is to be multiplied by W_N^n. Based on Eqs. 19.22 and 19.23, we can schematically show the evaluation of a decimation-in-frequency eight-point DFT in terms of two four-point DFTs as in Fig. 19.9.

We indicated in the previous section that when N is an integer power of two, then the FFT can be evaluated by successively splitting the output data sequence in even and odd parts. Table 19.2 shows the successive splitting of a 16-point output data sequence. Each splitting divides the output into even and odd parts. The column

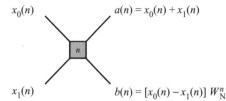

$x_0(n)$

$a(n) = x_0(n) + x_1(n)$

$x_1(n)$

$b(n) = [x_0(n) - x_1(n)] \, W_N^n$

Figure 19.8 The butterfly signal flow graph for a decimation-in-frequency FFT algorithm.

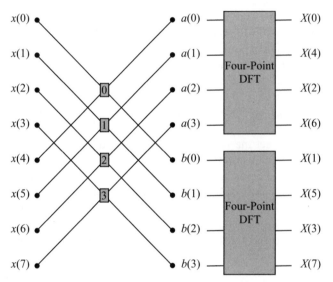

Figure 19.9 Evaluation of a decimation-in-frequency eight-point DFT based on two four-point DFTs.

Table 19.2 Successive Splitting of Output Data in Even and Odd Parts

Binary representation	Output sample natural order	First splitting length 4 DFT	Second splitting length 2 DFT	Binary representation
000	$X(0)$	$X(0)$	$X(0)$	000
001	$X(1)$	$X(2)$	$X(4)$	100
010	$X(2)$	$X(4)$	$X(2)$	010
011	$X(3)$	$X(6)$	$X(6)$	110
100	$X(4)$	$X(1)$	$X(1)$	001
101	$X(5)$	$X(3)$	$X(5)$	101
110	$X(6)$	$X(5)$	$X(3)$	011
111	$X(7)$	$X(7)$	$X(7)$	111

before last indicates that feeding in input samples in natural order will produce output samples in bit-reversed order. The first column of the table shows the binary address or natural order of the output data samples. The second column shows the output data when it is stored in the natural order in sequence. The third column is the output data ordering after the first splitting into even and odd data of length $N/2 = 4$. The fourth column shows the data after the second splitting. Note that at this stage, each sequence contains only two data samples where we can simply do a two-point DFT using additions and subtractions since $W_2^0 = 1$ and $W_2^1 = -1$. The fifth column shows the binary representation of the data index. This could be considered as their memory location, for example.

Compare the first and the last columns of the table. It shows what is known as bit reversal. The two-point DFTs produce output data that is the bit reverse of the natural order. Therefore, location 1, which is 001 in binary, will be bit reversed to 100, which correspond to output sample $X(4)$. The eight-point FFT will use the information in Table 19.2 for its operation. We start with the two-point DFTs, whose input data correspond to the data in the fourth column (second splitting). The outputs will be fed to four-point DFTs, whose input data correspond to the data in the third column (first splitting). The reader can try constructing a similar table for a 16-point DFT.

Now we are ready to construct the DG for the eight-point decimation-in-frequency FFT algorithm, which is shown in Fig. 19.10. The eight-point FFT consists of three stages since log2 8 = 3. Each stage contains $N/2 = 4$ butterfly operations. *Stage* 2 performs two-point DFT processes and the butterflies at that stage operate on data whose indices are 2^2 apart. *Stage* 1 performs two-point DFT processes and the butterflies at that stage operate on data whose indices are 2^1 apart. *Stage* 0 performs two-point DFT processes and the butterflies at that stage operate on data

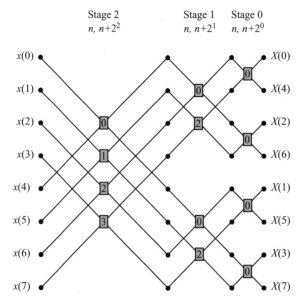

Figure 19.10 Eight-point decimation-in-frequency FFT algorithm.

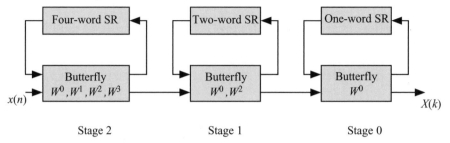

Stage 2   Stage 1   Stage 0

Figure 19.11   Cascade pipeline architecture for an eight-point decimation-in-frequency FFT algorithm using an R2SDF processor.

whose indices are 2^0 apart. The sequence of operations is from left to right; therefore, all operations in *stage* 2 must be completed before operations in *stage* 1 can start.

The FFT algorithm we described here when $N = 2^r$ is called radix-2 FFT algorithm because the input samples are divided into two parts and the butterfly operations involve two inputs and produce two outputs. Higher radix FFTs are possible. For example, radix-4 FFT assumes $N = 4^r$ and divides the input data into four parts and the butterflies operate on four data samples. The outputs of the butterfly would be

$$X_0 = x_0 + x_1 + x_2 + x_3 \tag{19.28}$$
$$X_1 = x_0 - jx_1 - x_2 + jx_3 \tag{19.29}$$
$$X_2 = x_0 - x_1 + x_2 - x_3 \tag{19.30}$$
$$X_3 = x_0 + jx_1 - x_2 - jx_3. \tag{19.31}$$

19.5 PIPELINE RADIX-2 DECIMATION-IN-FREQUENCY FFT PROCESSOR

Wold and Despain [121] proposed a pipeline FFT processor that is based on the decimation-in-frequency FFT DG of Fig. 19.11. Their design is usually referred to as an R2SDF processor. The structure assumes that input data $x(n)$ are available in word-serial format in natural order. This is why the processor at *stage* 2 delays the input sample by the four-word shift register buffer. For the first $N/2 = 4$ data words, the processor in *stage* 2 simply accepts the data words and moves them into the shift register buffer. After $N/2 = 4$ data samples have been shifted, the processor starts performing the butterfly operations on the input data and the data coming from the shift register buffer. The processor in *stage* 1 repeats the same actions for a period of $N/4 = 2$ delay and so on. A pipeline design for the radix-4 decimation-in-frequency FFT processor has been proposed by Despain [125]. The design is usually called an R4SDF processor and is shown in Fig. 19.7 for a 64-point FFT.

Chapter 20

Solving Systems of Linear Equations

20.1 INTRODUCTION

Solving systems of linear equations is found in almost all areas of engineering and scientific applications. A system of linear equations is generally expressed in matrix form as

$$\mathbf{Ax} = \mathbf{b}, \tag{20.1}$$

where $\mathbf{A}$ is the *system matrix*, which is an $n \times n$ matrix, $\mathbf{x}$ is the unknown vector of n components, and $\mathbf{b}$ is a vector of constants. Techniques for solving linear systems could be direct or iterative. Direct techniques are appropriate for small systems (small values of n) where computational errors will be small. Iterative techniques are more appropriate for large systems where an assumed solution is refined after each iteration while suppressing computational noise. Table 20.1 summarizes the different direct and indirect techniques used to solve linear systems. Reference 129 explains in detail how such techniques are used.

A comprehensive discussion on parallel matrix computations can be found in the standard textbook of Golub and van Horn [129]. We provide here a brief introduction and tie the algorithms to the techniques we discussed in Chapters 7, 8, 10, and 11.

Typically, the system matrix will have some structure due to the nature of the application. Before we start, we define some of these structures in the following section.

20.2 SPECIAL MATRIX STRUCTURES

The following subsections explain some of the matrices that have special structures and are relevant to our discussion here.

Algorithms and Parallel Computing, by Fayez Gebali
Copyright © 2011 John Wiley & Sons, Inc.

Table 20.1 Direct and Indirect Techniques Used to Solve Linear Systems

Direct techniques	Comment
Forward substitution	System matrix lower triangular
Back substitution	System matrix upper triangular
LU factorization	Convert system matrix to equivalent triangular system. L is lower triangular matrix and U is upper triangular matrix.
Gaussian elimination	Convert system matrix to equivalent triangular system
LDM^t factorization	Convert system matrix to three special matrices. L is lower triangular matrix, D is diagonal matrix, and M is a Gaussian transformation matrix such that the product MA produces an upper triangular matrix.
LDL^t factorization	Convert system matrix to three special matrices when system matrix is symmetric
Positive definite systems	System matrix is positive definite
Banded systems	System matrix is banded
Symmetric indefinite systems	System matrix is symmetric
Block tridiagonal systems	System matrix has special block structure
Vandermonde systems	System matrix has 1s in its first row
Toeplitz systems	System matrix is Toeplitz

Indirect techniques	Comment
Jacobi	Used when system matrix has nonzero diagonal elements
Gauss–Seidel	Like Jacobi but uses most recently available estimates
Successive over relaxation (SOR)	Like Gauss–Seidel but could accelerate convergence
Chebyshev semi-iterative	Like Gauss-Seidel but could accelerate convergence
Conjugate gradient	Used when SOR or Chebyshev methods prove difficult

20.2.1 Plane Rotation (Givens) Matrix

A 5×5 plane rotation (or Givens) matrix $\mathbf{G}_{pq}$ is one that looks like the identity matrix except for elements that lie in the locations pp, pq, qp, and qq. Such a matrix is labeled $\mathbf{G}_{pq}$. For example, the matrix $\mathbf{G}_{42}$ takes the form

$$\mathbf{G}_{42} = \begin{bmatrix} 1 & 0 & 0 & 0 & 0 \\ 0 & c & 0 & s & 0 \\ 0 & 0 & 1 & 0 & 0 \\ 0 & -s & 0 & c & 0 \\ 0 & 0 & 0 & 0 & 1 \end{bmatrix}, \tag{20.2}$$

where $c = \cos\theta$ and $s = \sin\theta$. The notation commonly used is that the subscript refers to the element that has the negative *sin* value, which is element at row 4 and column 2 in our example.

Givens matrix is an orthogonal matrix and we have $G_{pq}G'_{pq} = I$. Premultiplying a matrix A by G_{pq} modifies only rows p and q. All other rows are left unchanged. The elements in rows p and q become

$$a_{pk} = ca_{pk} + sa_{qk} \tag{20.3}$$

$$a_{qk} = sa_{pk} + ca_{qk}. \tag{20.4}$$

20.2.2 Banded Matrix

A banded matrix with lower bandwidth p and upper bandwidth q implies that all its nonzero elements lie in the main diagonal, the lower p subdiagonals and the upper q superdiagonals. All other elements are zero, that is, when $i > j + p$ and $j > i + q$. In that case, matrix A will have nonzero p subdiagonal elements and nonzero q superdiagonal elements. An example of a banded matrix with lower bandwidth $p = 2$ and upper bandwidth $q = 3$ has the following structure where $\times$ denotes a nonzero element:

$$
\begin{bmatrix}
\times & \times & \times & \times & 0 & 0 & 0 & 0 & 0 & 0 \\
\times & \times & \times & \times & \times & 0 & 0 & 0 & 0 & 0 \\
\times & \times & \times & \times & \times & \times & 0 & 0 & 0 & 0 \\
0 & \times & \times & \times & \times & \times & \times & 0 & 0 & 0 \\
0 & 0 & \times & \times & \times & \times & \times & \times & 0 & 0 \\
0 & 0 & 0 & \times & \times & \times & \times & \times & \times & 0 \\
0 & 0 & 0 & 0 & \times & \times & \times & \times & \times & \times \\
0 & 0 & 0 & 0 & 0 & \times & \times & \times & \times & \times \\
0 & 0 & 0 & 0 & 0 & 0 & \times & \times & \times & \times \\
0 & 0 & 0 & 0 & 0 & 0 & 0 & \times & \times & \times
\end{bmatrix}. \tag{20.5}
$$

20.2.3 Diagonal Matrix

A diagonal matrix D is a special case of a banded matrix when $p = q = 0$ and only the main diagonal is nonzero. A 5×5 diagonal matrix D is given by

$$
D = \begin{bmatrix}
d_{11} & 0 & 0 & 0 & 0 \\
0 & d_{22} & 0 & 0 & 0 \\
0 & 0 & d_{33} & 0 & 0 \\
0 & 0 & 0 & d_{44} & 0 \\
0 & 0 & 0 & 0 & d_{55}
\end{bmatrix}. \tag{20.6}
$$

We can write the above diagonal matrix in a condensed form as

$$D = \text{diag}(d_1 \quad d_2 \quad d_3 \quad d_4 \quad d_5), \tag{20.7}$$

where $d_i = d_{ii}$.

20.2.4 Upper Triangular Matrix

An upper triangular matrix $\mathbf{U}$ is a special case of a banded matrix when $p = 0$ and only the main diagonal and the first q superdiagonals are nonzero.

20.2.5 Lower Triangular Matrix

A lower triangular matrix $\mathbf{L}$ is a special case of a banded matrix when $q = 0$ and only the main diagonal and the first p subdiagonals are nonzero.

20.2.6 Tridiagonal Matrix

A tridiagonal matrix is a special case of a banded matrix when $p = q = 1$ and only the main diagonal, the first superdiagonal, and first subdiagonal are nonzero. A 5×5 tridiagonal matrix $\mathbf{A}$ is given by

$$\mathbf{A} = \begin{bmatrix} a_{11} & a_{12} & 0 & 0 & 0 \\ a_{21} & a_{22} & a_{23} & 0 & 0 \\ 0 & a_{32} & a_{33} & a_{34} & 0 \\ 0 & 0 & a_{43} & a_{44} & a_{45} \\ 0 & 0 & 0 & a_{54} & a_{55} \end{bmatrix}. \tag{20.8}$$

20.2.7 Upper Hessenberg Matrix

An $n \times n$ upper Hessenberg matrix is a special case of a banded matrix when $p = 1$ and $q = n$ and the elements of the diagonal, the superdiagonals, and the first subdiagonal are nonzero. An upper Hessenberg matrix has $h_{ij} = 0$ whenever $j < i - 1$. A 5×5 upper Hessenberg matrix $\mathbf{H}$ is given by

$$\mathbf{H} = \begin{bmatrix} h_{11} & h_{12} & h_{13} & h_{14} & h_{15} \\ h_{21} & h_{22} & h_{23} & h_{24} & h_{25} \\ 0 & h_{32} & h_{33} & h_{34} & h_{35} \\ 0 & 0 & h_{43} & h_{44} & h_{45} \\ 0 & 0 & 0 & h_{54} & h_{55} \end{bmatrix}. \tag{20.9}$$

20.2.8 Lower Hessenberg Matrix

A lower Hessenberg matrix is the transpose of an upper Hessenberg matrix.

20.3 FORWARD SUBSTITUTION (DIRECT TECHNIQUE)

The general form for a system of linear equations was given in Eq. 20.1. Forward substitution technique converts the square matrix **A** into a lower triangular form:

$$\mathbf{Lx} = \mathbf{b}. \tag{20.10}$$

Consider the 5×5 lower triangular linear system:

$$\begin{bmatrix} l_{11} & 0 & 0 & 0 & 0 \\ l_{2,1} & l_{2,2} & 0 & 0 & 0 \\ l_{3,1} & l_{3,2} & l_{3,3} & 0 & 0 \\ l_{4,1} & l_{4,2} & l_{4,3} & l_{4,4} & 0 \\ l_{5,1} & l_{5,2} & l_{5,3} & l_{5,4} & l_{5,5} \end{bmatrix} \begin{bmatrix} x_1 \\ x_2 \\ x_3 \\ x_4 \\ x_5 \end{bmatrix} = \begin{bmatrix} b_1 \\ b_2 \\ b_3 \\ b_4 \\ b_5 \end{bmatrix}. \tag{20.11}$$

If all $l_{ii} \neq 0$, then we can determine the unknowns according to the equations

$$x_i = \frac{1}{l_{ii}} \left(b_i - \sum_{j=1}^{i-1} l_{i,j} x_j \right) \qquad 1 \leq i \leq 5, \quad j < i, \tag{20.12}$$

where x_1 must be calculated before x_2 could be evaluated and so on. Thus, it appears that the calculations are sequential, with small opportunity for parallelization. However, the techniques we discussed earlier will help us derive parallel multithreaded and systolic architectures.

20.3.1 Forward Substitution Dependence Graph

The iterations in Eq. 20.12 use two indices i and j and we can use the results of Chapters 10 or 11 to study the parallelization of the forward substitution algorithm. Figure 20.1 is the dependence graph of the iterations in Eq. 20.12. Note that the

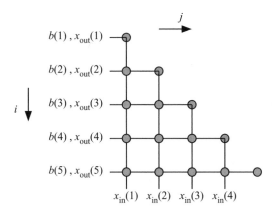

Figure 20.1 The dependence graph of the forward substitution algorithm.

variable x is an input/output variable and this explains why we have two sets of x, one set for the output instances of x and the other set is for the input instances of x.

Input instance $x_{in}(k)$ is a copy of the output instance $x_{out}(k)$. This is shown by the bends in the lines that appear on the diagonal nodes.

20.3.2 Forward Substitution Scheduling Function and Directed Acyclic Graph (DAG)

The choice of the scheduling function is dictated by the need to maintain the proper sequence of evaluating x_i. We know that $x_{out}(i)$ can be found only after $x_{out}(i-1)$ has been evaluated. We note that output instance $x_{out}(i)$ is obtained at the diagonal node (i, i) and is used by all nodes whose coordinates are $(i+k, i)$ where $k > 0$. Therefore, if the scheduling vector is $\mathbf{s} = [s_1\ s_2]$, then we must have

$$t[p(i,i)] < t[p(i+k,i)] \tag{20.13}$$
$$is_1 + is_2 < (i+k)s_1 + is_2, \tag{20.14}$$

and we can write the inequality

$$s_1 k > 0. \tag{20.15}$$

Since $k > 0$, we must have $s_1 > 0$ too. We can choose $s_1 = 1$ and we have our scheduling vector as

$$\mathbf{s} = [1 \quad s_2]. \tag{20.16}$$

We can choose three possible scheduling vectors while satisfying inequality (Eq. 20.13):

$$\mathbf{s}_1 = [1 \quad -1] \tag{20.17}$$
$$\mathbf{s}_2 = [1 \quad 0] \tag{20.18}$$
$$\mathbf{s}_3 = [1 \quad 1]. \tag{20.19}$$

The resulting DAGs for the three choices are shown in Fig. 20.2. The scheduling vector $\mathbf{s}_1$ implies diagonal-based calculations since each iteration requires simultaneous access to the elements of a diagonal. The choice of $\mathbf{s}_1$ will produce a DAG where output sample $x_{out}(i)$ is obtained on the left edge of the diagram. However, this output sample must be fed back to node (i, i) for use by later calculations. Depending on the projection vector chosen, we might have to provide communication between the left nodes and the diagonal nodes. The work W at each time step would start at N, then decrease by one at each time step thereafter.

The scheduling vector $\mathbf{s}_2$ implies row-based calculations since each iteration requires simultaneous access to the elements of a row. The work W at each time step would start at 1, then increase by one at each time step thereafter.

The scheduling vector $\mathbf{s}_3$ implies column-based calculations since each iteration requires simultaneous access to the elements of a column. The work W at each time

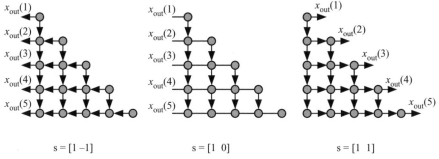

Figure 20.2   The DAG graphs of the forward substitution algorithm for the three possible scheduling functions.

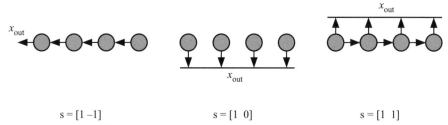

Figure 20.3   The $\overline{\text{DAG}}$ graphs of the forward substitution algorithm for the three possible scheduling functions.

step would start at 1 for the first two operations, then increase by two at the next two time steps. The maximum work is encountered halfway during the operation, and then work starts to decrease by 2 after each two time steps thereafter.

We can use nonlinear scheduling to control the total workload at each iteration. However, the work done at each time step will not be uniform.

20.3.3 Forward Substitution Projection Function

Three projection directions are possible:

$$\mathbf{d}_1 = \begin{bmatrix} 1 & -1 \end{bmatrix}^t \tag{20.20}$$

$$\mathbf{d}_2 = \begin{bmatrix} 1 & 0 \end{bmatrix}^t \tag{20.21}$$

$$\mathbf{d}_3 = \begin{bmatrix} 1 & 1 \end{bmatrix}^t. \tag{20.22}$$

The simplest projection directions to use would be $\mathbf{d}_2$ and $\mathbf{d}_3$.

Let us consider the case when $\mathbf{d}_2$ is used. The reduced DAG ($\overline{\text{DAG}}$) is shown in Fig. 20.3. We can use nonlinear projection to control the workload of each thread or each processing element (PE) in the systolic array.

20.4 BACK SUBSTITUTION

The general form for a system of linear equations was given in Eq. 20.1. Back substitution technique converts the square matrix $\mathbf{A}$ into an upper triangular form:

$$\mathbf{Ux} = \mathbf{b}. \tag{20.23}$$

Consider the 5×5 upper triangular linear system:

$$\begin{bmatrix} u_{1,1} & u_{1,2} & u_{1,3} & u_{1,4} & u_{1,5} \\ 0 & u_{2,2} & u_{2,3} & u_{2,4} & u_{2,5} \\ 0 & 0 & u_{3,3} & u_{2,4} & u_{3,5} \\ 0 & 0 & 0 & u_{4,4} & u_{4,5} \\ 0 & 0 & 0 & 0 & u_{5,5} \end{bmatrix} \begin{bmatrix} x_1 \\ x_2 \\ x_3 \\ x_4 \\ x_5 \end{bmatrix} = \begin{bmatrix} b_1 \\ b_2 \\ b_3 \\ b_4 \\ b_5 \end{bmatrix}. \tag{20.24}$$

If all $u_{ii} \neq 0$, then we can determine the unknowns according to the equations

$$x_i = \frac{1}{u_{ii}} \left(b_i - \sum_{j=i+1}^{5} l_{i,j} x_j \right) \qquad 1 \leq i \leq 5, \quad j > i \tag{20.25}$$

where x_5 must be calculated before x_4 could be evaluated and so on. Thus, it appears that the calculations are sequential, with small opportunity for parallelization. However, the techniques we discussed earlier will help us derive parallel multi-threaded and systolic architectures. The procedure we used to derive scheduling and projection functions for forward substitution can be used here.

20.5 MATRIX TRIANGULARIZATION ALGORITHM

This section shows the algorithm to convert a square matrix $\mathbf{A}$ to an upper triangular matrix $\mathbf{U}$. Once we obtain a triangular matrix, we can use forward or back substitution to solve the system of equations.

Assume we are given the system of linear equations described by

$$\mathbf{Ax} = \mathbf{b}. \tag{20.26}$$

The solution for this system will not change if we premultiply both sides by the Givens matrix $\mathbf{G}_{pq}$:

$$\mathbf{G}_{pq} \mathbf{Ax} = \mathbf{G}_{pq} \mathbf{b}. \tag{20.27}$$

Premultiplication with the Givens matrix transforms the linear system into an equivalent system

$$\mathbf{A'x} = \mathbf{b'} \tag{20.28}$$

and the solution of the equivalent system is the same as the solution to the original system. This is due to the fact that premultiplication with the Given matrix performs two *elementary row operations*:

1. Multiply a row by a nonzero constant.
2. Add multiple of one row to another row.

Let us assume we have the following system of linear equations

$$\begin{bmatrix} 1 & 2 \\ 3 & 4 \end{bmatrix} \begin{bmatrix} x_1 \\ x_2 \end{bmatrix} = \begin{bmatrix} 5 \\ 6 \end{bmatrix}. \tag{20.29}$$

To solve this system, we need to convert the system matrix to an upper triangular matrix. So we need to change element $a_{2,1}$ from 3 to 0. After multiplying by the Givens matrix $\mathbf{G}_{21}$, element $a'_{2,1}$ is given by the equation

$$a'_{2,1} = -sa_{1,1} + ca_{2,1} = 0. \tag{20.30}$$

Therefore, we have

$$\tan \theta = \frac{s}{c} = \frac{a_{2,1}}{a_{1,1}}. \tag{20.31}$$

For our case we get $\tan \theta = 3/1$ and $\theta = 71.5651°$. The desired Givens matrix is given by

$$\mathbf{G}_{21} = \begin{bmatrix} 0.3162 & 0.9487 \\ -0.9487 & 0.3162 \end{bmatrix}. \tag{20.32}$$

The transformed system becomes

$$\begin{bmatrix} 3.1623 & 4.4272 \\ 0 & -0.6325 \end{bmatrix} \begin{bmatrix} x_1 \\ x_2 \end{bmatrix} = \begin{bmatrix} 7.2732 \\ -2.8460 \end{bmatrix}. \tag{20.33}$$

The solution to the system is $\mathbf{x} = [-4 \ 4]^t$.

Givens rotations can be successively applied to the system matrix to convert it to an upper triangular matrix as shown in the following steps.

Assume our system matrix is 5×5 as shown below where the symbols $\times$ indicate the elements of the matrix.

$$\begin{bmatrix} \times & \times & \times & \times & \times \\ \times & \times & \times & \times & \times \\ \times & \times & \times & \times & \times \\ \times & \times & \times & \times & \times \\ \times & \times & \times & \times & \times \end{bmatrix} \quad \begin{bmatrix} \times & \times & \times & \times & \times \\ 0 & \times & \times & \times & \times \\ 0 & \times & \times & \times & \times \\ 0 & \times & \times & \times & \times \\ 0 & \times & \times & \times & \times \end{bmatrix} \quad \begin{bmatrix} \times & \times & \times & \times & \times \\ 0 & \times & \times & \times & \times \\ 0 & 0 & \times & \times & \times \\ 0 & 0 & \times & \times & \times \\ 0 & 0 & \times & \times & \times \end{bmatrix}$$

Initial system matrix	Insert zeros in first column	Insert zeros in second column

$$\begin{bmatrix} \times & \times & \times & \times & \times \\ 0 & \times & \times & \times & \times \\ 0 & 0 & \times & \times & \times \\ 0 & 0 & 0 & \times & \times \\ 0 & 0 & 0 & \times & \times \end{bmatrix} \quad \begin{bmatrix} \times & \times & \times & \times & \times \\ 0 & \times & \times & \times & \times \\ 0 & 0 & \times & \times & \times \\ 0 & 0 & 0 & \times & \times \\ 0 & 0 & 0 & 0 & \times \end{bmatrix}$$

Insert zeros in third column	Insert zeros in fourth column.

20.5.1 Givens Rotation Algorithm

We now show the algorithm that converts the system matrix to an upper triangular matrix so that back substitution could be used to solve the system of linear equations. Algorithm 20.1 illustrates the steps needed. We can see that the algorithm involves three indices i, j, and k and the graph technique of Chapter 10 might prove difficult to visualize. However, the graph technique is useful as a guideline for the more formal computation geometry technique of Chapter 11.

Algorithm 20.1   Givens rotations to convert a square matrix to upper triangular

---

Require: Input: $N \times N$ system matrix $\mathbf{A}$

1: for $k = 1 : N - 1$ **do**

2:   **for** $i = k + 1 : N$ **do**

3: $\theta_{ik} = \tan^{-1} a_{ik}/a_{kk}$; // calculate rotation angle for rows k and j

4: $s = \sin \theta_{ik}$; $c = \cos \theta_{ik}$;

5:

6:   //Apply Givens rotation to rows k and i

7:   **for** $j = k : N$ **do**

8: $a_{kj} = c\, a_{kj} + s\, a_{ij}$;

9: $a_{ij} = -s\, a_{kj} + c\, a_{ij}$;

10: end for

11:

12: end for

13: end for

Since estimation of rotation angle θ_{ik} is outside the innermost loop, we choose to have it estimated separately. In the discussion below, we ignore estimation of the rotation angle and concentrate on applying the rotations.

Algorithm 20.1 is three-dimensional (3-D) with indices $1 \leq k < N$, $k < i \leq N$, and $k \leq j \leq N$. Thus, the convex hull defining the computation domain is pyramid-shaped as shown in Fig. 20.4. The figure shows bird's eye and plan views of the pyramid shaped or layered structure of the dependence graph for the matrix triangularization algorithm when system matrix has dimensions 5×5.

Figure 20.5 shows the details of the dependence graph on a layer-by-layer basis when system matrix has dimensions 5×5. This way we can think of the dependence graph in terms of multiple two-dimensional (2-D) dependence graphs that are easier to visualize. We see that variable θ_{ik} is propagated along the j direction. Variable a_{kj} is propagated along the i direction. This variable represents an element of the top row in each iteration, which is used by the lower rows to apply the Givens rotations.

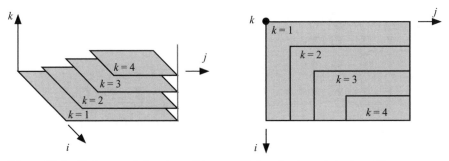

Figure 20.4 Bird's eye and plan views of the pyramid-shaped or layered structure of the dependence graph for the matrix triangularization algorithm when system matrix has dimensions 5×5.

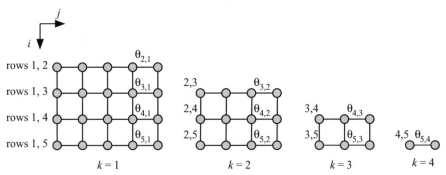

Figure 20.5 Dependence graph for the matrix triangularization algorithm when system matrix has dimensions 5×5.

20.5.2 Matrix Triangularization Scheduling Function

The scheduling vector **s** assigns a time index value to each point in our computation domain as

$$t(\mathbf{p}) = \mathbf{s}\mathbf{p} = is_1 + js_2 + ks_3. \tag{20.34}$$

The reader will agree that a 3-D computation domain is difficult to visualize and to investigate the different timing strategies. However, there are few observations we can make about the components s_1, s_2, and s_3.

At iteration k, a node at row $i + 1$, for example, a node at location $(i + 1, j, k)$, is proceed after node (i, j, k) has been evaluated. Thus, we have

$$t(i+1,j,k) > t(i,j,k) \tag{20.35}$$

$$s_1 > 0. \tag{20.36}$$

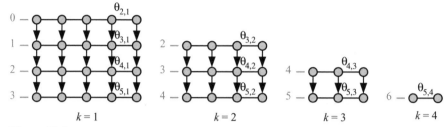

Figure 20.6 DAG diagram for a 5×5 system for s_2 scheduling function.

At iteration k, once the rotation angle has been evaluated, all the matrix elements in the same row can be processed in any order. Thus, we have

$$t(i, j-1, k) > t(i, j-2, k) \quad \text{or} \quad t(i, j-1, k) = t(i, j-2, k)$$

$$\text{or} \quad t(i, j-1, k) < t(i, j-2, k) \tag{20.37}$$

$$s_2 = 0, \pm 1. \tag{20.38}$$

The rotation angle at iteration $k + 1$ uses the node at location $(k + 2, k + 1, k)$. This angle estimation can proceed after node at location $(k + 2, k + 1, k)$ has been processed. Thus, we have

$$t(k+2, k+1, k+1) > t(k+2, k+1, k) \tag{20.39}$$

$$s_3 > 0. \tag{20.40}$$

We can choose three possible scheduling vectors while satisfying the above observations:

$$\mathbf{s}_1 = \begin{bmatrix} 1 & +1 & 1 \end{bmatrix} \tag{20.41}$$

$$\mathbf{s}_2 = \begin{bmatrix} 1 & 0 & 1 \end{bmatrix} \tag{20.42}$$

$$\mathbf{s}_3 = \begin{bmatrix} 1 & -1 & 1 \end{bmatrix}. \tag{20.43}$$

Perhaps the simplest scheduling function to visualize is s_2. The DAG for this function for the case of a 5×5 system is shown in Fig. 20.6. The figure shows the different layers separately for clarity.

We can see from the figure that the work done at each time step starts at a value N for the first two time steps then increases to $1.5N$ for time steps 2 and 3 and so on.

20.5.3 Matrix Triangularization Projection Direction

Based on the three possible scheduling functions discussed in the previous section, we are able to choose appropriate projection directions. Possible simple projection vectors are

$$\mathbf{d}_1 = \begin{bmatrix} 1 & 0 & 0 \end{bmatrix}^t \tag{20.44}$$

$$\mathbf{d}_2 = \begin{bmatrix} 0 & 1 & 1 \end{bmatrix}^t \tag{20.45}$$

$$\mathbf{d}_3 = \begin{bmatrix} 0 & 0 & 1 \end{bmatrix}^t. \tag{20.46}$$

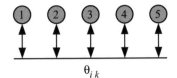

Figure 20.7   Reduced DAG diagram for a 5×5 system for $\mathbf{s}_2$ scheduling function and $\mathbf{d}_1$ projection direction.

For illustration, let us choose $\mathbf{s}_2$ and $\mathbf{d}_1$. The reduced DAG $(\overline{\mathrm{DAG}})$ is shown in Fig. 20.7. This choice of projection direction produces a column-based implementation since each thread or PE operates on a column of the system matrix. The rotation angle θ_{ik} is broadcast to all the threads or PEs. At iteration k thread T_k or PE_k is responsible for generating $N - k$ rotation angles and propagating these angles to all the threads or PEs to its right side.

20.6 SUCCESSIVE OVER RELAXATION (SOR) (ITERATIVE TECHNIQUE)

Iterative techniques are suited for large matrices. A simple iterative technique for solving linear equations is the Jacobi iteration, which is suited for matrices that have nonzero diagonal elements. Assume we are given the system of linear equations

$$\mathbf{Ax} = \mathbf{b}, \tag{20.47}$$

we can express the ith row of the above system explicitly:

$$\sum_{j=1}^{i-1} a_{ij}x_j + a_{ii}x_i + \sum_{j=i+1}^{N} a_{ij}x_j = b_i, \tag{20.48}$$

where we have isolated the term involving x_i. We can "solve" for x_i from the above equation as

$$x_i = \frac{1}{a_{ii}} \left(b_i - \sum_{j=1}^{i-1} a_{ij}x_j - \sum_{j=i+1}^{N} a_{ij}x_j \right). \tag{20.49}$$

Of course, we need to iterate several times before we converge to the correct solution. At iteration k, we can estimate x_i^{k+1} as

$$x_i^{k+1} = \frac{1}{a_{ii}} \left(b_i - \sum_{j=1}^{i-1} a_{ij}x_j^k - \sum_{j=i+1}^{N} a_{ij}x_j^k \right). \tag{20.50}$$

Gauss–Seidel iteration differs from the Jacobi iteration in that it uses the most recently found values of x_{ij}^{k+1} in the iterations:

$$x_i^{k+1} = \frac{1}{a_{ii}} \left(b_i - \sum_{j=1}^{i-1} a_{ij}x_j^{k+1} - \sum_{j=i+1}^{N} a_{ij}x_j^k \right). \tag{20.51}$$

The order of evaluation of the algorithm is to find x_1^{k+1}, x_2^{k+1}, ... , x_N^{k+1}. Note that in the Gauss–Seidel iteration, we use the most recent information for the first sum on the right-hand side (RHS).

Jacobi and Gauss–Seidel iterations might be very slow and SOR is meant to speed up the convergence. SOR iterations are described by the equation:

$$x_i^{k+1} = \frac{\omega}{a_{ii}} \left(b_i - \sum_{j=1}^{i-1} a_{ij}x_j^k - \sum_{j=i+1}^{N} a_{ij}x_j^k \right) + (1-\omega)x_i^k, \tag{20.52}$$

where $0 < \omega < 1$ is a *relaxation parameter* chosen to speed the algorithm. The order of evaluation of the algorithm is to find x_1^{k+1}, x_2^{k+1}, ... , x_N^{k+1}.

20.6.1 SOR Algorithm

Algorithm 20.2 shows the SOR in algorithmic form.

Algorithm 20.2   SOR algorithm

Require: Input: $N \times N$ system matrix A, ω, k_max

1: **for** $k = 1 : k\_max$ **do**
2:    **for** $i = 1 : N$ **do**
3:       $sum\_1(i, k) = sum\_2 = 0$;
4:       **for** $j = 1 : i - 1$ **do**
5:       $sum\_1(i, j + 1, k) = sum\_1(i, j, k) + a(i, j)x(j, k)$;
6:    **end for**
7:    **for** $j = N : i + 1$ **do**
8:       $sum\_2(i, j - 1, k) = sum\_2(i, j, k) + a(i, j)x(j, k)$;
9:    **end for**
10:    $x(i, k + 1) = omega * (b(i) - sum\_1(i, i, k) - sum_2(i,i,k)) + (1-\omega)x(i, k)$;
11: **end for**
12: **end for**

The SOR algorithm is 3-D, with indices $1 \le i \le N$, $1 \le j \le N$, and $1 \le k \le k\_max$. The convex hull describing the computation domain is a rectangular prism. We show in Fig. 20.8 only one layer for a given value of k.

Figure 20.5 shows the details of the dependence graph at a certain iteration when system matrix has dimensions 5×5. This way we can think of the dependence graph in terms of multiple 2-D dependence graphs, which are easier to visualize. We see from the algorithm that matrix element a_{ij} is represented by vertical lines along the k-axis and intersects the computation domain at points $(i, j, 1)$ and (i, j, N). Element

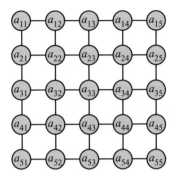

Figure 20.8   Dependence graph for the SOR algorithm for a given iteration when system matrix has dimensions 5×5.

b_i is represented by a plane whose normal is along the i-axis. The horizontal lines represent information flow for the sum_1, sum_2, and input variable x_i^k. The output variable x_i^{k+1} is shown by the vertical lines.

20.6.2   SOR Algorithm Scheduling Algorithm

A 3-D scheduling function has the form

$$t(\mathbf{p}) = \mathbf{sp} = is_1 + js_2 + ks_3. \tag{20.53}$$

There are several restrictions on the values of the scheduling vector based on the nature of the SOR algorithm. Node (i, j, k) is used to calculate the product $a_{i,j}x_j^k$. The valuation of variable x_i^{k+1} is performed at location $(i, i, k + 1)$ because it requires the all the product terms at the following locations:

- (i, j, k) for $i < j \leq N$
- $(i, j, k+1)$ for $1 \leq j < i$

This translates to the following restrictions on the scheduling vector components

$$t(i,i,k+1) > t(i,i-n,k+1) \quad n > 0 \quad \text{for} \quad sum\_1 \tag{20.54}$$
$$t(i,i,k+1) > t(i,i+n,k) \qquad n > 0 \quad \text{for} \quad sum\_2. \tag{20.55}$$

The above two inequalities produce

$$s_2 > 0 \qquad \text{for} \quad sum\_1 \tag{20.56}$$
$$s_3 > ns_2 \quad \text{for} \quad sum\_2. \tag{20.57}$$

The largest value for n is when $n = N$. Therefore, we can write the inequality as

$$s_2 > 0 \qquad \text{for} \quad sum\_1 \tag{20.58}$$
$$s_3 > Ns_2 \quad \text{for} \quad sum\_2. \tag{20.59}$$

Let us choose to have a scheduling function of the form

$$\mathbf{s} = \begin{bmatrix} 1 & 0 & N \end{bmatrix} - N - 1. \tag{20.60}$$

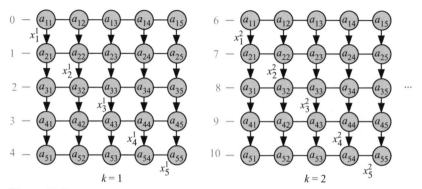

Figure 20.9   DAG for the SOR algorithm at the first two iterations when system matrix has dimensions 5×5.

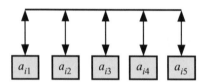

Figure 20.10   Reduced $\overline{\text{DAG}}$ for the SOR algorithm.

The $-N - 1$ term on the RHS is meant to ensure that time starts with value 0 when $i = k = 1$ initially. Figure 20.9 shows the DAG for the SOR algorithm at the first two iterations when system matrix has dimensions 5×5. The time needed to complete the iterations would be equal to N^2.

20.6.3   SOR Algorithm Projection Direction

The work done at each time step is N and the work done at each iteration is N^2. Therefore, it makes sense to obtain a reduced DAG ($\overline{\text{DAG}}$) that is one-dimensional and contains only N nodes. We can accomplish this using two projection directions

$$\mathbf{d}_1 = \begin{bmatrix} 1 & 0 & 0 \end{bmatrix}^t \tag{20.61}$$

$$\mathbf{d}_2 = \begin{bmatrix} 0 & 0 & 1 \end{bmatrix}^t. \tag{20.62}$$

The corresponding projection matrix can be obtained using the Chapters 10 or 11 as

$$\mathbf{P} = \begin{bmatrix} 0 & 1 & 0 \end{bmatrix}. \tag{20.63}$$

A point (i, j, k) in DAG will map to point j in $\overline{\text{DAG}}$. The resulting reduced DAG ($\overline{\text{DAG}}$) is shown in Fig. 20.10.

20.7 PROBLEMS

20.1. Study the parallelization of the back substitution algorithm.

20.2. Study the parallelization of the Gaussian elimination algorithm.

20.3. Explain how the LDM^t algorithm in Table 20.1 can be used to solve for the unknown vector x. Study the parallelization of this algorithm and relate it to the forward and back substitution algorithms.

20.4. Study the parallelization of the banded matrix–vector multiplication algorithm.

20.5. Study the parallelization of the banded matrix–matrix multiplication algorithm.

20.6. Study the parallelization of the Gauss–Seidel algorithm.

Chapter 21

Solving Partial Differential Equations Using Finite Difference Method

21.1 INTRODUCTION

Finite difference methods (FDMs) are used for numerical simulation of many important applications in science and engineering. Examples of such applications include

- Air flow in the lungs
- Blood flow in the body
- Air flow over aircraft wings
- Water flow around ship and submarine hulls
- Ocean current flow around the globe
- Propagation of sound or light waves in complex media

FDMs replace the differential equations describing a physical phenomenon with finite difference equations. The solution to the phenomenon under consideration is obtained by evaluating the variable or variables over a grid covering the region of interest. The grid could be one-, two-, or three-dimensional (1-D, 2-D, and 3-D, respectively) depending on the application. An example of 1-D applications is vibration of a beam or string; 2-D applications include deflection of a plate under stress, while 3-D applications include propagation of sound underwater.

There are several types of differential equations that are encountered in physical systems [48, 130, 131]:

Boundary value problem:

$$v_{xx} = f(x, v, v_x) \qquad 0 \le x \le 1, \tag{21.1}$$

where $v_x = dv/dx$, $v_{xx} = d^2v/dx^2$, and f is a given function in three variables and v is unknown and depends on x. The associated boundary conditions are given by

Algorithms and Parallel Computing, by Fayez Gebali
Copyright © 2011 John Wiley & Sons, Inc.

$$v(0) = v_0 \tag{21.2}$$
$$v(1) = v_1, \tag{21.3}$$

where v_0 is the value of variable v at the boundary $x = 0$ and v_1 is the value of variable v at the boundary $x = 1$.

Elliptic partial differential equation (Poisson equation):

$$v_{xx} = f(x) \qquad \text{1-D case} \tag{21.4}$$
$$v_{xx} + v_{yy} = f(x, y) \qquad \text{2-D case.} \tag{21.5}$$

These equations describe the electrical potential and heat distribution at steady state. For the 1-D case, when $f(x) = 0$, the above equation is called the Laplace equation. For the 2-D, Laplace equation results when $f(x, y) = 0$.

Parabolic partial differential equation (diffusion equation):

$$av_{xx} = v_t, \tag{21.6}$$

where a is a constant and $v_{xx} = \partial^2 v / \partial x^2$ and $v_t = \partial v / \partial t$. This equation describes gas diffusion and heat conduction in solids in 1-D cases such as rods.

Hyperbolic partial differential equation (wave equation):

$$av_{xx} = v_{tt}, \tag{21.7}$$

where $v_{tt} = \partial^2 v / \partial t^2$. This equation describes the propagation of waves in media such as sound, mechanical vibrations, electromagnetic radiation, and transmission of electricity in long transmission lines.

In the following section, we will study the wave equation as an example. The analysis can be easily applied to the other types of differential equations.

21.2 FDM FOR 1-D SYSTEMS

We start by explaining how FDM is applied to a 1-D system for simplicity. Assume the differential equation describing our system is second order of the form

$$av_{xx} = v_{tt} \qquad 0 \leq x \leq 1 \qquad \text{and} \qquad t > 0. \tag{21.8}$$

Note that we normalized the length such that the maximum value of x is 1. The associated boundary conditions are given by

$$v(0, t) = v_0 \qquad t \geq 0 \tag{21.9}$$
$$v(1, t) = v_1 \qquad t \geq 0 \tag{21.10}$$
$$v(x, 0) = f(x) \qquad 0 \leq x \leq 1, \tag{21.11}$$

where v_0 describes the value of the variable at $x = 0$, v_1 describes the value of the variable at $x = 1$, and $f(x)$ describes the initial values of the variable. Note that the boundary conditions at $x = 0$ and $x = 1$ might, in the general case, depend on time as $v_0(t)$ and $v_1(t)$. Usually, a is a simple constant. In the general case, a might depend both on time and space as $a(x, t)$.

It might prove difficult to solve the system described by Eq. 21.8 when the boundary conditions are time dependent or the medium is inhomogeneous and/or time dependent. To convert the system equation to partial difference equation, we need to approximate the derivatives v_x and v_{xx}. Using Taylor series, we can describe the first derivative as

$$v_x(x, t) = \frac{v(x + \Delta x, t) - v(x, t)}{\Delta x} \qquad \text{forward difference formula} \qquad (21.12)$$

$$v_x(x, t) = \frac{v(x, t) - v(x - \Delta x, t)}{\Delta x} \qquad \text{backward difference formula,} \qquad (21.13)$$

where Δx is the grid size. The value of Δx is determined by the number of grid points I:

$$\Delta x = 1/I. \qquad (21.14)$$

From these two expressions, we can express v_x in the *central difference formula*:

$$v_x(x, t) = \frac{v(x + \Delta x, t) - v(x - \Delta x, t)}{2\Delta x} \qquad \text{central difference formula.} \qquad (21.15)$$

Likewise, we can obtain v_{xx} and v_{tt} using the formulas

$$v_{xx}(x, t) = \frac{v(x + \Delta x, t) - 2v(x, t) + v(x - \Delta x, t)}{\Delta x^2} \qquad (21.16)$$

$$v_{tt}(x, t) = \frac{v(x, t + \Delta t) - 2v(x, t) + v(x, t - \Delta t)}{\Delta t^2}. \qquad (21.17)$$

The value of Δt is determined by the number of time iterations K and assuming that the total simulation time is 1:

$$\Delta t = 1/K. \qquad (21.18)$$

Our choice of Δx and Δt divides the x-t plane into rectangles of sides Δx and Δt. A point (x, t) in the x-t plane can be expressed in terms of two indices i and k:

$$x = i\Delta x \qquad 0 \le i \le I \qquad (21.19)$$
$$t = k\Delta t \qquad 0 \le k \le K. \qquad (21.20)$$

Using the indices i and k, we can rewrite Eqs. 21.16 and 21.17 in the simpler form:

$$v_{xx}(i, k) = \frac{v(i+1, k) - 2v(i, k) + v(i-1, k)}{\Delta x^2} \qquad (21.21)$$

$$v_{tt}(i, k) = \frac{v(i, k+1) - 2v(i, k) + v(i, k-1)}{\Delta t^2}. \qquad (21.22)$$

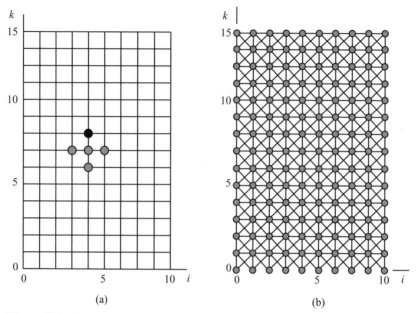

Figure 21.1 Dependence graph for the 1-D finite difference algorithm for the case $I = 10$ and $K = 15$. (a) Showing the dependence of the node at the black circle on the data from the gray circles. (b) The complete dependence graph.

Combining Eqs. 21.8, 21.21, and 21.22, we finally can write

$$v(i, k+1) = rv(i+1, k) + 2(1-r)v(i, k) + rv(i-1, k) - v(i, k-1) \qquad (21.23)$$

with

$$r = \frac{a\Delta t^2}{\Delta x^2}. \qquad (21.24)$$

Thus, we are able to compute $v(i, k+1)$ at time $k+1$ knowing the values of v at times k and $k-1$.

Equation 21.23 describes a 2-D regular iterative algorithm (RIA) in the indices i and k. Figure 21.1 shows the dependence graph for the 1-D finite difference algorithm for the case $I = 10$ and $K = 15$. Figure 21.1a shows how node at position (4,8) depends on the data from nodes at points (3,7), (4,7), (4,6), and (5,7). Figure 21.1b shows the complete dependence graph.

21.2.1   The Scheduling Function for 1-D FDM

Since the dependence graph of Fig. 21.1b is 2-D, we can simply use the results of Chapter 10. Our scheduling function is specified as

$$t(\mathbf{p}) = \mathbf{sp} - s \qquad (21.25)$$
$$= is_1 + js_2 - s. \qquad (21.26)$$

Assigning time values to the nodes of the dependence graph transforms the dependence graph to a directed acyclic graph (DAG) as was discussed in Chapters 10 and 11. More specifically, the DAG can be thought of as a serial–parallel algorithm (SPA) where the parallel tasks could be implemented using a thread pool or parallel processors for software or hardware implementations, respectively. The different stages of the SPA are accomplished using barriers or clocks for software or hardware implementations, respectively.

We have several restrictions on $t(\mathbf{p})$ according to the data dependences depicted in Fig. 21.1:

$$
\begin{array}{rclcl}
is_1 + (j+1)s_2 & > & is_1 + js_2 & \Rightarrow & s_2 & > & 0 \\
is_1 + (j+1)s_2 & > & (i-1)s_1 + js_2 & \Rightarrow & s_1 + s_2 & > & 0 \\
is_1 + (j+1)s_2 & > & (i+1)s_1 + js_2 & \Rightarrow & s_2 & > & s_1 \\
is_1 + (j+1)s_2 & > & is_1 + (j-1)s_2 & \Rightarrow & 2s_2 & > & 0.
\end{array}
\qquad (21.27)
$$

From the above restrictions, we can have three possible simple timing functions that satisfy the restrictions:

$$\mathbf{s}_1 = \begin{bmatrix} 0 & 1 \end{bmatrix} \qquad (21.28)$$
$$\mathbf{s}_2 = \begin{bmatrix} 1 & 2 \end{bmatrix} \qquad (21.29)$$
$$\mathbf{s}_3 = \begin{bmatrix} -1 & 2 \end{bmatrix}. \qquad (21.30)$$

Figure 21.2 shows the DAG for the three possible scheduling functions for the 1-D FDM algorithm when $I = 5$ and $K = 9$. For $\mathbf{s}_1$, the work (W) to be done by the parallel computing system is equal to $I + 1$ calculations per iteration. The time required to complete the problem is $K + 1$.

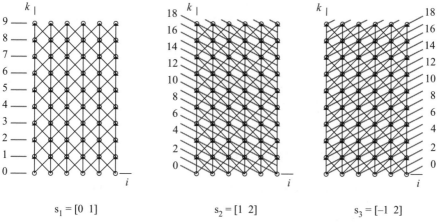

$$\mathbf{s}_1 = \begin{bmatrix} 0 & 1 \end{bmatrix} \qquad\qquad \mathbf{s}_2 = \begin{bmatrix} 1 & 2 \end{bmatrix} \qquad\qquad \mathbf{s}_3 = \begin{bmatrix} -1 & 2 \end{bmatrix}$$

Figure 21.2 Directed acyclic graphs (DAG) for the three possible scheduling functions for the 1-D FDM algorithm when $I = 5$ and $K = 9$.

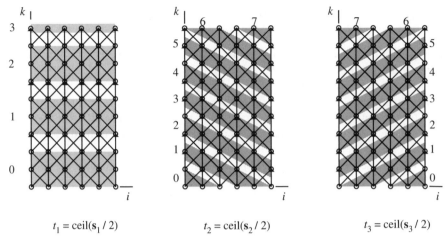

$$t_1 = \text{ceil}(s_1 / 2) \qquad\qquad t_2 = \text{ceil}(s_2 / 2) \qquad\qquad t_3 = \text{ceil}(s_3 / 2)$$

Figure 21.3   Directed acyclic graphs (DAG) for the three possible nonlinear scheduling functions for the 1-D FDM algorithm when $I = 5$, $K = 9$, and $n = 3$.

For s_2 and s_3, the work (W) to be done by the parallel computing system is equal to $\lceil I/2 \rceil$ calculations per iteration. The time required to complete the problem is given by $I + 2K$.

Linear scheduling does not give us much control over how much work is to be done at each time step. As before, we are able to control the work W by using non-linear scheduling functions of the form given by

$$t(\mathbf{p}) = \left\lfloor \frac{\mathbf{sp}}{n} \right\rfloor, \tag{21.31}$$

where n is the level of data aggregation.

Figure 21.3 shows the DAG for the three possible nonlinear scheduling functions for the 1-D FDM algorithm when $I = 5$, $K = 9$, and $n = 3$. For nonlinear scheduling based on s_1, the work (W) to be done by the parallel computing system is equal to $n(I + 1)$ calculations per iteration. The time required to complete the problem is $\lceil K/n \rceil$. For nonlinear scheduling based on s_2 and s_3, the work (W) to be done by the parallel computing system is equal to K calculations per iteration. The time required to complete the problem is given by $\lceil (I + 2K)/n \rceil$.

21.2.2   Projection Directions

The combination of node scheduling and node projection will result in determination of the work done by each task at any given time step. The natural projection direction associated with s_1 is given by

$$\mathbf{d}_1 = \mathbf{s}_1. \tag{21.32}$$

In that case, we will have $I + 1$ tasks. At time step $k + 1$, task T_i is required to perform the operations in Eq. 21.23. Therefore, there is necessary communication between tasks T_i, T_{i-1}, and T_{i-1}. The number of messages that need to be exchanged between the tasks per time step is $2I$.

We will pick projection direction associated with s_2 or s_3 as

$$\mathbf{d}_{2,3} = \mathbf{s}_1. \tag{21.33}$$

In that case, we will have $I + 1$ tasks. However, the even tasks operate on the even time steps and the odd tasks operate on the odd time steps. We can merge the adjacent even and odd tasks and we would have a total of $[(I + 1)/2]$ tasks operating every clock cycle. There is necessary communication between tasks T_i, T_{i-1}, and T_{i-1}. The number of messages that need to be exchanged between the tasks per time step is $3[(I - 2)/2] + 4$.

Linear projection does not give us much control over how much work is assigned to each task per time step or how many messages are exchanged between the tasks. We are able to control the work per task and the total number of messages exchanged by using nonlinear projection operation of the form

$$\bar{\mathbf{p}} = \text{floor}\left(\frac{\mathbf{Pp}}{m}\right), \tag{21.34}$$

where $\mathbf{P}$ is the projection matrix associated with the projection direction and m is the number of nodes in the DAG that will be allocated to a single task. The total number of task depends on I and m and is given approximately by $3[I/m]$.

References

[1] M. WEHNER, L. OLIKER, and J. SHALF. A real cloud computer. *IEEE Spectrum*, 46(10):24–29, 2009.

[2] B. WILKINSON and M. ALLEN. *Parallel Programming Techniques & Applications Using Networked Workstations & Parallel Computers*, 2nd ed. Toronto, Canada: Pearson, 2004.

[3] A. GRAMA, A. GUPTA, G. KARYPIS, and V. KUMAR. *Introduction to Parallel Computing*, 2nd ed. Reading, MA: Addison Wesley, 2003.

[4] Standards Coordinating Committee 10, Terms and Definitions. *The IEEE Standard Dictionary of Electrical and Electronics Terms*, J. Radatz, Ed. IEEE, 1996.

[5] F. ELGUIBALY (GEBALI). α-CORDIC: An adaptive CORDIC algorithm. *Canadian Journal on Electrical and Computer Engineering*, 23:133–138, 1998.

[6] F. ELGUIBALY (GEBALI), HCORDIC: A high-radix adaptive CORDIC algorithm. *Canadian Journal on Electrical and Computer Engineering*, 25(4):149–154, 2000.

[7] J.S. WALTHER. A unified algorithm for elementary functions. In *Proceedings of the 1971 Spring Joint Computer Conference*, N. Macon, Ed. American Federation of Information Processing Society, Montvale, NJ, May 18–20, 1971, pp. 379–385.

[8] J.E. VOLDER. The CORDIC Trigonometric Computing Technique. *IRE Transactions on Electronic Computers*, EC-8(3):330–334, 1959.

[9] R.M. KARP, R.E. MILLER, and S. WINOGRAD. The organization of computations for uniform recurrence equations. *Journal of the Association of Computing Machinery*, 14:563–590, 1967.

[10] V.P. ROYCHOWDHURY and T. KAILATH. Study of parallelism in regular iterative algorithms. In *Proceedings of the Second Annual ACM Symposium on Parallel Algorithms and Architecture*, Crete, Greece, F. T. Leighton, Ed. Association of Computing Machinery, 1990, pp. 367–376.

[11] H.V. JAGADISH, S.K. RAO, and T. KAILATH. Multiprocessor architectures for iterative algorithms. *Proceedings of the IEEE*, 75(9):1304–1321, 1987.

[12] D.I. MOLDOVAN. On the design of algorithms for VLSI systohc arrays. *Proceedings of the IEEE*, 81:113–120, 1983.

[13] F. GEBALI, H. ELMILIGI, and M.W. EL-KHARASHI. *Networks on Chips: Theory and Practice*. Boca Raton, FL: CRC Press, 2008.

[14] B. PRINCE. Speeding up system memory. *IEEE Spectrum*, 2:38–41, 1994.

[15] J.L. GUSTAFSON. Reevaluating Amdahl's law. Communications of the ACM, pp. 532–533, 1988.

[16] W.H. PRESS. Discrete radon transform has an exact, fast inverse and generalizes to operations other than sums along lines. *Proceedings of the National Academy of Sciences*, 103(51):19249–19254, 2006.

[17] F. PAPPETTI and S. SUCCI. *Introduction to Parallel Computational Fluid Dynamics*. New York: Nova Science Publishers, 1996.

[18] W. STALLINGS. *Computer Organization and Architecture*. Upper Saddle River, NJ: Pearson/ Prentice Hall, 2007.

[19] C. HAMACHER, Z. VRANESIC, and S. ZAKY. *Computer Organization*, 5th ed. New York: McGraw-Hill, 2002.

[20] D.A. PATTERSON and J.L. HENNESSY. *Computer Organization and Design: The Hardware/Software Interface*. San Francisco, CA: Morgan Kaufman, 2008.

[21] F. ELGUIBALY (GEBALI). A fast parallel multiplier-accumulator using the modified booth algorithm. *IEEE Transaction Circuits and Systems II: Analog and Digital Signal Processing*, 47:902–908, 2000.

[22] F. ELGUIBALY (GEBALI). Merged inner-prodcut processor using the modified booth algorithm. *Canadian Journal on Electrical and Computer Engineering*, 25(4):133–139, 2000.

[23] S. SUNDER, F. ELGUIBALY (GEBALI), and A. ANTONIOU. Systolic implementation of digital filters. *Multidimensional Systems and Signal Processing*, 3:63–78, 1992.

[24] T. UNGERER, B. RUBIC, and J. SLIC. Multithreaded processors. *Computer Journal*, 45(3):320–348, 2002.

[25] M. JOHNSON. *Superscalar Microprocessor Design*. Englewood Cliffs, NJ: Prentice Hall, 1990.

[26] M.J. FLYNN. Very high-speed computing systmes. *Proceedings of the IEEE*, 54(12):1901–1909, 1966.

[27] M. TOMASEVIC and V. MILUTINOVIC. Hardware approaches to cache coherence in shared-memory multiprocessors: Part 1. *IEEE Micro*, 14(5):52–59, 1994.

[28] F. GEBALI. *Analysis of Computer and Communication Networks*. New York: Springer, 2008.

[29] T.G. LEWIS and H. EL-REWINI. *Introduction to Parallel Computing*. Englewood Cliffs, NJ: Prentice Hall, 1992.

[30] J. ZHANG, T. KE, and M. SUN. The parallel computing based on cluster computer in the processing of mass aerial digital images. In *International Symposium on Information Processing*, F. Yu and Q. Lou, Eds. IEEE Computer Society, Moscow, May 23–25, 2008, pp. 398–393.

[31] AMD. Computing: The road ahead. http://hpcrd.lbl.gov/SciDAC08/files/presentations/SciDAC_Reed.pdf, 2008.

[32] B.K. KHAILANY, T. WILLIAMS, J. LIN, E.P. LONG, M. RYGH, D.W. TOVEY, and W.J. DALLY. A programmable 512 GOPS stream processor for signa, image, and video processing. *IEEE Journal of Solid-State Circuits*, 43(1):202–213, 2008.

[33] B. BURKE. NVIDIA CUDA technology dramatically advances the pace of scientific research. http://www.nvidia.com/object/io_1229516081227.html?_templated=320, 2009.

[34] S. RIXNER, W.J. DALLY, U.J. KAPASI, B. KHAILANY, A. LOPEZ-LAGUNAS, P. MATTSON, and J.D. OWNES. A bandwidth-efficient architecture for media processing. In *Proceedings of the 31st Annual International Symposium on Microarchitecture*. Los Alamitos, CA: IEEE Computer Society Press, 1998, pp. 3–13.

[35] H. EL-REWINI and T.G. LEWIS. *Distributed and Parallel Computing*. Greenwich, CT: Manning Publications, 1998.

[36] E.W. DIJKSTRA. Solution of a problem in concurrent programming control. *Communications of the ACM*, 8(9):569, 1965.

[37] D.E. CULLER, J.P. SINGH, and A. GUPTA. *Parallel Computer Architecture*. San Francisco, CA: Morgan Kaufmann, 1999.

[38] A.S. TANENBAUM and A.S. WOODHULL. *Operating Systems : Design and Implementation*. Englewood Cliffs, NJ: Prentice Hall, 1997.

[39] W. STALLINGS. *Operating Systems: Internals and Design Principles*. Upper Saddle River, NJ: Prentice Hall, 2005.

[40] A. SILBERSCHATZ, P.B. GALVIIN, and G. GAGNE. *Operating System Concepts*. New York: John Wiley, 2009.

[41] M.J. YOUNG. Recent developments in mutual exclusion for multiprocessor systems. http://www.mjyonline.com/MutualExclusion.htm, 2010.

[42] SUN MICORSYSTEMS. *Multithreading Programming Guide*. Santa Clara, CA: Sun Microsystems, 2008.

[43] F. GEBALI. Design and analysis of arbitration protocols. *IEEE Transaction on Computers*, 38(2):161171, 1989.

[44] S.W. FURHMANN. Performance of a packet switch with crossbar architecture. *IEEE Transaction Communications*, 41:486–491, 1993.

[45] C. CLOS. A study of non-blocking switching networks. *Bell System Technology Journal*, 32:406–424, 1953.

[46] R.J. Simcoe and T.-B. Pei. Perspectives on ATM switch architecture and the influence of traffic pattern assumptions on switch design. *Computer Communication Review*, 25:93–105, 1995.

[47] K. Wang, J. Huang, Z. Li, X. Wang, F. Yang, and J. Bi. Scaling behavior of internet packet delay dynamics based on small-interval measurements. In *The IEEE Conference on Local Computer Networks*, H. Hassanein and M. Waldvogel, Eds. IEEE Computer Society, Sydney, Australia, November 15–17, 2005, pp. 140–147.

[48] M.J. Quinn. *Parallel Programming*. New York: McGraw-Hill, 2004.

[49] C.E. Leiserson and I.B. Mirman. *How to Survive the Multicore Software Revolution*. Lexington, MA: Cilk Arts, 2009.

[50] Cilk Arts. Smooth path to multicores. http://www.cilk.com/, 2009.

[51] OpenMP. OpenMP: The OpenMP API specification for parallel programming. http://openmp.org/wp/, 2009.

[52] G. Ippolito. YoLinux tutorial index. http://www.yolinux.com/TUTORIALS/LinuxTutorialPosix Threads.html, 2004.

[53] M. Soltys. Operating systems concepts. http://www.cas.mcmaster.ca/~soltys/cs3sh3-w03/, 2003.

[54] G. Hillar. Visualizing parallelism and concurrency in Visual Studio 2010 Beta 2. http://www.drdobbs.com/windows/220900288, 2009.

[55] C.E. Leiserson. The Cilk++ Concurrency Platform. *Journal of Supercomputing*, 51(3), 244–257, 2009.

[56] C. Carmona. Programming the thread pool in the .net framework. http://msdn.microsoft.com/en-us/library/ms973903.aspx, 2002.

[57] MIP Forum. Message passing interface forum. http://www.mpi-forum.org/, 2008.

[58] G.E. Blelloch. NESL: A parallel programming language. http://www.cs.cmu.edu/~scandal/nesl.html, 2009.

[59] S. Amanda. Intel's Ct Technology Code Samples, April 6, 2010, http://software.intel.com/en-us/articles/intels-ct-technology-code-samples/.

[60] Threading Building Blocks. Intel Threading Building Blocks 2.2 for open source. http://www.threadingbuildingblocks.org/, 2009.

[61] S. Patuel. Design: Task parallel library explored. http://blogs.msdn.com/salvapatuel/archive/2007/11/11/task-parallel-library-explored.aspx, 2007.

[62] N. Furmento, Y. Roudier, and G. Siegel. Survey on C++ parallel extensions. http://www-sop.inria.fr/sloop/SCP/, 2009.

[63] D. McCrady. Avoiding contention using combinable objects. http://blogs.msdn.com/b/nativeconcurrency/archive/2008/09/25/avoiding-contention-usingcombinable-objects.aspx, 2008.

[64] Intel. Intel Cilk++ SDK programmer's guide. http://software.intel.com/en-us/articles/intel-cilk/, 2009.

[65] R.D. Blumofe and C.E. Leiserson. Scheduling multithreaded computations by work stealing. *Journal of theACM (JACM)*, 46(5), 1999.

[66] J. Mellor-Crummey. Comp 422 parallel computing lecture notes and handouts. http://www.clear.rice.edu/comp422/lecture-notes/, 2009.

[67] M. Frigo, P. Halpern, C.E. Leiserson and S. Lewin-Berlin. Reducers and other Cilk++ hyperobjects, ACM Symposium on Parallel Algorithms and Architectures, Calgary, Alberta, Canada, pp. 79–90, August 11–13, 2009.

[68] B.C. Kuszmaul. Rabin–Karp string matching using Cilk++, 2009. http://software.intel.com/file/21631.

[69] B. Barney. OpenMP. http://computing.llnl.gov/tutorials/openMP/, 2009.

[70] OpenMP. Summary of OpenMP 3.0 c/c++ syntax. http://openmp.org/mp-documents/OpenMP3.0-SummarySpec.pdf, 2009.

[71] J. Nickolls, I. Buck, M. Garland, and K. Skadron. Scalable parallel programming with CUDA. *ACM Queue*, 6(2):40–53, 2008.

[72] P.N. Gloaskowsky. NVIDIA's Fermi: The first complete GPU computing architecture, 2009. http://www.nvidia.com/content/PDF/fermi_white_papers/P.Glaskowsky_NVIDIA's_Fermi-The_First_Complete_GPU_Architecture.pdf.

[73] NVIDIA. NVIDIA's next generation CUDA computer architecture: Fermi, 2009. http://www.nvidia.com/object/fermi_architecture.html.

[74] X. Li. CUDA programming. http://dynopt.ece.udel.edu/cpeg455655/lec8_cudaprogramming.pdf.

[75] D. Kirk and W.-M. Hwu. ECE 498 AL: Programming massively processors. http://courses.ece.illinois.edu/ece498/al/, 2009.

[76] NVIDIA. NVIDIA CUDA Library Documentation 2.3. http://developer.download.nvidia.com/compute/cuda/2_3/toolkit/docs/online/index.html, 2010.

[77] Y. Wu. Parallel decomposed simplex algorithms and loop spreading. PhD thesis, Oregon State University, 1988.

[78] J.H. McClelan, R.W. Schafer, and M.A. Yoder. *Signal Processing First*. Upper Saddle River, NJ: Pearson/Prentice Hall, 2003.

[79] V.K. Ingle and J.G. Proakis. *Digital Signal Processing Using MATLAB*. Pacific Grove, CA: Brooks/Cole Thompson Learning, 2000.

[80] H.T. Kung. Why systolic architectures. *IEEE Computer Magazine*, 15:37–46, 1982.

[81] H.T. Kung. *VLSI Array Processors*. Englewood Cliffs, NJ: Prentice Hall, 1988.

[82] G.L. Nemhauser and L.A. Wolsey. *Integrand Combinatorial Optimization*. New York: John Wiley, 1988.

[83] F.P. Preparata and M.I. Shamos. *Computational Geometry*. New York: Springer-Verlag, 1985.

[84] A. Schrijver. *Theory of Linear and Integer Programming*. New York: John Wiley, 1986.

[85] D.S. Watkins. *Fundamentals of Matrix Computations*. New York: John Wiley, 1991.

[86] F. El-Guibaly (Gebali) and A. Tawfik. Mapping 3D IIR digital filter onto systolic arrays. *Multidimensional Systems and Signal Processing*, 7(1):7–26, 1996.

[87] S. Sunder, F. Elguibaly (Gebali), and A. Antoniou. Systolic implementation of two-dimensional recursive digital filters. In *Proceedings of the IEEE Symposium on Circuits and Systems*, New Orleans, LA, May 1–3, 1990, H. Gharavi, Ed. IEEE Circuits and Systems Society, pp. 1034–1037.

[88] M.A. Sid-Ahmed. A systolic realization of 2-D filters. In *IEEE Transactions on Acoustics, Speech, and Signal Processing*, Vol. ASSP-37, IEEE Acoustics, Speech and Signal Processing Society, 1989, pp. 560–565.

[89] D. Esteban and C. Galland. Application of quadrature mirror filters to split band voice coding systems. In *Proceedings of the International Conference on Acoustics, Speech, and Signal Processing*, Hartford, CT, May 9–11, 1977, F. F. Tsui, Ed. IEEE Acoustics, Speech and Signal Processing Society, pp. 191–195.

[90] J.W. Woods and S.D. ONeil. Sub-band coding of images. In *IEEE Transactions on Acoustics, Speech, and Signal Processing*, Vol. ASSP-34, IEEE Acoustics, Speech and Signal Processing Society, 1986, pp. 1278–1288.

[91] H. Gharavi and A. Tabatabai. Sub-band coding of monochrome and color images. In *IEEE Transactions on Circuits and Systems*, Vol. CAS-35, IEEE Circuits and Systems Society, 1988, pp. 207–214.

[92] R. Ramachandran and P. Kabal. Bandwidth efficient transmultiplexers. Part 1: Synthesis. *IEEE Transaction Signal Process*, 40:70–84, 1992.

[93] G. Jovanovic-Dolece. *Multirate Systems: Design and Applications*. Hershey, PA: Idea Group Publishing, 2002.

[94] R.E. Crochiere and L.R. Rabiner. *Multirate Signal Processing*. Englewood Cliffs, NJ: Prentice Hall, 1983.

[95] R.E. Crochiere and L.R. Rabiner. Interpolation and decimation of digital signals—A tutorial review. *Proceedings of the IEEE*, 69(3):300–331, 1981.

[96] E. Abdel-Raheem. Design and VLSI implementation of multirate filter banks. PhD thesis, University of Victoria, 1995.

[97] E. Abdel-Raheem, F. Elguibaly (Gebali), and A. Antoniou. Design of low-delay FIR QMF banks using the lagrange-multiplier approach. In *IEEE 37th Midwest Symposium on Circuits and Systems*, Lafayette, LA, M. A. Bayoumi and W. K. Jenkins, Eds. Lafayette, LA, August 3–5, IEEE Circuits and Systems Society, 1994, pp. 1057–1060.

[98] E. ABDEL-RAHEEM, F. ELGUIBALY (GEBALI), and A. ANTONIOU. Systolic implementations of polyphase decimators and interpolators. In *IEEE 37th Midwest Symposium on Circuits and Systems*, Lafayette, LA, M. A. Bayoumi and W. K. Jenkins, Eds. Lafayette, LA, August 3–5, IEEE Circuits and Systems Society, 1994, pp. 749–752.

[99] A. RAFIQ, M.W. EL-KHARASHI, and F. GEBALI. A fast string search algorithm for deep packet classification. *Computer Communications*, 27(15):1524–1538, 2004.

[100] F. GEBALI and A. RAFIQ. Processor array architectures for deep packet classification. *IEEE Transactions on Parallel and Distributed Computing*, 17(3):241–252, 2006.

[101] A. MENEZES, P. VAN OORSCHOT, and S. VANSTONE. *Handbook of Applied Cryptography*. Boca Raton, FL: CRC Press, 1997.

[102] B. SCHENEIER. *Applied Cryptography*. New York: John Wiley, 1996.

[103] W. STALLINGS. *Cryptography and Network Security: Principles and Practice*. Englewood Cliffs, NJ: Prentice Hall, 2005.

[104] A. REYHANI-MASOLEH and M.A. HASAN. Low complexity bit parallel architectures for polynomial basis multiplication over GF(2^m). *IEEE Transactions on Computers*, 53(8):945–959, 2004.

[105] T. ZHANG and K.K. PARHI. Systematic design of original and modified mastrovito multipliers for general irreducible polynomials. *IEEE Transactions on Computers*, 50(7):734–749, 2001.

[106] C.-L. WANG and J.-H. GUO. New systolic arrays for $c+ab^2$, inversion, and division in GF(2^m). *IEEE Transactions on Computers*, 49(10):1120–1125, 2000.

[107] C.-Y. LEE, C.W. CHIOU, A.-W. DENG, and J.-M. LIN. Low-complexity bit-parallel systolic architectures for computing $a(x)b^2(x)$ over GF(2^m). *IEE Proceedings on Circuits, Devices & Systems*, 153(4):399–406, 2006.

[108] N.-Y. KIM, H.-S. KIM, and K.-Y. YOO. Computation of $a(x)b^2(x)$ multiplication in GF(2^m) using low-complexity systolic architecture. *IEE Proceedings Circuits, Devices & Systems*, 150(2):119–123, 2003.

[109] C. YEH, I.S. REED, and T.K. TRUONG. Systolic multipliers for finite fields GF(2^m). *IEEE Transactions on Computers*, C-33(4):357–360, 1984.

[110] D. HANKERSON, A. MENEZES, and S. VANSTONE. *Guide to Elliptic Curve Cryptography*. New York: Springer-Verlag, 2004.

[111] M. FAYED. A security coprocessor for next generation IP telephony architecture, abstraction, and strategies. PhD thesis, University of Victoria, ECE Department, University of Victoria, Victoria, BC, 2007.

[112] T. ITOH and S. TSUJII. A fast algorithm for computing multiplicative inverses in GF(2^m) using normal bases. *Information and Computing*, 78(3):171–177, 1998.

[113] A. GOLDSMITH. *Wireless Communications*. New York: Cambridge University Press, 2005.

[114] M. ABRAMOVICI, M.A. BREUER, and A.D. FRIEDMAN. *Digital Systems Testing and Testable Design*. New York: Computer Science Press, 1990.

[115] M.J.S. SMITH. *Application-Specific Integrated Circuits*. New York: Addison Wesley, 1997.

[116] M. FAYED, M.W. EL-KHARASHI, and F. GEBALI. A high-speed, low-area processor array architecture for multipli- cation and squaring over GF(2^m). In *Proceedings of the Second IEEE International Design and Test Workshop (IDT 2007)*, 2007, Y. Zorian, H. ElTahawy, A. Ivanov, and A. Salem, Eds. Cairo, Egypt: IEEE, pp. 226–231.

[117] M. FAYED, M.W. EL-KHARASHI, and F. GEBALI. A high-speed, high-radix, processor array architecture for real-time elliptic curve cryptography over GF(2^m). In *Proceedings of the 7th IEEE International Symposium on Signal Processing and Information Technology (ISSPIT 2007)*, Cairo, Egypt, E. Abdel-Raheem and A. El-Desouky, Eds. December 15–18, IEEE Signal Processing Society and IEEE Computer Society, 2007, pp. 57–62.

[118] F. GEBALI, M. REHAN, and M.W. EL-KHARASHI. A hierarchical design methodology for full-search block matching motion estimation. *Multidimensional Systems and Signal Processing*, 17:327–341, 2006.

[119] M. SERRA, T. SLATER, J.C. MUZIO, and D.M. MILLER. The analysis of one-dimensional linear cellular automata and their aliasing properties. *IEEE Transactions on Computer-Aided Design of Integrated Circuits and Systems*, 9(7):767–778, 1990.

[120] L.R. RABINER and B. GOLD. *Theory and Application of Digital Signal Processing*. Upper Saddle River, NJ: Prentice Hall, 1975.

[121] E.H. WOLD and A.M. DESPAIN. Pipeline and parallel-pipeline FFT processors for VLSI implementation. *IEEE Transactions on Computers*, 33(5):414–426, 1984.

[122] G.L. STUBER, J.R. BARRY, S.W. MCLAUGHLIN, Y. LI, M.A. INGRAM, and T.H. PRATT. Broadband MIMO-OFDM wireless systems. *Proceedings of the IEEE*, 92(2):271–294, 2004.

[123] J.W. COOLEY and J.W. TUKEY. An algorithm for the machine calculation of complex Fourier series. *Mathematics of Computation*, 19:297–301, 1965.

[124] B. MCKINNEY. The VLSI design of a general purpose FFT processing node, MASc thesis, University of Victoria, 1986.

[125] A.M. DESPAIN. Fouier transform computer using CORDIC iterations. *IEEE Transactions on Computers*, C-23(10):993–1001, 1974.

[126] J.G. NASH. An FFT for wireless protocols. In *40th Annual Hawaii International Conference on System Sciences: Mobile Computing Hardware Architectures*, R. H. Sprague, Ed. January 3–6, 2007.

[127] C.-P. FAN, M.-S. LEE, and G.-A. SU. A low multiplier and multiplication costs 256-point FFT implementa- tion with simplified radix-24 SDF architecture. In *IEEE Asia Pacific Conference on Circuits and Systems APCCAS*, December 4–7, Singapore: IEEE, 2006, pp. 1935–1938.

[128] S. HE and M. TORKELSON. A new approach to pipeline FFT processor. In *Proceedings of IPPS '96: The 10th International Parallel Processing Symposium*, Honolulu, Hawaii, April 15–19, IEEE Computer Society, K. Hwang, Ed., 1996, pp. 766–770.

[129] G.H. GOLUB and C.F. VAN HORN. *Matrix Computations*, 2nd ed. Blatimore, MD: The Johns Hopkins University Press, 1989.

[130] I. JACQUES and C. JUDD. *Numerical Analysis*. New York: Chapman and Hall, 1987.

[131] R.L. BURDEN, J.D. FAIRES, and A.C. REYNOLDS. *Numerical Analysis*. Boston: Prindle, Weber & Schmidt, 1978.

[132] D.E. KNUTH. *The Art of Computer Programming, vol. 3: Sorting and Searching*. New York: Addison-Wesley, 1973.

Index

Algorithms and Parallel Computing, by Fayez Gebali
Copyright © 2011 John Wiley & Sons, Inc.

337